D0901587

BISON
BOOKS

© *Ferdinand Vogel*

SENATOR GEORGE W. NORRIS

Fighting Liberal

THE AUTOBIOGRAPHY OF

George W. Norris

SECOND EDITION

Foreword by Arthur M. Schlesinger Jr.

Introduction to the new Bison Books edition by
Bob Kerrey

University of Nebraska Press
Lincoln and London

Manufactured in the United States of America

First Nebraska paperback printing: 1992

Reprinted by arrangement with Marian Norris Nelson

"George Norris and the Liberal Tradition" originally appeared in the 1961 Collier Books edition of this book and is reprinted by arrangement with Arthur M. Schlesinger Jr.

Library of Congress Cataloging-in-Publication Data
Norris, George W. (George William), 1861–1944.
Fighting liberal: the autobiography of George W. Norris / George W. Norris; foreword by Arthur M. Schlesinger Jr.; introduction to the new Bison Books edition by Bob Kerrey.
p. cm.
Originally published: New York: Macmillan, 1945.
Includes index.
ISBN 978-0-8032-2676-0 (pbk.: alk. paper)
1. Norris, George W. (George William), 1861–1944. 2. Legislators—United States—Biography. 3. United States. Congress. Senate—Biography. I. Schlesinger, Arthur M. II. Kerrey, Robert, 1943–. III. Title.
E748.N65A3 2009
328.73092—dc22
[B]
2009028697

Introduction to the New Bison Books Edition

Bob Kerrey

I do not know for certain what motivated newspaper editor James E. Lawrence—a very interesting character himself—to push George Norris to write this book. It must have been a desire to record the history of Norris's forty years in the Congress. For Senator Norris's accomplishments are substantial. He achieved more than any other Nebraskan who has served there. The benefits of his work continue to be felt today; the laws he helped write made America more productive, safe, and just. However, the worthiness of this book lies less in its contribution to an understanding of history than in its use as a training manual for those who seek to serve in the public arena. The habits of Norris, the values of Norris, and the attitude of Norris are worthy of emulation. The success of democracy—and our experiment in self-government—depends on a lot more than ideas, eloquence, or charisma. Democracy needs men and women who value competency, effort, and the development of the skills needed to do the work.

So the hope that guides my writing is that the person who is holding this book and reading these words is a young person. Perhaps you have been required to read this book for a class on history or politics, or, better yet, for a first-year class in law school. Perhaps you have just been hired to work as a congressional staffer or have an ambition to serve in Washington yourself. If so, the lessons offered by George Norris will help you do your job well, and maybe, just maybe you might use Norris's stories—and the values that are woven throughout—to become as great a senator as he became. Oh, how this republic of ours needs that to happen.

This is not an autobiography or memoir that contains extensive self-examination or analysis. Norris gives us a paragraph or two to tell us about the deaths of his father and brother. Either could have been a moment to reflect on the progress of modern medicine or the advance of civilized living since his father died of pneumonia after chasing down a runaway horse, and his brother died of an infection following a seemingly minor wound suffered as a Union soldier in the Civil War. The understatement of the personal was an important value of Norris, but in the hands of today's reader it might be a turnoff. By today's standards the book is a little too dry and boring. He doesn't take enough time to tell us about the tragedies and losses of his life. There are only a few pages given over to the effort of making it obvious that he came a long way and overcame a great deal.

Norris was born in Ohio during the summer of 1861, the first year of the Civil War. He died in McCook, Nebraska, in the fall of 1944, the last year of the Second World War. He finished this book eight weeks before his death. And if you are a reader with an ambition for public service, you are lucky he did. From the example of his life there are a number of important lessons learned. I will extract a half dozen from among many.

First: Learn the rules. Norris learned and practiced the rules of parliamentary procedure beginning when he was a boy. You may not like the rules (and Norris clearly did not), but until you change them—and Norris changed many, including our Constitution—knowledge of the rules is a great source of power. And if you intend to use power to benefit the people you serve, this is knowledge you will use over and over again to good purpose.

Second: Make your own rules and live by them. Norris had rules about writing (he wrote all his own letters). He had rules about speeches on the Senate floor (he prepared but only read a speech once). He carefully researched those issues he chose to debate and did not debate if time or interest left him short of facts.

The personal research Norris did gave him extraordinary authority in debates. The 1932 Norris-LaGuardia Anti-Injunction legislation, which established a Federal right of an employee to join a union and prevented so-called Yellow Dog Contracts, was preceded by a considerable amount of work. The work was necessitated by the moral outrage he felt about the way workers were treated on the job. While campaigning in Pennsylvania against a candidate of his own party who he believed was corrupt, Norris met a coal miner whose story moved him. What he saw was wrong, and he wanted to do something about it.

But he didn't rush back to Washington and ask his staff to prepare a bill. In his words he "gave a great deal of attention to that subject long before formulating legislation to deal with it. I studied it to the best of my ability. I followed the developments in investigations that already had taken place, covering a period of eight years of research and legislative fight before an adequate law was enacted."

He chaired a subcommittee that held extensive hearings during which he "heard every syllable of testimony that was given." Unlike today, where oral testimony is limited to five minutes, no time limitations were imposed. Anyone who wanted to appear would be heard, and cross-examination of witnesses was permitted by either side. After the subcommittee produced a proposed law, they persuaded constitutional scholars to spend two full days examining the law to make certain that it would pass constitutional muster and survive a likely court challenge.

It is true that today's Congress would get a lot less done if every topic were given this kind of thorough examination. It is also true that whatever they got done would be of higher, more durable quality. Norris accomplished a lot because he allowed himself to move by things he believed were wrong and needed to be changed. He accomplished a lot because he was fearless in taking on vested political and economic interests in pursuit of change. He accomplished a lot because he did the necessary, time consuming, and unglamorous work of assembling facts before he began any effort to change the Constitution or the law.

Third: Don't give up. Norris persevered through long periods of reaction, public apathy, hostile opposition to his ideas, and legislative trickery designed to slow him down or prevent him from succeeding. It was ten years before he saw the passing of the Twentieth Amendment, which ended the lame duck congressional session, and very nearly as long before the Tennessee Valley Authority (TVA), the first comprehensive development of a U.S. river, was signed into law.

Fourth: Remain true to yourself. Norris wrote his own letters, made up his own mind what needed to be done, had a strong commitment to a personal code, and did not yield to the allure of flattery. He acquired a lawyer's mind and applied a frontiersman's discipline to the work of writing laws. He was familiar with despondency, frustration, and bitter disappointment. But he never lost an abiding faith in the people themselves, even when they voted him out of office in 1942 after thirty-six years in the Senate and four in the House of Representatives.

Fifth: Look for unlikely allies and arguments in favor of something you believe needs to be done. Look for simple reasons to do complicated things. This was his foundational thinking about the TVA: "I knew falling water, when properly harnessed, generated what some for want of a better name have called electricity. Its secret, even in the electrical age, which is dawning, is but partially known and understood science but its service to mankind is recognized—relieving men and women of drudgery which cannot be discharged in any other way. It drives the machines of production."

It's true the battle line was clearly drawn between public and private ownership of the development, with Norris fervently in favor of the public's right to own the project. However, Norris saw tremendous commercial and national security benefits. The electricity from the dams could be used to separate nitrogen from the air around us. In the First World War—which Norris opposed at considerable risk to his 1918 reelection—it became clear we needed a domestic source for nitrates. So he began to make the case that the electricity would make explosives in times of war and fertilizer in times of peace.

Sixth: Remember your home. Norris was an Ohioan by birth who came to Nebraska and fell in love with the place. He never lost that love, and it affected and shaped everything he did.

And most important of all: Build something beyond your lifetime. That was the advice Norris's mother gave him when they planted a fruit tree together. Someone other than you will enjoy the benefits of this planting. Long after you are gone—even if they do not credit you with the planting—others will enjoy the benefits of your labor. Norris took that advice to heart and all of us are the beneficiaries.

FOREWORD

George Norris and the Liberal Tradition*

By Arthur M. Schlesinger, Jr.

The liberal tradition is the grand and central tradition of our history. It expresses the basic American commitment to the development of a society which will offer the individual the fullest opportunity for creative fulfillment. It also implies the belief that mere humans will never achieve a perfect social order; that history is an unceasing process of change; that existing society has not yet realized the full promise of American life; that the liberal mission consequently becomes one of the application of human intelligence to the improvement of the social order in order to fulfill the imperatives of change; and that this mission becomes all the more urgent as the velocity of history increases.

This is liberalism in the broad sense. These are the essential liberal goals. Yet the strategy of liberalism has changed through our history to meet the changing circumstances of society. The social liberalism of the mid-twentieth century differs, for example, in important respects from the classical liberalism of Thomas Jefferson—differs not in the ends, but in the means according to which those ends are to be achieved.

It will be my contention today that George Norris was a key figure in the transition from classical to modern liberalism, that his life recapitulates basic episodes in the transformation of liberalism, that his story and his contribution represent an indispensable episode in the evolution of the American liberal tradition.

That tradition stretches back, of course, to the beginnings of the Republic. Its first great proponent was Thomas Jefferson; but it owes nearly as much to a man to whom liberals tend to be unfair—that is, to Alexander Hamilton.

*Address given at the Norris Centennial, Washington, D.C., May 16, 1961, when Schlesinger was Special Assistant to the President.

Hamilton was, I believe, in certain respects a more prescient and fertile statesman than Jefferson. It was fortunate for us all, for example, that Hamilton rather than Jefferson was the main architect of government in the first years of the Republic. Hamilton was right on two great issues on which Jefferson was wrong. One issue was the role of the national government, and the other was the future of the national economy. Hamilton believed that government, particularly the national government, had an affirmative and purposeful role to play in society. He believed, in addition, that the United States had an industrial future.

If Hamilton was right on these two great issues and Jefferson wrong, the fact remains nonetheless that Jefferson was right on two issues central to liberalism on which Hamilton was not only wrong, but passionately and fatally wrong. One of these questions was, of course, Jefferson's faith in government by the people, as against Hamilton's view that the only safe repository of government was the propertied elite. The other was Jefferson's insistence on the fullest freedom of conscience and expression against Hamilton's tolerance of such restrictive measures as the Alien and Sedition laws.

Jefferson's belief in democracy and in civil freedom amply entitle him to his reputation as the founder of the national liberal tradition. But what must be remembered about the liberal faith as expressed by Jefferson was that his liberalism emerged from what was basically an agrarian vision of American life. As we have seen, he rejected the industrial vision of Hamilton. He envisaged the United States in economically static terms, as a society of small farmers, each individual given a sturdiness of independence by the possession of a sufficiency of property—everyone tranquil and free under his own vine and fig tree. In modern terms, Jefferson was no champion of economic development.

Given this vision of national life, Jefferson assigned only a minimal role to government, and the least role of all to the national government. The economic function of government, as Jefferson saw it, was to employ various fiscal devices, like taxes, tariffs, and paper money to despoil the actual producer, the farmer yeoman, of the fruits of his labor for the benefit of the "paper aristocracy," an aristocracy founded on the issuance of paper money by banks. If the only function of an activist government was, as Jefferson thus believed, to transfer wealth from the farmer to the capitalist, then it followed logically, in Jefferson's view, that that government was best which governed least. Where Hamilton, in other words, affirmed a constructive role for government, especially for the national government, Jefferson wished, in theory at least, to confine that role to the minimum consistent with the survival and coherence of the nation. I say that this was Jefferson's position in theory. In practice, of course, Jefferson saw that the national government had its uses as an instrument of the people. His acquisition of Louisiana, for example, involved the assumption of extraordinary powers by the chief executive.

Under the next great president in the Jeffersonian tradition, Andrew Jackson, the national government acquired new strength and vigor. For one thing, Jackson revolutionized the whole conception of the presidency. Until Jackson the President had been regarded, in the main, as a passive executor of the Constitution and of the laws passed by Congress. It was Jackson who established the Presidency as a source of initiative, as a source of active and unrelenting national leadership, and thereby created the modern Presidency.

Moreover, Jackson's fight against the Second United States Bank established the principle that in a democracy the national government had to be more powerful than any private concentration of wealth within the community; that it was therefore inconsistent with the character of American democracy to permit a privately owned bank in Philadelphia to control the currency and credit of the nation. So, Jackson's policy in denying a recharter to the Second United States Bank was the symbol of this determination to vindicate the superior power of the democratic government. In the time of Hamilton, the business community had seen strong government as an ally, as an agreeable source of subsidies and charters and other special privileges. But it was now quick to draw new conclusions from the Jacksonian policies. Jackson obviously saw strong government as a means of chastening the business community, as a means by which what he called the "humble members of society" could rebuke and regulate the power of concentrated wealth. All this gave a new impression of the potential role of strong government. The business community, perceiving the future in Jackson, began a hasty retreat from the Hamiltonian position.

The age of Jackson thus saw the transformation of conservative philosophy from the Federalist philosophy of a strong national government to the Whig philosophy of a weak national government. It saw a similar transformation in conservative economic philosophy from a belief in mercantilism to a belief in laissez-faire. In this period businessmen began to move toward the Jeffersonian position that that government was best which governed least.

For their part, liberals in the Jackson period drew less clear-cut conclusions from the Jacksonian experience. Some, like Roger B. Taney, who after all was an ex-Federalist and therefore not antagonistic to the notion of strong government, was prepared to assert the power of the community over private wealth. "The object and end of all government," Taney said, "is to promote the happiness and prosperity of the community by which it is established; and it can never be assumed that the government intended to diminish its power of accomplishing the end for which it was created . . . the continued existence of a government would be of no great value if by implications and presumptions, it was disarmed of the powers necessary to accomplish the ends of its creation; and the functions it was designed to perform, transferred to the hands of privileged corporations." But most, while accepting the actuality of an interventionist state, tended to cling to the ideological framework of Jeffersonian anti-statism! This was true of Jackson himself, who believed that the new energy he had injected in the government was simply for the purpose of clearing away the underbrush and getting back to primitive simplicities; that the state had to be temporarily strong in order that it might be permanently weak.

Under the banner of anti-statism, Jackson thus had the ironic effect of making the national government more powerful than it had ever been before. But the framework of Jeffersonian ideology persisted. The concrete implications of the Jacksonian experience in favor of affirmative government were never codified, so to speak, in political philosophy. As a result, liberalism came out of the age of Jackson involved in activist government in practice, but still committed to negative government in theory.

One cannot say whether a prolongation of the Jacksonian effort would have produced a reformulation of liberal polticial philosophy. In the decades after Jackson, liberalism became increasingly preoccupied with a new and separate issue—the abolition of slavery—and the commitment of liberal thought and energy to the slavery struggle meant its withdrawal from economic reform.

The Civil War, in effect, interrupted the continuities of the liberal tradition. By the time after the war, in the 1870's, when reformers were beginning to return their attention once again to economic issues, the Jacksonians were dead, their experiments were unknown, their resort to the interventionist state forgotten. The "conventional wisdom" of liberalism was more Jeffersonian than ever.

This was the intellectual climate in which George Norris grew up. He was born a century ago on a farm in Sandusky County, Ohio. His boyhood had many characteristics of life on the frontier, though the frontier had by this time moved beyond Ohio. In particular, his early life imprinted on him moral traits which stamped his liberalism for the rest of his days. Norris wrote about the impact of this early experience in almost Jeffersonian terms:

"I learned to live most simply, and I learned to get a great joy out of work. . . . I grew up to believe wholly and completely in men and women who live simply, frugally, and in fine faith."

Norris thought that there developed unconsciously in his boyhood in this pioneer Ohio region an instinctive respect for justice and a great sympathy for the oppressed.

"As a boy," he said, "I saw with my own eyes the struggles of a democracy where the first problem is not the protection of the strong and the powerful, but instead, encouragement and inspiration for the weak and the unfortunate. In the organization of the life of this democracy, and in the development of its conceptions of social justice it has seemed to me is the spirit of America."

The conscientious historian is bound to comment that young George Norris did not immediately draw these lessons from Sandusky County. When he moved to Nebraska in 1885, at the age of 24, he was still an ardent Republican. As he later reflected, "I then thought the Republican Party was perfect." This had been the family faith. He maintained it with ardor for the next two decades.

Soon after he came to Nebraska, he encountered the Populist Movement of the late 1880's and the early 1890's. Farmers over the Middle West and South had begun to feel that they could stand economic deprivation no longer. They thought that by concerting their numbers and consolidating their organization they could secure enough political power to deal with the railroad owners and the processors and the bankers and the other groups upon whom they blamed their economic troubles. In face of the mortgage-ridden farmers, often unable to meet the cost of production out of the prices available to them, the young Norris remained staunchly conservative. Like Bob LaFollette in Wisconsin, he fought the Populists in 1892. In 1896 Norris, like LaFollette, supported William McKinley over William Jennings Bryan, who represented the Populist impulse within the Democratic Party. He did the same thing in 1900.

Still, as one looks back at the decade of the 90's in Norris's life, one cannot help feeling that he may to some degree have been educated by those whom he opposed.

The Populist platform of 1892 marks a watershed in the evolution of American liberalism. In that platform one finds the first clear, emphatic and decisive break with the Jeffersonian view of the state. "We believe," the Populists declared, "that the powers of government—in other words, of the people—should be expanded . . . as rapidly and as far as the good sense of an intelligent people and the teachings of experience shall justify, to the end that oppression, injustice, and poverty shall eventually cease in the land." They favored, in short, an enlargement of national powers in order to secure democratic objectives—Hamiltonian means to achieve Jeffersonian ends. Norris no doubt read that platform skeptically at the time, and remained strong in his Whig-Republican faith. But yet the posing of the issue could have had some effect. Certainly Norris's exposure as a district judge in Nebraska in the later 90's to the harsh realities of rural poverty unquestionably did something to drive the Populist lesson home to him.

He was still, nonetheless, a devout Republican when he went to Washington in 1903 as a Congressman. But by now the original ties of party loyalty were fraying away. A number of factors moved him steadily away from Republican orthodoxy. One factor was his increasing dislike of the reactionary and autocratic Republican organization in the House of Representatives, a dislike which finally led him to undertake his successful revolt against Speaker Joe Cannon. Another factor was his friendship with LaFollette. Another was his admiration for the great neo-Hamiltonian, Theodore Roosevelt. Another was his opposition to such business community measures as the Payne-Aldrich tariff. He later wrote, "Insurgency did not come easy to me," and this was so. But it came all the same, and it had behind it not superficial emotional enthusiasms or resentments, but rather the immovable integrity of a man who reached conclusions slowly and then stood by them.

Norris's political career was marked by a steady widening and deepening of his views. He went to the Senate in 1913 and soon became chairman of the Senate Agricultural Committee. In that role, he was among the first to understand that agriculture was no longer a local problem, that giving farmers a fair break in the economy required national action. He played a leading role in educating the nation to its responsibilities in agricultural policy.

Similarly service on the public lands committee brought home to Norris what he had already begun to learn from Theodore Roosevelt—the importance of conservation. He equally followed Roosevelt in understanding that the national government was the most reliable agency of conservation, that the national government was the best means of preserving the public resources, of building dams, of controlling floods, of improving navigation and ultimately of creating the conditions for the low-cost production of hydroelectric power. Others will speak to you of Norris's tremendous fight for Muscle Shoals and of the culmination of that fight in Franklin Roosevelt's establishment of the Tennessee Valley Authority. This was all part of Norris's evolving political philosophy. "A free people," he once wrote, "cannot permanently submit to the private monopoly of a necessity of life."

All this was accompanied by an increasing political independence. Though Norris supported Harding in 1920, he bolted the Republicans in 1924 to support his old friend Bob LaFollette on the Progressive ticket. In 1926 he made an even sharper challenge to the Republican organization when he went into Pennsylvania to campaign for William Wilson, who had been Woodrow Wilson's Secretary of Labor, against W. H. Vare, the conservative Republican millionaire, who seemed to typify to Norris the worst tendencies in the Republican Party. In 1928 Norris backed Al Smith. Soon he left the Republican Party for good, became an independent, and retained for the rest of his life a deep mistrust of any form of party organization.

The Pennsylvania campaign of 1926 strengthened another strand in Norris's liberalism. Coming from Nebraska, Norris had known most about problems of the land—agriculture, conservation, resources. What he saw in Pennsylvania now gave him an understanding of another dimension of the liberal mission—the cruel problems of organized labor. He would never forget the wreck of a man whom he saw in one Pennsylvania mine town, his spine contorted, his skin burned black by a mine explosion. Nor did he ever forget an epitaph he encountered in a mining town grave yard. The epitaph read,

> "For 40 years beneath the sod
> With pick and spade I did my task,
> The Coal King's slave, but now thank God,
> I'm free at last."

This experience led Norris to join with Fiorello LaGuardia, who was then a Congressman from New York City, in the campaign to eliminate the 'yellowdog contract' by which people, in accepting a job, agreed not to join unions. Their collaboration led to the passage in the early thirties of the Norris-LaGuardia Act. It also created a symbolic alliance—the alliance between the great progressive of the middle border, coming from the rural agrarian Jeffersonian tradition, and the first of the great urban progressives, who expressed the new energies of organized labor, of the immigrants and of the urban element in American liberalism. The alliance between Norris and LaGuardia, which began in the struggle for the Norris-LaGuardia Act, continued in the various Norris-LaGuardia committees set up in the elections of 1936 and 1940 as a means of rallying independent voters behind Roosevelt and the New Deal.

The New Deal, of course, came as a culmination of Norris's social hopes. Into the New Deal there poured the liberal currents of half a century preceding. No one more than Norris himself signalized the passage from the rural Jeffersonian liberalism of an earlier day to the industrial liberalism of the 20th century. Where many of his old friends among the pre-war progressives remained frozen in the clichés of their youth, Norris continued to see problems in fresh perspectives. He had no difficulty in giving his hand and heart to the basic direction and purpose of Franklin Roosevelt.

Norris signalized the transition in another field too—that is the field of foreign policy. Except for an early flirtation with Theodore Roosevelt's imperialism, Norris had been for most of his life a firm isolationist. In 1917 he had taken part in the filibuster along with LaFollette and others against Woodrow Wilson's bill to arm merchant ships. It was this filibuster that led Wilson to make his celebrated denunciation: "A little group of willful men, representing no opinion but their own, have rendered the great government of the United States helpless and contemptible." Norris compounded his offense in Wilson's eyes by being among the small handful to vote against the declaration of war. And, although Norris counted himself philosophically in favor of international organization, he voted against the ratification of the Treaty of Versailles. During the early thirties Norris remained secure in his isolationism. As late as 1937, on the occasion of the twentieth anniversary of his vote against our participation in the First World War, he issued a statement explaining why he still considered this action the high mark of his career.

Yet as Nazism began to disclose its aggressive purposes in 1937 and 1938, as Norris began to reconsider the moral obligation that he, as a man who cared deeply about people and freedom, owed to people whose freedom was under attack, as he perceived the moral implications of indifference to totalitarian aggression, Norris began to change his views. Reluctantly, but with a profound sense of moral and political lucidity about what he was doing, Norris moved from the isolationist position. Where others, like the brilliant son of his close friend Bob LaFollette, remained consistent in the isolationist faith, Norris, a much older man, saw the movement of events with superior clarity. He saw that Adolf Hitler had rendered isolationism obsolescent, and that both the political safety of the United States and the moral obligations of freedom required the United States to assist those resisting Nazi aggression.

Norris thus backed the leading measures by which the Roosevelt Administration sought ot help the opponents of Nazism. At a time when many of his old progressive colleagues were still clinging to the dream of an America which could seal itself off from the troubles of the world, Norris accepted the inevitabilities of the twentieth century.

One finds recorded in Norris's life the full transformation of the liberal tradition, both from negative to positive government, and from isolationism to internationalism. Franklin Roosevelt once called Norris "the very perfect gentle knight of American progressive ideals," and termed him "one of the major social prophets of America." This was surely so. No one, when I was growing up in the thirties, seemed to us to stand more completely and in such strength of commitment for the American liberal tradition. No one expressed that tradition with the purity and devotion of George W. Norris.

What was Norris's creed? He once tried to define the "greatest danger" which the American faith has faced. This danger, he said, consisted of the "consuming ambitions, both for power and for wealth; the greed and avarice of individuals and groups for wealth; the injection of privilege, favoritism and discrimination in national policy."

Such forces as these, Norris said, were the best allies of communism.

"Communism," he wrote, "does not breed in a country where people are happy and satisfied. . . . Communism is born where labor is denied its just reward and pressed down almost into human bondage. . . . The danger of dictatorship arises when the common people are unable to obtain justice under the laws, and when those who toil on the farm, in the workshop, and in the counting houses, are overburdened and bowed down with injustice at the hands of those who control the property of the nation."

One means by which democracy can combat the forces of entrenched and organized greed is through the use of government. "A government," Norris said, "in the truest sense is only a method to bring to humanity the greatest amount of happiness."

"That is what we are here for. That is what Congress is up there for. That is what your President ought to be there for. That is what you have your state governments for. That is what we ought to get out of government."

This was Norris's faith—a faith in the people and in their capacity to govern themselves prudently and wisely; a belief that the national government is an essential instrumentality of the people in their appointed pursuit of life, liberty, and happiness. It was an old-fashioned American faith, perhaps a little innocent and guileless to the sophisticates of a later generation. And yet there was incorporated in it the sturdy determination and the passionate integrity which have constituted the vital center of American liberalism. There resides in it the ideas and the commitments which have defined the great leaders of American democracy. As Franklin Roosevelt once said, "Senator Norris, I go along with you because it is my honest belief that you follow in their footsteps—radical like Jefferson, demagogue like Jackson, idealist like Lincoln, wild like Theodore Roosevelt, theorist like Wilson. You dare to be all of these." It was this daring which constituted Norris's greatness.

One can see intellectual defects in the formulation of Norris's political creed. He was not a political philosopher. He was a pragmatist, reacting with intelligence and compassion to a series of specific situations. But what mattered was not the consistency or profundity of his political ideas but the quality of his moral faith. It is this which represents his essential inheritance. It is precisely this that modern liberalism, for all the sophistication in which it takes such pride so desperately needs.

Norris used to remember how his mother, on a warm spring afternoon asked him to help her plant a seedling. She had dug a hole; and she wanted the boy to hold the tree upright while she shoveled the dirt around its roots and packed it all tightly in. George looked up at her. He saw the sweat running down her face, saw how worn she was and how tired she looked, and asked her finally why she worked so hard. "We now have more fruit than we can possibly use. You will be dead long before this tree comes into bearing."

As he recalled it many years later, her answer was slow to come. She measured her words and finally said, "I may never see this tree in bearing, but somebody will."

This concern for the future, this understanding that, as we act today, we act not just for our own time but for all subsequent generations, this perception that we are the trustees for our descendants—this was the heart of Norris's liberal faith.

He brought about in his day a moral renewal of the American liberal tradition.

It seems an appropriate occasion, on this centennial commemoration, to rededicate our own efforts toward a comparable moral renewal now.

Acknowledgment

For quite a number of years members of my family and hundreds of warm personal friends have urged me to write the story of my life.

Various reasons have been given, most of which did not appeal to me.

I could not see, and do not see now, just why people would be interested in the struggling and somewhat discouraging life that I have lived from boyhood.

When I left the United States Senate, this urgency on the part of my friends was intensified greatly. Literally thousands of letters came from all parts of the country, a great many of which were written by people who had never seen or heard me. Their ideas regarding me had been formed from what they had read in the magazines and in the newspapers, and in the reports of the various legislative struggles through which I had passed in my forty years' service in Congress.

Most of these letters were from young people—in many cases, just graduating from high schools. Many of them were from students and professors in various colleges and universities scattered from Maine to California and from the Canadian boundary to the Gulf of Mexico.

The beautiful, appealing language of so many of the letters made a great impression upon me.

The writers told of personal struggles—most of them, for an education—in which the story of my life would give them encouragement and greater hope. I was moved strongly by the appeals from the multitude of young people striving so earnestly for an education under the handicap of poverty. Most of them were doing what I had done when young: alternately attending classes while the money lasted, and teaching, perhaps, awhile, until their funds were replenished, and returning to college until their education was completed.

For six months after my retirement from the United States Senate these letters continued to come. Every letter was written from the impulse of some struggling young man or young woman, who was then seeking, under adverse circumstances, to better his or her condition and the conditions of the community in which he or she lived. Although I was impressed deeply, and although I felt honored by the fact that the battles that I had fought were an inspiration to many aspiring young people, I still could not see that a book about myself would accomplish what these friends thought it would, give hope to others faced with similar struggles.

While this struggle was going on in my heart, my old friend James E. Lawrence of Lincoln, Nebraska, whom I think one of the ablest editorial writers of the country, made several personal visits to my home in McCook, and with an eloquence far above the average possessed by mortal man, urged me to undertake the writing of my autobiography. He promised to help me—outlined what seemed to be a necessary work that I should undertake for the benefit of hundreds of thousands of my countrymen who apparently were appealing to me for help and comfort in a period of great national distress and confusion. I had not kept a diary of my early life, but under the urgent appeals of Mr. Lawrence, and with his assistance, I have undertaken to tell the story truthfully, however doubtful of its value.

In a volume of this size, only a part of the many struggles of a rather long and eventful life could be given in detail. One of Mr. Lawrence's tasks in examining the manuscript that I prepared has been to elaborate upon some parts of the material and to eliminate others in order to create a balanced story within the necessary limits. I want to say here and now that in my humble judgment, Mr. Lawrence is entitled to unlimited credit for his work of research, editing, and rearranging the material in its present form. It is safe to say that without his assistance, and his continual urging, the book never would have been written.

The book is truthful to my own experience, and I have tried to make it interesting. Whether or not I have succeeded will be for the readers to say. If it brings new hope to the generation now struggling on battlefields to preserve our country and to perpetuate the principles and the philosophy of government for which I fought throughout my public career, I shall be repaid fully for the effort.

G. W. NORRIS

McCOOK, NEBRASKA
August 10, 1944

Introduction

A VETERAN NEWSPAPERMAN, who has "covered" the White House and the deliberations of Congress for many years, said on a brief visit to Lincoln:

"The life of Norris is the story of America at its best."

This is the mature and critical judgment, not only of one correspondent, but many of the men writing in Washington.

It is true, the character of Senator George W. Norris of Nebraska has stamped itself permanently upon American political thought and action. His course so uniformly consistent—so faithfully consistent that friends and foes came to know what to expect of him—elevated him to rank as the outstanding liberal in Congress. Supporters and opponents could anticipate his position even before debate began or the roll call was taken. They knew the words he would speak, and they could foresee the vote he would cast.

That is the best measure of the extent to which he impressed his character upon the American public.

Ohio, his State of birth, almost as much as Virginia, has the right to be known as "The Mother of Presidents." Only Virginia has given more sons to the White House.

From Ohio came Ulysses S. Grant, commander of the Union army; Hayes, who was born on the fringes of the same section that gave birth to Senator Norris; Garfield, who kindled the boyish imagination of Norris; McKinley, whose Republicanism captivated the ardent young partisan of those days; Taft, during whose administration the young prairie insurgent was to lead his first brave fight against reaction; and Harding, during whose administration Senator Norris made some of his most gallant fights against reactionary tendencies in government.

There is some basis in the record for the conclusion that Ohio's greatest contribution to American government came from a son who spent his entire public life in Congress. Those Presidents Ohio gave America generally were of orthodox Republican pattern, willing symbols of party government, and as such, necessarily of smaller stature than the party they represented. The man who served forty years in the House of Representatives and the United States Senate was an independent throughout most of his public life.

The struggles in which Senator Norris took part are known in general outlines and results. Too little is known of the circumstances which projected them, and of the actual developments in connection with them.

The fight to overthrow Speaker Cannon did not end as Senator Norris had hoped it would. Results accomplished fell far short of the reform upon which he had set his heart.

His opposition to the League of Nations rested upon no flimsy foundation of fear that Article X of the Covenant would take from the American people their precious sovereign rights. He was willing to scrap the Monroe Doctrine. He insisted that, to achieve a peace, the American people had to sacrifice some of their notions—among them notions most dear to them.

This book concerns itself with the little-known circumstances of some of the most bitter congressional battles of the present century.

Senator Norris in his forty years in Congress demonstrated effectively that often the legislative branch of government lagged far behind the people it represented in political thought and action. Through two great wars on foreign soil, and through grave domestic strife and crisis, his eternally youthful vision, his courage and his honesty, gave strength, hope, and faith to millions of his countrymen.

Virtually alone in the early twenties in one of the most conservative eras of American history, he carried on the discouraging battle which led to the ultimate establishment of TVA. That victory established a sound, inspiring pattern for the conservation of natural resources, which has withstood a hundred powerful attacks.

Twelve years of congressional battle went into it.

He was the first to dare singlehanded an amendment to the Federal Constitution. The abuse and evils of the Lame Duck Congress were recognized widely long before Senator Norris proceeded to do something about them. Ten years were needed to overcome a powerful, reactionary congressional leadership in submission of the Lame Duck Amendment, which it took the American people, through their state legislatures, only eleven months to approve.

Senator Norris was the first to seek to correct abuse of the courts in this country by great corporate wealth, which utilized the legal process of injunction to oppress its workers. There were seven years of struggle for that new freedom which American labor now enjoys.

Agriculture, the forests, and the streams had in him a true and constant friend.

Throughout forty years Congress echoed to the voice of this Independent, who went to the prairie country as a young man, fell in love with it and its people, and for four decades represented the state of Nebraska on Capitol Hill.

Senator Norris never knew what it was to play. It was not unusual for him to work sixteen and eighteen hours a day in the handling of correspondence, in painstaking reading, in research and preparation. His passion for accurate information in Senate discussion was insatiable. If he did not have time to prepare himself properly on public issues, invariably Senator Norris refused to discuss them.

In personal and public life, simplicity, frugality, freedom from the restraints politics imposes upon most men, fairness and constancy are the qualities which have distinguished the man and the legislator.

For the first time, there is set forth fully his hard boyhood, his early manhood, and the struggles of a great American liberal, responsible for vast improvements in the tools of democracy.

In so far as possible, this book has been strengthened by study of the records of Connecticut and Ohio, and of Senator Norris's files and correspondence, all of which were drawn upon to supplement his vivid recollections.

The great wealth of available material included hundreds of columns of newspaper and magazine comment to which little reference could be made. There were the congressional debates of forty years, the long committee hearings, the inspiration of thousands of visitors and a voluminous correspondence.

In this book only those battles which Senator Norris thought may prove of some lasting consequence are set forth in the full details. He was in the thick of it for four eventful decades—the years took swift flight, and frequently when the end of one session found the issue unsettled, it was renewed in the next congress, and in some cases, the next and the next. That each separate legislative reform might be presented here in its most simple outlines, a strictly chronological arrangement had to be sacrificed in some cases.

He was the leader—both strategist directing the charge and doughboy back of the gun—in three far-reaching conflicts in progress simultaneously, overlapping one another during much of a ten-year stretch of war between reaction and liberalism. The battles for the TVA, the Lame Duck amendment, and the Anti-Injunction law were separate, distinct and wholly unrelated and yet each had its place in the development of national policy. The full measure of Senator Norris' effectiveness is provided by those three successful battles on three separate fields of action in a single cycle of national readjustment.

Senator Norris completed his dictation eight weeks before his death. The work upon which he embarked with doubts found him happy in its completion, and hopeful it would bring cheer to those for whom it was undertaken. "Unselfish faith," he said two weeks before he passed away, "will prove to be America's greatest resource in the difficult years ahead."

J. E. LAWRENCE

LINCOLN NEBRASKA
August 28, 1944

Contents

CONTENTS

ILLUSTRATIONS

Fighting Liberal

THE AUTOBIOGRAPHY OF

GEORGE W. NORRIS

1

AN OHIO FARM

IN THE YEARS before the Civil War there was a Chauncey Norris, of the northern Ohio countryside: my father.

He and my mother, my brother John Henry, and my sisters Lorinda and Sarah Melissa had come out of New York State in 1846 to seek a new home in Sandusky County in the "Black Swamp" country, not far from Lake Erie. There was in my parents the irrepressible craving for new country with all the satisfaction it gave to the adventurous spirit.

It was a settled community where their journey ended, nine miles from the waters of Sandusky Bay, yet a region which still retained, in the simplicity of its life, the strong twang of the frontier. Its thick timber of whitewoods, oak, and walnut waited the ax and the saw; there were large stretches of its soil still to yield to the plow.

For months during the autumn and winter of 1845 back in Batavia, New York, my father and my mother had talked quietly in the evening shadows, after the labors of the day, of joining her kin in Ohio—her brothers who wrote to her of the land that sounded so inviting. Then the death of a month-old daughter may have decided them.

By the first gray light of a morning in early summer, Father loaded Mother, the three children, and a few pieces of furniture into a wagon and headed the horses toward the highway over which thousands of emigrants had passed to the West.

My mother, Mary Norris, was magnificently endowed for her role as a home-maker in a new, raw country.

She had come to Rochester out of Pennsylvania, the Dutch blood in her veins reflecting the strength of those Pennsylvania colonists who became neighbors to the English, the Germans, and the Irish of the early settlements. Before her marriage, as Mary Magdalene Mook, she had been an expert spinner; and for years her spinning wheel, which now stands on the stair landing of my home in McCook, produced the fabrics which clothed my father, my brother, and my sisters.

My father and mother met at a house-raising—that good neighborly ceremonial of an early America, at which people gathered and pooled their labor to build homes for youths and maidens shortly to be married. A dark-haired, dark-eyed girl of twenty, she was betrothed to another when Chauncey Norris, at thirty-one, lost his heart to her. She must have seen something good in the disturbing stranger, who lived but a few miles away. It was a short and earnest courtship They were wed late on a Christmas afternoon and left Cayuga County a few weeks later for Monroe County only a short distance to the west.

* * *

My father's parents, of Scotch-Irish blood, came to America about the time of the American Revolution. They first appeared in Connecticut—Connecticut, the one American colony which in its first formal Orders establishing community governments made no mention of the British king, and matched Maryland in its statutes on religious tolerance.

In a world ruled by royalty, Connecticut started life with a framework of representative institutions of government long before the Declaration of Independence. There, where my forebears first settled, was example, inspiration, and confirmation of what came later at Philadelphia.

I like to think now, nearly two hundred years later, that Connecticut's aspiration toward the equality of men established by political processes was the beacon which first directed my grandparents to its soil.

There were five children—four girls and a boy. The boy,

Chauncey, my father, was the youngest; the oldest was a girl of fourteen when my grandparents, in the prime of life, died within a few short weeks of each other, one a victim of yellow fever, the other of pneumonia.

The fourteen-year-old girl, who at the bedside of her mother had promised to watch over her sisters and her brother, had only a single thought—and that was to keep the family as close together as circumstances would permit. She and her sisters and the five-year-old brother thus became a part of a trainload of children, westward bound to central New York for homes which needed their cheer, and needed even more the labor that they could furnish.

In Cayuga County, under the care of a German family named Martin, Chauncey Norris grew up beside his sisters, entered his teens, grew strong and straight, reached maturity. As a boy and a young man he was shy and reserved, little given to talk; but between him and his adopted parents there developed a deep bond of affection. Apparently he had no time for school, little time for reading. Habits of industry were ingrained deeply in him; simple and nourishing food made a strong man, and his zest in life rested upon work.

Both my father and my mother were uneducated, and it was with great difficulty that they wrote their names. Both were able to read, and it was in reading that my mother found her greatest pleasure.

* * *

So many times I have tried to turn the indistinct memories of my father into something tangible, something of flesh and blood—invariably to see, instead, the farm which he and my mother had carved out of the timber, the swamp, and the rock.

From the time I grew old enough and strong enough to work, that farm fully occupied my thoughts and my energies. Its acres were the most exacting of taskmasters, seemingly with a chore for every free hour of daylight. From daybreak to nightfall the farm cried loudly for attention, completely absorbing the strength and the thoughts of a growing boy.

My father had built a house—it still stands—and with pride had included a loft, pretentious for its day except among those of the well-to-do. Never did he find time to plaster and finish that loft. He cleared twenty-five acres of trees, south from the house to the sandy ridge which overlooked his land. The field was strewn with stones, flinty niggerheads: hundreds of smaller ones on the surface; scores of larger ones, up to seven or eight feet in length, and half a ton in weight, barely showing or buried in the soil. The smaller rocks had to be collected and carted off; the larger ones, covered over so that the plow would not hit them. Many times I would dig a deep pit, and then, using a tree trunk as a lever, roll great niggerheads into the pit and cover them with soil. Tree stumps, aged by the winds and the rains and the snows, had to be grubbed out.

This was the frontier home to which my parents came in search of peace and happiness; where my father died in the middle years; where my mother bravely raised a family of eleven children; and where I, as a boy, lived in the wonder of nature, in the hope of usefulness and knowledge and in the tender companionship of a family.

* * *

My tiny world consisted of flowering apple trees in the spring; wheat turning golden in the near-by field; the carefully tended vegetable garden; the haze-bathed horizons of the adjacent woods, beyond which we passed on rare occasions when Father loaded the family into the wagon to visit relatives and neighbors.

It was well these surroundings satisfied me, because my father was little given to visiting. He had lived so much to himself throughout all of his life. His face and bearing were habitually stern, and his only tender side was a love of flowers. His neighbors took note that Chauncey Norris attempted to screen the rails of the barnyard fences—rails which he had hewn from the timber with his own hands—with gay blooms.

I know that he was sensitive to the glory of the seasons.

In the winter the snow lay deep, blocking roads with drifts; and darkness closed in rapidly on the short, pale afternoons when the skies were overcast. Those winter nights, I was told, were times of cheer and companionship even when the nearest neighbors seemed far away, and the family occupied a little country of its own. There was meat in the smokehouse, the cellar was filled with vegetables and apples, the near-by woods provided an abundance of fuel. Inside, the glowing stove warmed that country home; and the winds and the snows and the cold outside only added to its magic.

My father knew the creatures of the field, the woods and the skies even as I, a growing boy, after his death, came to know them. The fall nights of cold pelting rain and low-hanging, scurrying clouds always beckoned to my imagination when flocks of geese in the darkness overhead broke the silence on their flight to the south. I looked forward to their return in the spring, to the tiny rivulets of snow-water, to the first green buds, and to the first robins. I reveled in the roll of thunder at the close of a hot summer afternoon, and the cool splash of water on my brow. I watched the trees sway in the gales, gathered the wild flowers, searched for berries, and like all youngsters of that era eagerly anticipated the first frosts which would bring the walnuts falling from the high branches.

* * *

My father died midway between my third and fourth birthdays; died as the aftermath of the only vivid experience that I was permitted to share with him. Even now, eighty years later, the recollections of it are sharply etched in my memory.

That first day of December, 1864, opened with a clear cold sunrise and a nipping north wind blowing from off the waters of the lake. A trip to the mill in Clyde with a load of wheat, which was to be ground into flour, was in prospect; and I, an eager adventurer of only three and a half years, wanted to go along.

The tears coursed down my cheeks when my mother objected that the day was too cold for a tiny boy to make the trip.

"Let him come along," my father said. "I will not leave the wagon."

Then my two sisters burst into tears: they, too, wanted to go. In the end my mother bundled us all snugly and warmly, and placed us in the rear of the wagon box; and I had my first glimpse of the miller, jolly and fat, and covered with white powder from head to foot.

All went well until we were nearing home on the return trip, when the sight of a neighbor at work in his field reminded my father of a borrowed cultivator which it was convenient now to carry home. He loaded it into the wagon, resting the handles against the endgate.

We had started on when a frightened rabbit dashed like a gray streak under the nose of the colt which Father was driving that day with an old mare. The colt, broken only recently to harness, was high-strung; and it plunged wildly and then broke into a run, taking the older horse along. Its terror increased as the wagon bounced over the frozen ruts and the iron handles of the cultivator rattled noisily against the endgate. The faster the horses ran, the greater the noise, and the greater their terror.

My father fought to bring them under control.

How my sisters and I laughed! We thought it was great fun.

My mother heard the noise of the pounding hoofs, and the rumble of the wagon, and she was waiting near the gate to the farm yard when Father brought the team to a stop a few feet beyond the point where normally he turned into the barn, one wheel tightly locked against a great boulder. Grabbing us in her arms, she removed us to safety.

"It is Providence," Mother said, her eyes resting upon the boulder which had checked the flight of the frightened horses.

But again they started to run, jumped the fence of the south field, tearing the rear wheels from the wagon. Around the field they raced, and jumped the fence a second time, when my father was thrown heavily to the frozen ground.

Apparently he was unhurt. He finally conquered the team, drove it for another hour, and then came into the house dripping with perspiration.

Late in the afternoon he was taken with a heavy cold, and in the night pneumonia set in.

In forty-eight hours my father was dead.

Years afterwards, as a boy and a young man, I hunted rabbits. Never did one spring from the weeds or the underbrush but my thoughts drifted back to that December day in Ohio.

Five days after the runaway, December 5, 1864, the neighbors, my mother's kin, and the family gathered at the little community cemetery to bury Chauncey Norris in the soil upon which he had built his hopes and dreams.

Only the grief of my mother and my sisters left an impression upon me.

When I grew older it seemed to me my father never had lived.

* * *

Some months earlier, my brother John Henry, strong and straight, a man of twenty-five years of age, had promised my mother he would not join the army. I know now that in the years before, with Gettysburg's bloody struggle fanning the patriotic fervor of thousands of the young men of Ohio, John had fought many a grim battle with himself. One afternoon I found my mother in tears; and, deeply distressed, I asked her why she was crying.

"John has broken his promise to me," was the only reply she made as she passed into the next room.

That was it.

I could not realize then the desolation my mother felt over John's enlistment in Company A, the Fifty-third Ohio Volunteer Infantry, which became a part of Sherman's column marching from Atlanta to the sea. I could offer no consolation when John, after suffering a slight wound in a skirmish at Resaca, Georgia, which he apparently dismissed as of no consequence, died of an infection on May 27, 1864.

One younger sister, Ida, was born in February of 1865, but she lived for only two years. John's death and hers left me—born on July 11, 1861—the youngest in the family and the only boy.

Three of the girls had married and had established homes of their own. Six sisters—Henrietta, Mary Adelaide, Elizabeth, Effie

Ann, Emma, and Clara—and I remained with my mother on that cold and bleak December day when my father was buried, to share the heritage of the Ohio farm.

And what was that heritage?

When finally the estate was divided, my share was $132; but the money that came to me was the least of my heritage.

There on that farm I lost all fear of poverty. I learned to live most simply, and I learned to get a great joy out of work. It never occurred to me in those years that the lack of money was of any consequence. I grew up to believe wholly and completely in men and women who lived simply, frugally, and in fine faith. I learned that fear was inspired in men and women who could not reconcile themselves to the possibility that hardship and sacrifice might confront them in battling for the right.

Unconsciously there developed in that pioneer Ohio region a great respect for justice and a great sympathy for the oppressed. As a boy I saw with my own eyes the struggles of a democracy where the first problem is not protection of the strong and the powerful but instead encouragement and inspiration for the weak and the unfortunate. In the organization of the life of this democracy, and in the development of its conceptions of social justice, it has seemed to me, is the spirit of America.

2

MY MOTHER

In my teens I came to understand to some degree my mother's struggle after father's death. Not for years, however, could I appreciate fully the remarkable, stoic gallantry of spirit which sustained her.

My mother was in her early forties at the time I was born, a mature woman, with a serious bearing that had a charming grace; but the weeks and months following my father's death gave her a new gravity—a gravity unnoted by me in my carefree childhood.

Winter in that part of Ohio was severe; snow covered the ground; the skies were leaden; and the trees my mother loved stood bare, gaunt, and grim against the fringes of that farmhouse, where her immediate problem was feeding, clothing, sheltering, and educating her children.

My father's death intensified mother's grief over the loss of John.

He had been such a comfort to my mother. Unlike father, he was buoyant, cheerful, and companionable; and, as is so frequently the case of a son in a large family of girls, my mother seemed to lean upon him and to shower an extra measure of affection upon him. When John attained young manhood my mother came to rely on his judgment implicitly. She was proud of his industry and gloried in his schooling, which included a year of college.

From the opening weeks of the Civil War—from Fort Sumter and Bull Run—my mother lived daily in fear John would enlist in the Union army. She decided to exact from him a promise not to enter the armed service. That gave her a temporary peace of mind; and then when John, no longer able to bear the spectacle of his friends marching off in uniform, went off like them, she gave herself the luxury of a few tears in my presence as she went about her household tasks.

Although the battlefields were far to the south and east, the war was very near to the farms of that section of Ohio, whose settlers had been drawn entirely from the New England and Middle Atlantic states. Antislavery sentiment was overwhelming, and the debates over that issue had fanned patriotic fervor. Commanding generals in the field had their fierce partisans at the stores, the schoolhouses and the public squares. Abe Lincoln had gripped the hearts of most Ohians.

Near Clyde was Fremont, named after an earlier American military leader and explorer; and in the heart of the community was the home of General McPherson, one of the great Union commanders whose grave and monument later furnished a constant reminder of the tide of Union sentiment that had swept most of the young men of the state.

In maturity I could understand John's struggle with himself. He had been raised in a rigid and unswerving devotion to all promises. A promise made was a promise to be kept. Undoubtedly it was with great effort that he told mother of his decision to enlist. My mother, like all mothers, hated war; but at the time I thought it was John's failure to keep his word to her that caused my mother's sharpest grief. Never before had he broken a promise. It was on this record of obedience that she had rested confidently.

When he went away she watched the mails for letters that came from him, with long waits in between. She treasured those letters more than any other possession, reading and re-reading them, and then tying them in a packet with red ribbon and placing them away carefully in a tin box. Red ribbon was scarce in that impoverished household of girls.

There was the initial shock when the news came that John had been wounded in the Battle of Resaca which preceded Sherman's triumphant entry into Atlanta. But the message itself was reassuring; a bullet had pierced his leg, and the wound did not appear to be serious. He had written that after receiving medical care he had been able to rejoin his company without delay and would continue the march, nearing its end. Then word arrived of his death from infection which had set in. And while he was sinking he wrote mother a letter seemingly inspired by the knowledge death was near. I treasured it for years until it disappeared from my safe in McCook, along with the watch which John had carried into battle. I have thought the letter and watch were taken when political enemies years later rifled that safe.

There was the illness and death of little Ida, a gurgling, laughing baby, born in February following my father's death, and dying in her third year.

I never heard a song upon the lips of my mother. I never even heard her hum a tune. Years later I understood why those years robbed her of the song of motherhood which has come down through all of the ages. She loved music. Her children were musical. The song of life, so natural to Mary Mook Norris, was silenced forever in the bitter grief and sorrow of those years between 1864 and 1867. The war ended, and the young men came back, but John slept in a soldier's grave in the blackened southern countryside. There were times when it seemed that her heartache over her son never would pass.

Mother was forty-six years of age when father died.

She was a confusing mixture of sternness, gentleness, and strength of will and purpose.

She had borne twelve children, and had buried three of them. When the harvest required it, she had taken her place in the field. She had planted and tended the vegetable garden. She had spun the cloth, and had made the clothes which my father, my sisters, John, and I wore. She had directed the girls in addition to performing her share of the household tasks. Spinning and weaving and sewing, washing and ironing and canning—she now undertook the financial planning for the family. Her hair was unstreaked; she walked erect. She rarely lost that unruffled composure which told completely the full strength of her spirit. She was a woman of great, simple faith: a faith so strong and so indestructible that it sustained and comforted her through all the years of a long and useful life. She was eighty-two in the summer of 1900, when she died in the farm home she and my father built.

Among my most vivid recollections of my mother is of her sitting straight and rigid in a chair, reading to us from the only book in our home, the Bible. Each year she read the Bible through. On Sunday afternoons she would gather us to her side and, opening the worn pages, read for hours. It never seemed strange that, devoted Bible student that she was, she was not a member of any church.

Not far away, very close to the Mount Carmel district school, was a small church where on Sunday mornings I went to Sunday school, often remaining for church services; and occasionally in the evenings I would attend revival meetings held there. All of the people of the community were very strongly religious, and I soon discovered my mother believed the Bible literally.

Those preachers in the little country church preached terrifyingly and with fervor of hell fire and damnation, and invariably, I was frightened when I reached home.

My mother, while she could not explain, sensed fully my fright, and managed to soften the harsh words of the preacher. Always she convinced me that the horrible prophecies from the pulpit would not descend upon me, and in the warmth of her love my fears disappeared.

Later, one of the first books to come into my possession was "The History of the Conflict Between Religion and Science," by John William Draper. Instinctively, I knew mother would object to my reading it.

She had opposed vigorously her children dancing, and in deference to her it was not until I left home that I attended my first dance. I remember how provoked I became at my sisters when, my mother having gone for a visit with her relatives, they arranged for a dance at our house. In protest at their disobeying her while she was away, I went to bed.

She did not approve of card playing. I was in my teens when my mother's scruples against cards suddenly and unexpectedly evaporated and she joined with my sisters one night in urging me to take part in a card game. I never knew why she relented.

So when that book came into my hands by loan I carried it home under my coat. I took it to my room, and cautiously hid it under the straw tick of my bed.

And there by candlelight, when the house was still and the others were asleep, I read it without my mother's knowledge, fascinated by the new worlds which it opened.

My mother was reading to me from the Old Testament one Sunday afternoon, and she came to Deuteronomy, the twenty-third chapter, second verse:

> A bastard shall not enter into the congregation of the Lord; even to his tenth generation shall he not enter into the congregation of the Lord.

Without fully understanding the words of the verse, I was shocked that the door of heaven seemingly was closed to innocent children, themselves guilty of no wrongdoing.

"What does it mean?" I asked mother.

"Do you not know what it means, Willie?" she asked. "You know—I shall call her 'Little Jennie.'"

I knew Little Jennie. She was a child of the easy conventions of the frontier. She was a beautiful little girl, so fair, so angelic of features, a golden crest of curls. She seemed filled with the joy of life. I was seized with seething rebellion. I wanted no heaven from a God who said Little Jennie might not enter the congregation of the Lord.

Passing Jennie's home on the way to school the following Monday, I could hear screams, high and shrill. I was troubled through the entire day. When I returned home after school I spoke to mother about it.

"You do not know what happened to Jennie?" she asked me.

I shook my head.

"She is dead," my mother replied.

It seemed that when Jennie's mother went to the kitchen that morning to prepare breakfast, her little girl obtained some matches, set fire to her little nightgown, and was burned so badly she died a few hours later. It was her screams of pain that I had heard on my way to school.

I was disturbed, and for years the incident tormented my mind, adding to my confusion over the church and religion.

That lack of education against which my parents fought throughout their lives made each of them, and particularly my mother, solicitous that all their children be educated to the extent that conditions permitted. There was no sacrifice too great for her to make toward her children's education. She saw to it that my brother, completing the common schools, was sent to Baldwin University at Berea, Ohio, for one term.

Even after the death of my father and John, my mother insisted that my older sisters continue in the country schools, frequently at great financial sacrifice; and when the family's straitened financial circumstances improved somewhat, and the schools of the region offered greater facilities, again she insisted that Effie, Emma, and Clara all go to the high school at Clyde, approximately three and a half miles away.

There, they secured positions with families and, under mother's constant urging, worked for their board while completing their studies. So firm was her resolution the children should have a greater opportunity than had been hers that she insisted Emma and Clara, who were just older than I, attend the university at Berea for a year.

I noted her interest in education ran contrary to the prevailing thought of most of the settlers. There were many families in much better financial circumstances, but these families did not seem to be interested in the education of their children. At the most they believed in the three R's: grammar, higher mathematics, and other studies were a waste of time.

Children could not have desired more encouragement than mother gave to us. It was she who gave warmth to the home and a security to the family.

There were few comforts in that home. The loft, uncarpeted, unfinished, unheated, where I slept, developed wide cracks between the shingles, and there were nights when I could see the

Acme Photo

GEORGE W. NORRIS AND HIS MOTHER, MARY MOOK NORRIS. THE CLOTHES WORN BY THE SON WERE SPUN BY THE MOTHER. AT THE TIME THIS PICTURE WAS TAKEN HE WAS APPROACHING HIS TEENS, BUT ALREADY HE HAD ASSUMED HIS PLACE IN THE FIELDS OF HIS MOTHER'S FARM. SHE WAS TO INFLUENCE HIS THOUGHT THROUGHOUT HIS LIFE.

stars twinkling in the Earth's celestial blanket. There were nights in the winter when the snow sifted in, too, laying a white blanket over my bed.

I remember the anticipation with which my sisters and I looked forward to the first coal-oil lamp, purchased after much planning and arduous saving, to replace the tallow candles. No one except mother was permitted to touch that lamp, for fear it might be broken. She cleaned it, trimmed the wick, lighted it, and placed it back upon its resting shelf when the family retired for sleep.

After mother remarried, my stepfather—Isaac Parker, an elderly, quiet Pennsylvanian of Dutch blood, and an expert wood worker—built a large desk for the house, which filled an entire corner of one room. It was an ornamental piece. He made a high stool for it; but frequently the stool was pulled out to the center of the room, the lamp placed upon it, and there in the circle of its light my mother plied her spinning wheel; my sisters either knit, at which they were adept, or buried themselves in their schoolbooks, and I did my lessons. It was on such occasions a closely knit family circle, earlier bound together by adversity and grief, self-supporting and undisturbed by the lack of cash and money, sensed the full happiness of home associations.

When I had grown to sturdy boyhood, Isaac Parker gave me one of those huge two-cent pieces on the Fourth of July that I might celebrate in Clyde. In the happiness that two-cent piece brought me, I lost no time getting to town. There I pooled resources with another boy of my age, who had five cents, to buy firecrackers to celebrate Independence Day. The ceremony which the holiday commemorates could not have been matched with a greater solemnity than the conference which followed purchase of the firecrackers as the two of us divided them on the basis of individual contribution to the joint fund.

It was not until I had attained my twenty-first birthday that I tasted ice cream; and then I tasted it not at home, but during a visit to a neighboring city. I thought I had never tasted anything so good, and I ate it slowly to make it last longer.

Early I developed a love of music.

I enjoyed singing, and it was the greatest ambition of my early boyhood to possess a violin. Again my mother's religious scruples intruded: while she also enjoyed music, her Puritan faith looked upon the violin as an instrument of the devil because it supplied the music for dancing. She finally told me I might have an accordion.

Her consent did not solve the pressing problem of money.

There were weeks when there was not a cent in our home. At that time the clothing I wore, and for some years to come my clothing, was handed down to me from others who had outgrown it. It was a great occasion for rejoicing when mother had the good fortune to sell one of the huge walnut trees on the farm for lumber for a few dollars.

Wants were few; no one in the community possessed money, it seemed, and the lack of it in all families made them unconscious of poverty. My mother's willingness to let me have an accordion made me very conscious of money for the first time in my life. She had ingrained in us a deep horror of debt, a revulsion against it never overcome. She had created in us the feeling that debt was a sin.

I knew that before I could think of buying an accordion, I must earn and save the money. At the foot of the near-by ridge and along the fringes of the woods were hazelnut thickets. Each fall we had gathered the nuts. And here, it came to me, might be a source of funds for the accordion. Each day after finishing the farm chores, I took a two-bushel sack and visited the hazelnut thickets, returning home only after it had been filled. When the hulls were dried, my mother and my sisters gathered in the kitchen and helped me hull the hazelnuts. It was slow work: it took a great many hazelnuts in the hull to make a quart of hulled hazelnuts.

I kept at it until I had five and one-half bushels.

With this treasure a nephew, Sam Higgins, who could play the accordion and I hitched up the old mare to the wagon, put in hay and grain for her, and started out for Sandusky City, eighteen miles away, confident we should find a ready market for the hazelnuts, and there among the music stores of Sandusky City find an accordion within reach of my limited financial means. I had never seen Sandusky City. I had never been that far away from home.

I discovered quickly no one wanted hazelnuts.

Long after the lunch hour I sold the lot to a grocer for $5.70 and, with Sam, started for the music stores. There were large stocks of accordions, but most of them were priced far beyond what I could afford. Finally one dealer brought out an accordion which Sam said would do. I experienced bitter disappointment when he said the price was $8.50. I had started to turn away when the proprietor called to me, suggesting that I take the accordion and pay the balance when I was able to do so. I could not go into debt. Again I started to leave, and then the proprietor called to me, told me I might have the accordion for the money I had in my pocket.

Sam and I returned to the square, harnessed the old mare to the wagon, started for home just before the sun sank at the western horizon, and shortly before midnight drove up in the farmyard triumphantly, while I played lustily: "Jesus, Lover of My Soul."

With Sam's tutoring I had learned it while riding home through the gathering darkness of that country road.

My mother became very fond of the accordion and proud of me.

She invited the neighbors in to hear me play, and we would sing the old familiar songs. It has been years since I looked at the copies of these songs; they still are in the cabinet at home.

My most faithful, constant companion was my dog, "Lion."

In the darkness of winter nights he would wait by the gate in the snow for me, and long before I reached it I knew he was standing sentinel there. His eyes glowed in the blackness; his bark and his wagging tail would run a race to determine which could express the greater joy; he would spring upon me in his joy and excitement, his paws striking me in the chest and knocking me over.

Together we would roll over and over in the snow.

I have been told frequently that my mother influenced my thought more than any other living person.

If that is so, I was not conscious of it. I recognized her deep concern for my welfare. Frequently I was moved to wonderment by the strength of her patience, and by a native wisdom acquired through hard labor, without books or teacher. We were never hungry, never cold, never miserable, and in all the hard work of that farm and the large family which it supported I cannot say we were conscious of hardships.

I recall all those cycles of the years—summer, fall, winter, and spring—with pleasure.

The feel of the warm sweet earth underfoot was good; the sight of the ripening grain, and the orchard with its trees of red-cheeked apples created a sense of well-being. There was a joy to those winter mornings, when in the early darkness and cold I would awaken, dress warmly, eat a hearty breakfast, and hurry to the timber with ax and wedges to spend the day splitting rails. There was a sense of triumph which only one who has split rails will understand when the wedge drove home and the tree trunk fell apart.

I was young, strong, and active, and long before I became a man I was able to do a man's work. I reveled in the tasks of the farm, early acquired the ability and the physical strength to husk corn with older men.

I became an expert shot in a region where the supreme sport was to shoot squirrels. My accuracy with a gun compelled the admiration of some of the best shots in the neighborhood. I remember there was a flying squirrel that had eluded all the hunters. I made up my mind I would kill it. I waited patiently at the foot of a great tree in which it had a nest until it put in its appearance, fired, and exulted when the squirrel came tumbling to earth.

Proudly I displayed it to the men and boys of the neighborhood, most of whom at one time had tried to bag it.

There was that warm spring afternoon when mother, who had been busy throughout the entire day, called to me to assist her in planting a tree. She had dug a hole, and she wanted me to hold the seedling upright while she shoveled the dirt in around its roots and packed it tightly. I looked up at her, and it came to me she was tired. The warmth of the afternoon and her exertions had brought small beads of perspiration to her brow.

So I said to her:

"Why do you work so hard, mother? We now have more fruit than we can possibly use. You will be dead long before this tree comes into bearing."

The little farm was well stocked with fruit. It had its apples, its peaches, and its sour cherries.

Her answer was slow to come, apparently while she measured her words.

"I may never see this tree in bearing, Willie," she said, "but somebody will."

That was the unselfishness of the pioneer era.

Its thought was not solely of itself.

In its planting of the fields it derived the satisfaction of growing things. Its planning was not only for the present but the future.

So many times in the battles in Congress, particularly in the fights relating to the conservation of natural resources, my mother's words that late spring afternoon came to my ears.

There is a substance to the faith that nations prosper and grow strong when that which is done today contributes to the happiness and well-being of those who will follow us.

3

EARLY EDUCATION

THAT PART OF OHIO where my parents settled was peopled largely by Pennsylvania Dutch.

Many of the older inhabitants continued to speak their native tongue, but they sent their children to the public schools and saw to it the children were educated in the English language.

Older than I, my sisters had been launched upon their education by mother.

I cannot remember the exact year I entered school. I looked forward to that first day. The Mount Carmel district school had been moved from the earlier location only half a mile from our home to one a mile and a half away. We walked along the country road to school, carrying our lunch, and then home again.

I remember that first day.

The teacher called all of us tiny beginners to his knee, and there undertook to instruct us in the first six letters of the alphabet. I was frightened; I had never seen the letters of the alphabet. I knew I could not get the lesson, and that feeling was fully confirmed the following day when I returned to school.

I did not know the six beginning letters.

But we were fortunate in having fine instructors for the Mount Carmel district school, particularly in the last two years that I attended the common grades. The teacher then, I. D. Speidell, who lived in Clyde, was an exceptionally well educated man, with great understanding of children and sympathy for them. With the exception of the Norris family, and two or three other families of

Vickerys, of English blood, each one of the latter with quite a number of children, all the pupils attending Mount Carmel were descendants of the Pennsylvania Dutch.

Today those incidents of school years which remain the most exquisite, warm recollections of American education during my boyhood would seem simple and unsatisfactory. But it was thorough, and it produced good citizenship. There had developed during the years the great rivalry of the "spelling bee"; it was the one tradition in which parents and pupils alike took a great interest. For many years the Norris girls were the leading spellers of the vicinity, and it was Mount Carmel's proud distinction to be able to "spell down" all the other schools of the region. When my sisters left, Mount Carmel lost its championship, although prior to their completion of the school term Jesse Vickery, two years my senior, had become a champion. Jesse had a sister, Flora, my age, and in the same classes.

In addition to the rivalry created by the spelling bees, the teacher in the primary arithmetic class took a great interest in teaching the multiplication table. He utilized the technique so effective in the spelling bee in order to stimulate interest in arithmetic. He would arrange the youngsters, varying in age from fifteen or sixteen, to much younger ones like Flora and myself, in a long row; and, starting at the head, he would question pupils in multiplication, allowing only a second for the answer.

When he snapped his fingers, if the pupil had been unable to answer, the question passed to the next one, and so on until finally everybody had been eliminated.

He was an excellent penman, and had prepared a prize which was to be awarded to the student who won the multiplication table contest. It was a splendid specimen of his penmanship, and in my heart I made up my mind to win it.

The news spread, and soon the entire district was talking about it; and when the hour of the contest arrived the schoolroom was packed with patrons. It took several hours to complete the elimination, but gradually the larger pupils went down one by one until no one was left except little Flora and me. We stood there for a long time while he shot questions at us, and as we gave the answers, gradually he shortened the time allowed us.

I remember when Flora missed.

The question which she had been called upon to answer was: "How much is 9 times 12?"

She answered instantly, "96."

The teacher snapped his fingers and I said, "108."

I was champion, and yet I felt ashamed.

I thought a great deal of Flora; in fact, Flora and I were little schooltime sweethearts. She was my first sweetheart, and I think that the memories of boyhood attach a special sentimentality to that first schooltime sweetheart. I remember in the various games we played at school how always it turned out that Flora was my favorite and, apparently, I was hers. We used to play "Drop the Handkerchief." Flora always dropped it back of me, and I do not believe Flora ever ran fast enough to escape being kissed.

In fact, it seemed to me that she did not try.

That night when I reached home, I thought how cruel it had been not to let Flora win that contest. Young as I was, I knew I should have been manly enough to surrender the prize to a beautiful girl. I remember crying myself to sleep when I went to bed alone in the loft where at that moment a multiplication table contest seemed to be the biggest event in a big world. It would have been understood and applauded, I reasoned, had I permitted Flora to win. I never talked to Flora about it; she never mentioned it to me; although I knew, without a word being spoken, she was grieved sorely.

In spite of such healthy rivalries, most of these pioneer people clung to the belief that the labor of their children on the farms was infinitely more important than the study of higher mathematics or grammar. There were none more poor, and none needing labor more than my mother, but she insisted I study as extensively as the facilities permitted.

Only three—Willis and Jesse Vickery and I—completed the course in grammar.

Mr. Speidell succeeded in interesting us in algebra. Under his teaching, we completed Ray's Highest Algebra so effectively that upon entering Baldwin University, I was able to plunge into mathematics in the beginning courses of geometry.

At the Mount Carmel school there was a debating society, composed mainly of farmers, which met every Thursday night.

Such debating societies flourished widely throughout the country. They were the natural offspring of the old form of Town Hall meetings which gave such vigor to American colonial life, and which stimulated so much interest in public discussion. They were healthy and invaluable to the development of American citizenship and to American political progress. Their gradual decline has been a loss to the nation.

One of the members of the Mount Carmel debating society was a wagon-maker, George Setzler. Except for Mr. Setzler and the teacher, Mr. Speidell, all the members lived in the country. For reasons unknown the older people never took part in the discussions of the debating society.

It was a great night when Mr. Speidell told the two Vickerys and me that he was going to place our names before the society, but only on the condition that we join actively in the debates.

The leader on my side was "Bill" Wagoner, a farmer, a very fine debater, but unfortunately inclined to imbibe a little too much. That was his plight the night we were to be presented to the debating society. He came to me and said:

"Now you are near the foot of the row on my side. Under the rules, you have about ten minutes, and I want you to talk the full ten minutes. If you should forget what to say, look at me, and I will raise my right hand, and when I raise it, you take up this particular point. If I raise my left hand, it will serve to remind you of that particular point."

It was hard to remember what Bill had suggested as arguments; harder to remember his arguments than to talk without prompting. But to my great surprise, when my time came, I talked the full ten minutes without great effort.

That debating society ushered me into a new life.

The night I became a member the question under discussion was: "*Resolved,* That water is more destructive than fire."

Bill Wagoner in a moment of inspiration recalled the destruction of Vesuvius.

"Now there is Pompoy," he said in a loud voice. Everybody laughed and Bill was stopped for a moment. "Now there is Pompee," he shouted a second time. Again there was laughter. Bill never did succeed in pronouncing Pompeii that night.

I remember on one occasion I proposed this question: "*Resolved,* There is more pleasure in living with a neat, cross woman than with a good-natured, slouchy woman." There was a great deal of laughter, but it was adopted by vote as the basis for discussion at the next meeting. I found I alone was willing to defend the slouchy woman. But the question had provoked a great deal of curiosity, and the schoolroom was crowded to capacity. Alone, I was given all the time I desired for argument and rebuttal, and when the three judges delivered their decision I was a unanimous winner.

More frequently the questions extended to history.

One was: "*Resolved,* That Grant was a greater general than Lee." Another was: "*Resolved,* That the Emancipation Proclamation of Lincoln was constitutional under the constitution at the time of the Civil War." Still a third: "*Resolved,* That under the constitution any state had the legal right to secede and withdraw from the Union."

I remember that one question in which I became greatly interested, and to which as a boy I devoted a great deal of study was: "*Resolved,* That man is a free moral agent." I was curious then concerning the independence of the individual to serve himself and fulfill his responsibilities to his fellow men. It was to bob up at the most unexpected times and under the most unlooked-for circumstances.

George Setzler was unmarried, about thirty-five years old. I had to pass his wagon shop each morning on the way to school. One day he said to me:

"I want to take you over to my room and show you my books."

It was just across the road, upstairs in a farm home. I thought his living quarters were the finest I had ever seen. There was a rug on the floor, and there were curtains at the windows. It was luxury beyond my dreams.

The furniture consisted of three ordinary wooden chairs; a little wooden table, unpainted, which he himself had made; and a bookcase consisting of three shelves about eighteen inches long, also homemade, filled completely with books.

I never had seen a library so large.

When he noted my deep interest, he told me to my delight I was welcome to any book.

All we had to read at home was the weekly newspaper, the *Cincinnati Times*, and the Holy Bible. I was hungry for books, and my pulse quickened at the thought of the nights of reading ahead of me.

Both Mr. Speidell and Mr. Setzler were skillful parliamentarians, and shortly the Vickerys and I found ourselves deeply interested in parliamentary procedure. George Setzler had a copy of Cushing's "Manual of Parliamentary Practice" which generously he loaned to us. The Vickerys and I got enough money together to get Robert's "Rules of Order." It was not long before we participated with all of the eagerness of veterans in parliamentary squabbles and were deeply engaged in parliamentary procedure.

One of the attributes of the American system of public education, to which Jefferson looked for the perpetuation and strengthening of the ideals of democratic institutions, is the imperishable memories of teachers and their influence upon young thought. Throughout my life in Congress, I was cheered and comforted by letters from these old school associates.

George Setzler married Miss Heater, who was my teacher in the last year that I spent in the public schools of Mount Carmel. Years later I learned that she was living at Caldwell, Kansas; and so on January 17, 1931, when she had reached the age of seventy-nine years, I wrote her:

> I have a distinct and vivid recollection of the time when I was a boy and you, as Lydia Heater, were my teacher. Neither can I forget the many kindnesses shown to me by your late husband, George Setzler. It

was he more than any other one person, who induced me to join the old debating society of Mount Carmel and started me in as a debater. I have often thought and I firmly believe that the experience I received in that old country schoolhouse, where we met once a week to debate various questions, was one of the main things which started me on my political career. I think of you and your husband always with a feeling of love and affection. I recall the days when I attended school and you were the teacher, with many pleasant recollections and with gratitude for your infinite patience and inspiration.

To which Mrs. Setzler replied:

I not infrequently recall my experience at Mount Carmel. It has long been one of my pleasures to watch the careers of a number of the pupils whom I enrolled at that time. I distinctly remember that you and your two classmates, Willis and Jess Vickery, always were studious and faithful. To me, it never seemed strange that later each one of you was able to do the things that made you so marked an honor, not only to your family and friends, but to your country as well. Permit me to congratulate you on always having the strength of purpose to stand by your honest convictions.

To another of the thinning circle of those early country-school days, Ambrose Jones, of Toledo, Ohio, from whose granddaughter, Irene Waranke, I had learned of his whereabouts, I wrote in 1937:

What great sport we had playing baseball, and when it was impossible to do this on account of the snow on the ground, we put in time playing "dog and deer." As I look back over the years, it seems to me those were some of the happiest days of my life.

I remember distinctly the occasion when Mr. Speidell told us of a debating society in the town of Clyde, called the Boanerges, which translated means "Sons of Thunder."

It was impressive for farm boys to walk into a meeting hall which had carpet on the floor, fine lights, and nice desks.

To our embarrassment, we found that the members were well groomed. They had white shirts and fine suits; while we wore our rough, crude high-top boots, trousers tucked inside as we dressed on the farm, shirts homespun without collars. But our embarrassment soon faded away. The young lawyers and the young doctors of this debating society revealed every consideration for us.

I remember that during the summer months when the society met I worked hard in the harvest field all day; when daylight faded, walked to Clyde, three miles away, for the debates, and was back in the fields soon after daylight the next morning. It was not difficult; it was a great privilege, and a great pleasure.

I did not know then—in fact, it did not occur to me until years later—that what I learned of parliamentary procedure by this rough road in the primitive country school and the pioneer town debating society was one of the best educations of my life. It gave me an understanding of parliamentary technicalities and of human nature itself that later became of great value in congressional battles. What I learned in this frontier Ohio community on many occasions helped me on the floor of the United States senate. Some of the bitterest, some of the most far-reaching congressional contests were determined by parliamentary tactics.

It was during these years that I learned of the unfulfilled romance of my brother John. Almost from the opening day of my attendance in the Mount Carmel district school, I noticed the deep interest which Lizzie Tuck took in me. She would come to the schoolhouse and occupy the big double seat assigned to me with another pupil. Whenever that seatmate was absent and Lizzie Tuck was present, she would sit down and visit. I resented those interruptions when I wanted to study. I resented even more when my schoolmates teased me about Lizzie Tuck. She was in her early twenties, a beautiful woman, gentle-voiced and friendly.

At the close of one term, I had looked forward to winning the prize awarded to the most consistent champion during the spelling bees. The afternoon of the spelling bee, Lizzie Tuck came to school and sat down with me. We were in McGuffey's Advanced Speller, the words were difficult, and I wanted to devote all my time to study, but she continued to talk to me.

I was angry.

That night when I went home, I told my mother of the interruptions.

"I think I should tell you, Willie," she said, "that Lizzie Tuck was to marry your brother, John Henry; they were engaged when he went away to war. They were to have lived on a near-by farm. She has been a great comfort to me. She calls to see me, and the reason that she is interested in you is that you remind her of John Henry. When I was not able to get letters from John Henry, she told me that my mail would go through if the letters were addressed to his company and his regiment, and then add the line: 'To follow the regiment.' That brought me my first communication with John."

I have thought Lizzie Tuck wrote many, if not all, of mother's letters to John. As long as I attended public school, her interest continued although John had been dead nearly a decade. For years I remembered Lizzie Tuck. She never married. My mother had told me she never would marry. She went to Chicago and became a successful artist, and years after I reached Congress she wrote to me.

When I entered my teens hard work had given me a physical strength far beyond my years. During the summer of those years in the Mount Carmel district school, I worked for different farmers in the neighborhood; and when at fourteen I finished the grades I was able to perform and was performing man's labor.

In early September, following the completion of Mount Carmel, my two sisters—Emma and Clara—and I went to Berea to attend Baldwin University. It was my first adventure beyond the parental roof. We rented the second story of a house—three rooms—including two small bedrooms and a larger one in between that had to serve as kitchen, dining room, and living room. I bought wood from a farmer, sawed it, split it, and carried it upstairs to our quarters. The two girls did the housework, cooked the meals. Both sisters were very attractive, and the closeness of our quarters embarrassed me, because when men students called upon them there was no place where I could go to study except that tiny bedroom.

When the term finished at Baldwin, again I returned to the farm and worked in the fields for the neighbors.

I was strong, active, ambitious, and hungry for education.

4

ON TO VALPARAISO

Now, AT EIGHTY-THREE, I plead guilty to the same healthy spirit of mischief that runs through all American boys: a mischievous streak from which my more tolerant political enemies said I never recovered in later years.

Others of those enemies, less charitable, had another name for it.

At Mount Carmel I think I contributed my share of pranks.

I had finished grade school when my mother and my stepfather became the victims of one of my innocent jokes which succeeded far beyond my expectations. They used to make trips to Whitehouse, Ohio, about fifty to sixty miles from our home. They drove the old mare, Fan, in traveling to and from Whitehouse by buggy. By starting before daylight, they could reach their destination by nightfall.

My stepfather, usually meek, took a great pride in this feat and used to boast continually about it. He thought old Fan, then well advanced in years and as gentle and leisurely as a kitten, was the finest horse in that region. She was the only horse on the place.

He thought it remarkable, and perhaps he was right about it, that he could drive the horse that distance in a day's travel.

Usually they took a week in getting ready for this trip, and it was the subject matter of conversation at home during this time as to what the outcome of such an undertaking would be. There had been a few times when he did not succeed in driving the entire distance in a day. He had relatives living at Maumee City, about sixteen miles from Whitehouse, and occasionally would stop with them if it had gotten late, going on the next morning. Maumee City was located at the terminus of the Maumee pike, and the town bore the same name as the pike.

I was alone at home with my mother and stepfather when a trip to Whitehouse again was under discussion.

In the sitting room at home was a grandfather's clock, taller than a man, and operated by two weights. It struck the hours regularly.

I conceived the idea when the trip came up in discussion, of testing my stepfather's ability to awaken early in the morning at the hour which he desired, and which continually he boasted he could do. In the lean-to on the south side of the main building was another clock, a cheap and ordinary timepiece which struck the hours in company with the grandfather's clock in the sitting room.

My stepfather as a rule went to bed early, but the night before they were to start on this trip both he and my mother retired soon after dark in order to get all the rest possible for an early start.

After they had retired and I was satisfied they were asleep, I went into the sitting room, opened the door of the grandather's clock, quietly and carefully lifted the two weights off their cords, and set them in the bottom of the clock; it, of course, stopped instantly.

But I knew that when he got up in the morning the first thing that he would do would be to look at the clock; and if he found it had stopped he would go into the kitchen to get the time there.

So, after I had stopped the grandfather's clock, I took the kitchen timepiece from its shelf, and with a screwdriver removed the striker and then turned the hands ahead three hours. I put the striking mechanism back and fastened it tightly and then went to bed.

I knew that when my stepfather saw the clock in the kitchen was still ticking, he would be disturbed in the belief he had overslept.

I hardly closed my eyes.

I knew exactly what would happen.

In the morning he opened the door, went out in the kitchen, and then I listened carefully. In my imagination I could see him holding the candle to the face of the clock, and I could even see the consternation when he discovered the time.

Immediately he called to my mother.

"We have overslept," he said. "Get up quick. We are too late. It is getting light in the east. We will never be able to make the trip."

I heard mother as she came out of her bedroom, looking first at the grandfather's clock, and then at the one in the kitchen. I heard her exclamation of disgust. Immediately she accused my stepfather of oversleeping, reminded him of his boasting, and scolded him roundly.

He was rather penitent, suggested that they not make the trip, and said he could not understand how such a thing had happened to him.

Mother had planned to go and would not put off the trip.

"No, we will have to drive the mare a little faster."

My stepfather was very angry, slammed the door, and started for the barn to feed Fan.

Mother continued to talk to herself while preparing breakfast. I could hear her pushing the griddle about on the stove. The coffee was not ready when my stepfather returned to the house, complaining it was getting later; she was too slow, she should have had breakfast ready, and now they would have to wait for her to finish her work.

That started another spirited discussion.

Finally they set out, three hours too early, in the darkness, and reached Fremont before the first streaks of the rising sun broke through the gray mists in the east. They made the trip, reached Whitehouse on schedule, and after their return, still were discussing how they came to conclude they had overslept.

I chid my stepfather about neglecting to get up in time, but I never did tell him or my mother what I had done.

I never heard him boast again about his ability to awaken at any hour he desired.

There was no urging needed to kindle a desire to continue study after completing the country school.

I was eager to go on.

Again, the greatest difficulty was money.

When I finished Mount Carmel, I was physically strong as a result of hard work and outdoor living, and filled with the dream that when I grew to manhood I would become a practicing attorney. I had visited the neighboring justice court, and was fascinated by the atmosphere of the courtroom. In my fancy I could see myself standing in front of the judge, arguing the law.

I did not realize then that continuing study meant constant interruption: a brief period in school and then dropping out to work and save money, then returning to my books.

Something else was taking place.

Unconsciously I was being confirmed in an unflinching, devoted Republican party faith. My mother was a Republican. Most of the farmers of the region were Republicans; most of Ohio adhered to Republicanism.

In those early years I was as intense a partisan as could be found.

Rutherford B. Hayes, later President, lived in Fremont, very close to Clyde, my home.

When Hayes was nominated, I, a boy, caught up in the enthusiasm that swept over his homeland and carried away by the red lights, the marching bands, stole my stepfather's old mare to ride to Fremont to hear Hayes make his acceptance speech.

Along with all the others I thought he was a great Republican.

The trip to Fremont was not without its regrets. There had been a special train from Clyde; but I had no money, and so, as the next best thing, late in the evening I slipped down to the pasture quietly, got the old mare, Fan, started out and rode to the home of Uncle John Harpster, who lived in Fremont, put her in the barn where Uncle John had chained a fierce dog.

Then I went to the rally.

It was inky black when I came back to the barn, and Uncle John and Aunt Sue were fast asleep. Remembering the dog, which growled and strained at the leash, I climbed astride old fat Fan and rode her through a small side door of the barn. There was a cistern in the back yard, the top of which was badly rotted, and when old Fan stepped upon it, down she went, her hind legs in the water, her front legs holding on the cistern rim. I rapped at Uncle John's bedroom window, got him up; and after he had recruited help from town we got old Fan out by using a plank as a derrick.

It worried me, and I exacted a promise from Uncle John not to tell.

The next day when my stepfather, Isaac Parker, went to the pasture, he discovered old Fan was the worse for wear.

"Where have you been, old Fan?" he said to her. "How did you get that?"

I was watching him carefully; but I did not tell him of the night's happenings, and Uncle John never betrayed my secret.

There was Elder Long, a big, fine-looking man, with a long beard. My mother thought everything of him, and often he came to our house. She told me on one occasion that Elder Long had said to her he did not believe a Democrat could go to heaven.

Regularly the *Cincinnati Times* came to our home. It was supporting Hayes, and I read every line in it. In the Republican convention at Cincinnati in 1876, Robert Ingersoll made the great speech nominating Blaine but Hayes emerged as the compromise nominee.

Then fifteen years old, I devoured every line of the report of it carried in the *Times*.

I was saturated with the Republican ardor. The fight between Conkling and Blaine; the speech with which Garfield so captivated a convention that he himself was nominated for the Presidency in 1880, strengthened my Republican faith through those years until that early partisanship changed the entire course of my life.

While teaching a term, I lived with a family, the Calvin Hubbells, who were residents of Monclova, on the outskirts of Cleveland. Calvin Hubbell was a remarkable man, and the family itself exemplary. In those months I made my home with the Hubbells, I never heard a cross word from the parents to the children, or from the children to their parents. The older son fell victim to a scourge of typhoid fever which swept through that region. The daughter, and the younger son, were taken sick. I remember vividly carrying the daughter from an upstairs room where the noise of squeaking stairs disturbed her in her distress, down the narrow flight to place her on the bed in which her brother had died. There were no nurses. I had become deeply attached to the Hubbells, and for a week I nursed them through the fever.

The mother, grieving over the death of her older son, and worn with the sickness of her other two children, was near collapse.

When the younger son and daughter recovered, and my school was nearing its close, Calvin Hubbell came to me and told me that he thought I was making a mistake to leave the settled state of Ohio for new country.

He had been active in Democratic politics, and was county manager for Representative Frank Hunt Hurd of Toledo.

"I have talked to Congressman Hurd about you," he told me. "I have told him honestly what I think of you. I have asked him to take you into his law office at Toledo. He has one of the most extensive practices in Ohio. He has told me that he believes you are the young man he has been looking for. So many of the city boys he has taken into his office have been disappointing; he will give you some business and push you along as rapidly as possible. I think it is a great opportunity for you."

I was not ungrateful, but I never called on Hurd. He was one of Ohio's most widely recognized lawyers. He represented two railroads as legal counsel. But he was a Democrat, and in those days of my bitter partisanship, I did not want to be associated with a Democrat. A few years later, after experiencing the hardships of drouth and of depression, I picked up a paper and read that Frank Hurd had died. I was to have been his partner.

There was no simple, clearly etched pattern for those years of schooling and teaching.

I was in college; then in the harvest fields in the summer; and teaching the school terms to get money.

That year at Baldwin and the school term at Whitehouse softened me, and it took me several days to regain the rhythm of the ax and keep steadily at clearing the timber without aching muscles. Summer's heat surprisingly bothered me in the beginning, but soon I found I was enjoying woodcutting.

After teaching a term at Whitehouse I went in the fall to Valparaiso.

I had heard of a private school there, which in many respects was a remarkable institution. At the time it was the largest normal school in the United States, with an attendance of fifteen hundred pupils. It was known as the "poor boys' school": hardly a student enrolled, either boy or girl, but was in part working his way through. They were young men and young women, hungry for education. They would teach, then complete one term, drop out again to teach and save a little money, and then come back to school.

It was a private institution, the owner of which was H. B. Brown. There was the tradition—true or untrue, I never knew—that Mr. Brown had gone to a normal school as a very poor boy, and that in his senior year his class had levied an assessment of five dollars upon each member to raise funds to cover the expenses of the ceremonies. He did not have the five dollars.

He did not think his classmates had any right to levy the assessment and refused to pay it. Then the class officers took it up with the school authorities, who summoned Mr. Brown to appear before them. He told them he lacked the money, would not pay it, with the result he was not permitted to receive his diploma; but his last word had been that, if under the circumstances he was not allowed to graduate, in ten years he would have a school larger than the one he was attending.

He kept his word.

He induced some businessmen of Valparaiso to join him in the new school; he secured a competent corps of teachers, and launched his institution. He had a remarkable aptitude, and an amazing understanding of the undertaking in which he was engaged. He sought in every way to strengthen his faculty. He sent the faculty members to other institutions for additional training.

He added new branches constantly to the curriculum, until it covered every field. He developed the physical plant as circumstances permitted.

One of the things I remember is Flint Hall, a large three-story building which provided furnished rooms and board for men for $1.40 a week. Another building, known as East Hall, housed the girls, and they were given board and room for $1.60 a week. The tuition was $18 per term, and there were five terms in the year—four terms of eleven weeks each and a fifth lasting six weeks—which meant that study at Valparaiso was practically continuous. I completed the classical and the elocution courses here, and then turned to law.

Very few of the pupils came from rich families. As a result, there was on the campus of Valparaiso a spirit of democracy and of deep companionship; and I was not long in recognizing that my associations there were to have a profound influence on my life. I have met graduates of this institution, which now is known as Valparaiso University, in all parts of the United States. In June of 1942, I delivered the commencement address, and among the law alumni present were lawyers from nearly every state in the Union. In the Senate and the Lower House at Washington I came in contact with graduates of my alma mater.

At Valparaiso I discovered that debating clubs, which I had thought were so helpful and beneficial, formed a large part of the school life. The course in debate was especially valuable. The members of that class were organized by its instructors into clubs, or the students were allowed to perfect their own organizations, subject only to the supervision and control of the professors in charge. I fell in with the latter idea. It seemed that it offered greater educational opportunities. Under the plan of organization, four of the twelve club members each week would take part in the discussion; a fifth acted as president, the sixth as secretary, the seventh as critic, and the remaining five as judges. Automatically the members moved from one position to another. The member who served as secretary one night became president at the next meeting. A member who took part in the discussion after four nights became a judge.

We had in collaboration arranged the questions to be discussed long in advance. One semester they would be issues arising out of English history; the next, questions precipitated by American history.

At the same time we gave great attention to the study of parliamentary procedure. It seldom happened that the minutes kept were approved without debate; and every decision handed down by the president was criticized in order to present a new, deeper knowledge of parliamentary law.

The discussions inevitably inspired a great deal of research.

So impressed was I that later, in my work as a teacher, I followed somewhat the same plan of organization in establishing debating societies in the schools. Every Friday afternoon I would divide the schools I taught into two different sections. I appointed one pupil to occupy the chair, another to serve as secretary, circulated among the students, aided them in raising parliamentary questions, and frequently had to take charge to restore order.

I was delighted to observe the development that took place.

My attendance at Valparaiso extended over quite a number of years, but only once was I able to continue through an entire year. Every other year I had to stop school in order to raise money, so that at least half the time I was out in the field at work. Now, it seems to me remarkable that I was able to remain there as long as I did. The life that I had to lead would have been intolerable had it not been that nearly everyone else was in the same position. All the social activities were inexpensive. There were as many girls as boys at Valparaiso, and the girls likewise paid all their expenses by working.

I had but two shirts, only two or three handkerchiefs, two pairs of socks of the very cheapest kind. Some of my clothes were second-hand. I bought a used overcoat for five dollars that lasted me for several years. I washed my handkerchiefs and my socks and sometimes my underwear in order to save money. I took my shirt, and perhaps a collar, to the washwoman; then at the end of the week brought them to my room, changed clothes, and carried the soiled clothes back to be done.

In all of the boarding houses and institutions where the students lived I do not remember seeing one bathtub.

Our baths were entirely sponge baths except in the summertime, when we would go to Sager's pond, a mile or two distant, for fine swimming, but we had to swim at night because none of us had a bathing suit.

Not until years later did I know the luxury of a nightshirt.

When finally I was graduated in law, I went home to see my mother, as I had tried to do at least once every year. On this occasion she asked why I did not teach at the old school; she wanted me to live at home that winter. I knew I should need money to establish myself in a law office, and it seemed that this presented the opportunity. I made application, and to my delight the school board employed me to teach in the same old building where first I started as a small boy to learn my ABC's.

My mother still occupied the farm where I was born, although she had sold part of it so that there were only eighty acres left; and we talked of the possibility of selling the farm and going out west, where I could set up a law practice and mother could establish herself upon the land.

5

THE L.U.N. (LUNATICS UNDER NORRIS)

NEAR THE CLOSE of my school days at Valparaiso there was formed an organization of students which had a very great influence upon my entire life—the L.U.N.

For several years there had been two great factions in the Crescent literary society—of nearly equal strength. Without any conscious effort on my part, gradually I became the leader of one of these factions. A bitter contest developed over the election of a president of the society, and I found myself a candidate of one faction, opposed by a classmate named Hummer.

It was an exceedingly spirited and acrimonious contest.

In the atmosphere of the campus it took on the importance, and became as real as the election of a President of the United States. I was defeated by one vote. The opposing faction was jubilant, and celebrated hilariously, and under the circumstances was entitled to celebrate. The election had been fair, and the contest entirely legal.

A few days later my associates came together in my room, all members of the society but one, and he had been an employee of the school, in charge of the library. He was as much interested and wielded as much influence as if he had been a member himself. It was suggested then, while we all were bemoaning defeat, that we should form an organization of some kind to meet occasionally after we had separated and gone to our homes. Again with all the exuberance of youth it was proposed that a written constitution be drawn up, and a committee was appointed with myself as chairman. We were to meet in a few days and decide whether we wanted to form an organization of a permanent character by which we could maintain the friendships and the pleasant relationships that had existed through college.

Out of it came the organization known as the L.U.N., the only secret being the name itself. It was provided that under no circumstances, and at no time, might the real name be disclosed to nonmembers. The campus buzzed in its curiosity; among the names bandied about by the other faction was one: "Lunatics Under Norris." But from it sprang associations that continued throughout the next sixty years; associations which all of us prized highly; and associations that influenced each of us greatly.

So far as I know, no other organization of a similar character has ever existed in any American college or has passed through so many years of happiness and joy.

It was stipulated in the constitution that we would meet once every year as long as we lived, to celebrate the friendship that had grown up between us and that had survived defeat in the campaign for the presidency of the Crescent society. The constitution provided that no new members should ever be admitted, and that no change in it be made except by unanimous consent.

Some time during the month of August there was to be a banquet at a place to be designated.

We started the organization with a banquet in the Merchants' Hotel at Valparaiso on the sixth day of August, 1883. From then on the L.U.N. held an annual reunion and banquet. As "chief worthy" I presided at the first banquet. The "vice worthy" was reelected each year because he kept the books and financial records.

Again the next year we met at Valparaiso. Not one of the members had started in business yet, and not one had married. During those early years of L.U.N. it took practically all the money I could scrape together to get back. It came to us all that we who had worked our way through school would be scattered over the United States, and soon we decided to establish a common fund so as to apportion the expense of the reunions equally and fairly among the members.

After several years it became evident Valparaiso was not suited for the reunions. The lakes attracted us, and we met at Okoboji in Iowa, Lake Delavan and Brown's Lake in Wisconsin, and a number of others. Then we gathered at the Grand View Hotel overlooking Rainbow Lake, one of the most beautiful lakes in the United States and one of a chain of sixteen frequently called the Switzerland of America; and there beside the blue waters and the pines L.U.N. acquired a permanent home: L.U.N. Cottage. With but one single exception—when one of the members, H. H. Harrington of Waukesha, Wisconsin, could not attend because of illness, and we went to him—we gathered there from that time on, although we discovered that the cottage which L.U.N. had purchased was too small to accommodate us and our wives, who were present usually during the reunions.

Time went on; a few of the friendships formed in school days waned, and the membership decreased; two members were dropped, and one was expelled. As death cut down the ranks, the meetings became more and more solemn until the fifty-ninth banquet brought us together at Haleiwa Cottage on August 30, 1941. Finally the membership dropped to two, and automatically I became chief worthy and Ermon E. Smith of Dodge City, Kansas, vice worthy. In 1942 I was not able to travel from Washington and Mr. Smith was unable to join me. For the second consecutive summer, because of war conditions, L.U.N. could not meet in 1943, nor again in 1944.

The banquets always were quite formal in their nature: a printed program, and a speech from each member. Some speeches were prepared in advance; all were invariably short; and all were models of dignity. Many referred to incidents of years ago in school, keeping alive memories that had become sacred emblems of the past, memories that were still fresh in our hearts.

There was an L.U.N. song, which began:

Out from among the memories of school days past and gone,
We cherish the remembrance of lasting friendships formed.

Another stanza of the song explained the effect the organization was to have and did have upon the lives of its members:

We separate and wander among the paths of men,
But at the time for banquet, we all return again;
Then, brothers true and noble whate'er your lot with men,
Stand up for our sacred order, be true to the L.U.N.

The printed program of the forty-fifth annual reunion, held at Rainbow Lake from August 6 to August 13, 1927, which I had prepared as chief worthy, was headed "With apologies to James Whitcomb Riley," as follows:

Once there was a lazy boy who ran away from school.
The L.U.N. took after him and ducked him in a pool;
They quenched his thirst with castor oil, put pepper in his eyes,
Then filled his mouth with angleworms, and made him eat
some flies.
They took him to the woods and tied him to a log,
They cut him up in pieces and fed him to a hog.
So you better do your duty and be kind to all about,
Or the L.U.N. will get you if you don't watch out.

At that time the membership had been reduced to three, and addresses were delivered as follows:

"The Sands Are Running Low," by the Philosopher H. H. Harrington; "But the Fishing Is Still Good," by the Expert E. E. Smith; "True Justice Needs No Mercy to Temper It," by the Vagabond G. W. Norris.

At the first reunion held after my oldest child, Hazel, was born, the then chief worthy Lardin assigned me the task of responding to the toast, "The Responsibility of Parenthood."

My response follows:

Of all the joys that life can bring,
The baby is the best,
I've learned to laugh and cry and sing,
And miss at night my rest.

And when at night from heavenly dreams,
I'm brought to earth a spell,
It's all because I think, it seems,
I've heard the baby yell.

To music of inferior brand,
  All clothed in robes of white,
With baby in supreme command,
  I march the floor at night.

But when those little eyelids close,
  In slumber peaceful, sweet,
I kneel beside my slumbering rose
  And kiss her on the cheek.

And kneeling there, in accents mild,
  I send up thanks to God,
And ask Him to protect my child,
  When I'm beneath the sod.

Then fill the flowing goblets well,
  And drink with joy serene,
To her whose charms I love to tell,
  My pride, my love, my queen.

The little child whose virtues I was then extolling has traveled by my side practically all of my mature life. Her steady hand now guides me. She has been a constant joy and still is a beacon of light and hope.

These reunions of L.U.N. added greatly to our lives, made us all better men, better citizens, and better fathers. The friendships formed extended to our families. And beneath the solemnity, and the companionship, there was always close to the surface a bubbling spirit of fun.

Smith, who then lived at Mendota, Illinois, and I, on a visit to him, decided to pay our respects to Lardin, teaching a country school approximately six miles from Mendota. It was winter; snow covered the ground, and sleighing was excellent. We did not let Lardin know, and arrived about the noon hour while his pupils were playing in the school yard. Immediately he called them from the yard, in order that he might dismiss earlier in the afternoon. After listening to several classes he told the pupils they were "very much honored by the presence of two very noted visitors," teachers in eastern colleges who had promised to address them. It was a complete surprise to both of us, and when Lardin called on "Professor Smith" first he simply said he had nothing to say and asked to be excused.

Lardin expressed keen sorrow that Professor Smith had declined to speak, but took consolation in saying: "We still have Professor Norris, who is a doctor of national renown. I know he will not disappoint us."

Walking down to the front of the room, I admitted everything that had been said about me, adding that I had been a professor in college for a great many years and in spite of appearances was much older than their teacher, who had been one of my pupils. I indicated how ignorant he was when he came to me, and said I had taught him all that he knew. He left the room at that point.

Lardin was a fine penman and had placed some specimens of penmanship on the blackboard for his pupils to follow. I called attention to the specimens and, taking the slate of a small girl who had been practising from them, not very successfully, I held it up to the class and said that when their teacher first had come to school he could not write as well as this little girl. Then I told them that since their teacher had deserted them I was in charge, and I was going to give them a holiday.

School dismissed, the pupils and I filed out of the room, and found both Smith and Lardin holding their sides.

We came to that year when there were seven vacant chairs. The happy, the pleasant associations of the past gradually spread themselves before our eyes. Without much effort we could fill the vacant chairs. So real were the reunions that those comrades of our youth seemed to be there in person.

These friendships in L.U.N. meant much to me. Through the years I continued to correspond with these associates. They wrote me fully and frankly, frequently upon matters of national concern. They followed the deliberations of Congress with avid interest. The outcropping sentiment of the regions with which they came in contact reached me in letters from them, presenting a faithful picture of America's march. I recall especially Harrington's most thoughtful letter from Wisconsin when Fighting Bob La Follette was facing one of the critical struggles of his career. Year after year Harrington, Smith, and Lardin wrote with devoted loyalty.

And yet each reunion brought us the reminder that soon the organization would pass out of existence: one of the most unique, one of the most useful—and one of the most enjoyable of any established among the college traditions in America.

6

WASHINGTON TERRITORY

ONE YEAR MERGED into another during that period of teaching, work in the harvest fields, and college study, and there was little difference between the year that preceded and the year that followed.

The teaching position at Whitehouse, in Lucas County, Ohio, was typical both of the times and of the country. I was sixteen when I accepted this, my first teaching post.

During the five-month term, for which I was to receive $150, I spent the week ends with my older sister and her husband, on a farm at the fringe of the little village.

For five days each week, I boarded with the Lahr family, who occupied a log house a story and a half in height. On the lower floor were a bedroom and sitting room to which Mr. Lahr had added a "lean-to" to provide a kitchen and dining room.

My quarters were over the lean-to.

The eaves of the roof did not fit snugly, and it was common to get out of bed in the morning on an uncarpeted floor, covered with snow which had drifted in through the crevices. I drew no money until the close of the term, then received $150 in a lump—the largest sum I ever had had at one time. Out of it I paid Mr. Lahr for board at the rate of two dollars a week.

A year at Baldwin University followed. Then another season in the harvest fields and a winter in the schoolroom gave me enough money to resume college. I was nineteen, when on August 3, 1880, at the Valparaiso commencement exercises, I received my first

GEORGE W. NORRIS AND HIS SISTERS EMMA AND CLARA. HE WAS ONE OF TWO BOYS IN A FAMILY OF TWELVE CHILDREN.

diploma from that institution, representing not only study, but corn-husking, wood-splitting, timber-clearing, and self-denial.

I listened to my mother's plea that fall not to leave the farm, and upon her suggestion made application to teach the school at Mount Carmel which I had attended as a boy. Again I returned to Valparaiso to study law.

My mother had grown weary of the struggle on the old farm. The unceasing battle against rocks and stumps had been an unequal one for her, which, during the rearing and educating of her children, she had faced without complaint.

Now she had a chance to sell the old home at a price that appealed to her; and something of her love for the soil was rekindled by reports from the West. Colonization agencies in Ohio were directing attention to the opportunities which Washington Territory offered, and she listened eagerly to the glowing descriptions of the new lands.

After talking it over with mother, I decided to go West to Washington Territory and establish a law business there, with the understanding that, if I found it as attractive as it was said to be, mother would join me.

It took virtually all my savings to purchase a ticket on the emigrant train from Clyde to Walla Walla. The journey lasted nearly two weeks, and I rode second-class from Clyde to St. Paul—third-class from there to Washington Territory.

I felt lonely in St. Paul, a city throbbing with life as the gateway to the Northwest country, but I made up my mind that under no circumstances would I show it. Before going on, I purchased what was to be my cushion and my mattress—a long bag of ordinary calico, stuffed with coarse straw, that had neither shape nor softness. The only baggage I had was a small grip which contained a few pieces of extra clothing.

At St. Paul, I looked over my traveling associates with a great deal of curiosity. They, it seemed to me, were setting forth with the same purpose of establishing a new home. In their ranks were a number of miners and prospectors.

The emigrant car in which I rode was made up largely of passengers going to Coeur d'Alene, Idaho, to work in the mines. They were rough in speech and dress; not overly sociable; and virtually all of them spoke a foreign tongue. They kept much to themselves.

There were no seats in the car, only berths built of boards along the walls: berths, both upper and lower, bare of upholstering or pads. Most of the passengers schooled in travel, had brought wraps and blankets upon which to sleep at night, and to sit during the day.

For bunk mates I had two old men, neither able to speak a word of English, and a young man apparently of my own age who only could speak German. I was assigned to the upper berth with one of the old men, who appeared to be about sixty years of age; the young German, who showed some signs of sociability, to the lower berth with the second old man.

The train pulled out of St. Paul after dark, and I was embarked upon my first long journey, confident that the new country to which I was going would compensate me fully.

That first night rest was impossible. I could not lie on the mattress, which was a mass of lumps. Throughout the entire night I rolled, twisted, and turned, and scarcely closed my eyes.

The old gentleman seemed to sleep through it all.

There was no dining car. At the frequent stops, peddlers of food always put in an appearance, selling bologna, cheese and crackers mostly. Our car was equipped with a large stove at one end, where passengers who had coffee or fresh meat might cook a meal.

I became acquainted with the young man the next day, and we decided to propose an exchange of berths to our bunk mates. They gave assent, and so for the remainder of the time I had the young German for a companion.

During the entire trip I did not have a single morsel of hot food. Those people bound for new country did not reveal hospitality at any time.

My desire for a warm meal nearly got me into trouble at one train stop of some length. There was a dining house near the station, but I found inside that I should have to pay fifty cents for a meal. Feeling that I should not spend the money, I started to leave; but the proprietor stopped me and demanded pay. When I told him I had eaten nothing he replied that I had passed the door, and it was up to me to pay the price of the meal.

The argument grew more serious and more heated.

To my relief the conductor, who had heard the discussion, came forward and insisted I be permitted to return to the car.

Walla Walla was not the promised land that I had anticipated. It was dusty, and dirty, and desolate, and uninviting. It was no place for my mother. My money was running low. I tried vainly in every way to procure work of some kind, suffering failure after failure. I was becoming worried and desperate. Finally, I hired out as a sheep herder on the condition that I was to get the job if the herder who had filled it for two years did not return. That next day as the hour of noon approached, I became anxious. I was so sorely in need of work. And then, just before twelve, the absent herder reappeared and the position that had revived my hopes slipped through my fingers.

It then occurred to me that I might be able to get a school.

I inquired for the county superintendent, who proved to be an eastern college graduate and a very fine man, living on the outskirts of Walla Walla, and I presented to him a letter of recommendation from President Brown of Valparaiso, and another from the members of the board at Monclova, where I had taught one year. These recommendations seemed to be pleasing, and the superintendent issued a temporary permit.

Unfortunately, there was only one school open, and that was near Bolles Junction in a remote part of the country. Its patrons, he said, were anxious to have a school but had no facilities to board the teacher.

It was Saturday.

I told him I would take the chance, and left Walla Walla on a train operated by the Oregon Railway and Navigation Company. Bolles Junction appeared prominently marked on the map and apparently one line of the railroad led from it to Spokane and the other to Dayton.

It was dark when I reached my destination.

The depot was boarded up, and there was no railroad agent. There I was alone on the platform, with no person or house in sight. I had been instructed to find a man named Lee, a former Kansan, who was president of the district and lived about a mile from the station.

In the darkness I took the wrong direction.

Across the hills I saw a light at some distance, and I left the railroad tracks to make my way to it. I stumbled over brush and depressions in the ground. Twice I fell heavily and was bruised. And then I reached the house and found it occupied by a homesteader. He was gruff, suspicious, and inhospitable, but he gave me instructions when I told him I was hunting for Mr. Lee's place.

I reached the railroad tracks again, retraced my steps to Bolles Junction, and continued until I found Mr. Lee's home. He and his wife were still awake; their children had gone to bed. I introduced myself, told him of the letter from the county superintendent, and he invited me in.

The house consisted of a small living room, two bedrooms, and a lean-to kitchen.

He was anxious to have school—he had two children of school age himself; but he also said there was no place where a teacher could find board and lodging. He said most of the people there were old settlers, unfriendly to the railroad that had just been built, and against breaking up the large ranches.

That night I slept on the floor.

In the morning I found that Mr. Lee was the foreman of a gang of Chinese, who took care of the railroad maintenance, and after breakfast I started to visit the people of the district. Not one of them was willing to take me in as a boarder. In midafternoon I retraced my steps to Mr. Lee's house and told him of my failure.

I was desperate.

I insisted that I would teach the school even if I had to sleep out in the open air: a place to sleep worried me less than a place to eat.

We walked down the tracks together, and I saw a small building of crude construction which had housed the Chinese maintenance crew brought in by the railroad. It was a sorry place, filled with machinery, the ugly, bare boards thrown together so roughly that large cracks let in the sunlight and outlined the grim interior, covered from roof to floor with dirt and dust.

I offered to clean it, sleep in it, if I might board with him.

At first Mr. Lee demurred, protesting that the house was so filthy no man should sleep in it. But I got a pail of water and a brush, scrubbed it thoroughly, built a rough bunk of boards, filled a mattress with straw. Motherly Mrs. Lee, taking pity on me, provided me with blankets. There, when darkness closed in, I fell into an untroubled sleep, with a teaching post to replenish my finances. That shack was my home for the entire school term.

The next day school opened with seven children present.

The schoolhouse was built from lumber cut in the neighborhood, without any attempt to fit the boards together, and there were big openings where the green lumber had warped. It was not uncommon for a woodpecker or for some other bird to fly through the schoolroom.

Inasmuch as school closed at noon, my afternoons were free.

Lee and I became great friends. He would pick me up, with a gun and ammunition, and we would set off for the creek to hunt. There were trout in the stream, and frequently we had a nice catch of the speckled beauties to take home.

At the close of the school term Mr. Lee and I visited the new city of Dayton, of which he had heard glowing reports, and where he thought I might desire to establish a law practice.

The main building of the new town was a brewery. We visited it and had a glass of beer.

There was a logging gang there, headed by a huge man, well over six feet, with powerful shoulders, a hairy chest exposed by his rough shirt open at the neck, a heavy growth of whiskers, and a great mop of hair. This boss was intrigued when he learned I was a schoolteacher, and apparently sensed some fun for his men. They were lined up against a bar, and he was determined that I join them every time they ordered a round of drinks.

I asked the bartender for a cigar, instead.

The logging boss flushed angrily. It was evident that he was accustomed to having his way, and that he ruled his gang with his fists.

"Schoolmarm, you'll drink," he growled, and took a step forward. I was backed up against the bar, the men in front of me and on both sides.

Something inside me exploded; I remember calling him names and reaching in my pocket for a gun. I warned him that if he took one step more I would shoot.

Just then, Mr. Lee came running from the other end of the bar, pushing his way through the circle.

"For God's sake," he said to the boss, "leave him alone! He's a dead shot, and he will kill you."

There was a short silence, and then the logging boss said:

"Schoolmarm, you can have your cigar."

I had had enough of Washington Territory. Whatever thoughts I may have had of establishing a law practice there died that afternoon in the brewery.

At the end of the week, with the funds I had accumulated, I bought a ticket east for Nebraska.

7

A LAW PRACTICE

SEVERAL YEARS BEFORE, my mother had bought eighty acres of land in Johnson County, Nebraska, near Tecumseh.

She had made a trip there to visit David Mook, whom she had known in New York State where they grew up as children. His own mother had died, he had lived with my mother's family and looked upon her as his sister.

I came into Nebraska on the overland train of the Union Pacific, Abe Lincoln's connecting link between the East and the West, and reached the Nebraska capital to discover that I should have to wait until the following morning to take the "Irish Mail" for my destination.

On the street I met Kate Stoddart, a classmate at Valparaiso, an exceptional student, and valedictorian in the graduating exercises.

I had a great admiration for her but was ashamed to meet her, dirty as I was. As soon as I could, I got away.

At Tecumseh, I spent several days with Mr. Mook, and then he drove me by buckboard to Beatrice. On our way I passed a farm where my sister Effie and her husband had settled. Those first impressions of Beatrice were very favorable and led to a decision that I would locate there and practice law.

But I was out of money, and again I returned to the schoolroom in Ohio. I got a place teaching in a private school at Warrensville. My sister Melissa lived on a near-by farm, and I boarded at her home; the school children came from the neighboring farm homes. Warrensville was then a crossroads, but the school building was two-story and of substantial character. This particular school was devoted to advanced education. It was one of the most pleasant of teaching experiences. I enjoyed it particularly because most of the students were in advanced classes of algebra, geometry, and philosophy.

In 1933, while serving in the Senate, I received a memorial prepared by a committee representing the former students of the old Warrensville institution, inviting me to attend a reunion for which elaborate preparations had been made. I should have enjoyed returning for those festivities; I had noted with satisfaction the progress some of the students had made; but there was the business of the Senate in a period of great national crisis.

My sister Melissa was one of the finest women I ever knew. She had saved carefully and at that time had over $300 from the sale of butter and eggs. When I again left to return to Nebraska, she lent me these savings. My mother gave me a deed to the eighty acres of Johnson County land. And my savings from teaching, together with the loan from Melissa, constituted the capital out of which I bought a modest law library, some office furniture, and embarked upon practice in partnership with H. H. Harrington. He had been a schoolmate at Valparaiso.

Those early months were disillusioning. We had nothing to bring us business—no associations and no connections. We found rooms with a private family in the suburbs, but after a few months with no business it seemed that we should quit.

In less than a year, the partnership was dissolved.

I had met in Beatrice a man from Beaver City named Hawkins, who told me about the Beaver valley, which he said was a beautiful, fertile district, but without railroad facilities.

I sold my Johnson County land for $1,500; and with it and what I had left I started for Beaver City. The train took me to Arapahoe, on the Republican River in the northern part of Furnas County, and from there it was necessary to travel overland by wagon.

I can never forget the day I reached Beaver City.

We had started out driving from Arapahoe on Saturday; there were few well outlined roads; travel was over the line of least resistance, frequently through fields of corn. It was just getting dark when we approached Beaver City at about eight o'clock in the evening, and the road ran diagonally through a field of corn that I thought was the finest I had ever seen. I had been raised on a farm, and here I was in a field that grew so tall I could not see for any distance. On that September day of 1885, I said that I had never seen better corn grow out of the ground.

The little hotel at Beaver City was crowded: many settlers were flowing into the new country.

The next day—the Sabbath—I walked up the gentle slope to the divide overlooking the town.

The skies were clear and blue; the sun was brilliant and pleasantly warm.

I lay down on the buffalo grass and let my eyes drink in the glory of the Beaver valley. It was covered with a fair growth of timber; the soil seemed to be perfect, without stumps or stones; and the evidence in front of the eyes was convincing that the land would produce.

Doubt assailed me: I wondered if I hadn't made a mistake.

Here was the place of all places where it seemed to me everything was designed for the happiness and prosperity of the farmer. I knew about farming; I had completed my law studies, was admitted to the bar, but I knew practically nothing about the practice of law.

I felt that day I wanted to hold a plow again in my hand and turn over the sweet-smelling earth of this fertile valley. I wanted to live and work on a farm as I had done during most of my lifetime in northern Ohio.

The human flood pouring in was mostly young people of my age, coming into new country, seeking homes. Many of them were highly educated, graduates of eastern colleges. They looked out upon the pleasant skies and the prosperous valley—an outlook that was cheering and invigorating. The air was pure and healthful, and the soil was fertile as the valley of the Nile.

God was smiling upon this country with its abundant crops.

The first houses were mostly of sod, but they were built with willing hands upon homesteads under which these young men and women acquired title to 160 acres of Uncle Sam's domain. To these new homes the brides were coming to help build up a new world. Children were going to be born, to grow into manhood and womanhood, to give strength to the highest kind of civilized society.

The girl of my choice was waiting for me on an Indiana farm, waiting for me to prepare a home for her. My meeting with her had been by chance. I had gone to call upon a college classmate named Betty Hayes, and while waiting for her saw this girl in an adjoining room combing her beautiful hair; she did not know that the reflection of her head and her locks came to my eyes. When she had finished, she came into the room where I was seated, and that evening I took her buggy riding.

Friendship ripened into love, and when I left for the West it was with the understanding I would return for her. But before I returned to my old Ohio home again, I had experienced the hardship of the Nebraska frontier, and our romance ended.

Now on this Sabbath day, looking over as fair a country as man might desire, I was full of hope and ambition, moved by the glory of the new country, and certain in my heart that here on the prairie there would be a civilization second to none in all the world.

In association with a nurseryman, I bought a quarter-section of land half a mile north of Beaver City; and I opened a law office south of the square. The first money I made in Nebraska was in the land business, and often I made more money in the land business than in the law business. We sold the farm that we had bought for a profit of a few hundred dollars, and it was not long before I started to pay back to my sister the money she had lent me.

Gradually my law business increased until I was devoting all my energies to it. Although the fees were small, I worked just as hard as though millions had been involved, and advanced until I was interested in practically all litigation of importance in the county.

My business and my hopes went up and down with those of the farmers. When the crops failed and withered, and suffering came to those who were tilling the soil, my business declined. A whole season's labor, with the promise of a fine crop of wheat and corn, would often be made vain when the crops were nearly matured by a few days of hot winds that destroyed and burned everything.

Men and women became hardened, their spirits and their natures changed.

But on that bright Sunday morning as I lay on the prairie, my thoughts were far from bitter strife and the battles against drouth and discouragement. All was clear and serene.

The solid friendships of the early years were enduring.

I had been a member of the Odd Fellows lodge at Clyde from the time I was twenty-one years old. Immediately upon arriving in Beaver City, I transferred to the Beaver City lodge. In early May of 1932, I received a beautiful jewel as a testimonial of my membership there.

In a letter which I wrote, all the happy memories of those years found expression:

> One of the brightest spots in life centers around the short-grass country. This was particularly true in the early days when every man's latchstring was out, and when the atmosphere was pervaded with a spirit of brotherly love.
>
> . . . The first Friday night after I reached Beaver City, I went to lodge. Chance Inman was conductor; Bob Scott, warden. The next Sunday night I went out to visit Bob in his brown-colored mansion just a little northwest of town. I shall never forget my first sight of that house. The walls, I think, were at least three feet thick, and the house looked like many other buildings I have since seen in Boston and New York, only they were much larger and were called "brownstone."
>
> Bob's house had only one story.
>
> As we sat in front of the mansion, a lone jackrabbit appeared over the hill. Bob took off his coat and shoes and started after it. In fifteen minutes he had run it down, or said he had, when he returned, triumphant, carrying the jackrabbit over his shoulder. He explained to me rather minutely that was the only proper method by which a frontiersman obtained the meat for his livelihood. We cooked the jackrabbit; it was one of the finest meals I have ever eaten. Jackrabbit stew makes a meal fit for the gods.

So many times I have thought of that country in that day in these closing lines:

"If those who live in this great world of ours today could go through the same experiences and have the same fine training as the fine people of the early settlements, crime largely would be unknown, criminal courts largely would be unnecessary, and we should have in truth and in fact 'brotherhood of man and the fatherhood of God.'"

8

AN ARDENT REPUBLICAN

Soon I became firmly established in that fertile Beaver valley of Nebraska to which, as a young man, I had come.

The country itself, and its people, gave me a sense of great contentment.

It was so different from the Ohio I had known.

Although it was new country, it was different from that section of Washington Territory which I had visited.

Growing crops always have thrilled me throughout my life. These newly broken fields, lush and green, created a feeling of security and well-being from early spring, when the freshly plowed soil scented the air, until the arrival of the harvest in all of its glory.

I never grew weary of it.

But along with the prosperous seasons, when Nature in her most generous moods smiled upon the earth and the earth smiled back, I was to see many heartbreaking failures in that Beaver valley.

Fortunately, I was young; the people about me were young; adversity wore upon them lightly when in the beginning, first the disappointment and then the pinch of crop failures would make themselves felt. I was so happy to be located in a land where the plow could bite into the earth without encountering hidden rocks.

In a modest way, I became interested gradually in the political controversies which arose.

I was an ardent Republican.

With youthful enthusiasm, I thought the Republican party was perfect. I had no personal ambition to hold a public office, I was in love with my profession, I wanted to have a family, and I wanted to live and grow up in this great expanding West. It seemed to me at that time no one could wish for a more ideal life than I had determined upon. My law practice was growing; gradually it extended itself into practically all of the adjoining counties, and to a less extent into several counties in neighboring Kansas, only a few miles to the south.

My loyalty and zeal as a Republican never faltered in those years. I became acquainted with nearly every man in Furnas County; and without any definite plan or effort I became in a slight way a party leader.

The Populist party was in its formative stages in Nebraska and Kansas about the time I was becoming established; but my first experience with the independence and insurgency of a farming region, which later was to acquire national significance, made no impression upon me.

Men and women who had been carefree and lighthearted were turning bitter, and there was a sudden, unheralded, spontaneous outburst of resentment over the hardships resulting from crop failures, or from low prices for farm commodities in the years of abundance, or from a combination of both. Populism spread like an uncontrollable prairie fire in the region that had become my home, gathering in practically all the farmers, and many of the businessmen in all of these communities of the West.

Many of its leaders, I soon discovered, were honest, earnest, intelligent citizens; but others were unscrupulous, insincere, bent upon exploiting to the fullest a most natural and distressing discontent. I found myself importuned frequently to become a Populist, but I remained loyal to my Republican faith.

In later years, I have felt that I was often as unreasonable and as unjust to the Populists as could be.

I campaigned ardently for the Republican nominees and spoke in schoolhouses all over the county. But the Populists succeeded.

They carried everything before them; elected all the county

officials. At the high tide of the Populist rebellion, it took a brave man to predict the speedy disintegration of this political uprising and a most gifted man to foresee its rapid fall.

Some of the Populists elected were competent, able, and performed their duties faithfully; others appeared to be moved entirely by a bitter, unreasonable political spirit unfaithful to the principles which they so ably had advocated.

After the storm had spent itself, I could see nothing unnatural about this Populist movement. It represented human misery and poverty. It came into existence as naturally as the seasons. Its ardent advocates in the Beaver valley enlisted with high hopes of success. They and their associates dominated not only a majority of the counties in Nebraska, but the entire state as well.

The Republican party, previously in power, was blamed for crop failures which actually came from nature itself. Some of the Republican leaders were unfaithful, some dishonest; and at that time any effective political organization largely was controlled by machine politicians.

Still, I never weakened in my Republican allegiance.

I was blind to a great extent, perhaps, to the errors that were committed in the name of the Republican party. I refused to censure or condemn Republican candidates even when I knew they deserved condemnation.

It was in this period that I became a candidate for prosecuting attorney of the county, and was defeated by the Populist nominee although I ran ahead of the Republican ticket.

I am inclined to think I deserved defeat.

My opponent in this contest was a very talented, industrious lawyer named McClure who had settled in the Beaver valley and was growing up with the country. He and I were the two outstanding lawyers of the community. While we remained personally friendly, we were bitter political enemies.

He, in reality, was a Democrat, although it was the Populist wave which carried him into office in this contest for prosecuting attorney. If all the leaders of the Populists had been as able and as honest as McClure, they would have continued to rule Nebraska and a number of agricultural states of the Middle West for many years.

Later, I again was to match political swords with McClure in a campaign for the district bench. That was the much-discussed election at which I was elected district judge. I entered the campaign very much against my own wish and will. I was elected; but throughout my entire political life men opposed to me harked back to it to charge that I was not elected on the face of the actual returns.

Before my own candidacy, I had refused to be considered under the most peculiar circumstances.

Furnas County, including the Beaver valley, had been a part of the judicial district presided over by Judge Cochran of McCook. When the legislature reapportioned the judicial districts of the state, the governor appointed Judge Cochran to fill the new judgeship until the next election.

He had acquired a large following, earlier had been nominated by the Republican party and elected. It was while he was on the bench that the Populist wave had gotten under way.

The Populist candidate was Judge D. T. Welty of Cambridge.

I think Judge Welty was an honest man who did his best to be a good judge; but his association with some of the corporations, especially the railroads, changed the course of his activities greatly. I favored the reelection of Judge Cochran, and was supporting his nomination in the Republican convention.

That idea of becoming a candidate myself never entered my mind until the Republicans of Furnas County met to select delegates to the Republican judicial convention. To my surprise, I discovered a rather bitter opposition to the renomination of Judge Cochran. As his friend, I had not realized fully how deep-seated and how widespread this opposition was even in my own town. I had done some work in his behalf, thinking there would be no difficulty in getting a delegation favorable to his renomination.

On the morning of the convention the farm delegates came in, and after a little discussion with them I found they were opposed to sending a delegation to the Republican judicial convention favorable to Judge Cochran. Even now, fantastically, I can recall how disappointed I was when it developed that they were almost unanimous in the desire to name a delegation which would work for my nomination.

Judge Cochran knew I favored his nomination, and he had left Furnas County to me in the confident belief its delegation would support him.

But these farmer delegates could not be won over: they were determined I should become a candidate.

I remonstrated with them; told them I could not do it; told them frankly I was working for Judge Cochran with his knowledge, and he was depending upon me; that, under the circumstances, I could not change my attitude and become a candidate against him. They were a determined group of men, all friendly to me, and all equally opposed to Judge Cochran.

After discussion with my friends, in the end, it was decided that the delegation to the judicial convention would support me if I should conclude that Judge Cochran had no chance of renomination. I was to do everything faithfully I could to secure his nomination. I was permitted to select the delegates from our county convention, with this understanding, and I chose a delegation loyal to me, which at the same time, in its opposition to Judge Cochran, was moderate enough not to repudiate him.

In a few days the judicial convention took place.

Meanwhile I had sought immediately an interview with Judge Cochran. I explained to him what had taken place. I told him I should have to accept the nomination if it came to me, but the Furnas delegation, while true to my candidacy, would stay by him as a second choice. I had been able to secure that concession from the delegates. He was entirely satisfied, and I entered the judicial convention confident that the arrangement that had been made would spare Judge Cochran a bitter fight. There were eight counties in the district, and after several ballots our delegation and several others went over to Cochran and he became the nominee of the convention.

The "Pops" had nominated Judge Welty. His practice had been

very limited; he seldom tried cases in the district court; he was not an outstanding lawyer, but the intensity of the Populist uprising swept him into office. I campaigned for Judge Cochran, but it was impossible to make a dent in the Populist ranks.

Men listened with respect but were not convinced.

Judge Welty served one term of four years, and near the close of it, I became an active candidate for judge. I went into the other seven counties, and did not have very great difficulty in getting sufficient delegates to secure the Republican nomination.

It was an exceedingly bitter contest.

I did everything that I could to be elected. I turned my guns upon Judge Welty's relationship to the railroads. I made a speaking campaign over the district. Although the Populist party still was considered to be the majority party, I had a majority of just 2 when the votes were all counted and canvassed.

The closeness of the vote resulted in a contest that was to be injected in subsequent campaigns.

Judge Welty brought a quo warranto proceeding against me in the supreme court of the state. After settlement of several of the preliminary proceedings, the case reached the point where the court was to appoint someone to take evidence. I, with my attorney, went from Beaver City to Lincoln to attend a meeting of the supreme court at which we expected the naming of a commissioner to take evidence. We were very happily surprised when we discovered that Judge Welty had dismissed his action.

In all the discussions of later years, its echoes were injected in nearly all the congressional campaigns. I have never referred to this district-bench contest. I was satisfied that I was elected legally and honestly. I did most of the legal work and practically all of the investigational work in connection with the contest. I had delved into every precinct in the district for the purpose of ascertaining if through technicalities I might be able to throw out even one vote. In the end, I was satisfied then, and I state now, if this contest had ever been tried, and the evidence taken, I should have won the contest by between 50 and 100 votes. I have no knowledge of what disclosures my opponent intended to make.

There never was a direct decision by the Nebraska supreme court on this contest. Its only order, made in a collateral proceeding, was in effect against me: The court ordered the canvassing board to reassemble and canvass the vote. The boards did this without bringing about any change.

We had opposed the action although not afraid of the recount.

This contest left some very deep bitterness. The result was that, when I went into office as judge, I had been painstaking enough in my investigation to conclude that a recount would have resulted in a gain of several votes. Afterwards, Judge Welty and I became friends, although the charges of fraud that had been made on both sides were of the bitterest character. I think both realized there probably were errors and mistakes on both sides even in the voting, but neither one of us in my judgment was guilty of doing anything wrong or illegal. Many of our ardent friends had gone further than they should and further than the law would permit, but many years before Judge Welty died the bitterness in his heart had disappeared entirely.

Some of the particulars of that campaign I have never related.

I had charged in my answer to the contest that quite a number of illegal votes had been cast for my opponent in northern Frontier County. These illegal votes, I claimed, had been obtained by the use of railroad passes issued by A. R. Curzon, a banker at Curtis. I further charged that he had purchased quantities of whisky and had given the liquor to the voters. He had been very active in the campaign against me. Earlier in the fight to secure the nomination, I had visited Curtis, called upon him, and introduced myself. He had been quite prominent in Republican politics.

In the private office of his bank while we were talking, he was very frank. He said he wanted to see me, wanted to support me, but had to be very satisfied on one point before he would do it. And then he said:

"During the term of the judge who will be elected next fall, there will be a county-seat contest in Frontier County between Stockville, the present county seat, and Curtis, and I am not going to support any man for judge until I know how he stands on that subject."

His statement almost took my breath away. It practically ended the conversation.

I told him that under no circumstances would I make him or anyone else any promise as to my attitude upon any official matter that would come before me as a judge if I were so fortunate as to be elected. I did ask him how he knew my opponent was set on the question. If he did know, why was he trying to induce me to make a disgraceful, dishonorable, and illegal pledge? At last he said that he preferred to support me because he did not think my opponent had made a good judge, but that his information made him sure that Judge Welty would be all right on the county seat.

He fought me very bitterly, and because he was respected there was no doubt but his influence and his work had a very material effect in that section of the district. I set all this forth in the answer.

A year later I met this man in Omaha at a Republican gathering which was scheduled at the same time as a meeting of the Masonic grand lodge. He was exceedingly friendly, and asked a friend to take his wife back to the hotel so that he could join me. We walked down the street, and he told me how glad he was that I had been elected: while he had fought me bitterly, he regretted it, and, anticipating I would be a candidate for reelection, he wanted to do everything to help.

Then he requested me to make an open statement for publication in the newspapers of the county to the effect that further examination had proved the charges I had made against him in the answer to the quo warranto proceedings to be without foundation.

I told him frankly I could not do this: I had only made the charges after thorough investigation and believed them to be correct; and I had never had an occasion to change my opinion.

This brought on another bitter quarrel.

He told me he was going to sue me for damages, and I should be served with a summons the next day before I could leave Omaha.

I really believed that the man was bluffing; but, bluffing or not, I told him very frankly that I should be delighted to have him sue me for the opportunity to prove the truth of the charges that I had made.

He never filed suit.

The next time I saw him was in Boise, Idaho. He had sold his banking interests in Curtis, had gone to Boise, and had made investments that turned out to be very profitable. I was in Boise campaigning for Theodore Roosevelt, who then was the Progressive candidate for the Presidency of the United States. I met Mr. Curzon at the hotel while I was eating breakfast, and discovered that he also was engaged in an active campaign in Idaho to carry the state for Roosevelt.

I discovered that his financial standing had given him great prominence.

He was one of the leaders in the Progressive movement there, and although in that presidential contest the Roosevelt electors had to be written in by the voters, Roosevelt came very near carrying the state of Idaho.

While in Boise, Mr. Curzon really took charge of me, introduced me to the prominent men of the city and invariably took occasion to say we had been old friends in Nebraska and had worked together for many years in the Republican party of that state.

Near the close of my senatorial career, I was seated in the shade of a friendly tree in my back yard one summer afternoon, when a young man put in an appearance unexpectedly. I never had seen him before, I was certain; but, fearful that my eyes were playing a trick upon me, I greeted him cordially. He introduced himself.

He was Judge Welty's son, and was a resident of the state of Washington.

He told me that his father often had told him about the bitter fight for the judgeship, and in telling him about it, had spoken gently and warm-heartedly of me.

It was like a refreshing breeze on that hot summer afternoon.

I sat there musing, after he had left, on the great fairness and sense of justice that ultimately triumphs in this country. I thought how amazing it is that the second generation should show such consideration. Only in America are the ancient enmities forgotten, to be replaced by understanding and friendship. It is a fortunate nation that escapes the continuing bitterness of political differences.

9

CONCEPTIONS OF JUSTICE

THE SEVEN YEARS I spent as a judge on the bench were the most satisfactory period of my life. I liked the work. I had no ambition to leave it, and I have wondered throughout all my service in Washington if I did not make a serious mistake when I did leave it.

It brought before my eyes human nature in all of its nobility and goodness; and in all of its weakness and error. During the seven years I served as a district judge, my sympathies were to be broadened, my understanding of life enriched, and my conceptions of simple justice strengthened. The circumstances which confronted me year after year could not other than implant in me a very deep respect for law.

Here, frequently, were poverty and distress.

Here was a none too settled country, largely peaceful and orderly only because of the character of its people.

The eight counties of the district embraced the extreme southwest corner of the state. Periodically man's greatest trouble there was hot winds, intense heat, and a lack of moisture during the growing season. Law could not do anything about that, but it had to take that into consideration in dispensing justice. It had to adjust itself to the circumstances under which people lived.

Most of the settlers came into possession of their land under the Homestead Act and had no cash capital, so that immediately after final proving up for homestead rights their first thought was to borrow money to construct improvements for the farm. Mortgage companies were eager to loan, and the new landowner was equally eager to borrow. The new arrival had only one question in his mind. It was: "How much money can I borrow on my 160 acres of land to which the government has given me title?"

Naturally, many unsound loans were made. The appeal of ten per cent interest silenced any scruples the insurance companies may have had, and the only competition resulted from the efforts of the landowners to get a larger loan. The result was extremely heavy indebtedness. In seasons of damaged or completely destroyed crops, the farmer could not and did not pay his taxes; he neglected his interest; and scores of foreclosure suits developed. It was apparent to me that, unless some restraining hand delayed these foreclosures, the country would soon become subject to absentee ownership.

My term as a judge followed close after the years of crop failure and low farm prices that had inspired the Populist uprising. There was that single, blistering afternoon in 1893 when hundreds of thousands of acres of corn were burned by a scorching wind from the south. There was the amazing paradox in 1896 of a bountiful crop sold for eight and ten cents a bushel, with farmers burning corn in place of fuel.

The years immediately after were little better. One of the first things I had to contend with when I became judge was this condition, and I adopted a rule that became almost universal through the district.

Stripped of all technical legal reasoning, it was simple; and yet I thought it was just: if in my judgment the farmer was going to be able, under ordinary circumstances, to meet his indebtedness, I would postpone confirmation of the sheriff's sale and give the farmer an opportunity to pay it. At first the rule was bitterly opposed by the attorneys for the mortgage holders; but after it had been applied for two or three years there was almost universal satisfaction with it.

This principle was crystallized in some of the moratorium legislation enacted by the legislatures of agricultural states during the period of great distress in 1933.

And yet, if anything, the remedy from the bench was more effective than the cure provided by the legislation for a serious economic malady in the farm regions. When the mortgage had been foreclosed, the decree rendered, and the stay of nine months allowed, it was the practice of the clerks to issue an order of sale to the sheriff. The sheriff would procure appraisal of the land, make the sale, at which, with few exceptions, the mortgagee would buy the land in; but before a deed could be issued to the purchaser the sale had to be confirmed by the court.

Here I thought I saw the proper place for the court to fortify and strengthen justice: by simply continuing the case and giving the defendants an opportunity to make payment whenever the conditions clearly warranted such action—that is, whenever they were men and women who loved their farm homes and were honest and upright, and had failed only in that nature had failed them—so that they still might retain their lands. The mortgagee did not want the land in most of these cases: he wanted his money. It soon became evident that the rule I had adopted was the best possible way for him to get his money. If the owner, bound by ties of affection to his land, industrious and frugal, wanted to save his farm home, I made it possible for him to avoid the expense of hiring an attorney to represent him in court in the move to postpone confirmation of the sale.

Many attorneys at that time gave their services without cost.

Only those who have lived in the heart of the nation's food-producing regions know fully the agony of these cycles of crop failure, heavy indebtedness upon the land, and ruinous farm commodity prices. If the evidence clearly showed that the indebtedness was much in excess of the value of the land, and it would not in the end benefit the owner to postpone confirmation, I confirmed the sale at once. If it appeared to me that under normal conditions the farmer would be able to pay out, I postponed confirmation until the next term. I took into account the value of the land, the amount of the indebtedness, and the means that the farmer had to meet his obligation. I would give a reasonable length of time for him to do so. I required the debtor to pay into court any cash that he possessed, and any income he could anticipate from crops not yet marketed.

I forced him to pay the taxes.

In the end, hundreds of farmers paid off their mortgages, and hundreds of farms that otherwise would have become vacant or operated under absentee ownership, remained in the hands of those who settled upon the soil. With proof of bad faith on the part of the farmer, I promptly confirmed the sale. And that seemed to me to be a rule of justice that could be inspired only by diligence upon the bench; by humane consideration of facts; and by recognition both on the part of the borrower and on that of the lender that national welfare and progress are stimulated by any system of capitalism which provides for the widest distribution of the natural resources of soil and its use by the largest number of legal owners.

In this new and somewhat primitive country, home life and marriage both prospered and failed.

There was the usual number of divorce cases.

The one I remember most distinctly was tried at Beaver City during my second term as judge, when I was living in McCook.

The plaintiff, the well-to-do owner of two farms clear and unencumbered, with a considerable amount of money in the bank, had sued his wife for divorce on the ground of adultery. He was wholly lacking in refined and cultured instincts. He seemed to me to be almost inhuman. He was a hard worker, he stayed out of debt, he had been successful financially; but his treatment of his family in my judgment was brutal. He and his wife had one child, a boy then twelve or thirteen years of age. That father had kept his son out of school, compelling him to work on the farm day and night. He used to whip the boy unmercifully. I saw the scars where the father's lash had bitten into the flesh. He also was cruel, coarse, and abusive to his wife, a modest-appearing woman, fairly well educated, clean and neat. His niggardliness forced her to dress poorly. All of her life seemed to be tied up in this child, whom she loved with an affection that I have rarely seen.

At the trial her attitude proved that, while considerable property was involved in the case, she gladly and willingly would surrender all of her claim if she could have custody of the child.

On a near-by farm lived a man who had lost his wife several years before. I had long known him through association on the county Republican central committee and in several campaigns. He was a leading citizen, and I had a great respect for him. I had never known him to advocate anything which was dishonorable or disreputable. Unconsciously at first, it appeared, he had attempted to lighten the load of the boy and the mother. The natural thing, it seems to me, took place: the man and the woman fell in love. The divorce case followed, with an adultery charge, and the evidence presented by the husband's two very able lawyers fully substantiated the charge, I thought.

During the trial, which lasted several days, I could see that the woman was filled with fear that her son was to be taken from her. I could see that she was ready to sacrifice everything for the boy. I could only say that the evidence sustained the charge of adultery. She never made a direct denial, and she never made a direct admission in examination. At the conclusion of the hearing, the husband's attorneys and her counsel agreed finally upon a decree giving most of the property and the custody of the child to the father, which they submitted to me. After I had examined it, I said to the attorneys:

"I will not sign this decree. I am not going to render that kind of a decree in this case."

There was a very spirited argument, and the attorneys became very angry. They threatened to carry the case to the supreme court if necessary, in order to get action.

"I know you can take this case to the supreme court, and you may reverse me. I have not decided what I am going to do, but I am not going to do what this decree provides. I am not going to give the custody of the child to the father. I am not going to give the bulk of the property to the father. I will prepare the decree myself, and you will appear in the court the next day."

When the courtroom had emptied, I called to the clerk, Tom Boyd. I asked him to consult an elderly couple in Beaver City who were in modest means, a couple I knew well and had boarded with, and to find whether they would be willing to provide a home for this boy if the court made reasonable allowance to compensate them. Tom Boyd reported to me the following morning they were delighted and would do the best they could to give a home to the boy. I then prepared the decree, dividing the property equally between the husband and the wife, giving the custody of the child to this elderly couple, and providing for modest payments by the husband for the child's care and support.

It did not, however, dispose of that case.

I have thought of it many times. I assume that in the instance of a shocking charge of adultery, public conscience would be extremely sensitive. The husband was very much dissatisfied, principally because he had to pay for the support of the child. Through the clerk, I discovered that he never came in except on the last day of the month, that he never went to see his son, and that he continually threatened to suspend payments. The mother visited her boy once a week. She never came without bringing him some little present that she had made with her own hands. I kept the case on the docket anticipating something was going to happen.

At the start of the school term, I found that the boy might not be permitted to attend.

His father did not live in the district, but one of the attorneys who had represented him also represented a bank in Beaver City; and the president of that bank was the president of the schoolboard. The attorney told the school-board president the board had no right to admit the child into his school. At a meeting of the board, it was decided that it could not allow the boy to attend school unless tuition was paid. I knew the president of the bank very well; he was a fine man, honest, upright, and public-spirited. I decided to act energetically. I wrote him a letter, setting forth that I understood the board would not permit the boy to attend school unless he paid tuition. I told him he was taking a course at variance with his own private life; that he himself was a father and knew that the boy lacked education and should be admitted to the public schools. I told him I had kept the case on the docket, and if it became necessary I was going to call a special term of court, summon the school board to appear. If the board persisted in its attitude, I would enter an order compelling it to admit the boy to school and would hold it for contempt if it refused. The result was that the boy got to school.

In less than a year, the mother and the man with whom she had been guilty of adultery married. I modified the decree, gave the custody of the child to the mother and rescinded the court order requiring the father to pay into the court for the support of the child. I was moved largely in this case by consideration for the boy. I could not see a third life, his life, jeopardized because of circumstances of which he was entirely innocent.

I did not know it at the time of the trial, but the Methodist minister in Beaver City was in the courtroom and heard all of the evidence. He apparently had known of the case, and had become greatly interested.

Years later (I believe it was in 1930), when I was in the Senate, I closed a campaign meeting at University Place, a Methodist town and the site of a Methodist college. Tom Boyd and his wife had moved there, and they asked me to spend the night at their home. There he told me about the minister, who, he said, had been completely convinced that I had done the right thing under difficult circumstances, and had been singing my praises all these years.

"This man is dying now of consumption," Tom said, "and his wife has told me that he wanted to see you."

I walked over to the minister's home. He was pitifully weak and near death, and talked only with the greatest difficulty. He said that he had admired me always since that trial in court when I had a controversy with the attorneys, and when I entered the decree which I did. He said he had wanted to see me and tell me that he had admired me for giving the mother, who was not free from wrongdoing, the custody of the boy, and silently had been singing my praises in his heart.

In that frontier county naturally there was violence.

A number of murder cases came before me for trial. One involved the slaying of a Kansan, a man of considerable wealth, who had mortgages against a large number of farms in Furnas County.

One of his debtors was a man named Hawkins, who could neither read nor write. The Kansan, Jensen, disappeared. Weeks passed, and still no trace could be found. Then slowly the murder unraveled, and it came to light that Hawkins, apparently with three associates, had killed Jensen, thrown the body down an abandoned well, and partially covered it over. The trial was long and tense. The evidence was wholly circumstantial but convincing. Not only had Jensen been killed, but before his death he apparently had been tortured to procure information about his property.

Only the chance discovery that Hawkins was attempting to fill up an old well led to the final solution of the murder.

The jury retired late in the afternoon, shortly after returned a verdict of guilty, and fixed the penalty at life imprisonment.

To permit the attorneys for the defense to prepare a motion for a new trial, I adjourned court until eleven o'clock the next day. At the time appointed the defense attorneys were not quite ready with their motion, although the defendant had been brought into the courtroom. The courtroom was crowded to the doors.

Just as the lawyers finished their motion, the sheriff came into the room, took the defendant by the arm, and led him into the clerk's office without saying anything to me. Shortly after, he brought him back. I overruled the motion for a new trial and sentenced Hawkins to the penitentiary for life.

Later, I asked the sheriff why he had taken the man out of the courtroom without asking permission. He reached into his pocket and pulled out a .38-caliber revolver with just two loads in it.

"That is why I took him out," he said.

Apparently someone had given Hawkins the gun.

During the trial he had formed a very unfavorable opinion of me and had come to the conclusion that I was favoring the prosecution.

He sat not more than six feet from the elevated bench.

He knew that, if he killed me, he would be mobbed, and he had a second load in the gun for himself.

A second murder case remained long in my mind. It took place in Dundy County at the home of a well-to-do rancher named Morse, only a few miles from Benkelman. One of his employees was an old man, quite well known in the community, who had a habit of carrying a large, long pocketbook in an inside coat pocket. There was also on the ranch a lad possibly eighteen years of age. When the proprietor went to Benkelman one day, this boy got a gun, loaded it with buckshot, crept up on the old man who was sawing a two-by-four, and shot him to death. Then the boy harnessed a horse, fastened the rope around the body, and dragged it to the river about half a mile distant, where he dumped the body into a hole in the ice.

It was months before the evidence was fully marshaled, but ultimately the facts came out. And it developed that the boy had no regard for human life; desperately wanted to become an outlaw.

The jury properly found the boy guilty, and I sentenced him to life imprisonment.

He looked younger than actually he was. He seemed to enjoy the trial more than anyone else connected with it. In describing his life, he told the jury that he had been in every town in Nebraska that had a railroad but never had paid a cent of fare.

Then the case reached the governor of the state, John H. Mickey, on the plea of delegations of women seeking clemency for the boy. I told the governor I thought that the evidence sustained the verdict; but he, much opposed to capital punishment, much given to leniency, an honorable man, honest and reliable, received one of the delegations in his office. At the governor's suggestion they all knelt in prayer. When the prayer ended, the governor, convinced the boy was innocent, issued a pardon and set him free.

Shortly after, the boy turned up in Missouri where he served three years for horse stealing. Upon his return to Nebraska, he was arrested in Omaha and sent to the state prison for safekeeping while awaiting trial on a charge in Omaha. In an attempted escape from the prison with a gang of criminals, he was shot and killed by one of the guards.

The case, always clear in my mind, demonstrated to me that citizens ought not to join in movements to procure clemency for criminals, unless they have personal knowledge of the facts.

10

MARRIAGE AND HOME

THE NEW COUNTRY to which I had come, which in its beauty and promise satisfied all my cravings, breathed the spirit of the homesteaders and the timber-claim settlers.

There were hundreds of them.

Some of them were young men and young women, recently married, and embarked upon the adventure of establishing homes along the new frontier. Some of the men had come west first, filed upon their homesteads, built their sod houses, and then sent for the women of their choice.

That spectacle of settlement made a lasting impression upon me that was reflected later when I became a member of Congress.

After the more fertile and productive valley lands along Nebraska streams became settled, I outlined a plan while a member of the House of Representatives to increase the homestead rights from the original 160 acres to 640 acres.

All that remained in Nebraska, and in some of the neighboring states, was submarginal land, and I felt that at least 640 acres were necessary for the support of a family.

This idea was incorporated in what is known as the Kinkaid Homestead Act, under the provisions of which the old cattle empire of western Nebraska, of magnificent distances and sweeping vistas, was broken up. I had outlined the plan in a newspaper interview and Representative Kinkaid wrote a bill incorporating it.

Then, near the close of my service in the United States Senate, I succeeded in having the Daniel Freeman homestead northwest of Beatrice, near the mouth of Cub Creek, set aside as a national park. It was the first homestead taken under the provisions of the act signed by Abraham Lincoln. Daniel Freeman, a soldier in the Union army, had filed upon it in 1863, in the early morning of the New Year's Day, shortly after the Homestead Law became effective. It commemorates one of the great developments in American history. Under that Homestead Law, more than a million American families established themselves upon the land.

The little valley of Beaver Creek, where I located, was once a part of the greatest buffalo hunting country on the North American continent. For years great herds of the shaggy beasts had fed upon the thick grasses and had slaked their thirst in the clear streams.

It was to this region that Buffalo Bill brought Crown Prince Alexis of Russia for a buffalo hunt, thereby doing his part to pave the way for the Alaska purchase.

Long before I came, the buffalo had been slaughtered systematically by professional hunters armed with long rifles, rough men living dangerously and adventurously under the sun and the stars. There was not a remaining vestige of the thousands of buffalo which frequently covered the plain as far as the naked eye could see.

There were quail, prairie chickens, and grouse.

My old love of the gun returned to me within a short time after locating in Beaver City; and there were many occasions when the meat of a prairie chicken (grouse) or the tender rabbit furnished a welcome change in the scanty diet which a new country provided. They added glory to the table in the late fall and during the winter.

Many of the men were as good marksmen as I, or better, and were infinitely more familiar with the habits of the game.

Early, there befell me a hunting accident which at the time, I thought, meant an end to usefulness, and hence to life itself.

Four of us had gone hunting for quail when one in the party, one of my closest friends in those early days of settlement, whose name I never have mentioned, fired at a covey of quail.

I remember even now the noise of the explosion, the sharp

pain that ran through me, and then the darkness as I fell to the ground, dropping my gun. Some of the small shot from the charge had entered the flesh of my cheek and around my eyes. Only the distance at which I stood possibly averted a fatal climax to that hunting trip.

I do not know how long I was unconscious; it seemed hours, but probably only a minute or two elapsed before I recovered my faculties. It came to me in darkness that I had lost my eyesight, and I began groping for the gun in terrible agony.

I could not bear the thought of living on and on in blindness.

My associates administered to me immediately, and then procured medical assistance. The doctor discovered the shot had not penetrated the eyes; and after a hasty examination he removed the pellets and told me that all the vital tissues had escaped permanent injury. The sight of one eye had returned partially before he arrived; and the joy of emerging from darkness into light, and of again seeing that tiny world I had come to love, swept away all thought of the accident and made me doubly solicitous to relieve the distress of my hunting associate.

When I first reached Beaver City, the county seat of Furnas, it was an inland town with no rail connections. Supplies had to be freighted from the railroad, adding sharply to the cost of everything. Freight rates on coal from the mines to western Nebraska, plus the cost of transporting it overland, frequently doubled or more than doubled its price.

That winter I burned corn to heat the little two-room building, twenty-two feet by fourteen, which I had put up. The corn came from the 160-acre tract near the town site which I had purchased, in company with Charles Hikes, immediately after my arrival. I husked it, used a team and a wagon owned by Hikes to haul it to town, and piled it on the ground near my office building, thus saving the expense of storage.

Later I dug the corn out from under the white blanket of snow, carried it indoors; and it provided warmth for my combination of office and sleeping quarters: a large outer office, behind which was a small room that served the dual purpose of bedroom and private office. There I lived for a number of years.

My mother still was occupying the old farm in Ohio, and she sent me bedclothes and a feather bed. Strangely, she sent also—to me, in the heart of what had been the choicest buffalo hunting ground in the United States—one of the largest buffalo robes I have ever seen, which she had acquired in Ohio for only a few dollars. Afterward, when I moved to McCook, buffalo rugs had become scarce and in great demand, and I sold it for $100.

It was the common practice in Beaver City, and throughout all the region, to heat homes and storerooms with corn. The crops had been abundant, and grain prices were low. Corn made a very hot fire, the difficulty being that it soon burned out and had to be replenished frequently; but selling for eight cents a bushel, it was much cheaper than coal.

I was deeply impressed with the rapid changes in corn prices in those years. Not uncommonly corn would sell at eight and ten cents a bushel through the fall and winter, and then spurt to fifty or seventy-five cents in the spring. Many men made a great deal of money simply by buying corn when it was cheap, storing it, and holding it for a dry growing season.

I continued to live in the little room in the rear of my office until I married on the opening day of June, a day filled with bright, warm sunshine, in 1890.

I married Miss Pluma Lashley, the daughter of David H. and Sarah Lashley, an attractive girl, tall, lithe, dark-eyed, who had been of great encouragement and inspiration to me.

Her father and mother had come from Iowa to Beaver City shortly after its founding, and Mr. Lashley had quickly risen to a position of influence in the community. He was a man of ability, with an unusual capacity for inspiring confidence. He had a great faith in the new country. He built a gristmill, operated by water power, on Beaver Creek about a mile from the town itself.

The stream was one of those clear, winding, lazy creeks, fringed by clumps of willow and other trees, twisting in snakelike fashion between the hills and flowing, winter and summer, in steady volume.

The settlers brought their grain to that mill to be ground into flour, and it continued prosperous until Mr. Lashley's death in 1894. There in season the farmers, their wagons filled with wheat, exchanged the news or discussed political issues. It seemed to me that the gristmill was one of the institutions which softened the primitive frontier.

After the ceremony on that June day my brother-in-law and I loaded Pluma's trunk into a lumber wagon, and he drove it to the little four-room cottage which I had rented and furnished. For a honeymoon trip, Pluma and I walked the short distance from her father's home to our cottage. It had a large room, a kitchen, and two bedrooms. I had removed a partition to increase the size of the bedrooms. Together, we had carefully selected the simple furnishings, and I remember my delight and my pride as I glanced over the house and noted these. After Mr. Lashley died, my wife and I moved into the large house which he had built, and where she had spent her girlhood.

Four children were born to us: a boy and three girls. Just a week prior to the birth of my first-born, I was taking my wife out for a ride as I did every pleasant day. I had purchased the horse as a colt; she was a beautiful animal, sensitive and high-spirited, but gentle in every respect and obedient to my command.

We had started out just before the sunset of a beautiful day, driving down Beaver valley. The road crossed the first bottom, and then was graded steeply in order to be above the frequent floods of Beaver Creek. In approaching the bridge that led to this steep high grade, we met a farmer's daughter on horseback, going to town. I turned out from the road a little, and the girl also turned out to pass, but just then a strong gust of wind blew her riding habit almost into the face of my horse.

As quick as a flash, the horse jumped clear from the embankment of the road.

I do not understand now what spared the buggy from overturning, but it remained upright; I yelled at the horse, and she obeyed my voice, quivering in her fright at the bottom of the ditch. She soon regained her calm, and I succeeded in driving out of the ditch and back onto the road again.

But my wife also was frightened, and the shock was intensified greatly by her condition. Just seven days later the child was born—born dead; and the attending doctor was of the opinion that this little boy would have been born alive and healthy the evening of the accident, had it not been for that tragic fright.

Three girls—Hazel, Marian, and Gertrude—followed. Hazel and Marian came to add sunshine to our home in Beaver City, and, our little daughter, Gertrude, was born after we had moved to McCook. The birth of Gertrude proved fatal to my wife, and left three baby girls in the hands of a helpless father.

Thus passed out of my life and out of the lives of her daughters one of the loveliest and most motherly of women ever to bless a family fireside.

Greatly as I had enjoyed the robes of a judge, they had taken me away from home much of the time; and my grief at Pluma's death was intensified when the need of holding court at different towns compelled me to be absent from home.

My girls needed me, and we all missed their mother.

The life that I lived at that time and the lives my children were compelled to live were not satisfactory to me. I knew that every day motherly care was missing. It seemed to me that in this dark period the building hand had disappeared from our lives. It seemed some necessary thing was missing in our home.

Thus we lived for nearly three years.

After my election to the House of Representatives, but before I was sworn in, I had quite a serious experience with my teeth, the culmination of difficulties and troubles extending over a period of years. I always have been very sensitive when in the dentist chair, but had arranged for an appointment with a Grand Island dentist, a Dr. Miller, who had examined my teeth earlier. For a week, both forenoon and afternoon, he worked on me, until I was almost a nervous wreck. There was still another day's work left, and Dr. Miller suggested my taking a rest for two or three months and coming back to have the work finished; but I insisted he complete the job.

I remember the last of his work had to be done by artificial light. I was in a terrible condition, and went to bed in the hotel without waiting for dinner. Dr. Miller, who had been apprehensive when I had left his office, came to my room and insisted upon getting a physician; but I objected, fearing that the physician would not permit me to take the train for home in the morning.

When I reached home, I summoned a doctor. After several days he became discouraged and said he wanted to have a consultation with some other physician. I thought of a young physician and surgeon in Beaver City by the name of C. C. Greene, who had become widely respected and had developed a warm friendship for me.

Dr. Greene came to McCook and stayed for several days because of the friendship between us. It was the talk in McCook that I had blood poisoning, but this was not true. I apparently had lost control of myself and was suffering from nervous disorder, aggravated by an acute attack of erysipelas. After several days, Dr. Greene reached the conclusion that I was in a dangerous condition, and I remember how gently and kindly he told me that I could not recover unless I gave him some assistance, which I was not giving. The truth is that I had made up my mind that I did not want to live.

"You are battling against every bit of medicine that I give you," Dr. Greene said. "Without your assistance, I have no hope for your recovery, and I think it is up to you to decide now whether you are going to die or going to live."

I did not tell him so, but in my own mind I thought it better under the circumstances I die.

It was in the fall of the year; the leaves had fallen from the trees, covering the ground thickly. My three little children were all small, and the neighborhood youngsters had come over to play.

My bedroom was on the bottom floor, and I could hear them distinctly as they were playing in the leaves. It sounded as if they were making houses out of rows of leaves that they had pushed up with their feet. It seemed to me that they were carefree and happy, and not old enough to realize the condition I was in or to have any interest in my illness.

My oldest child, Hazel, persisted in sitting in the room where I was. My eyes had been covered with bandages, and I was in complete darkness; but I realized that Hazel was standing by my bed, and I said to her:

"Ought you not to go out and play with the other little children—those guests who have come to play with you?"

She very solemnly and calmly replied she would rather sit in the room with me.

I still tried to persuade her to join the other children, and finally she said:

"Father, if you want me to, I will go out and play with them, but I would rather stay here with you."

Through the darkness I saw light that I had not seen before. If my little girl, then motherless, could give up the delight of playing because she wanted to sit in the darkened room with me, what must be my manhood to turn her away from my bedside?

The thought came to me if I died she would have no protection. What manner of man must I be to think of leaving her? So I reached over in the darkness, and took her little hand and said:

"Hazel, I wish you would stay here with me. If you want to stay, I would be more than pleased to have you stay."

I solemnly breathed a prayer then and there to live, and I think that change of attitude saved my life.

I lived under the influence of these little children, saw them grow up from babyhood to womanhood, and I have always thought that what little I did to bring them up to be worthy has brought me the greatest pay that I ever received in my lifetime.

My present wife was Miss Ellie Leonard of San Jose, California, who for several years had been a teacher in the public schools of

McCook, where I met her. When we were married on July 8, 1903, there came into my home at once a real mother to my motherless children.

To her more than any other person, my family owes a debt of affection. In reality, she has been the only mother that my children knew, and never was there a more considerate or a more tender-hearted, loving mother. She entered into our lives like an angel from heaven. She gave a warmth to the home that I could not give; that only a mother gives, and no man can impart. She shared the joys and the sorrows of the girls and their schooling, planning with them, anticipating their needs, watching over them, administering to them, and guiding them from babyhood to womanhood—girls now all happy in homes of their own.

I know it gave her great joy.

I know of her love for these children.

After this marriage, and while I was serving as a member of the House, in Washington, on February 23, 1906, Mrs. Norris gave birth to twin boys. During that night of bitter struggle, her life hung precariously, but just before daylight the word was brought home my wife was safe; and it was followed by the news that the twins had died.

It was a shadow that never lifted completely from us.

After she regained her strength, her spirits, we shared the life of Washington, the summers in the woods by the clear waters of the lake, rebuilt completely the home in McCook, where now the books and radio and magazines and newspapers and correspondence of days past fill my hours as I sit writing this.

I have loved the woods in all their stately garb.

I have loved the singing streams.

I remember one little stream near Washington, deep in the wooded hills, a place of peace and beauty as the night comes on. When the clouds close in, and the rain falls, that silent little brook becomes a roaring creek.

Among other of the happy Washington reflections were those Sunday evening suppers at the home of my daughter, Gertrude, now Mrs. Gordon Rath, with the grandchildren playing about. Always in America, it has been its homes which bring the greatest satisfaction.

I love the peace of that park across the street from my home in McCook where I have watched the trees grow from small saplings into stately giants, and where in summer the children play, and in fall the birds gather in preparation for the flight to their southern home. I love the veranda that opens upon the lilac and the bowers formed by the trees in my back yard, with the sun streaming down, in its benediction as the visible master of the skies.

There are the years which we have passed together—Mrs. Norris and I—years of struggle, years of great fight, years in the shadows, the defeats and the victories, for causes often misunderstood, bitterly assailed and criticized, frequently unavailing, and as frequently triumphant.

I came back to Nebraska a year ago because Washington, in all those years, never seemed to be home. The only home I can remember in all of its distinctiveness is Nebraska. I am a part of its soil, and its soil is a part of me. During those recent years when it was tortured by heat, and by drouth, when its skies were black and its sun a coppery hue, I had only to step to my window in the Senate Office Building and gaze out towards the gardens and the green stretches of the Capitol grounds, in order to realize clearly the struggle through which my people were passing.

I knew through the experiences of my young manhood, the thoughts that were pressing down upon them. I knew how anxiously they were watching the skies. I knew what hope a simple cloud along the horizon could stir. I knew the emotion when green and growing fields became seared and brown in the space of a few swift hours.

It is, or it should be, the simple things of life that contribute most to culture and civilization. Men have been establishing homes, building factories, harnessing streams, bridging canyons, conquering the earth and the skies. And yet rich are the people in this world to whom trees, and water, and growing things bring hope and happiness.

11

RELUCTANT DECISION

I HAD SERVED three years of my second term as judge—seven years in all—when I was elected to a seat in the House of Representatives at Washington. It was with great reluctance that I left the bench—work which I had enjoyed, and for which I felt that I was much better qualified than legislation.

At first I had declined positively to be a candidate.

I told the persuasive political leaders, who were out to reclaim the Fifth District from the Populists—it was then represented by A. C. Shallenberger of Alma—that I had no desire to get into the political field. But my success in breasting the Populist tide had attracted wide-spread attention among the Republicans of that district, and had been noted by a portion of the press. Finally, with some misgivings, and with a great deal of regret, I yielded to the politicians.

I knew, when I gave assent, that if I were successful in the election a spirited rivalry would develop among the lawyers of the district for the appointment by the governor to fill my unexpired term upon the bench. I knew who the candidates would be: men who were my friends, and upon whom I was dependent for support in the congressional fight. It led to a decision to see personally every one of these potential candidates and indicate plainly to them that unless they agreed among themselves on a recommendation I would refuse to attempt to influence the governor in his appointment. I made the understanding very definite that in consenting to run for Congress I was under no circumstances to be asked to seek the appointment of any particular man to the bench.

Later, successful in the election, I kept that agreement to the letter. The governor at that time was Ezra P. Savage, of Sargent, and after the November election, he asked me for my recommendation of a successor upon the bench. I told him of the agreement and of my determination to keep it. This did not relieve me from very great pressure from various quarters, but Governor Savage made his appointment without knowing what my preference was.

So the Fifty-eighth Congress of the United States received as a new member a bitter Republican partisan. In my early forties, I was and always had been a member of the Republican party. I took every opportunity of advocating the election of candidates on the Republican ticket—sometimes, I now know, without regard to their qualifications. I believed that all the virtues of government were wrapped up in the party of which I was a member, and that the only chance for pure and enlightened government was through the election of only Republicans to office. I was conservative, and proud of it—sure of my position, unreasonable in my convictions, and unbending in my opposition to any other political party, or political thought except my own.

At that time it was not important that soon these stanch and bright ideals of the purity and wholesomeness of Republican politics and Republican candidates were to be shattered. Even as a boy I was influenced, and influenced deeply, by the belief of my mother. This illustrates how bitter and how deeply founded was my partisanship; yet I can say truthfully that I held this belief honestly, only to awaken to its lack of logic, to its unfortunate result in so many instances, and to the distortion of patriotism in the terrible injury inflicted by blind and unreasoning partisanship upon any country founded under democratic ideals.

I served five consecutive terms in the House beginning with the Fifty-eighth Congress of 1903, and five consecutive terms in the United States Senate, for a total of forty years. I saw men come and go, living their hour of glory in the heat of bitter battle, forgotten and broken in their hour of defeat. I saw the panorama of forty years of national progress as it was mirrored in Congress; and frequently from a seat in the House, or in the Senate, it was possible to see what was not mirrored for the public's eyes.

My first congressional opponent, A. C. Shallenberger of Alma, supported by both Democrats and Populists, occupied the seat in 1902 when I became a candidate. It was a close race, after an exceedingly intense, spirited, and vigorous campaign. When the votes were counted it was revealed that I had received 14,927, to 14,746 for Representative Shallenberger.

My opponent whom I met in a series of joint debates, was one of the ablest campaigners developed by the Middle West. He was a man of impressive personal appearance, with piercing eyes, handsome features, a fine head set upon an athletic body, and a fine speaking voice. He was just as bitter a partisan as I was.

Mr. Shallenberger lived on a fine farm near Alma; but his main business was running a bank, which he did in a very able manner. In his campaign he talked chiefly as a farmer, telling of his fine farm, emphasizing that he had grown up on the land and that his sympathies were entirely with the farmer; and many people in the district did not know he was the owner of a bank.

He leveled his guns upon me as a lawyer although at the time I was a judge. Just as unreasonably, I exaggerated the influence that the banker had over the destinies of the farmer. I pictured how the farmer was held in chains because of the excessive interest that he had to pay to the local banker. In one of these joint debates our friendship for the farmer clashed.

Before a large audience in McCook composed chiefly of farmers, Mr. Shallenberger made an eloquent plea in which he endeavored to convince them that they could not be represented properly in Washington by a member of the legal profession. I followed him with a review of his business in an effort to convince them that a banker was not the proper person to represent farmers in Congress.

The heat of the debate precipitated an incident of which I was never very proud.

There was a great crop of corn in Nebraska that year, one of the best crops ever produced, and corn picking was at its peak. I challenged Mr. Shallenberger to a corn-husking contest, which would demonstrate to the people of the district who was the real farmer candidate. I proposed that we select a field in the vicinity of McCook and decide the issue without delay: go out into the field the next day and husk corn from sunrise until sunset, stopping an hour for dinner from twelve to one. And then and there I gave my pledge that, at another meeting to be held in the same hall in the evening after the husking contest, I would withdraw as a candidate for Congress if I did not husk more corn than Mr. Shallenberger—with the understanding that he would do the same if he lost.

It was unstatesmanlike, foolish, but it had a wonderful effect on my audience. Over and over again, I dared him to accept my challenge. I knew that when I was on the farm I had possessed the ability to husk corn; without knowing how good a corn husker he was, I thought I stood a better chance of winning that contest than I did of winning the election. The audience was fairly evenly divided between Republican and Democratic parties, and although he did not accept my challenge and sought to make light of it, I knew that it appealed to a great many men who would have liked to see the election settled in the cornfield.

After his defeat, Mr. Shallenberger became a candidate for governor, won; and he was again my rival in my first campaign for the United States Senate. Defeated for this, he became a Democratic candidate for the House, was elected, and then reelected, and gained the respect of his colleagues to an exceptional degree.

In 1904, and again two years later in 1906, I had comparatively easy campaigns during the ascendency of the star of Theodore Roosevelt, to whom I had become deeply attached. But in 1908 I participated, I believe, in the closest political contest of the congressional elections of that year. I had thrown off the cloak of bitter partisanship and had become identified to some degree with the Progressive wing of the Republican party. I had incurred the ill will of the party leaders and had aroused the suspicions of the organization workers. My margin of victory was 22 votes. William Howard Taft had been chosen, with the blessing of Theodore

Roosevelt, as the Republican candidate for the Presidency. My fellow Nebraskan, W. J. Bryan, was the Democratic standard-bearer. Taft visited Nebraska, flashed his best campaign smile before an audience in that state; and Mr. Bryan made an aggressive campaign, closing with a great rally in his home community that fanned the patriotic fervor of his friends and neighbors to a white heat.

I had been unopposed in the primary that year, but the smallness of the primary vote, 6,936, should have given me warning. The Democrats and the Populists centered upon Fred W. Ashton of Grand Island, and in the primary he came within approximately 1,500 votes of polling the same number I received.

Mr. Ashton was a lawyer. He had been a devoted party worker, never seeking anything for himself, spending his time and his energies in behalf of the Democratic party. He had powerful newspaper support in the district, and in the press outside the district. He was a charming and engaging man, over six feet in height, magnificently built, his features enhanced by a head of silvery hair. Where he went, he made friends, and he had the active support of the conservative elements in both parties directing a well knit organization. When the votes were counted, I had 20,649, and he 20,627.

I knew then that my independence, which was just beginning to bud and flower, had been resented by party leadership, and the first clouds of those battles that were to come later were along the horizon. But again in 1910, midway in the Taft administration, Progressive spirit was rising, with the storm to break two years later nationally, and I won an easy victory in my final race for the Lower House, scoring the most convincing triumph of my career up until then.

My majority was over 4,000.

My ten years' service in the House of Representatives was not a happy one. I had been nominated first at a convention as the Republican candidate. I soon was to go through the experience that cooled the ardor of my partisanship. I discovered that my party organization I had supported so vigorously was guilty of virtually all the evils that I had charged against the opposition. One by one,

I saw my favorite heroes wither. Slowly but clearly, and with absolute certainty, I was compelled to abandon my belief in the lofty character of the Republican party.

In that first congressional campaign Representative Joseph W. Babcock was chairman of the national Republican Congressional Committee. I had entered into some correspondence with him during the campaign, and he had sent me several thousand copies of speeches which Republicans had made in the House of Representatives. These I circulated over the district. He sent me a thousand dollars as a contribution to my campaign fund. I never had seen him, and it was natural that I should form a very high opinion of him.

Before he sent out the great bulk of these speeches for circulation, he mailed me some samples, possibly a dozen, and asked me to select the ones I should like to circulate. Several were speeches by Babcock himself, bitter, partisan, but they suited me exactly at the time.

They arrived by the dray load.

Then the day came when I had taken farewell of Nebraska and was to be sworn in at the opening special session of Congress called by Theodore Roosevelt, and I was assigned a seat beside Representative Wesley Jones of Washington. He had served two terms, and it was from him that I acquired the first lesson of procedure in the House. He was a very agreeable man, conscientious, intensely partisan (as I realized when I came to know him better), but moved by the highest motives and convictions. I did not know on that day when I first became acquainted with him that our association was going to be so friendly as it afterward became. And I did not know I again was going to sit beside him in the Senate of the United States.

One of the first things I requested him to do was to point out to me veteran statesmen I knew by reputation. One of the first men I asked about was Joseph Babcock of Wisconsin.

In my mind I had constructed Babcock as a bold warrior, with flaming eloquence. I told Mr. Jones how wonderful I thought Babcock's speeches were, and I never can forget the hint of a smile that went over his countenance when I told him how I looked forward to the time when Babcock would take the floor.

Again there was that shadowy smile.

Then he told me that Representative Babcock did not make many speeches; he pointed him out, and I confess that I was disappointed in the appearance of the man, who had occupied such a large position in my mind. Still I was unsatisfied. I asked how it was, if he seldom spoke, that so many of the speeches he had kindly sent me could appear in the *Congressional Record*. With another whimsical smile Wesley Jones said:

"We have a way here of putting speeches in the *Record*. It does not always follow that those speeches are actually delivered on the floor of the House and, knowing Mr. Babcock as I know him, I doubt very much whether he actually made the speeches to which you refer."

I could hardly believe what Jones was telling me.

Recalling the incredulity and astonishment that filled me on that opening day, I know that for many freshmen entering Congress in high hopes the sun passes under a cloud immediately upon being seated.

But I was persistent. My idol was not to disappoint me so easily. I questioned Mr. Jones further about putting these speeches in the *Record* when they were not actually delivered. He said that Representative Babcock was a very fine man and a very able one, but was not an orator; he himself had never heard him make a speech in Congress although he had been there for some time.

Throughout the ten years that I served, I never heard Babcock make a speech. He was chairman of the Committee on the District of Columbia, had charge of bills that pertained to the government of the District, and later I heard him get the consent of Congress to publish something without reading. When I examined it afterwards in the *Record*, it appeared to be a great speech. I soon was to learn that he held the position of chairman of the national Republican Congressional Committee because of his ability to get great contributions from great corporations to the Republican cause.

It must not be inferred that a member of Congress cannot serve well unless he is an eloquent speaker, able to make great speeches; on the contrary some of the most useful and some of the best members of Congress do very little talking. But through all the years, in which new faces have appeared and old faces disappeared, those first impressions of the national legislative assembly remain sharp; and I continue to be troubled by the erroneous ideas the American people may form from reading in the *Congressional Record* reputed speeches to the House, with frequent indications that they were received with great applause, when as a matter of fact there was nothing of the kind.

My heart was set upon becoming a member of the House Committee on Public Grounds and Buildings, and I had procured the backing of leading Republicans. The committees then were appointed by the Speaker, and every two years the Speaker of the House had it in his power either to reappoint or to refuse to reappoint to any committee position. My wish was gratified, and now years later I wonder why I was so anxious for this recognition. It was of no consequence and gave me no particular influence nor power.

After I had landed the assignment the initial meeting of the committee was called by the chairman, Representative Charles W. Gillet. The object of the meeting, he said, was to bring the committee together and to enable its members to become acquainted; and back of that was the discussion of the possibility of bringing in an omnibus building bill. I was new and uninitiated, and I had no idea of what it was all about. Entirely untutored in the power of the machine, I had no idea of the autocratic power that the rules of the House gave to the Speaker.

Congressman Joseph Cannon had just been elected for the first time to that office. I supported him gladly and voted with my party for him.

At this initial meeting of the committee, nevertheless, I was dumfounded by the developments. Discussion arose as to whether the committee could draft a public building bill, and it seemed to be taken for granted that the decision was to be made by the Speaker. The senior Democratic member of the committee, Representative

Bankhead of Alabama, long since dead, actually made a motion that the chairman of the committee should seek a conference with the Speaker and ascertain whether or not we should be allowed to have a public building bill at that session. I could not understand why the Speaker should have anything more to say about it than anyone else, and especially the members of the committee.

Bankhead's motion carried unanimously.

It was a severe shock to me. Then, right then, I believe the light dawned upon me and I began to see for the first time that the Republican party was subject to influences similar to those that I believed controlled the Democratic party; and soon I learned there was no difference between the parties in this respect. Both of them were machine-controlled, and the Democratic and Republican machines often worked in perfect harmony and brotherly love. That impression was heightened as the years passed.

In a short time the chairman of the Public Grounds and Buildings Committee reported to his committee colleagues that the Speaker finally had decided the Fifty-eighth Congress would have an omnibus public building bill. Naïve as I was, it was pleasing news to me, as it was to other members of the committee. I entered ardently into the preparation of that bill. In hours of reflection I anticipated a great fight on the floor of the House when the bill was reported. It seemed to me there were a great many provisions written into it that had at least two sides; and I seriously doubted the justice and wisdom of many of the provisions.

Imagine my surprise, my disillusionment, and my awakening, on this first introduction to the great American institution known as the pork barrel, to find that it aroused virtually no opposition. When the bill came up for consideration, discussion lasted only a few minutes, and it went through with a whoop in convincing demonstration that the Fifty-eighth Congress was unanimous for the distribution of pork that the bill contained. I had not served in the House very long before I became aware that my partisanship often led me astray, and that I followed pliantly partisan leaders many times when my conscientious convictions revolted. It caused me to think and to ponder over the practice of following a blind leadership which frequently led into illogical positions, and to dealing out legislative favors to men who were unworthy. I soon learned that if I was to get any favors in the way of appointments, it would be necessary that I be ever faithful to my party leadership.

It was the basis of the first speech that I attempted to make in the House of Representatives. I knew that many such appointments were being made, and that there were more appointments than there were members; and it soon dawned upon me that the reason I was not recognized in appointments was that gradually the leadership was beginning to suspect my loyalty to the Republican party.

I soon lost my good standing with the leading politicians of my party. The direct cause was my resentment against the party caucus. When I first reached Washington it was the general practice of members to follow implicitly the decisions of the caucus. After I announced that I would not be bound by any such action that did not agree with my conscientious convictions, I discovered that many other members felt as I did; and during the years I remained in the House this feeling increased to such a degree that ultimately the party caucus was abolished, and the attempt to control the votes of the members in this way was given up.

Washington had emerged from the gay nineties in men's attire when I reached the national capital. Generally the members of the House wore a stiffly starched shirt, with a detachable collar which either completely enclosed the Adam's apple or, if the wearer gave a thought to comfort, was of the wing variety. The tie usually was a bow, although the Ascot had its followers.

The coat fitted snugly, with narrow lapels; trousers were tight around the hips and in the legs.

There has been so much talk of Washington's expansion.

When I reached the National Capital, Potomac Park, now a place of beauty, still was a swamp. There was no Senate or House office buildings. Where the Senate Office Building now stands, there were rows of houses. The Union Station, which thrills most Americans on their first visit to Washington, had not been constructed. I remember the dirty, grayish B. & O. Depot, and the Pennsylvania Station, which was of red brick, approximately at Seventh and Pacific avenues. It was there that Garfield was shot.

Many of the streetcars had trailers—the operator stood at his post unprotected in all kinds of weather. Pennsylvania Avenue was lined with souvenir hunters to the west of the Capitol. Every hour of the day echoed to the sound of the horses' hoofs. The Lincoln Memorial in all its majesty had not been built; the cherry trees along the Potomac had not been planted.

In the forty years that followed, the nation's march revealed itself strikingly in the physical changes which completely changed the face of Washington.

12

PAYNE-ALDRICH TARIFF BILL

My education in party government was continued in the House of Representatives through a course in tariff legislation.

In 1909 the Payne-Aldrich bill passed, and thereafter throughout my service in Congress I heard and participated in every debate which took place over a tariff law.

To the end of that period, there was virtually no change in the technique of tariff legislation. New duties might be proposed, or existing levies might be increased; but always the methods utilized bore a startling likeness, and the forces back of every measure were the same. The means taken to determine duties, the consideration and debate of those levies, and the passage of the bill either in its original or in its amended form, followed a fixed pattern, which had been polished until it glistened.

Recent years have brought much controversy over subsidies for favored groups or classes. Paternalism in government began with adoption of the high protective tariff principle. In its practical operations, the high protective tariff is a subsidy pure and simple though indirect; for the benefit conferred upon the producers of industrial commodities, through those tariff walls which Congress built higher and higher, exacting enormous profits from the consumers for the manufacturers, embodies the idea of a subsidy. In time, the insatiable appetite for higher tariffs was responsible for the most flagrant nationalism ever developed in this country.

I had barely emerged from the freshman class as a member of the House when what is known as the Payne-Aldrich tariff bill was being drafted.

It was written in reality in its entirety by the Republican members of the Ways and Means Committee of the House.

Representative Sereno E. Payne was chairman of the committee. He was a man of very high character, exceptionally well posted upon tariff legislation, and had had a part in drafting the McKinley and the Dingley tariffs. If he had been granted a free hand the bill he drafted would have made as good a tariff law as could have been drawn. Unfortunately, Mr. Payne was invariably obedient to the wishes of the Republican party machine, and often he sacrificed his own true judgment in order to retain his high standing with the party bosses.

The committee at its initial session referred the tariff bill to a subcommittee of twelve Republican members, and this subcommittee proceeded with hearings and with the formalities of preparing the bill.

It may be enlightening to the American people to hear that the first agreement reached by the members of the subcommittee, all Republicans, in preparing the Payne-Aldrich tariff bill was that they would settle all disputed questions of duties in the subcommittee hearings; then, after the measure was drawn and approved as a whole, the members of the subcommittee would consider themselves bound, as Republicans, to oppose any change by the full committee.

The result was that a bare majority of the subcommittee, which in itself fell short of constituting a majority of the full Committee on Ways and Means, was able to control the action of the full committee.

Under that procedure, a minority of the most powerful House committee directed in iron-fisted fashion the actions of the entire group. It constituted a tariff dictatorship repugnant to men of independent thought.

The committee had twelve Republican members, and these twelve Republicans made up the subcommittee considering the Payne-Aldrich tariff law. Seven thus constituted a majority of the subcommittee, and for all practical purposes the same seven amounted to a majority of the full committee. Which meant that interests selfishly concerned in establishing tariff rates satisfactory to themselves had to control or to win the support of but seven members of the subcommittee in order to triumph both in the subcommittee and in the full committee, bringing the tariff bill out on the floor of the House with the unanimous backing of the Republican members of the Ways and Means Committee.

In time the abuses of this control aroused the resentment of the American people, and the bill to which I refer became one of the hottest controversial issues of an era of America history, and the storm center of a national political campaign.

One of the items in that Payne-Aldrich tariff law figured very conspicuously in the congressional campaign which preceded the election of the members of the Fifty-eighth Congress. It was the amount of tariff that should be levied upon "petroleum and its products." The widespread public sentiment to place them on the free list was well recognized, and throughout the campaign there had been virtual agreement among congressional candidates that petroleum and its products should be placed on the free list. No member, seeking election at the time, undertook to advocate substantial protection for petroleum and its products.

In the subcommittee, petroleum and petroleum products were unanimously placed on the free list.

But the machine had other plans.

When the action became known to House Speaker Joe Cannon, he asked Chairman Payne to call a meeting of the subcommittee immediately for the purpose of reconsidering its decision.

A bitter debate developed. Some of the members protested hotly that they owed it to the country to place petroleum and petroleum products on the free list, and that the great oil companies would be the only beneficiaries of this tariff. But the Speaker insisted that the Republican members of the committee should abide by the promise which party leaders had made to the oil interests to place a tariff on petroleum and petroleum products. The Speaker said that if the Republican party was to be loyal to its leaders the agreement had to be carried out. Finally the item came to a vote, and the subcommittee stood seven to five in favor of putting a tariff on petroleum and petroleum products.

Representative Edgar D. Crumpacker of Indiana, an old friend and colleague of mine, was one of the seven who opposed the tariff most bitterly; but they all, having agreed in advance to abide by the action of the subcommittee, felt honor-bound when the bill came before the full committee to vote to sustain the subcommittee.

The result was that the bill, as finally reported to the House, contained a tariff of 25 per cent on petroleum and its products.

The fight had been won in the committee.

The bill was considered in the House under a special rule. Under the procedure it was impossible to offer an amendment placing petroleum and its products on the free list. The only amendments that were in order were such as to change the amount of the duty. I secured the floor and offered a motion to change the duty on petroleum and its products to 1 per cent; and after some debate the motion prevailed, with the result that the House practically returned petroleum to the free list. Committee Chairman Payne then told the House that the duty as amended would not pay the cost of collection; and he asked unanimous consent that petroleum and its products be placed on the free list, which was done.

On the roll call Representative Crumpacker had not voted. The following day he told me that during all his service in Congress he had never dodged a vote before; but he had thought this tariff on petroleum so wicked and so unjustified that, when the vote was to be taken, he left the chamber.

There was nothing in 1909 to suggest the extent and degree to which petroleum and its products would touch the lives of the American people. Less than twenty years later the same element of American leadership was proclaiming proudly that nearly every home had its automobile.

Here was just one commodity of common use among the hundreds of items incorporated in every tariff law. For centuries, by a geological miracle oil had been forming in lakes far beneath the surface of the earth. Men had little to do with it. Then its use spread, and men began developing the supply. In the infancy of a great industry a sanguine, stubborn battle was fought in Congress to prevent a few men from strengthening their monopolistic control of petroleum.

Now in 1944 much has been said and printed about the danger of exhaustion of America's oil reserves. The enormous drain of modern, mechanized warfare, with its tanks, its motorized equipment, and its planes, may have cut deeply into the country's supply.

Great fortunes, some of the largest in America, have been made from oil. It and precious metals have caused the spilling of more blood in the struggles between nations than any other spoils over which men fight and kill each other.

But in the battle over the petroleum duty in the Payne-Aldrich tariff bill there was no expression of the thought that the day might come, and soon, when the American people not only would welcome shipments from other regions of the world but, in the absence of such shipments, would be forced to readjust their lives drastically. The only concern then was larger profits and a more airtight monopoly.

Oil was only one item in the tariff bill. There were hundreds.

That frenzy for higher and higher protection, walling America in from the rest of the world, touched not only the comforts and luxuries but the simplest necessities of life. It reached to the family table, to the homes and the activities of people.

I saw partisanship twisted to commit a great wrong.

In the years which followed, there were more violent battles over tariff legislation. There was a mounting tide of opposition in America as the new levies piled injustices and inequities one upon another.

The Middle West, my home, was exploited and bled white. Its people, true, had been lulled into a false sense of benefits by tariffs upon agricultural products which failed to provide full protection for commodities sold upon a world market. These farm families found themselves faced with mounting financial problems, with a disparity between agricultural and industrial income that became more and more marked. Among them, revolt was taking form.

I had come to Congress an ardent Republican.

I respected the tariff policy of my party.

I believed honestly there were instances where the protection given by a tariff justified the duties and made them beneficial.

But in that initial baptism, I became impressed with the autocratic power held by the Speaker of the House over tariff legislation.

In the case of this Payne-Aldrich bill he, standing alone—not even a member of the committee—and bowing his head to promises made in a political campaign, had been able to ram a duty on petroleum and petroleum products down the throats of members of the subcommittee after there had been an agreement petroleum should go on the free list.

He was able to make the members of the subcommittee jump rope, and under the rules he could force the Republican members of the committee to back him in his position regardless of their own conscience. He compelled them to place a duty on an item upon the demand of special interests.

I then and there concluded that the institutions of democracy needed some reformation, and needed it badly.

In all the tariff struggles which followed, I saw the same spectacle. Powerful, well entrenched interests came to Washington, and enforced their demands upon members of Congress.

The lobby grew more arrogant, and at times more contemptuous.

Out in the open, unabashed and confident, the dread of a flood of foreign commodities at the close of World War No. 1 made the task of writing the Fordney-McCumber tariff law a simple, easy one. All thought of the consumer was silenced by the fearsome spectre of an invasion of American markets by European industry and labor.

Nationalism was becoming the most strident note in the world.

Tariff walls were thrown up hastily in defense against other tariff walls.

Trade was languishing.

Then came the final act under Mr. Hoover, with the Smoot-Hawley tariff legislation, originally projected as a program of revision, convincing me the time had arrived to renounce the uninterrupted upward sweep of tariff duties. I voted against the Fordney-McCumber tariff law; spoke against it; asked to be placed upon record against the Smoot-Hawley law.

I talked with a few of my associates. Among them were men whom I knew to be most devoted and public-spirited legislators.

I asked one old friend, for whom I have had the highest regard, why he did not oppose duties upon products which I knew were being produced in insufficient quantities here in the United States. We had left the Senate chamber to loll in the sunshine.

I shall never forget his answer:

"I could not be reelected," he told me, "if I voted against those duties. My people would slaughter me."

"What difference does it make?" I answered. "I would rather go down to defeat than vote for those duties."

It was my experience in the House and Senate that fear of resentment among the beneficiaries of a few items in a tariff bill, providing protection for limited commodities produced locally, has been the chief factor in the development of America's tariff policy. Men of great courage in most matters shrank from what they thought would incite opposition from a few or a considerable number of constituents. They chose to swallow the whole dose rather than resist levies they individually thought were wrong and unjust.

Less than three terms in the House had made me ripe for rebellion.

There was that embarrassing experience when in innocence and inexperience I inadvertently had voted to support a motion offered by a Democratic representative to observe the birthday of George Washington. I alone of the Republican membership had given it support, and the displeasure of my party colleagues registered so clearly in every Republican's face. I had balked at the caucus. I had been told many times it was the solemn duty of every good Republican to go along.

I made no effort to disguise my irritation. I was not in good standing—and, worse, I did not seem to care.

I undertook in these years of legislative education no major matters of legislation. One bill in which I was interested deeply sought to correct a railroad shipping inequity in my district. I had given considerable study to it and had gathered an impressive array of evidence. At the committee hearing the railroad representatives flatly contradicted my charges, and the committee was unwilling to call the witnesses I needed to establish the charges. What I charged was true, but its truth was of little consequence.

There were bigger battles just ahead.

13

THE UNHORSING OF SPEAKER CANNON

GREAT POWER tends to make men contemptuous of opposition.

In the early hours of the struggle to strip Speaker Joe Cannon of those official prerogatives which enabled him to bend the House of Representatives to his will, Mr. Cannon probably failed to sense any grave danger in the challenge which the insurgent group tossed to him.

He and the loyal regular Republican organization were taken by surprise in that St. Patrick's Day uprising of 1910. Arrogance—born of a firm belief that the long-standing rules of the House would continue in force without substantial change—blinded them.

The factor of surprise contributed generously to the success of the fight I led against Cannonism, while millions of Americans looked on.

Now, more than thirty-four years later, I think the country gave us credit for more than actually was accomplished in reform, probably because, for the first time, there had been a challenge to the autocratic power of the Speaker of the House. Even then the nation did not understand the technicalities and the parliamentary peculiarities of that struggle. It knew that Boss Cannon had been beaten, and that was enough for it. Since then, other millions of men and women have come to voting age; and to them that battle of March, 1910, is but a fleeting memory of an event long past.

In its essence, though in different form, that same fight goes on constantly in this country. The individuals participating are of only passing importance; the fact of the struggle is all that really counts. The unceasing effort to make democratic government really and truly responsive to popular will, and to human welfare, may present itself as it did in the Cannon fight, or under entirely different aspects.

Under the rules, the channels of legislative expression were not free and open. Speaker Cannon could shut them off at his desire. He was literally a czar, with power to be used for good or evil.

Mr. Cannon was no better and no worse than many men in Congress. He was capable in machine politics. He was, perhaps, the most efficient and the most articulate representative of that blighting philosophy in America which places loyalty to party at the top of the list of duties and responsibilities of citizenship. In personal appearance and in habits, he was fitted ideally for the part he played in that particular period of American history. He was disarming in his attitude toward newcomers in the House. Frequently he was brusque and curt, and when aroused he pulled no punches; but in customary contact he had a mellowness that attracted men.

I came under his displeasure early, because I would not stay hitched to his cart; and I never really knew Joe Cannon until after he was licked.

Hedged in as he was in the powerful post of Speaker, he lost contact with the members of the House in the months preceding that insurgent uprising, and did not sense the full measure of the revolt that was in progress.

From the day that I was sworn into office, I noted the rising resentment against his autocratic rule. The natural result was the organizing of members known as insurgents. I know it to be a fact that the single objective which brought these men together was the taking from the Speaker of the vast, brutal power which the rules of the House gave him to control the action of individual members.

Speaker Cannon should not have been caught off guard: there was abundant evidence of growing discontent, in the atmosphere of the chamber when the House was in session, and the cloakroom gossip. It was Mr. Cannon's genuine confidence in party discipline that made him so fearless; and this confidence was his undoing.

Yet, only a short time before, there was a development which clearly foretold what would happen if the right opportunity arose.

There had been many rumors in Washington about the leasing of coal and timber lands in Alaska by President Taft's Secretary of the Interior, Richard A. Ballinger. The President's dismissal of Chief Forester Gifford Pinchot had not terminated a controversy over the policy of conservation of natural resources. It had in fact fed the flames. It became common knowledge that a congressional investigation of the Department of the Interior and the Bureau of Forestry would accomplish what executive action had failed to bring about; Secretary Ballinger was to be vindicated; the investigators were to apply a copious coat of whitewash. The press openly speculated upon the men who might be selected to make the investigation.

A concurrent resolution was introduced in both branches of Congress calling for the appointment of a joint committee. It passed the Senate, and the Vice President was authorized to name the five members from that body.

When the resolution came up in the House, I had made up my mind to take the appointment of its investigators from the Speaker, if possible, and to permit them to be named from the floor.

While the resolution was under consideration, Representative John Dalzell of Pennsylvania was serving in the chair (Mr. Dalzell performed the chores regularly for Speaker Cannon). He was a staunch Republican regular, and I could not expect to get recognition from him to offer my substitute for the concurrent resolution.

Representative Dalzell was a precise man, and I had observed his luncheon habits:

Regularly at one o'clock, he would leave the chamber for a sandwich, a cup of coffee, and a piece of pie at the House restaurant. That practice was as fixed as the clock itself.

When Representative Dalzell vacated the chair, Walter Smith followed him as the presiding officer. Representative Smith, who also was a regular, was a close personal friend and had been thoughtful and considerate on many occasions. While the discussion continued, I eyed the clock anxiously: as the hour hand moved towards one, Representative Dalzell started down the aisle. When he neared the door, I walked over to Smith and asked him if I might have a little time.

"How much do you want?" he asked me.

"Not over two minutes," I answered.

"I'll give you five minutes," he replied. "Just as soon as the present speaker finishes, I will call on you."

It was exactly what I desired. I had hardly gotten back to my seat before Congressman Smith recognized me. I had hastily written out the substitute proposal, and without any delay presented an amendment to the resolution, by which the House as a body would make its own appointments to the investigating committee, instead of authorizing the Speaker to make the appointments.

My substitute carried by the narrow margin of 149 to 146, with insurgents and Democrats supporting it; and an investigation launched as a gesture to political expediency turned into a thoroughgoing overhauling which had considerable influence in the next presidential election.

That victory gave the insurgents new heart in their weary fight: they had scored against the Speaker, and his power, after attaining a cancerous growth, had suffered a setback.

Those who have received the ballot since the struggle against Speaker Cannon should observe the practical effects of the rules under which the House was functioning until Speaker Cannon's overthrow. Those rules, as applied by Mr. Cannon, disfranchised the minority. This had been true for a long time. Under both Republican and Democrat majorities the Speaker, when the need arose, had the power to hold the House under rigid control.

Every special rule first has to be agreed to by the House, and frequently the question was asked: "Why did the members of the House vote for these tyrannical special rules?"

Often I asked myself the same question. The rules seemed so obnoxious no fair-minded man could support them. But in a parliament as large as the House of Representatives, it is necessary to expedite business by the adoption of special rules governing the consideration of much of the legislation which comes before it. The unwieldiness of the membership of the House meant that unless there was some curtailment of debate, and some limitation of the freedom to offer amendments, it would be unable to proceed in an orderly manner or to advance legislation, and would be beset and weighted down by interminable delay.

Failure to limit debate and amendment of a tariff bill, for example—containing thousands of items affecting all regions of the country—would have meant months, or even years, of delay in the passage of the bill.

It was the abuse of the rules, and not the purposes for which they had been drafted, which was at fault. They left so many tempting loopholes. Every two years the members knew they were confronted with the appointment of the various standing committees; and one man, the Speaker, possessed absolute authority to do what he pleased in these selections. He held in his hands the political life of virtually every member. He could reward the faithful, and he could punish the "guilty."

I doubt if any Speaker in the history of Congress was as ruthless as Joe Cannon sometimes was.

Through his domination and control of the Committee on Rules, he likewise had a formidable lever to dictate the action of the House itself. Speakers chosen from the ranks of both political parties had had the same power, but no one could have made more effective use of it.

Inevitably members knew they would be pleading on bended knee before the Speaker for favors to perpetuate themselves in office.

Specifically, these obstacles made the path of reform difficult:

An ordinary procedure to amend the rules was blocked because there was no way at that time to discharge the committee.

There was no procedure under which a committee could be compelled to report upon either a resolution or any bill referred to it.

So when resolutions to change the rules were introduced—and

there were thousands of them—all that the Committee on Rules had to do was to pigeonhole them and permit them to die a slow, lingering death: it became the graveyard of resolutions.

Quite by accident, in the unguarded moment I knew would come, the opening for a reformation of those rules presented itself. The Constitution provided, "Each House may determine the rules of its proceedings."

In this usage I thought there could be no doubt that the word "may" was to be construed as meaning "shall." Otherwise, there was no method provided by the Constitution to establish the rules for the United States Senate or for the House of Representatives. The two legislative branches created by the wise framers of government would have been powerless to accomplish anything without rules to govern their deliberations. It seemed so plain, so clear, so logical to me that the constitutional provision was in effect compulsory upon each House to adopt proper rules.

The Constitution likewise stipulated: "The actual enumeration [to determine the membership of Congress] shall be made within three years after the first meeting of the Congress of the United States, and within every subsequent term of ten years, in such manner as they shall by law direct." This is in Section 2, Article I, of the Constitution.

Representative Edgar Crumpacker of Indiana, chairman of the Committee on Census, reported a bill which provided for the taking of a new census.

Apparently it had been overlooked until the session was well advanced. It was placed on the House calendar, but under the rules it could not have been reached in the regular order of business prior to adjournment. The general House rules decreed bills should be taken up in the same order they were reported to the House by the committee. Always after Congress was in session, many bills were reported out and placed on the calendar without any chance of consideration.

Representative Crumpacker's census bill was far down on the list.

Nevertheless, he undertook to call it up for consideration, out of the regular calendar order. A point of order was made promptly against his motion to advance the census bill; but Speaker Cannon ruled Mr. Crumpacker's motion was in order because the constitutional provision, which gave it preference, superseded the general House rules.

An appeal from the Speaker's decision resulted in Mr. Cannon being overruled. The House itself decided it was not in order to take up the census bill, notwithstanding the Constitution. I thought the Speaker's decision was wrong and the House action in overruling him correct, and I voted to support the appeal from the Speaker's ruling. The next day the Cannon forces had arranged to have all faithful followers present, and Representative Crumpacker offered the same motion which had been rejected the day before.

The machine had been oiled properly this time. When the appeal was taken from the Speaker's decision ruling the Crumpacker motion in order, Mr. Cannon was sustained by the votes of the Republican regulars. They therefore decided, on that fateful day, that the constitutional provision conferred a constitutional privilege supreme over the general rules of the House.

It was the hour for which I had been waiting patiently.

I had in my pocket a resolution to change the rules of the House. Unknown to anyone, even to my closest insurgent colleagues, I had carried it for a long time, certain that in the flush of its power the Cannon machine would overreach itself. The paper upon which I had written my resolution had become so tattered it scarcely hung together. That was the best evidence of long waiting for the minute that had come, and the frequency with which I had studied it alone in my own office.

I had become convinced that, if a constitutional provision for taking the census was entitled to precedence over the general House rule, then the constitutional provision giving to both branches of Congress the right to make their own rules must receive the same recognition.

What was sauce for the goose had to be sauce for the gander.

In the debate that followed, and in widespread public discussion, it was charged I was illogical because each time I had voted against the Speaker on the appeal taken from his decision, and by so voting had established that I did not believe the constitutional provision applied.

Even now, as I see it, there was no inconsistency in the course that I followed. My resolution to change the rules of the House was entitled to the same consideration—no more and no less—than Speaker Cannon and the Republican majority accorded to Representative Crumpacker's census bill. It was the House that decided the issue; and it was my duty as a member to accept that judgment, and follow it, even if I believed the construction which had been adopted was erroneous.

The smoke of battle over Mr. Crumpacker's census bill still hung in the House chamber when I sent my resolution forward to be read, and arose to claim for it constitutional privilege.

I remember a feeling of curious detachment from the ripple of surprise, and the new tenseness that set in, as the resolution was read. I had formulated no definite battle lines although I had weighed the possibilities with great care. So in that moment it seemed to me triumph was near. I felt I knew the temper of the House, growing resentment against the ironclad orders Mr. Cannon had imposed. I had waited so long, watchful day after day during weeks of weary frustration, for the opportunity I felt would present itself in good season.

Here it was.

Every member of the House knew full well the stakes of this battle.

The resolution I introduced provided that the Committee on Rules in the House of Representatives should be constituted as follows:

> That the country be divided into eight separate districts, that each district shall contain as near as possible the same number of representatives of the majority party represented in the house. Then in each one of these districts, the members of the majority party shall meet and select one of their own party, who would become a member of the committee on rules, and that they should certify their action to the clerk of the house.

That the country should be divided into seven districts, each district containing as near as practicable the same number representing the minority members of the house, and that such districts should meet and select one of their party, and should immediately report action to the clerk That members thus reported should become the committee on rules of the house of representatives.

That the committee should select its own chairman from its own members.

That the speaker should not be a member of the committee on rules.

This resolution provided a Committee on Rules of fifteen members, eight representing the majority party, and seven the minority party, distributed throughout the entire country so that each member was representative of the entire country.

It took from the Speaker the right to appoint anybody on the Committee on Rules, and the committee thus constituted was to have the power and duty of appointing the members of all the other standing committees of the House.

It stripped the Speaker of his power, thoroughly and effectively.

I felt these provisions likewise would distribute the committee appointments over the country, making it impossible to pack any committee with members from any section, representing any special interests. It would be a thoroughly democratic organization of all the committees of the House. It would free any member of the House from obligation to the Speaker.

I think it was the most democratic plan ever proposed in Congress in the selecting of committees. It would necessarily have placed the power to select committees in the hands of a representative House group from all sections of the country, and while it would have given majority control to the party in power it, nevertheless, would have divided responsibility much more closely between the two parties.

The words of the resolution hardly had died on the air when the Republican floor leader, Representative James Mann of Illinois, raised the point that my resolution was out of order.

Decision, of course, rested with the Speaker.

The entire membership knew with equal sureness that Mr. Cannon would sustain that point of order, and that I would appeal at once. It was then up to the House to decide whether my resolution was in order, and whether the House desired to consider it.

If Speaker Cannon's emotions rose he held them well in check. Under parliamentary law, he had the right to ask for debate when it became his duty to rule on a point of order. If he desired, he could call upon individual members to express their opinion and to offer arguments either for or against sustaining the order. If he ruled immediately upon the appeal a vote would follow; and if the Democratic and insurgent members stood solidly in support of my resolution I should be sustained. In that event, the resolution would come to an immediate vote.

In the uncertainty of the attitude of Democratic members, and the absence of some of his supporters, he decided to play for time in the hope of reorganizing his lines. It seemed to me I could read his thoughts as he looked over the chamber. My resolution had come up so unexpectedly that among the absentees were members who had gone out of the city. Mr. Cannon's hope rested solely upon bringing them in or recruiting some support from Democratic members. He decided to keep the House in session and the point of order under debate while he reserved his decision.

I did not believe any parliamentarian, giving proper consideration to the decision which the House had reached, upon Representative Crumpacker's bill, could exclude my resolution.

All of us knew that the debate, however long and extended, would have no influence upon the Speaker's decision. It continued through the late afternoon and throughout the night, supposedly for the enlightenment of Mr. Cannon in ruling properly on the question of order. He was not in the chair during those dragging hours of discussion, or for a share of the following day. The debate which he had set in motion progressed without the guest of honor. He was at his hotel. The shadows gathered, darkness closed in, crowds thronged the gallery. On the floor groups of members gathered. The clock moved past the midnight hour, then into the early morn and gray dawn.

While the debate was in progress, the Republican insurgents

held several meetings, and Democratic members of the House caucused, recognizing that unless they stood by in support the struggle to change the rules must fail. The Democrats knew their votes meant victory, and a split in their ranks would result in defeat.

As the spokesman for the insurgent bloc, I conferred on a number of occasions during the night with Representative Champ Clark, the Democratic floor leader, and his close parliamentary officer, Representative Oscar Underwood of Alabama, deservedly recognized as one of the best parliamentarians of the House.

To my surprise Mr. Clark and Mr. Underwood told me the Democrats would not support us. They said they did not like my method of selecting the Committee on Rules, and did not believe the authority which my resolution gave the committee should prevail. In order to get the Democrats solidly behind it, they told me, I should have to agree to an amendment to my resolution providing simply that the power to select committees should be taken from the Speaker.

I was stunned.

For a moment I saw victory, which I had felt was so near, slipping away. My spirit was chilled although afterward I was told I was the calmest man in the chamber and seemed to incarnate confidence.

The House itself, they insisted, should elect members of the Committee on Rules.

It seemed to me we could not win in this fight without agreeing to the Democratic proposal, which would make a definite improvement over existing conditions but contained many serious faults.

Yet, in the heat of battle, I hated to give it my approval.

I reported the facts to my insurgent colleagues, and they expressed dissatisfaction. Many of them were opposed to making the concession to the Democrats; but after full discussion they reached a conclusion to which I agreed, that bitter as the dose was, we must take it in order to be sure of obtaining some improvement such action would bring about.

I reported to Clark and to Underwood that we would agree to their proposal, and offered to substitute for my resolution the simple proposal that the Committee on Rules should be elected by the House itself.

I have always been deeply regretful that the Democratic members of the House took this position at that time. Many of the Democratic members were sympathetic with the position the Speaker had taken. They were expecting confidently to control the House in the next election, and they wanted to acquire the great power for a Speaker of their own choice which we were endeavoring to take away from Joe Cannon.

Late in the afternoon of the next day Speaker Cannon announced he was ready to rule, and the debate came abruptly to an end.

The Speaker began to talk in matter-of-fact tones of the rights of the majority. In the deep silence of the floor and the galleries, men listened intently. At the end of ten minutes, he announced his ruling, sustaining the point of order against the proposal I had presented.

Promptly an appeal was taken, this time by the Democrats, and a vote ordered, which resulted in Mr. Cannon being overruled, 182 to 160.

Thus, my amended proposal for the selection of the Committee on Rules by the House came to a vote, was accepted 191 to 156, and the long dynasty of the all-powerful Speaker came to an end.

I never thought it was personal pique which prompted Speaker Cannon to submit his resignation immediately as soon as the tumult of the decision had been brought under control.

I regretted the motion which was made to accept it, voted against it, and was pleased when it was defeated. I was criticized severely at the time for my opposition to accepting Mr. Cannon's resignation. Some of my insurgent colleagues condemned me sharply because of my failure to vote with them. I was in an embarrassing position as a result of the fight that I had led. But I had no personal feeling against the Speaker. My opposition was solely to his frightful abuse of power. I saw no logic in his resignation, and that feeling was shared by some of the other insurgents, including Representative Gardner of Massachusetts, one of the best parliamentarians of the

House. I had not prepared that resolution to punish an individual. I was shooting at the system. I wanted simply to take from Mr. Cannon the autocratic powers which his office and the old rules of the House had conferred upon him.

I have never ceased to regret that the original resolution had to be sacrificed in order to terminate an unbearable condition in American government I felt and still feel the original resolution would have strengthened the institution of Congress.

While the overthrow of Joe Cannon awakened rejoicing, and represented a great victory for democratic control of the House, it did not place the power where it would be exercised in the most practical and democratic way.

It left appointment of the standing committees largely to the partisan machines.

It left the deliberations largely to powerful monopolies.

That night I returned home triumphant in a decent fight, and disappointed that its fruits could not have been even greater. That is the struggle which the people of a democracy face. Frequently they must compromise in order to achieve partial reform. If victory were full and complete, there would be no new political battlefields in due time. Progress and change are constant and eternal.

14

THE ARCHBALD IMPEACHMENT

THE COURTS, and the administration of justice, held my unflagging interest throughout my service in Congress.

I served on the Judiciary committees of the House and the Senate.

In that capacity, matters of justice which otherwise would have escaped me came to my attention. I had the opportunity to examine the workings of the federal judiciary, and the qualifications of men wearing the robes of the judge. I took active part in the Senate in a number of the tense struggles over confirmation of presidential judicial appointments.

Near the close of my service in the House, much against my wishes at the start, I found myself cast in a leading role in one of the few instances of congressional action, which resulted in the impeachment of a federal judge. Reports had reached Congress of the reputed misconduct of a member of the federal bench in the state of Washington. He resigned. And then attention shifted to Pennsylvania where Circuit Judge Robert W. Archbald, originally appointed by McKinley and later promoted by Taft, was under criticism.

It came about in this way.

William P. Boland, owner and president of the Marian Coal Company, of Scranton, Pennsylvania, came to me with a story of injustice that stirred me deeply. From childhood he had been identified with mining; as a young man, he had worked in the anthracite fields. He was a giant physically, and extremely intelligent. I was impressed immediately with his thorough, comprehensive knowledge of the coal business. On the occasion of that first visit, I judged him to be, perhaps, fifty years of age. He was a type the American people held in deepest respect—thrifty, industrious, and ambitious. Through habits of saving, he had established himself in the coal business under the firm name of the Marian Coal Company, which, I concluded, he and his wife owned outright.

His business reached back to the earlier years of anthracite coal mining in Pennsylvania, when the methods of removing impurities from the coal were very crude. After the coal had been separated from the other useless materials, the debris was piled conveniently on the ground, and these accumulations become known as "culm dumps."

It had gone on for years until the dumps grew into huge hills, sometimes the size of mountains. As the years passed, they became covered with an undergrowth of grass, scraggly brush, and trees until they no longer were recognizable. Many were hidden so completely that they resembled forests in the second growth.

But they contained a large amount of coal, because of the imperfect processes of early mining.

When Mr. Boland embarked in the coal business, new and improved methods of washing and reclaiming anthracite from the discarded "culm dumps" had been developed, and a great, flourishing, and extremely profitable industry followed.

The Marian Coal Company was engaged in this business.

The rediscovery of these huge culm dumps was as important to profitable operation as capital and machinery. That is where Mr. Boland came in. He was a very valuable man, an expert in this line, because of his earlier mining knowledge. He had become a rather wealthy man.

His success attracted the attention of other coal companies and corporations. They became interested until the struggle for rights in the culm-dump region became intense, and a great impetus was given to this type of "recovery mining" in the hard-coal regions of Pennsylvania. The impeachment of Judge Archbald in the House of Representatives, resulting in his conviction by the Senate and removal from office, grew out of charges that he was unduly friendly with some of the corporations fighting Mr. Boland.

As a member of the House Judiciary Committee, I brought the resolution of impeachment against Judge Archbald only after long and exhaustive investigation of all the facts which I could assemble. I was reluctant to initiate it. It seemed to me that a member of the Pennsylvania delegation in the House more properly should sponsor it. I had declined at the outset to go into the case, feeling so strongly as I did; but the spirit and determination of Mr. Boland, together with the evidence he placed before me, finally convinced me I should take action.

I never regretted it.

The accumulating evidence revealed some of Judge Archbald's friends were engaged in the business of locating and then working these culm dumps.

Among competitors of the Marian Coal Company was the Delaware, Lackawanna & Western Railroad Company, owning both rail lines and coal lands. It was charged it had utilized the railroad to break the Marian Coal Company and ruin Mr. Boland. It was clear to me the Marian Coal Company could not continue to compete against a rival possessing the advantage of transportation because one of the chief items of expense was the cost of moving the coal from the culm dump to the point of consumption. It was immaterial to the Delaware, Lackawanna & Western whether it made its money on the transportation of coal, or on the sale of coal itself.

The relationship was close.

The general manager of the railroad company was the general manager of the coal company. He could haul the coal reclaimed for greatly reduced freight rates and could compensate himself in the sale of the coal for any loss sustained. Mr. Boland had to pay a higher freight rate than his competitor. He had resorted to litigation; but the cases had been heard mostly in the federal court presided over by Judge Archbald, and invariably he had been unsuccessful. He became convinced he could not win a case in Judge Archbald's court, whatever the evidence was. He saw his fortune melting away, and I think it affected his mind.

Finally, he carried his fight to the Interstate Commerce Commission.

After his first visit to my office, I found he had been doing things I could not tolerate. He was writing letters to members of the United States Supreme Court, including Edward D. White who then was Chief Justice. It became necessary to tell Mr. Boland that unless he ceased addressing letters to the court, I would drop his case.

Yet I knew the man was tortured and laboring under a great mental strain. There were many nights when, long after the midnight hour, I walked with him through the Capitol grounds, getting the facts and assisting him to prepare his case.

It was at this time that I discovered the eagerness with which representatives of several of the principal competing companies sought out Mr. Boland for information relating to these old culm dumps. He had been most generous with them in that respect. The older the dump, the more valuable it was, because the methods used to extract the coal had been cruder.

Outwardly, Mr. Boland continued to befriend those competitors who sought him out in every way that he could, for the purpose of getting the evidence. Out of that came a plan which put him in possession of letters and other evidence of invaluable aid in the impeachment proceedings before the Judiciary Committee.

He secured a little frame house of two rooms, purchased a photographic machine, hired a confidential secretary and stenographer, in whom he could place implicit faith, and then took his secretary into his full confidence.

In talking with coal men who came to see him about culm dumps, he was shrewd enough to inquire into all the details and to bring out in elaborate fashion the evidence that connected Judge Archbald with those companies competing against his anthracite business. Frequently the men with whom he talked brought correspondence and discussed various statements in the letters referring to the culm dumps, their location, and the method of handling them. He would engage such men in conversation, and get them so avidly interested that they forgot everything about the correspondence.

When he had detached the particular paper in which he was interested, he would press a buzzer; his secretary would come into the room, move around, and pick up what appeared to be a letter. Taking it into the other room, she would photograph it, come back, and replace it without anyone knowing.

Later the general manager of the railroad company was on the witness stand.

I was questioning him about controversies between his company and the various coal companies. He answered that there had been many. Then I asked what happened if a controversy arose between the railroad company of which he was general manager and the coal company of which he was also general manager.

He replied that he passed on that controversy as general manager of the railroad company, but at times there were bitter controversies.

I asked him how he expected to decide in a case of that kind where the claim of the coal company of which he was general manager conflicted with the interests of the railroad company of which he was general manager.

Before he had finished on the stand he had made many statements later disproved by his own letters, photographic copies of which I had in my pocket. After he had tied himself in a knot, I would pull a letter from my pocket and insist he explain what he had meant when he wrote it.

Once when a letter of his own contradicted his testimony he came very near fainting on the witness stand.

When my resolution of impeachment was introduced, there was much laughing, and the prevailing opinion was that it would be pigeonholed, and never would receive any genuine consideration. But I had not talked with anyone on the Judiciary Committee, and none of its members knew the evidence I had accumulated. I insisted the resolution be taken up in the committee. When the evidence developed, day after day, and it became clear that the subject had attained a deep importance, the atmosphere changed. Before the hearings were concluded, the Judiciary Committee had become convinced that Judge Archbald should be impeached, and my resolution was reported to the House with a recommendation that it pass.

At that time the most powerful Republican political machine in Pennsylvania was backing Judge Archbald.

The Senate set a day for hearing, and the trial commenced.

I had been placed on the committee chosen to manage the case in the Senate. Serving with me was Representative John W. Davis, of West Virginia, who afterward became the Democratic candidate for President of the United States. Mr. Davis, then a young man, was an excellent lawyer. I had formed a great affection for him, and we had become warm personal friends. We worked together on this committee, and we joined in the trial by submitting a written agreement signed by each of us, outlining the case as we saw it, the evidence supporting the charges, and the law that applied.

Neither Representative Davis nor I had been on the Judiciary Committee of the House long enough to be put on the committee managing the trial in the Senate; and we found ourselves there only because the chairman of the House Judiciary Committee appointed seven to the trial committee instead of five—with the avowed purpose of giving Representative Davis and me places.

The chairman was Representative Henry D. Clayton of Alabama, afterwards appointed as federal district judge in Alabama, a post which he filled until his death.

The Senate found Judge Archbald guilty and not only removed him from office but passed a resolution, provision for which is made in the Constitution, prohibiting him from ever holding any office of profit or trust under the federal government.

After his impeachment Judge Archbald opened law offices in Scranton.

His original appointment to the federal bench had been upon the recommendation of Pennsylvania's Senator Boies Penrose, who never was convinced of his guilt, and during the impeachment proceedings voted against every count that was brought against Judge Archbald.

In private practice Judge Archbald was not a success, and in the tragic termination of his career he became a subject of charity. But in those closing years that forgiving trait of human nature which so distinguishes American life, furnished a truly beautiful ending to the impeachment of Judge Archbald. I have understood one of the men who aided him in dire need was Mr. Boland, although Mr. Boland never told me of his assistance.

Those conferences with Mr. Boland, stretching over a period of many months, come back to me in all of their intimate detail.

Generally they took place at night.

It was our custom to walk in the park surrounding the Capitol. When he first came to me he was so wrought up that often it was difficult to get a coherent story from him of the various transactions. It was on one of these occasions that he felt that I was suspicious of his mental condition.

He broke down to tell me of the source of his agony and hurt:

"I know, Mr. Norris, that you are worried about my condition. There is one thing that I have never told you about my troubles. It may sound foolish, but I have made up my mind to tell you. The Marian Coal Company started out with bright prospects. It was a success. It was making a fair profit on the operation of a number of culm dumps when I saw all my efforts frustrated.

"All my machinery on one occasion was burned and I never have had any doubt but my enemies set fire to it.

"There is something secret about that name.

"We had a bright, beautiful little daughter named Marian, and my wife and I decided to name this coal company after her.

"When our financial troubles and difficulties piled up, when it looked as though the company was going to fail, our little Marian was taken sick, and after a short while died.

"I could not bear to have anything that bore her name turn out to be a failure.

"When it looked as though we were about to lose all that we had accumulated, my greatest sorrow and agony was that the company named after our child was about to fail. I could endure the thought of becoming a pauper, but I could not endure that thought. It is this that has affected me. I do not expect your sympathy, I do not expect the sympathy of anyone, or the understanding that I have been moved so greatly in what I have done by the mere thought that the name of my little child was to be brought into dishonor and disgrace through no fault of hers but through the power and influence of men, who for financial reasons are attacking me."

Mr. Boland's sentiment made a deep impression upon me and sharpened my determination to see that he was vindicated.

I told him while we walked on in the silence of midnight in the Capitol park I did not regard this attitude as foolish and that I, too, was the father of a bright little girl named Marian.

That night while we talked my mind went back to my own daughter Marian. She had once committed some small childish misdemeanor, and I decided to punish her by shutting her in a closet off from the dining room.

Just as I was about to close the door my daughter's eyes looked out from the semidarkness, betraying fright. Every feature revealed dismay and terror.

I threw the door open.

I held out my arms, and my daughter sprang to me and threw her arms around my neck, and together we mingled our tears.

I can see even to this day those beautiful eyes looking through the darkness piercing my anger and throwing light into the very depths of my soul.

While Mr. Boland was talking I saw his love and affection for that little child who was only a memory.

Unable to speak, he and I looked at each other through tears, and silently I said to myself:

"No stone shall be left unturned; nothing shall be left undone to bring out all the evidence in this terrible case and if possible get justice for this man."

The memories of that night gave me strength in a one-sided struggle.

The impeachment of Judge Archbald brought about a great change in the life of Mr. Boland. Once again the Marian Coal Company became prosperous and successful.

In the burden of Senate labors the case had passed far from my mind, and I had become engaged in a bitter struggle for re-election when one day he walked into my office, having read of my fight. He and his wife were on their way to Florida on an extended vacation, but he wanted to make a contribution to my campaign.

In his hand was a check for $500.

I told him I could not accept it—there was no special use for the money as far as I was concerned, and I did not intend to spend large amounts in the campaign; but I gave him the name of the committee having charge of the campaign in Nebraska and he made it a contribution of $500.

When that contribution was reported as required by statute, my political enemies at once jumped at it as a gift from "a millionaire coal company" which was a part of the coal trust. But Mr. Boland followed his contribution with a letter telling briefly the story that I have set forth here.

In a later campaign he prepared a lengthy statement which he placed in the larger daily papers of the state, and the attacks that had been made against me, based on his contribution to my campaign, aided materially in reelecting me to the United States Senate on at least two occasions.

15

THE PARTY RAWHIDE

I ALWAYS HAVE BEEN grateful that Joe Cannon subsequently revealed to me a quality of character he seldom permitted the American people to see. After his defeat over the rules, and after his own district had repudiated him in the congressional elections which followed, that trait revealed itself during an unexpected visit.

I had gone to the Republican cloakroom one afternoon and, finding it completely deserted, had seated myself on a sofa, facing the large open grate.

It was a long, narrow room under the gallery which extended completely around the House chamber. Speaker Cannon came in. He stood with his elbows resting on the mantel of the grate, only a few feet in front of me, his traditional cigar tilted out of the corner of his mouth, his eyes fixed upon me. He was silent for a brief period. Then he said:

"Norris, I have been defeated for reelection to the House of Representatives, and you have been elected to the Senate."

I wondered what was coming.

I fully expected a personal quarrel and a farewell tongue lashing—which I was in no mood to accept, although anxious to avoid disagreeable discussion.

Virtually from the day I took my House seat, Mr. Cannon had refused to recognize me even when we chanced to meet in the corridor or in the elevator. I was surprised, dumfounded, but immensely pleased when these words followed:

"I never have had any personal enmity towards you, Norris. I am an old man, and you are a comparatively young man. I anticipate you will have a long and continuous service in the Senate. The probabilities are that I am passing out of public life forever; and I have wanted to say to you that I have no personal grievances against you. I have no apologies to make. I would act the same if I had it to do over again, even though I knew in advance that it meant I would be driven from public life."

Those words meant a great deal to me. I could respect the courage and the sincerity they embodied even while disagreeing fundamentally and violently with the views of public service to which Mr. Cannon referred.

He continued:

"Throughout our bitter controversy, I do not recall a single instance in which you have been unfair, or wherein you have taken an unfair advantage of me. I am of the opinion that you have been perfectly conscientious in all that you have done. I cannot say this of many of your associates; but this may be the last time I will have the opportunity to talk to you, and I want to say to you now that if any member of your damned gang had to be elected to the Senate, I would prefer it be you more than any of them."

I was delighted by this unexpected utterance of Mr. Cannon not solely because it showed such confidence in my sincerity in the fight against him, but even more because it was such a perfect expression of a noble, American ideal of tolerance and generosity in political battle. Men and women should be able to differ, and to differ sharply, without ascribing to each other unworthy and sinister purposes.

I could say truthfully to Mr. Cannon then—and never have I known the time when I felt differently—my position had been free of malice. I have fought throughout my public life. Every difference with friends and associates brought sorrow and heartache.

I recognized my comparative youth and short service in Congress, by contrast to Joe Cannon's venerable years and long service, entitled him to a greater consideration.

I told him this as we stood there in the afternoon light in the quietness of the cloakroom; and we shook hands and separated as friends.

This friendship lasted as long as he lived. He did not fade out of public life, but again became a candidate and was reelected to the seat in Congress which he had filled for so many years. Frequently he came over to the Senate, and we had many pleasant conversations in the Senate cloakroom. Now he is gone, but I feel that he was as happy as I was at reaching a friendship which had not existed prior to that battle over the rules, and which, until the cloakroom meeting, had no basis for existence.

He had served the state of Illinois a great many years, and I had no doubt that from beginning to end his public attitude represented his conscientious convictions, although earlier I had felt his personal feeling led him often to treat me with an unjustified contempt.

It was a system, a political condition worthy of close examination, to which this struggle pertained.

From beginning to end of the battle between the insurgents and the Speaker, Representative James R. Mann of Chicago had been Republican floor manager. The controversies on the floor had been very bitter, and he had displayed no inclination to be lenient. He was one of the hardest workers in the Lower House, one of its best parliamentarians.

The change in the rules by which committee members were to be elected, instead of being appointed by the Speaker, conferred upon Mr. Mann only slightly less power in the naming of these than had belonged to Speaker Cannon. He took great pains to make a fair tentative selection among the Republicans for the different committees—being dominated, of course, by what he considered to be the party rights of members; and I never knew his choice to be influenced by personalities. This selection was submitted to a party caucus; and, if the caucus approved, his assignments were invariably voted by the House. I think the Democrats pursued the same method.

The first Congress after the change in rules was about to launch itself when Representative Mann surprised me with a telephone call asking me to come to his office for a conference.

There he frankly asked what committee assignments I desired.

The change in procedure almost took my breath away, and before I could answer he said:

"I have always felt, Mr. Norris, that you ought to be a member of the Judiciary Committee of the House."

Ever since I had been in the House, I had been anxious to become a member of that committee. And I told Mr. Mann assignment to it suited me exactly.

In this manner I became a member of the House Committee on Judiciary, on which I continued to serve until I went to the Senate.

In the years preceding, committee assignments and patronage were the rawhide used to promote party subserviency and to crush any spirit of independence. Patronage was especially effective in checking rebellion and solidifying party lines. In those years it hung over the heads of members of Congress day and night.

I remember my acute disappointment on the occasion of the death of Representative Lovering at the height of the insurgent fight.

Mr. Lovering was a man much older than I, and was one of the original members of the insurgent group. I had formed a great affection for him, and sought his advice on many occasions. He had considerable means, and our group often met at his home on Massachusetts Avenue.

It was my desire to be appointed on the committee which would represent the House of Representatives at the funeral. At the time I felt I could not afford the expense, but felt more strongly that my association with Representative Lovering dictated I should stand it.

I hoped the Speaker, recognizing my close ties with Mr. Lovering, would accord me the privilege of paying my respects to a very dear friend, as a member of the House committee. Without seeing the Speaker about it personally, I had one or two friends approach him; and they reported he refused absolutely to approve my selection. It was a long time before the deep resentment which this roused in me disappeared.

One of my first assignments in the House was to the Committee on the Election of President, Vice President, and Representatives in Congress, of which Joseph H. Gaines of West Virginia was chairman. It was not the most desirable assignment; but in the regular course of affairs I gradually advanced in seniority until I stood next to the chairman. Under an unwritten rule of House procedure, I was in line for advancement if death, retirement, or any other development left the chairmanship open.

The advantage in those days of being chairman of a standing committee, even one of no importance, was that the chairman had an office, stationery to the amount of $125 each session, and other prerogatives. This was before there was a House Office Building. Members of the House who were not committee chairmen commonly used their living quarters for office purposes. I felt it necessary to have an office, which always I paid for out of my own pocket. Usually I got a reasonably cheap room. Elevation to the chairmanship under the House practice would not only have added to my prestige but have saved me considerable money.

Representative Gaines and I worked together closely on the committee, and had become warm friends in spite of the fact that he was a firm and steadfast follower of the Speaker; and he told me more than once in conversation of his anxiety to gain a place on the Ways and Means Committee—the most powerful committee of the Lower House, and the most coveted assignment.

Another unwritten rule which had been adhered to with very few exceptions was that a Congressman appointed to the Ways and Means Committee must give up the chairmanship of any other standing committee. Representative Gaines recognized this. He was willing to relinquish the chairmanship of the Committee on the Election of President, Vice President, and Representatives in Congress, and was almost as anxious as I to have me succeed him as its head—which would take place automatically under the rule of seniority. And I know he did everything in my behalf that he could.

The Speaker would not have it.

The final result was that when Representative Gaines was

advanced to the Ways and Means Committee, the Speaker made an exception to House practice and reappointed Mr. Gaines to his old post.

That was the way recalcitrant Congressmen, who had conflicting ideas on legislation, were punished in the effort to force them to submit to the party caucus and party organization.

All this I knew that afternoon Mr. Cannon and I visited, and I chose to accept his expression on that occasion as a genuine change which had been brought about through the battle which had taken place.

Infinitely more oppressive was the whiplash of patronage. The abuse of patronage was one of the great evils of public life; and, although to a much lesser degree, it still is. My experience with it made me a stanch and unyielding advocate of Civil Service in governmental agencies: I could not other than believe passionately in the merit system after my opportunities for observation.

When first I entered the House, appointments to West Point and Annapolis were based usually upon party considerations. To me this was an abhorrent method of selecting young men from among whom would come future generals and admirals. I immediately adopted a method of making appointments to West Point and Annapolis on the basis of recommendation by the district committees, to which all applicants writing me were instructed to apply.

I had worked out arrangements through which these committees conducted examinations, actually graded the papers of the applicants, and reported the individual standings to me. Without exception, my recommendations for appointment rested upon the standing of the applicants. Even this method was not entirely satisfactory, for some unsuccessful candidates charged I had influenced the decision of the committees. This was not true.

Finally other members, encountering the same difficulties as I, delegated all examinations for appointment to West Point and Annapolis to the Civil Service Commission; and through such action we eliminated a common cause for complaint.

I felt the antagonism and displeasure of the party leader wherever I went. My congressional colleagues quickly expressed their hostility to my independent attitude. In the personal contacts and in the formal discussions on the floor, their criticism was sharp-pronged; and they had a very practical method (at least it seemed practical to them) of spanking me: I lost my patronage.

The loss aroused no regrets on my part: it was a relief to be freed of the responsibility, and I was certain that in the end, the denial of patronage to me would be a positive benefit. But I resented the causes which had brought about the withdrawal.

Not all of my associates among the insurgents shared my attitude; many of them were very much perturbed. They talked to me about it and clung to their patronage with a tenacity which was surprising.

In the abstract sense, it always had seemed to me no member of Congress had a legal right to patronage. To take one simple example, the Constitution confers the power to appoint postmasters upon the President of the United States. Naturally, a President cannot have personal knowledge of the qualifications of thousands of applicants for postal positions, and it is necessary for him to depend upon advice.

More to set forth my view of the tactics adopted to punish the insurgents than for any other purpose, I wrote to President Taft on January 6, 1910, in part in this language:

There was published in the newspapers of January 5 a dispatch to the effect you had decided to deprive the insurgents in Congress of all executive patronage. The article purported to come direct from the White House, and inasmuch as it has remained unchallenged and undisputed I feel warranted in assuming that it is true and has your approval. I am likewise led to this conclusion because the recent recommendations from insurgent Republican Congressmen have not received the favorable consideration by the heads of departments formerly accorded. In the article referred to the matter is summed up in this language: "Since the Representatives have taken the stand against the present administration and continue to align themselves with the opposition to the President's policies, they are to receive no consideration in matters of patronage. . . ."

The so-called insurgents were organized and stand for but one proposition—a change in the rules of the House that will take away from the Speaker some of his power which we believe to be unreasonable, detrimental to good government, and at times tyrannical. We have gone into this movement on principle because we conscientiously believed it to be right, and will not be enticed away from it by the promise of political patronage or driven therefrom by the threat of its withdrawal. . . . The insurgents of the House have taken no "stand against the present administration," and I regret exceedingly, Mr. President, that in the very beginning of your administration you took a stand against us in the fight to change the rules of the House. The present move can be nothing but a second step in that direction. . . . In other words, we are to be punished for our fight against Cannonism and for the freedom of representation in the House of Representatives, while the country is told that our punishment is inflicted for an entirely different reason—a reason that in fact does not exist. I frankly admit, Mr. President, that you have the legal right to deprive us of all patronage. I admit that you can do so without giving any reason therefor, but I do insist that, if you give a reason, common fairness and justice demand that you give the correct one.

The following day I received from President Taft this note in reply to my letter to him:

I have your letter, and it contains such misstatements that I must answer it. In the first place, I have made no announcement or statement that I am going to deprive the so-called insurgents of patronage. In the second place, I took no part in the fight over the rules in the House. What I declined to do was to join those who differed from a majority of the Republican party and stayed out of the caucus, when, as a leader of the party, I am dependent upon party action to secure the legislation that has been promised. It did not then seem to me, and it does not now seem to me, that, as titular leader of the party, I should take sides with fifteen or twenty who refuse to abide by the majority voice of the party, but that I should stand by whatever the party decides under the majority rule, whatever my views as to the wisdom of the rules, which are peculiarly a matter for settlement in the House itself. It has been the custom for a Republican administration to honor the recommendations of Republican Congressmen with respect to local appointments, subject, however, to the condition that the candidates recommended should be fit for the place. This custom has grown up with a view toward securing party solidarity in acting upon party questions. The only indication that I have given has been that, with respect to legislation that I have recommended and I am recommending, there should be party action to discharge the promises of the party platform, and that those who feel no obligation in respect to it cannot complain if their recommendations are not given the customary weight.

The next day I wrote Mr. Taft at greater length, challenging his statements that he had taken no stand against the House insurgents.

I referred to the Ballinger case first and then added:

Quite a number of these insurgents claim they had a personal interview with you and that you labored with them to induce them to support the Speaker in his effort to adopt the old rules, and to make no fight. If you were taking no part in this fight, then you were most woefully misrepresented by some of your closest advisers. . . . Under no circumstances do I want you to get the idea that I am making a plea for patronage. I shall not be swerved a hair's breadth from what I believe to be my duty in the House by the giving or taking away of all the patronage within your control. I desire to say that I am not in any way piqued or grieved that executive patronage has been taken away from me, and I do not desire to be understood as in any way seeking its return.

Again the following day President Taft wrote that patronage would not be used to influence legislation:

If I conclude to withhold the patronage from any person who ignores the obligation of the party platform to support the legislation which I am recommending to Congress, it will not be for the purpose of compelling him to vote for the legislation or to frighten him into it, but will be for the purpose of preventing his use of patronage in the district which he represents to create opposition to the Republican administration. . . . I have the most reliable information that, in certain districts in this country, their patronage which is being dispensed by my hand is being tendered to fortify opponents of the administration and opponents of the declared policies of the Republican party. Personally, I should be glad if there were no local patronage and every public office were covered by the Civil Service law; and it will be my policy during this administration to cover under the Civil Service law as many offices now outside of it as it is practicable to include therein.

I was happy to be freed of the burden of patronage.

In the beginning, I had followed the general custom of recommending the appointment of postmasters. Never had I appealed to the successful candidates to contribute to campaign funds.

I grew tired of recommending candidates. I could see no honest reason why a postmaster in Nebraska should be a member of the political party in power in Washington. I felt strongly postmasters should be removed from partisan politics; and, as nearly as possible, patrons of post offices should be permitted to make their own selection. I supported and advocated all measures to broaden and strengthen the Civil Service. I rejoiced as each year showed advances by the merit system; and it has gratified me in recent years that this has received a greater application than ever before in American history.

Surely three little experiences, of more than three decades ago, which are still vivid in my mind, should encourage faith in the merit system.

One of these was at Doniphan a town of about 400 people in central Nebraska, then the center of a rich farming community, where the illness and death of the postmaster had created a vacancy. Business having taken me to Harvard, not far from Doniphan, it occurred to me when I missed my train, that by hiring a livery team I could go to Doniphan and make a personal examination of the postal situation there, and still get back to my home in McCook nearly as quickly as if I remained in Harvard.

My only acquaintance in Doniphan was a candidate for appointment to the office, a member of the county central committee—a fine man so far as I knew, fairly representative of his people. Invariably he had attended county conventions, and usually he had appeared as a delegate to the district or state conventions. I expected to appoint him to fill the vacancy.

Upon reaching Doniphan, I went to a general store to inquire the names of prominent Republicans in the community. It so happened that this business house was owned and operated by a Democrat, who recognized me. I explained to him I was anxious to hear from the people themselves, to discover whom they wanted for postmaster. He sent me across the street to his competitor, who also recognized me, was most gracious and helpful and finally provided me with a small vacant room in which to interview the townspeople.

From ten in the morning until darkness set in, they came in a steady stream. After interviewing practically every patron of that post office, except the candidates, I found all except two were in favor of the acting postmaster, a woman, who had performed all the work and had given excellent service during the long illness of the postmaster. Of the two who objected, one was a relative of the applicant and the other a temporary resident who had been asked by the Republican committeeman to appear in support of his candidacy.

When I asked the townspeople why they objected to the appointment of the Republican leader, invariably they told me he was a political boss, had been running the politics of the town for many years, insisted upon his own way in all caucuses, consulting no one about what should be done, and was arbitrary. They were tired of his control.

The interviews completed, I went to the train after dark. Before I boarded it the Republican committeeman, who expected to get the appointment, met me. I had not completely analyzed the record, but said to him that I could not recommend him because his townspeople did not want him to be their postmaster.

He followed me through life in every convention and at every primary election as an embittered enemy.

My education was enriched by a bitter post-office fight in Trenton, county seat of Hitchcock County, directly west of my home community. There were seventeen candidates for the office. I was well acquainted in Trenton, where I had sat many times as judge of the district court, and felt a deep personal interest in its affairs.

After giving notice that I would visit Trenton on a certain day, in an effort to settle the post-office appointment, I was amazed in stepping from the train to be greeted by a delegation of seventeen, all candidates for the appointment except one, who represented a candidate unable to be on hand himself. I followed the same general procedure I had used in Doniphan.

Before beginning the interviews, I took advantage of the opportunity to address the candidates, reminding them only one would be selected. Although all of them were my personal friends, sixteen would be disappointed. It was sixteen to one. I told them I was willing to trust their judgment and, without promising definitely, expected to be able to recommend the one they selected as their choice. I offered to retire from the room and let them settle it.

Not one would agree. Each one was relying on my friendship and personal acquaintance in the belief the appointment would come to him. When they failed to take this opportunity, I invited them to leave.

One of the seventeen candidates had served four years as sheriff, and an equal period of time as county treasurer. He was, I thought, a very fine man, industrious and influential. To my amazement, I discovered during the day that he was not nearly as popular as he thought he was, and he had made a good many enemies while he was in control of the party in the county.

At the end of the examination, I had reached no decision of the relative merits of candidates.

For several days I went through the notes I had taken. The man finally selected, on the basis of popular expression, never had figured in political contests so far as I knew. He had genuine ability and was very popular. Two men, in particular, became my political enemies—the sheriff and the clerk of the court—and fought me on every occasion. The unsuccessful sixteen invariably revealed the bitterest animosity.

I remember still a third post-office fight at Macon in Franklin County, located nearly in the center of the county, with notions that it was destined to become a city. The Post Office Department in Washington had issued an order discontinuing the post office there.

Its citizens were greatly perturbed at the proposal to serve it by rural carrier from Franklin. I never doubted but the order had been justified on the ground of economy alone, but I succeeded in having it set aside before it went into effect.

The patrons were evenly divided between the two candidates, and I received letters from both factions stating frankly that if the postmaster they wanted was not chosen, the writers either would get their mail at Franklin, or would have it delivered to them by rural carrier.

So I made a visit to Macon, notified both factions, and with practically all the patrons present, told them of the threats that had come and of my intention, if the threats were carried out, never to lift a hand again to save their post office.

The desired effect followed. I finally succeeded in persuading the farmer who lived about a mile from Macon to take the appointment; and not only went out of town to get the postmaster, but made arrangements for a small office to serve him as a post office.

One of my earlier rivals in the Democratic party lost election later in the House of Representatives because of a bitter post-office fight in which a business man of Grafton insisted upon the selection of his candidate. The qualifications of that congressman had nothing to do with it.

It was these experiences, and many more, that led to my belief that a congressman should not be mixed up in postmaster selections.

16

FOR THE GRAND OLD PARTY

THAT PERIOD OF INSURGENCY in Congress, in my judgment, had a permanent, wholesome influence upon American life. I recognize the conservative follower of either Republican or Democratic doctrine honestly may take sharp exception.

I have reflected frequently upon what would have been the consequences had reaction continued unchecked.

I believed fully in William McKinley. I voted for him for President against a fellow Nebraskan, W. J. Bryan, who was leading the fight against conservative Republicanism. Again in 1900 I supported Mr. McKinley against Mr. Bryan, and in 1904 my growing liberalism seemed to flower in the election of Theodore Roosevelt over the Democratic conservative, Judge Alton B. Parker. Those years opened new vistas in Mr. Roosevelt's advocacy of so many reforms which I thought American life needed badly.

President Taft, I was certain, would follow the path Teddy Roosevelt had blazed, and again I voted against Mr. Bryan and for Mr. Taft in complete confidence progress would continue.

Those next forty months changed American history profoundly.

The insurgent uprising in the House, which filtered slowly to the Senate and took root in the hearts of millions of Americans, was unselfish in its aims.

Several of my colleagues among the insurgents felt keenly and with a spirit of prescience the course which they had adopted would lead to defeat and retirement to private life.

It is only fair to say that, if Nebraska had not adopted the primary system of nominating candidates, I should have been defeated long before I completed five terms in the House of Representatives. Equally clear, if it had not been for the adoption in Nebraska of the "Oregon system," I should not have been elected to my first term in the United States Senate. At home, I had incurred the enmity of a large number of the regular Republican leaders. It continued undiminished throughout all the years of my public life. I frankly confess I never thoroughly understood it.

I suspect it was not confined solely to Republican regulars.

There were occasions later when the stanch, conservative Democratic leaders from Nebraska revealed an opposition fully as marked and as deep-seated.

I have lived long enough to accept it with tolerance, understanding, and philosophical spirit. In the end, the sureness of the justice of the American people in considered judgment invariably decides the right and the wrong of political differences.

From a grandstand seat in Nebraska I had seen the full depth of the emotional tides of the election of 1896. I had come in direct contact with agrarian discontent as a judge of the district court. I was shocked and dismayed by the more unreasonable and unjust demands, but I understood and sympathized with the underlying economic causes that expressed themselves in political action.

So I have spoken of the insurgent movement in which I had a part with the mixed emotions of one born and reared in the Republican faith, believing my party could do no wrong, and taking my faith in it from the inspired and enlightened leadership of Abraham Lincoln. That party training was most complete. I have read every life of Lincoln time has permitted.

I was not yet four years old when his assassination took place, and it was long before the full import of that tragic development made its impression upon me.

Much nearer to me was the Garfield assassination. As a boy I had followed Garfield with an eagerness that made him my hero. He lived only a short distance away from my mother's farm, and his assassination seemed to release a rage that had been growing in me through the years as I meditated upon the fearful deed that had struck down Abraham Lincoln.

I had gone to work on a farm in the harvest field near the shores of Sandusky Bay. I was then not quite twenty, but so muscular and vigorous that a man's work was easy for me. My helper was a drifter.

I remember that early afternoon when word came Garfield had been shot. The harvest helper told me he had been in Philadelphia, harnessing a team as a helper in a livery stable, when the news came that Lincoln had been shot by Booth.

He was so happy, he said, he dropped his work, the harness partially buckled, and went out to the street to celebrate.

I sprang at his throat.

He was a burly man, well along in years, but powerful, and he would have overpowered me if the owner of the farm had not intervened and separated us.

Even in my most ardent Republican days, I never could understand the depths of partisanship.

The poignant tragedies of Lincoln, of Garfield, and of McKinley have weighed upon me throughout my life.

It was in Garfield's campaign that I engaged in my first political activity. While teaching school at Monclova, I took part in one of those old-fashioned parades which Republican leadership of the era arranged. I rode in a horse troop which had drilled for weeks. Our uniforms, I remember, included a cap to which a gasoline torch had been attached. Our instructor, a former cavalryman, taught us a number of intricate formations. In the parade we made a fine appearance and won the first prize. A group of young women from the same neighborhood, all dressed in white, rode on a float which created equal enthusiasm.

Under such early associations, insurgency did not come easy to me.

It represented pain.

It involved hours of regret.

But the more I became acquainted with political machinery, as typified by the leadership of that period, the more I lost my ardor for many of the leaders and for the party.

I remember my first meeting with Theodore Roosevelt.

I had just been sworn in as a member of the Fifty-eighth Congress, which had been convened by Mr. Roosevelt in special session. Senator Charles H. Dietrich of Nebraska had invited me to accompany him to the White House, explaining that he desired to introduce me to the President.

While we sat talking, Edward Rosewater, who was the founder and editor of the Omaha *Bee,* a paper of national reputation by virtue of his militancy, came into the President's receiving room and joined in the conversation.

In the course of that discussion, Mr. Rosewater related the details of what apparently he believed had been a very smooth, adroit Republican maneuver in the presidential campaign of 1900. In the absence of an official ballot, he said, he and several other Republicans had thought out the plan of printing a lot of ballots, headed by the names of the Democratic candidates for President and Vice President, followed with the Republican presidential electors. Several thousand of these ballots, apparently Democratic, but in reality Republican, were printed, distributed, voted; and, when counted, naturally they added to the vote of the Republican candidates for the presidential electors.

I never had heard this story, and if it was true I never discovered any confirmation of it.

The thing that impressed me was the effect the story had upon Mr. Roosevelt. He clearly demonstrated what he thought of it in what he said to Mr. Rosewater, to Senator Dietrich, and to me. He was disgusted, and he thought it dishonorable and disgraceful. With these words he switched the subject, and never again was that story referred to during the conference. The look that spread itself over his face lived in my memory for years.

I followed Mr. Roosevelt implicitly in the liberal views that he took, and was impressed always with his sincerity and integrity. I believed particularly in the doctrine he advocated on the conservation of the natural resources: a cause to which I had not given much attention, but of which in time I became an ardent supporter.

Often those years I followed him when I had some doubts as

to the righteousness of his course. It seemed to me that his intense sincerity frequently led him to believe the object he wanted to accomplish justified the means.

Several times I heard this story, of the authenticity of which I have had doubts, used to illustrate this characteristic of Teddy Roosevelt:

It was after the new Union Station was constructed in Washington. Congress had contributed very liberally by appropriation to it, the Union Station costing a vast amount of money. The old Pennsylvania Station was in the Mall, one of the Capital's beautiful parks; it was an eyesore, and President Roosevelt was anxious to get rid of it. Congress had passed no law authorizing it to be torn down or to be moved away.

The story goes that Mr. Roosevelt called the Attorney General to the White House, and inquired if he had legal authority to have this station removed, and if there had been congressional action providing for such steps. The Attorney General is said to have informed him he did not believe the President had legal authority to remove it. Whereupon Mr. Roosevelt requested him to examine if any statute permitted him to act.

A few days later the Attorney General returned to the White House, reporting that investigation had failed to disclose any law granting power to the President to remove the station.

Still persisting, Mr. Roosevelt then asked the Attorney General if there was any statute that prohibited him from removing it, to which the Attorney General replied in the negative.

President Roosevelt decided to act immediately, ordered removal of the old Pennsylvania Station, and it was taken away entirely.

I was impressed by the scrupulous honesty and high motives in the attainment of public good that characterized Theodore Roosevelt. He was a man of action, quick to weary and become disgusted with delays and interferences; and it was this impetuosity, it seemed to me, and this irritation with the technicalities of law that sometimes prevented him from carrying out great national developments.

Yet he built the Panama Canal after other governments and a

great corporation had spent a vast amount of money and had failed in their efforts. He threw his heart into the construction of this waterway, whose long useful service has caused the struggle for it to be forgotten; but during its progress the means by which the Panama Canal was accomplished in some respects seem doubtful to me. I followed him step by step in that fight. Doubts assailed me at the time, and I have since reached the conclusion that our government's decision to establish the new republic of Panama, which in reality prevented Colombia from defending her own territory with her army, was open to argument. The United States through appropriations has indirectly made amends so that relationships with Colombia fortunately are on the most friendly basis.

My devotion to Theodore Roosevelt was such that in 1912, when he ran as the Bull Moose candidate for President on the Progressive ticket, I supported him, although at the time I was a member of the Republican party, and the legal Republican nominee for the Senate in the same campaign.

I became acquainted with William Howard Taft, his opponent, when he served as Secretary of War in the Roosevelt cabinet, and our relations were pleasant. I thought then and I have always thought he was at heart a real progressive, but moved and controlled by those about him to such an extent that he surrendered his own convictions.

Much later, when Mr. Taft was appointed as Chief Justice of the Supreme Court, I therefore was not pleased; but afterwards we had many conferences and our relationships became pleasant and somewhat confidential. I was serving as chairman of the Judiciary Committee of the Senate, and in frequent conferences with the chief justice of a most private character, I gradually came to think a great deal of him.

There were associations that ran through the years. My friendship for Representative Augustus P. Gardner, the son-in-law of Senator Henry Cabot Lodge, developed from an admiration for his great parliamentary capacity. He was a man reputedly of great wealth and one not naturally to be expected in a band of reformers. It is one of the pleasant recollections of my life that in gratitude for the great contributions that he made to the progressive cause I went to Massachusetts and campaigned on two occasions for his reelection.

Still another of these old associates was Victor Murdock of Wichita, the editor of the Wichita *Eagle* and a man of great ability, much more informed on public affairs in the national sense at the time of our first meeting in Washington than I was. Mr. Murdock had a broad, comprehensive view of national policy; he was honest and extremely courageous; unlike Representative Gardner, who took the lawyer's viewpoint, adhering to all the principles of law and precedent, Mr. Murdock did not care much for technicalities. This young man from Kansas knew what he wanted to accomplish, and he did not overlook things that he believed to be wrong. Through his efforts in a bitter committee fight and on the floor of the House, two reforms were adopted in the pay that railroads were receiving for the carrying of mail. The country owes him more than it has realized for the vast savings that his fight accomplished. He was appointed by President Wilson as one of the first members of the Federal Trade Commission and served upon it until 1924, when he resigned after having served as its chairman for four years.

His work was outstanding and difficult.

My association with him was close and confidential. Not only were we personal friends, but we were bound by the same faith and the same philosophy of government. Only once did we part company. When the fight for modification of the House rules was over, and Speaker Cannon tendered his resignation, Mr. Murdock was in favor of accepting it. I was opposed because I thought it would place the insurgents in a false attitude.

Still another leader for whom I had great affection was Edmond H. Madison of Dodge City, Kansas, a magnificent lawyer, splendidly equipped to serve on the Supreme Court of the United States. Both Mr. Madison and I had been lawyers, both of us had served as judges. He was courageous almost beyond belief. I happen to know some of the pressure that was applied to force him to withdraw from the insurgent uprising.

Still another House memory that lingers is of Representative William C. Lovering, a very wealthy man, but a genuine liberal in spite of it.

These recollections of personalities from those years suggest the compensation the fight brought in the personal friendships along with the enmities. In the terms of public benefits, I felt long ago the popular verdict was delivered. Some of the reforms made possible remain permanently as a part of the nation's institutions. Some were the inspiration for continued improvement.

It was reported the insurgents were seeking to gain control of the Republican party in order to place a man of their own liking and faith in the White House. I know that in the beginning the revolt against party rule did not contemplate party control.

I myself hoped to strengthen my party in its position in this country, and to free it from influences which in my eyes were lessening its usefulness and destroying its opportunities to be a party of service to the American people. Many of my associates felt about it exactly as I did. They had no personal ambition to satisfy. They believed in their party, and they believed the attitude they represented strengthened it with the people.

Ahead of the Republican national convention of 1912—several months ahead of it—Theodore Roosevelt had no intention of becoming a candidate for the Presidency. It was discussed among the intimates of the insurgent bloc and those who had been drawn to the conclusion there should be an insurgent candidate leaned upon Senator La Follette as their choice.

My fifth term in the House was drawing to a close.

Many of my friends in Nebraska were urging me to become a candidate for governor. I had no desire to occupy the gubernatorial office, and I had fully determined not to become a candidate for reelection to the House. I had to continue to keep up a campaign, expensive and burdensome, and I discovered that the Republican leaders and the Republican machine in their control were more bitterly opposed to me than the Democrats.

It was at this point that the weariness and the constant struggle, uneven in the continued opposition of the Republican organization, that I decided to become a candidate for the Senate, even though it did not seem to me that I then would succeed.

Before I had announced my candidacy; in fact, before I had reached a definite decision, a Nebraska lobbyist called upon me in Washington, a man well known throughout the state. I never had had anything in common with him or with anything he represented, and I was dumfounded when in my office he announced he wanted to talk with me about becoming a candidate for governor.

I was equally surprised at his frankness.

"The interest I represent always fought you," he said.

In the main he was the spokesman for liquor interests, and also to a very large extent the railroads. It was no secret in Nebraska. He belonged to the school that aligned itself with the most conservative faction of the Republican party, although, like all lobbyists, he did not care very much about political alliances, supporting Democrats as readily as Republicans. It was because he and the interests he represented had supported a Democrat for governor in the preceding election, and had been "sold out," that they had agreed to support me for governor.

He painted a very bright picture.

It would be easy, he assured me, to win the governorship; all I would have to do would be to announce my candidacy. He could assure me there would be a united effort by the "special interests" to bring about my election. They had raised a fund of $15,000, which he had brought with him, and would turn over to me if I would announce my candidacy for governor.

"You will not need it in the campaign," he said. "You will not be called upon to spend even half of that amount. We will make the fight for you. Your progressive friends will support you, and without making any fuss about it we will quietly give you our support. I think I can assure you there will be no opposition against you as there always has been in the past, because we will control that opposition completely."

As we sat there quietly talking, I masked my feelings and tried to find out why the interests he represented would support me when it was well known those interests had been my bitterest enemies. The explanation he gave me was that it was better to support a man whom they regarded as honest and truthful than one who would make all kinds of promises and then not fulfill them. He mentioned that he had been fooled in the signing of what became known in Nebraska as the eight o'clock closing law of saloons.

I told him the governor was right when he signed the bill; that I would have signed the bill if I had been governor. There was a great agitation in the state over the so-called county option. Existing statutes permitted each municipality to decide for itself whether it would have saloons; but, under the county option proposal, counties would vote as a unit, and the decision reached by the county would govern all the political subdivisions in the county.

My visitor said his people were much opposed to county option, which probably would be the main issue in the next election. They understood I would favor passage of county option, and while they would be very glad if I would oppose it, and announce that I would oppose it, they did not expect me to. In announcing my candidacy they expected I would say nothing about county option, keep out of it during the campaign, and they would not attempt to exact my promise.

When I told him I was for county option, and would campaign for it publicly, he said even that would not change their offer.

Unable to understand why these interests were so anxious for me to become a candidate for the governorship, and unable to persuade myself they would support me for any office, I reached the conclusion then and there they had thought I would be a candidate for the Senate, and would be elected. They would rather have me in the governorship than in the United States Senate, where they thought I would be more injurious to their ideas of government.

I firmly and positively told him I would not be a candidate for governor and had not decided fully I would be a candidate for the Senate; but shortly after his visit I announced myself.

Senators at the time were elected by legislatures of the several states; the amendment to the federal Constitution providing for the election of senators by a direct vote not having been adopted.

Nebraska was under what generally over the country was called the Oregon plan, under the provisions of which candidates for the state legislature could, if they desired, have printed on the official ballot a statement that if elected they would vote for the candidate for the United States Senate who had received the largest number of votes in the general election. The law was popular in Nebraska, and nearly every candidate for the legislature printed on the official ballot a statement to the effect he would abide by the result of the general election, and be guided by the preferential expression of the people.

Under the Oregon plan the political parties were able to nominate candidates at the primaries for the United States Senate. I won the Republican nomination, and A. C. Shallenberger, who was my opponent in the first contest for the House, and who had served as governor of the state, was the Democratic choice.

I had unseated Norris Brown, a regular Republican, in a furious primary battle.

Mr. Shallenberger and I fought out the campaign in 1912 in precisely the same fashion that we would have campaigned had there been a direct vote as the final step to election. We had accepted the pledge made by candidates to the state legislature as binding, although its action was merely a matter of honor.

In the November election a strange development took place. I defeated Mr. Shallenberger, to discover that the majority of the members of the legislature were Democrats. Among some of the more reactionary Democrats a feeling quickly developed they should endeavor to induce members of the legislature to disregard the pledge given under the Oregon plan and elect a United States senator who was a Democrat. It was nipped in the bud before it got very far. Statements from a few of the most prominent Democrats who had been chosen to serve in the legislature, that they considered themselves honor-bound to fulfill their pledge, and that they intended to vote for me for the Senate even though I was a Republican, quickly settled the move of these reactionary Democrats.

When the legislature in joint session convened to cast a ballot for United States senator, I received the solid vote of all the members regardless of politics, with perhaps two exceptions.

In that same campaign I had supported Theodore Roosevelt, the Progressive candidate against President Taft. Nebraska, like all the states, was divided bitterly. I made no secret of my preference for Theodore Roosevelt.

I had attended the conventions in Chicago—sitting on the fringes of the regular convention which renominated Mr. Taft, and presided over by a fellow Nebraskan, Victor Rosewater. I had seen the committee on credentials unseat the Roosevelt delegates, and it seemed to me that a great injustice was committed. I attended the Progressive convention at which Theodore Roosevelt was nominated, shared the enthusiasm which gripped his followers, and which gave the struggle elements of a crusade. I was in a fight for the Senate, and the state itself was torn in the clash between Progressives and Republican conservatives. Theodore Roosevelt was popular in Nebraska; he had carried it overwhelmingly against Judge Parker. Nebraska was aroused over the monopoly question; it had been profoundly disturbed by the revelations of the sugar trust; and although it gave its electoral votes to Woodrow Wilson by a margin of 41,000 votes in the three-cornered race, it sent me to the Senate by 38,071 votes.

17

NO FRIENDLY ATMOSPHERE

UPON TAKING my Senate seat the following March I found that my reputation had preceded me.

Many of the leaders were cool and unfriendly, looking upon me as a party outcast, a troublemaker, and a faultfinder. Many of the leading Republicans in the Senate had an aversion to me because of my unwillingness to accept instruction by the political bosses.

They were perfectly conscientious in their attitude towards me, and it included no personal ill will.

I was placed upon the Committee on Agriculture to my delight, and became an active worker on the committee. On it was Senator C. S. Page, a most honest, conscientious man who would not intentionally injure any associate. He attended committee sessions regularly, participated actively in deliberations, and we became very warm friends. He had been governor of Vermont before his election to the Senate. He took just pride in the fact that he answered to all roll calls, never ducked a vote, and was present at every committee meeting. But he was imbued with a bitter partisanship which often destroyed his usefulness in the Senate, and led him invariably to follow the leaders of the Republican machine.

He was a very wealthy man. Prior to his entry into politics, he had been engaged in the tanning business, and had been most successful.

I had been in the Senate for several months when a mutual friend told me of a conversation relating to me which Senator Page had with a fellow senator. He had told this senator that while he often disagreed with me we had no personal quarrel and had become fast friends. Because of the reports that had preceded me to the Senate, Senator Page said, he had watched me closely at work, and had come to the conclusion I was honest.

In time we came to have many confidential conferences.

Because of his previous business activities, he had had relationships with the great packers over many years; and one day we were visiting pleasantly in the Agricultural Committee room when the subject of the packers came up. He told me that he had had transactions mounting into the millions with the largest packing houses, and the relationship that he had always had had been fair and honest.

On election to the Senate, he said, he had quit the tanning business, because he felt the public interest would require all of his time. A representative of one of the packing interests came to congratulate him, reminding him of the business relations between them that had extended over so many years and had been so satisfactory, and expressed regret that Senator Page had decided to go out of business. He said they had talked the matter over, and wanted to show their appreciation of those long and happy business relations by placing him upon their salary roll at a reasonable salary.

Senator Page answered that he could not accept their offer, did not need the money, and, while he appreciated the sentiment that was expressed, it was his duty to decline it.

After telling me this he said:

"During all the conversation never once was there any mention made that my vote would be expected to be influenced by this salary."

I regarded the omission as a testimonial to the uprightness and honor of the great corporation; and yet the packing institutions of the country often were deeply interested in national legislation and at the very time of the reported conversation the Committee on Agriculture was engaged in an investigation of the packing industry.

I always believed that Senator Page was conscientious and honest in every vote that he cast either in the committee or in the Senate; but it seemed quite clear to me that in offering to place him on their salary roll—at $5,000 annually, as I remember it—they raised in his mind a doubt as to whether he honorably could accept the offer.

Gradually my associations in the Senate became more pleasant. In addition to the Agriculture Committee I was placed on the Public Lands Committee. There I got first introduction to a fight which, in all its successive stages, was to occupy my remaining years in the Senate.

For more than a century the national assembly has been legislating on various phases of conservation. Damage by flood waters of the many rivers has amounted to billions of dollars—more billions than now is represented by America's national debt. Each year in some region of the great Mississippi valley, millions of dollars' worth of property is destroyed, large amounts of fertile soil are washed away from the valley lands, and the productivity of this great food region is impaired.

Congress has appropriated hundreds of millions for the improvement of navigation and the prevention of damage by flood waters to life and to property. Channels of rivers have been deepened and straightened, dikes have been built, and still the floods come and go along the Mississippi and its tributaries.

The Father of Waters divides the United States into two parts.

In its slow sweep from northern Minnesota to the Gulf of Mexico it winds through a region more intensively developed for agriculture, and providing more food for the world, than any similar area on any other continent. Each spring when the melting snows and the driving rains add to the waters of its tributaries, they all pour into the Mississippi. When the tributaries rising in the Allegheny watershed overflow simultaneously with tributaries whose headwaters are in the Rockies, those lower Mississippi disasters with which the American people are familiar become inevitable. The great flood of 1927 in the lower Mississippi basin, following a fall and winter of abundant rain and snowfall both in the Rocky Mountain and in the Allegheny watershed, may have played a part in hastening the economic collapse of 1929.

The main loss occurred annually in Louisiana and Mississippi, although other southern states suffered heavily and could look forward to floods that would inundate large sections of fertile land. Then why not store these waters as near the source as possible? Why not build reservoirs high up on tributaries which would hold back such floods as, in rolling down the Mississippi, had carried millions of tons of rich silt, had built a great delta extending far out into the Gulf of Mexico? Why not now be busy against the day when the hillsides and the flat valleys would be stripped of fertile topsoil?

From the lengthy study I had made, I had reached the conclusion that the American people were not pursuing a proper course to control these floods. The sensible step was to take advantage of reservoirs that Nature had provided at different spots in the Mississippi valley, to build a dam at the mouth of every such reservoir, to store the flood and waste water, and then to release this water when the Mississippi was at low stage—thus reducing or eliminating the danger to property or life.

It was then that a bill was introduced, passed the House, and came to the Senate, providing $10,000,000 for improvement chiefly of the Mississippi River channel as it wound through these southern states, I became more interested than ever. Its advocates insisted that, by spending a large amount of money at one time for the construction of dikes and levees and the dredging of the bed of the stream, the flood waters could be held within the banks.

A very short time before, the Pathfinder Dam in Wyoming had been completed and brought into operation. Its purpose was to hold back the flood waters of the North Platte for use for irrigation. Under the authorizing law, the farmers who used the water were to bear the entire cost of the dam. But without the dam these waters would ultimately have found their way to the Mississippi River, where, mingling with flood waters from other tributaries at the peak of the spring floods, they would have increased and multiplied destruction of crops, property, and human life in the lower Mississippi valley.

Furthermore, the best place for storing water was in the soil. Irrigation of these dry lands on the eastern slopes and in the watershed of the Rocky Mountains fitted into the plan of Nature.

Plainly, every gallon of water impounded behind the Pathfinder Dam aided in the prevention of flood damage in the lower Mississippi valley, and it was unjust to farmers sorely in need of irrigation to burden them with the entire cost of the dam. Therefore the cost of constructing this dam should be divided between the farmers, using the water for irrigation, and the federal government, seeking to protect the vast valleys of the Missouri and the Mississippi from floods.

The prevention of floods and the improvement of navigation early found approval in the courts as being in the province of the federal government. It should not be any great shock to the courts, I felt, for the federal government to bear a portion of the cost of building a dam even though the dam was far distant from the Mississippi.

I had reached no conclusion as to how the cost ought to be divided—what proportion should be paid by the irrigator, and what proportion the federal government should bear. Even if it became necessary to use an arbitrary formula for the division of the expense, I felt there was solid foundation for taking these steps.

To the bill then pending in the Senate, I offered an amendment which arbitrarily provided that half of the cost of constructing the Pathfinder Dam should be paid out of the federal Treasury, and half by persons utilizing the stored water for irrigation.

In support of my amendment I argued that construction of dams like the Pathfinder was of great help toward flood control in the Mississippi valley, and that we should build more dams to hold back the late winter and early spring floods.

I did not expect the amendment to meet with approval—I could not have said just what the division of expense should be if some opponent had insisted I justify the formula offered; but, after debate, I was very agreeably surprised at the small margin by which the amendment was defeated. It was one of the steps then necessary to educate the people of the country to the unfairness of charging to the irrigator the entire expense of a dam which held back flood waters. This was long before river developments for flood control, navigation, irrigation, and power assumed the outline so familiar today.

Even among engineers there was no agreement upon the effectiveness of my proposal of flood control. Many of them laughed at the idea of averting floods by storing the waste water of tributaries in reservoirs, and said that the program would cost billions of dollars and would require many years for completion. Invariably I admitted that the cost would be enormous, and that it would take many years to complete the work.

I have lived to see the idea which I proposed then advocated by some of America's greatest engineers. I have lived to see it accepted as a scientific approach to flood control, as an improvement in navigation, and as an economy in averting hundreds of millions of dollars' damage in floods. And I have lived long enough to see it increase the production of farm products enormously.

So today generally, I believe, it is agreed that the best way to control floods is to store flood waters in reservoirs at points where the lay of the land makes these possible, lending itself to the construction of dams at the least possible expense.

I have seen the fulfillment of the dream: the lessening of floods and of their destruction, the expansion of irrigation, the liberation of farm families trying to live in semi-arid regions on marginal lands, and finally a great increase in the food production of the American people. All that is involved is the conservation of natural resources.

The job is far from finished.

This program of controlling the surplus flood waters of the great Mississippi valley by storage in natural reservoirs situated on the main stream and along the tributaries is an immense one. It may never be fulfilled. That depends entirely upon the vision of the American people. It will require a vast amount of money to complete it; it will take years of planning and of labor to meet fully all of its factors; and yet it offers the only promise discovered by men for the effective control of floods and efficient conservation of natural resources.

One other great benefit I have not mentioned naturally follows the storing of flood waters: the possibility of producing vast amounts of electric power. We have been living in an electrical age not fully explored. Perhaps, in all of the comforts and conveniences which electricity already has provided, only the dim outlines of the electrical age have been sketched. There may be an airplane of tomorrow driven by electrical energy. The rail transportation of another generation may extend infinitely those lines already electrified. We may live in homes heated and lighted exclusively by electricity, and we may fight a war—if we fail in the peace settlements of the present conflict—in which the dread weapons will be electrical: not only electric planes, but giant tanks rolling over the ground driven by electricity.

This struggle for hydroelectric development in America, in which I was privileged to have a large part, may have been an invaluable service to us in the prosecution of the present conflict.

But the production of electrical power and the clash it brought on have made these fights to conserve water and land long, tedious, and bitter. By the expenditure of only a small additional amount, every one of these reservoir dams would produce an untold amount of electricity, which naturally would interfere with the plans of private power companies.

I have found little difference to the opposition that develops in every part of the United States. The power trust is the greatest monopolistic corporation that has been organized for private greed. The investigations instigated by the Federal Trade Commission, covering a period of years, have revealed some of the most disgraceful, distasteful, and disreputable means by which it attempted to perpetuate its control of the natural resources of the nation. It has bought and sold legislatures. It has interested itself in the election of public officials, from school directors to the President of the United States. It has succeeded in placing its friends in office unbeknown to the people. Its representatives have been carefully placed in seats of honor and trust. Its lobbyists have control of legislation in practically every state of the Union. It has managed to infest farm organizations; it has not hesitated to enter the sacred walls of churches and religious organizations. It has influenced, wherever it could, the election of judges in the various state courts, and the appointment of judges to the federal bench.

The fight has never ended. It is still in progress, sometimes secret, sometimes bold, but consistently against the construction of all great national undertakings like the TVA, Bonneville, Grand Coulee, and the Little TVA of my own home state. The power trust has fought the development and advancement of rural electrification by the national government. It has endeavored to bring about the defeat of municipal ownership in villages, towns, and cities.

It will continue to fight; and the people must be on guard, because it is resourceful, intelligent, and relentless.

Every stream in the United States which flows from the mountains through the meadows to the sea has the possibility of producing electricity for cheap power and cheap lighting, to be carried into the homes and businesses and industry of the American people. This natural resource was given by an all-wise Creator to his people and not to organizations of greed. No man and no organization of men ought to be allowed to make a financial profit out of it. Every drop of water that falls from the heavens to the earth beneath should perform its proper share of preserving the blessings God intends to bestow upon his people.

This issue is by no means settled. It is one of the greatest issues presented to the American people in the last century and it remains in the indecisive stage. It is in reality the same question I raised when I offered my amendment in the Senate to a bill whose object was the prevention of floods in the great Mississippi valley.

I became a storm center because it seemed to me that the development and conservation of these resources ought always to be under public control, public ownership, and public operation.

18

HETCH HETCHY

A PART OF THE national park preserves and on the fringes of the natural glories of Yosemite National Park in the California Sierras is known as the Hetch Hetchy watershed.

Among other assignments which fell to me when I entered the United States Senate in 1913 was one to the Public Lands Committee.

It had before it the bitterly controversial issue of developing the water and power resources of the Hetch Hetchy watershed for the benefit of the people of the city and county of San Francisco.

There could be, in my judgment, no better example of the slow and painful processes through which the American people ultimately in their wisdom may come into the full benefits of some of the great natural wealth which belongs to them.

Now, thirty years later—three full decades—the powerfully intrenched private interests which prevented San Franciscans from enjoying what belongs to them still thwart the express will of the American Congress, the clear-cut mandates of the federal courts, and the Department of the Interior, under both conservative and liberal administrations. Strangely, these forces flaunt their defiance seemingly with the approval and support of the government of the city of San Francisco, and indirectly its people, for whom the project was undertaken and to whom Congress granted rights with certain sound limitations.

Hetch Hetchy is worthy of examination for the light that it sheds on the exact character of a fight which has been in progress for years.

Hetch Hetchy's development called for the construction of a 430-foot dam on the Tuolumne River—blocking the north end of the valley, and impounding the waters in an artificial lake approximately three miles in length and from one-quarter to three-quarters of a mile in width. It was to create a lake not far from some of the most magnificent trees of America, giants of the forest, which tossed their branches to the skies and, through sunshine and storm, impressed millions with the true grandeur trees can attain.

What could have been more natural than that sincere lovers of nature should be disturbed by the prospect that this region upon which God had bestowed beauty with a lavish hand was to be marred?

The road that leads northward from the Yosemite valley proper to the Hetch Hetchy project winds its way through the Tuolumne Grove of big trees—and they are really giants. Then it opens upon forests of sugar pine and red fir. In the valley itself the walls of sheer granite rise precipitously, with the crests and the pinnacles reaching an elevation of 4,000 feet above the surface of the waters. The valley took its name from the Indian name, *hatchatchie,* descriptive of the grass which grew in profusion there and had an edible seed.

I reached the conclusion, after listening intently to all the evidence, that the beauty of the region would not be injured in any sense by the construction of O'Shaughnessy Dam. If anything, a lake would accentuate its loveliness.

I could see the shadows of the canyons and the trees mirrored in deep waters. The birds and little creatures of the wild still would pursue the even tenor of their ways. The impressive solitudes of a national park preserve would not be destroyed by the dam or the lake that formed behind it.

Yet many honest and conscientious men in and out of Congress, including some of the leading progressives in the Senate, were opposed to the development—among them, Senator John D. Works of California and Senator W. E. Borah of Idaho, both now dead.

No one doubted the sincerity of these men. I had full trust in their honesty and sincerity and, as a newcomer, was impressed with their unmistakable conscientiousness, but I felt they were making a great mistake. I could come to no other decision than that, if we believed in the conservation of natural resources in America, the construction of a dam so magnificently located and so promisingly useful could not be opposed. I did not then recognize the inspiration, in other quarters, for a newly awakened interest in nature.

Through months of fight which flared and flamed to new bitterness, the project embraced in the House Resolution 242 finally won approval and became known as the Raker Act.

A simple eleven-line clause—Section 6—was the center of a savage battle continuing for months until the bill became law on December 19, 1913. Constantly through a period of thirty years since that day, that fight has gone on.

It would never have begun if Section 6 had not dedicated the power developed by Hetch Hetchy to public benefit.

The section reads:

> The grantee [the city and county of San Francisco] is prohibited from ever selling or letting to any corporation or individual, except a municipality or a municipal water district or irrigation district, the right to sell or sublet the water or the electric energy sold or given to it or him by said grant; provided that the rights hereby granted shall not be sold, assigned or transferred to any private person, corporation or association, and in case of any attempt to sell, assign, transfer or convey this grant shall revert to the government of the United States.

It is this language which dedicates Hetch Hetchy to the use and benefit of the people. It was this language which also inspired the savage opposition of private utilities to the proposed development in the early years of the Wilson administration. The will and purpose of the Congress was clear and unmistakable.

I am certain that, had it not been for Section 6 under which San Francisco was given valuable rights in a national park reserve and the Stanislaus National Forest to obtain both a water and a power supply, the Sixty-third Congress, and possibly any succeeding Congress, would not have given approval. I am equally certain that, in the absence of this restriction, there would have been no fight by the privately owned utilities.

In Congress itself, then in the courts, and through one municipal election after another, sometimes subtly under cover and on other occasions out in the open, the battle went on unnoted by millions of Americans.

In the House discussion Congressman Raker bluntly said it was the purpose of his bill to have San Francisco supply electric power and water to its own people. In the Senate, speaking in defense of the safeguard provided by Section 6, a colleague, Senator Key Pittman, told the members the bill "provides absolutely that neither this water nor this power can ever fall into the hands of a monopoly."

And in the course of the debate, speaking in similar vein to many others, I said:

"This bill is not giving to a private corporation any power. It is giving to the people of this locality of San Francisco the right to use a cheap power when it is developed. . . . Why do we want to develop water power? Will we give it to the public or to a private individual or corporation? Here is an instance where we are going to give it directly to the people, if we pass this bill. It is going to come into competition with power companies and corporations that have, or will have, if this bill is defeated, almost a monopoly, not only in San Francisco, but throughout the greater portion of California."

I underestimated the resourcefulness of the Pacific Gas and Electric Company.

When I spoke so hopefully and so confidently (not only I but many others) it was incredible that a great utility could control the policies of city government in San Francisco, with all of the resources at its command could battle through the courts to defeat—only to stave off that defeat by delaying rear-guard actions, and then reappear in the halls of Congress itself to renew the fight, and at all times and under all circumstances continue to defeat the original purpose and spirit of Hetch Hetchy.

But it has done all this.

The work progressed slowly, and the project was not finished until 1937. The dam created a lake containing 1,466,000,000 gallons of water. In its preliminary stages it was discovered that the power transmission line, instead of terminating in San Francisco where there was a market, actually delivered the electricity developed by Hetch Hetchy to Newark, where the Pacific Gas and Electric Company had transmission facilities, and where there was no market except through the Pacific Gas and Electric Company.

In all particulars San Francisco proceeded without delay under the limitations of Section 6 to the distribution of supplemental waters stored for the convenience and supply of a great metropolis. It distributed that water to the consumers in San Francisco without rake-off by or profit to any private company.

It was not until 1925, more than a decade after the congressional authorization had been given, that Hetch Hetchy electric capacities were developed to furnish any substantial amount of electricity.

But from the beginning the city made no substantial effort to comply with the restrictions imposed by Congress, and openly violated the limitations in Section 6 by selling its power to private companies for resale to the consumer. In 1925 the project reached the point where electricity was produced in most substantial volume, and it seemed highly desirable a new arrangement be made.

With this in mind, the San Francisco Board of Supervisors passed a resolution which stated:

> The Board of Supervisors is unalterably and unequivocally opposed to the policy of entering into any contract, lease or agreement of any kind or character for the distribution of Hetch Hetchy electricity to or through any private corporation.

That expression of public purpose was refreshing.

It gave promise that the aims of Congress finally would be carried out.

The resolution was drawn by Supervisor Rossi, later to become mayor of San Francisco. Unfortunately its effect was short-lived: only a few months later a majority of the supervisors, including Mr. Rossi, agreed to a contract executed on July 1, 1925, under the terms of which Hetch Hetchy power was turned over to the

Pacific Gas and Electric Company for resale to the consumer—naturally at a handsome profit.

The people of San Francisco arose in wrath.

All of the supervisors who had voted in favor of adopting this contract were defeated less than a year later in the municipal election. It was unfortunate that the contract itself was not on the ballot, so that the citizens of San Francisco could have had the opportunity to terminate its trouble-making existence once and for all.

The legality of that contract, challenged almost immediately by the Department of the Interior, swung back and forth without definite results.

The then Secretary of the Interior, Ray Lyman Wilbur, a Republican and a Californian, took up the fight to induce San Francisco to comply with all the terms of the agreement under which the municipality had been authorized to construct Hetch Hetchy Secretary Wilbur's attitude as a member of President Hoover's official family left no question of the undoubted high purpose back of this effort to add to the usefulness of the pioneer preservation development.

Harold L. Ickes, who followed Mr. Wilbur in office, made painstaking investigations as Secretary of the Interior, and then appealed to the Attorney General of the United States to bring suit against San Francisco to compel compliance with the congressional limitation governing the distribution of electricity generated by Hetch Hetchy. In June of 1938 the United States District Court, Northern District of California, held the troublesome contract between San Francisco and the Pacific Gas and Electric Company to be in violation of Section 6 of the Raker Act. The court enjoined the city from further disposing of power in an illegal manner.

Still the power company was not licked.

It had the resources to continue the fight through the courts. Its appeal to the Supreme Court of the United States was duly prosecuted, and once again the decree of the lower tribunal was upheld fully.

In an opinion written by Mr. Justice Hugo Black, expressing the judgment of an eight-man majority, the congressional limitation dedicating Hetch Hetchy power to the beneficial use of the public was sustained.

That decision was handed down on April 22, 1940.

Again San Francisco came in with pleas to save Hetch Hetchy revenues during the necessary period of transition to full compliance with the Raker Act. As a result of those pleas, enforcement of the injunction which had been sustained by the Supreme Court's rulings was delayed three times by stays.

Finally out of it all emerged still another plan under which the Pacific Gas and Electric Company in a practical sense would have retained its tight grip upon Hetch Hetchy electricity. This plan was rejected by Secretary Ickes; and the city of San Francisco, weary of the fight, placed upon the ballot a proposal for a charter amendment under which the community was to finance with revenue bonds the purchase or construction of its own distribution system.

The campaign which followed has had its counterpart in scores of American cities and towns. Time and again I have spoken of the familiar tactics employed by the utility interests to defeat the popular will. I have spoken on the floor of the Senate of those methods by which the public so frequently has been misled. The people of San Francisco were told that the bonds imposed a general obligation upon the taxpayers instead of being payable entirely from income derived through distribution of Hetch Hetchy power. Civic organizations in militant opposition sprang up like mushrooms. Amazingly after two decades there was the counter proposal to amend the Raker Act. The battle cry in that campaign became: "Vote down the bonds, and amend the Raker Act." It was successful in spite of all that had gone on before.

And on the day in 1939 following the defeat of the bonds California's Congressman Rolph introduced a bill in the Lower House to reopen consideration of the original enabling legislation.

So through the long years Hetch Hetchy came down to that Sabbath day which produced the Japanese sneak raid on Pearl Harbor, with the Pacific Gas and Electric Company still triumphan·

in its fight to prevent electric power from being distributed in San Francisco in accordance with the congressional mandate.

Again the controversy was back in the lap of Congress, and at the hearing before the Public Lands Committee of the House in January of 1942, Secretary Ickes said in part:

"I suggest that it would be more fitting for the officials both of the city and of the company to appear before you and tell you what they will do to comply with the law. If the Pacific Gas and Electric Company should cease to be the dominating partner in the Hetch Hetchy conspiracy, I am sure that, overnight, all of the difficulties of carrying out the Raker Act would cease. If the Pacific Gas and Electric Company ceased pouring forth a stream of gold and flood of propaganda, all would be clear sailing. It is using the present emergency as a cloak behind which to obtain exoneration for complicity and lawlessness and as a warrant for the continued future flouting of an act of Congress. . . .

"I see no cause for concern or for relaxing our resistance upon compliance with the Raker Act merely because the people of San Francisco have voted down several times bond proposals. It took a number of attempts before they got their water distribution system. . . . When the people of San Francisco realize that this Congress is not going to forgive and forget almost two decades of law violation; that it declines to sanction a grab of Hetch Hetchy by private interests, then much of the confusion will have been dispelled. . . .

"Hetch Hetchy is only a minor front in the grand strategy of the Pacific Gas and Electric Company in California. It fought the great Central Valley project with every weapon in its arsenal. Since it was not successful in completely blocking that project, it has undertaken the capture tactic. I want to stress the fact that the Raker Act does not represent an instance where the federal authority was exercised for the purpose of influencing the city of San Francisco to undertake the distribution of power. On the contrary, it was a case where the city of San Francisco besought the right to acquire federal park land. There was a reluctance on the part of Congress to grant this right. It wanted to be satisfied completely that no private interest was involved. But the city of San Francisco, having gotten its grant, is now trying to destroy the condition to which it freely agreed in order to obtain the grant."

This has happened so frequently in varied ways in the United States. If it is not public lands it is vast sums of public funds, poured out for public developments, which great private interests seek to utilize to their own selfish gain.

There was still one more episode in the Hetch Hetchy battle to unfold.

It was the proposal of a contract under the terms of which it was computed that the Pacific Gas and Electric Company would receive $4,900,000 annually for use of its distribution system. It was to get $21,667.67 for rental of the transmission line from Newark to San Francisco. It was to receive $58,333.33 monthly for 70,000 kilowatts of stand-by power. It was to be reimbursed for unemployment insurance and other items, and a group of its employees was to be transferred to the city pay rolls at the prevailing wages paid. More significant, it was to have complete authority over budgets for the maintenance and betterment of the distribution system of San Francisco. That last condition still left it in control, it would seem, so that it could be asked reasonably whether the Pacific Gas and Electric Company actually was relinquishing its grip or was fattening itself and tightening its strangle hold.

Hetch Hetchy power now turns the equipment of a great factory for the production of a vital war metal, and is making its contribution to the struggle in which America became engaged. Looking ahead, there is now a proposal the city acquire its distribution system.

Why have I returned time and again to the attack in these developments of the natural resources of America?

Why has this uncompromising, irreconcilable struggle gone on and on?

This fight affecting one American city—a beautiful city from which ships sail through the Golden Gate to the ports of the world, a city which was tumbled by earthquake and blackened by fire and yet had the spirit and vitality to rise again—stretches through my service of six terms in the United States Senate. It began in those opening freshman months when I was enrolled there in 1913.

It was not finally and conclusively ended when I took leave of Washington in the opening days of January, 1943.

An intrenched power of that kind is an impressive force.

I think back over those thirty years during which the future of Hetch Hetchy with its promise of great usefulness was uncertain. They were tumultuous years. They included two great wars. In between, the American people shivered in the economic dislocation of a depression which clutched their soil and the soil of much of the world. At its height millions saw darkly and lost hope, only again to emerge into sunlight; and it has seemed to me that life here in America, seeking to survive, has cast a glow of warmth frequently penetrating the chill and the darkness beyond these shores. Those older lands know fully the price of indifference, of greed, and of exploitation.

Hetch Hetchy, to me, is a symbol.

Since it first took shadowy form not far from the tall redwoods and the glistening peaks of the Sierras, with their tumbling mountain streams, I have seen the people of southern California, reaching out for both water and light, go eastward to the course of the Colorado River to construct Boulder Dam. Far to the north in the woods and rocks of Washington and Oregon, Grand Coulee and Bonneville have impounded the waters of the Columbia River which flows majestically to the sea.

Hetch Hetchy as it unfolded before me, in the quickening, growing interest in the conservation of natural resources, has come to be one of the symbols, and one of thoughtful memory because it marks a beginning. It is, in all the frustration that has marked its history, one of those developments through which the American people have sought to express their purpose to make the best use of the waters of the land. I have no doubt this splendid vision will in due time spread to all sections of the United States and to other regions of the world. It offers so much of hope against exhaustion and despair. Those who may visit Hetch Hetchy, those who may stand on the banks of the Columbia beside Grand Coulee or Bonneville, and those who may journey in the old valley of the Tennessee past its many dams and its many lakes will gaze upon the miracle.

Hetch Hetchy embodies the story of the ages.

The snows of winter wrap the peaks of the Sierras gently in a deep white blanket or, in howling gales, fill the deep canyons with ice and snow. And then spring follows, and spring's warm sun, and snow water happily courses down the mountain side, gathering in tiny creeks which rush rapidly to the river, seeking the sea.

Men may build dams to pile those waters back in lakes, averting floods and providing cities with water and light.

That is the miracle which embodies the wisdom of an intelligent and competent people.

It is the plan through which a modern world enters upon an electrical age.

19

DEATH KISS BY FILIBUSTER

For the first fifteen months following the inauguration of Woodrow Wilson the American people busied themselves with improving the inner structures of democracy.

In fact, it was not until Europe was well along in the third year of war that the full danger of American involvement impressed itself upon the public.

In the United States Senate, curiosity rather than concern was uppermost when news came on June 28, 1914, that a Serbian youth, a flaming nationalist, had shot and killed Archduke Francis Ferdinand of Austria and his royal consort.

That day, and in the weeks that followed, very few if any members of the Senate anticipated that Europe would be blanketed with war in a few months, and the United States would ultimately become involved. That indifference was a most revealing reflection of American thought.

Under Mr. Wilson's leadership, the American people had embarked upon a pretentious course of internal readjustments. Tariff revision had occupied the energies of Congress with months of debate. I welcomed the overhauling of tariff duties but noted with regret that precisely the same caucus tactics which had inspired me to opposition earlier as a member of the House of Representatives dominated the framing of this new tariff proposal. I sought vainly to procure the same treatment for wheat, produced by the middle western farmer, which was given rice, produced by the southerner. I hoped a nonpartisan tariff commission would be established.

I rejoiced in the legislative proposals leading up to an income-tax law, which in my judgment could have been strengthened by amendments. I sponsored a companion inheritance tax proposal. I was happy to support the legislation creating the new Federal Reserve System, although I thought its control and operation should be vested in the people rather than given to the banking interests.

Those were months, however, when America was concentrating upon long neglected business of government; and whatever misgivings and disappointments arose were offset by my sympathy in the objectives these legislative steps sought to attain.

Congressional discussion reflected the mounting demands of Europe for food and weapons. America was feeding many millions, and its factories were producing vast quantities of munitions. The mounting tension created by the interchange of notes over blockade regulations and ship sinkings created an uneasiness among some of us, but it seemed that pent-up impatience and irritation gathered and broke in the short space of thirty-six days.

Of course, this crisis had been developing for months. It did not reach a head as a result of any single development.

There had been the British proclamation establishing a blockade against food and munitions for the Central Powers, followed by a retaliatory German order of blockade against the British Isles in the attempt to starve out the British people. There had been the continual search and seizure of ocean-going vessels, and ship sinkings. There had been the stories of atrocities. And finally there was the German decree of unrestricted submarine warfare under von Tirpitz.

I always have felt that the issue of war was presented in Mr. Wilson's request for congressional authority to arm American merchant ships. It was defeated through a filibuster in which I took a most active part. Not even the declaration of war, which followed slightly more than a month later, precipitated more intense feeling and bitterness on the floor of the Senate. The public fully sensed the issue, which had been reduced to the simplest terms by a declaration of war. Then, as on most other occasions, it did not comprehend all the minute details at issue in a struggle in which a filibuster became a desperate weapon of Senate action.

GEORGE W. NORRIS IN 1903, AT THE TIME OF HIS ELECTION TO THE HOUSE OF REPRESENTATIVES IN WHICH HE SERVED FIVE TERMS BEFORE PROMOTION TO THE SENATE.

Filibusters often have been a national disgrace.

The filibuster is a legislative weapon to be employed sparingly if at all. It should be understood in all of its mechanics.

The tradition that makes a filibuster possible is the practice which has governed the Senate throughout its history of debate without limitation. Its members have taken great pride in the fact that debate in that tribunal is unrestricted.

No curtailment of discussion on any issue has been permitted.

In theory, and generally in practice, the Senate thereby became an open forum for discussion of all public questions. No machine and no organization has had the power to interfere.

If a permanent adjournment of the Senate is fixed definitely, either through constitutional limitation or otherwise, a filibuster can be successful although indulged in by only a few senators. The Lame Duck amendment, which came later, is a very effective method to prevent the filibuster. Prior to it the practice of Congress was to adjourn "sine die" if in session at noon on the fourth day of March, the hour and the day when the terms of office of all the representatives and of a third of the senators expired.

It was the end of a Congress.

Singlehanded, one member of the Senate could carry on a filibuster at the close of a Congress if he could talk from the time that he obtained the floor until noon on March 4. It was easy, indeed, to prevent action by the Senate if the issue in question came up for debate on the closing morning. It was necessary to talk only an hour or a few hours before it became the duty of a presiding officer to declare the Senate adjourned without delay. If he instigated his filibuster the day before, he would have to continue talking and, perhaps, be unable physically to achieve his result. And if a filibuster came a few or several days before, and was indulged in by a sufficient number of senators to consume all of the time up until the hour of adjournment, then again the filibuster would be successful.

Filibustering is made possible under the rules of the Senate and not under any law. It could be prevented largely by a simple rule; but the jealous pride with which the Senate guards its tradition of open, unlimited debate makes the adoption of the rule difficult, if not impossible; and this, to many senators, a sacred right often put the Senate in a very ridiculous and sometimes, I think, unpatriotic position

Any man who engages in a filibuster assumes a very heavy responsibility. If he succeeds in his purpose, he not only defeats the measure against which the filibuster is directed, but makes impossible any other action by the Senate. For example, a filibuster started when an appropriation bill awaits action by the Senate, and carried on until the hour of adjournment, will defeat the appropriation bill —which may contain items absolutely necessary if the government is to continue to function.

Only a special session of Congress could correct that abuse of the filibuster.

Finally the Senate adopted a rule placing a limitation on debate.

I have always felt, especially since the adoption of the Lame Duck amendment, there ought to come a time under fair and judicial Senate procedure when useless and unnecessary talk should cease, and a majority of the Senate should be able to express its will.

But on a number of occasions I became a party to filibustering.

Accepting the great responsibility involved, I took such actions only when I thought the legislation was of such importance as to warrant it.

I felt the passage of the proposed bill to give Mr. Wilson authority to arm merchant ships would automatically plunge the United States into the war.

Under the circumstances I was bitterly opposed to pushing our government into the war as an actual combatant.

Feeling so strongly, I thought the filibuster was justified in spite of my repugnance to the method. The ship bill had passed both the House and the Senate, but in amended form, and under the rules had been referred to a conference committee. The House and Senate conferees had completed their labors, and the House had agreed to the conference report. The bill would become a law as soon as the Senate gave its approval.

No other legislative step is more difficult to defeat through filibuster than a conference report. By its very nature a conference report cannot be amended; and the only question that comes before either Senate or the House is:

"Shall the conference report be agreed to?"

There is but one motion to be voted upon—but one opportunity for delay, and that is to defeat the motion.

If it passes, that ends it.

A filibuster against a bill itself can be prolonged easily by the offering of amendments and by other parliamentary procedure that will bring about delay.

In the tense, anger-filled atmosphere which developed over a proposal to give Mr. Wilson authority to arm ships, there was only one chance for a triumphant filibuster. Opponents to the conference report had to be ready to debate that question. Unless they were alert and careful, the motion carrying approval could be agreed to in less than a moment's time.

The conference report came before the Senate in the afternoon of March 1, 1917, slightly more than a month before the war declaration. Those members opposed to the proposal, who had determined upon a filibuster in order to defeat it, were ready. They knew fully the unpopularity of the course upon which they were about to embark.

Under ordinary parliamentary procedure, when a question is under debate those who speak are required to talk to and about the issue, and failure to do so paves the way for a point of order the presiding officer will sustain. Under another ancient unwritten rule of the Senate it always was held that the man who had the floor was himself the judge as to whether what he was saying had some relevancy to the pending question. Frequently it brought about some most absurd discussions in the Senate.

As we prepared for the battle, the older senator, Fighting Bob La Follette of Wisconsin, became the acknowledged leader of the filibuster, although the parliamentary procedure was not handled directly by him. On the other side, interested in having the conference report adopted, was Senator Gilbert M. Hitchcock of Nebraska, the ranking member of the Foreign Relations Committee.

Its chairman, Senator William J. Stone of Missouri, belonged to the ranks of the filibusterers; and because he was very much opposed to the adoption of the proposed conference report he arose in the Senate to announce he felt someone who favored it should have charge of the debate on that side of the question.

While I was not a member of the Foreign Relations Committee, by common consent I was given charge of the parliamentary procedure in opposition to the adoption of the conference report.

The little group of us openly opposed gave careful thought to our battle strategy. We came to the conclusion that, since it would be necessary to consume a great deal of the Senate's time in order to succeed in the filibuster, Senator La Follette should be held back to make the concluding speech. We anticipated in excess of seventy-two hours of debate. La Follette had indicated he desired to speak for about three hours. Therefore, I arranged matters so that we should keep the debate open and in progress until twelve o'clock noon on the fourth day of March, with Senator La Follette, given the privilege of the closing argument, taking the floor at nine on the final day of that Congress. It was felt he would consume all of the time until the presiding officer under the rules would have to adjourn the Senate.

The debate got under way.

I had arranged for speakers so there was no possibility of a break in the discussion.

I warned each member of the filibuster that he must be ready when the senator who had the floor surrendered it, and that he must immediately address the presiding officer. If we permitted a moment to elapse, the presiding officer would put the question, and the conference report would be agreed to.

It is a matter worthy of public attention that there were many senators opposed at heart to the proposal for arming of merchant ships but publicly supporting the motion to agree to the conference report and prepared to vote for it. Among them were those who felt that party regularity was of extreme importance. They knew that the sentiment of the country seemed to be almost unanimous in favor of the bill. Some of these men privately came to me, committed as they were to vote for the conference report, and urged me over and over again while the filibuster was in progress to be sure to have somebody ready to speak, so that the issue would not come to a vote.

Invariably, I said to these men that the thing we needed was somebody to talk. We did not care whether it was in support of the report or against it. Strangely, two senators made an agreement with me, and actually spoke at long length in favor of the conference report; but as time went on during the filibuster it became more dangerous for any senator on that side of the question to use the Senate's valuable hours because he opened himself to the charge he was helping the filibuster.

The plan I had arranged and endeavored to carry out called for three senators on the floor all the time in addition to the floor manager. When any senator relinquished the floor, they immediately would jump up and address the chair.

Hour after hour, that went on until late on the 3rd of March.

Then I knew, or felt that I knew, that the filibuster was going to succeed.

Late in the afternoon of the third day, through unanimous agreement with Senator Hitchcock, the majority leader, I arranged for a brief recess. I told Senator La Follette I sensed victory as we walked away from the Senate chamber.

During the night, I remained at the Senate chamber to guard against eventualities.

The hours of darkness dragged slowly. To fill out the time, I consumed two or three hours of discussion myself. I was talking when the first tints of the sunrise colored the eastern sky and the mists which overhung the Potomac.

It did not appear there was any loophole in the filibuster program.

I knew others were ready to follow me when needed.

My associates had been notified to go home and rest; they would be called before their turn to speak arrived; but they must not fail to be on the floor of the Senate at least thirty minutes in advance.

There were empty seats and empty galleries as the hands of the clock dragged wearily around the dial and the debate went on monotonously.

It began to dawn upon Senator Hitchcock and the advocates of arming merchant ships that probably we should be able to consume all of the remaining time. I think then they came to the conclusion that, if the motion to adopt the conference report was going to be defeated by filibuster, it might be excellent strategy for friends of the proposal to talk so that, instead of a one-sided record, arguments friendly to it would appear. Apparently, they decided to do this and at the same time to prevent Senator La Follette from securing the floor. They saw to it they had a man in the chair at all times friendly to their side, ready to seize the slightest opportunity of putting the question of adoption of the conference report if there was the slightest hesitation on the part of its opponents.

Up to that time there had been no argument of any great length in favor of it. All of the discussion had been against it. So far as the proposal was concerned, it seemed to have no friends, and during the night it had been condemned in the most caustic language.

But it had the votes, and we knew it.

I had told Senator La Follette that, inasmuch as he had a three-hour speech which was to close the filibuster, he should return to his apartment and go to bed. I think he did rest most of the night. His absence convinced the supporters of the proposal that he was being held back. They knew he would make a powerful speech, and they entered fully into the fight to prevent him from obtaining recognition. It appeared to us they had worked out an understanding with the presiding officer that when Senator La Follette attempted to gain the floor, one of their number would claim it at the same time, and the chair, exercising the privileges of a presiding officer, would recognize the senator who he knew was favorable to the conference report.

Thus, Bob La Follette was handcuffed in a struggle which I believe affected him more deeply than any other among the many historic battles in which he engaged.

Try though he did, he was not permitted to get the floor.

I saw his face flush, his eyes flash, and his anger rise. He made many attempts to speak, and his failure to get recognition clearly established what had been agreed upon. I could appreciate his feelings, but the battle was being won, and could not be lost unless some untold development arose. So I walked over and undertook to quiet him. I sat down beside him and begged him to do nothing which would upset our carefully prepared program.

He was furious.

In undertones he insisted he would gain the floor regardless of the efforts to prevent him.

Joe Robinson was presiding, and at one time, as I recall it, Senator La Follette threatened to toss a spittoon to attract his attention.

Thus, the closing hours of the historic filibuster were consumed not by us, but by those who favored the legislation, although many times they offered to terminate the discussion if we would agree to a vote; as the floor leader, I always promptly rejected the offer. Since they would not permit us to talk, we reasoned we could make them talk; and while they made bitter speeches against us, denouncing the filibuster, we knew and they knew they were carrying out the program which we had mapped.

Those final minutes live in my memory.

The words which filled them were without meaning.

In that chamber, men became slaves to emotion. The clash of anger and bitterness, in my judgment, never has been exceeded in the history of the United States Senate. La Follette, his face contorted with anger, writhed in the humiliation of being unable to get the floor. He was on his feet one minute and then back in his seat. Not far away was Ollie James of Kentucky, a huge man of great physical strength. And hovering on the heels of James was Harry Lane of Oregon, small, frail, and even then in the early stages of a mortal illness, watchful of every move by the Kentuckian.

The hour hand dragged toward twelve, and when it pointed to the arrival of noon, the chair announced adjournment.

The filibuster had won.

The conference report, which would have authorized the arming of merchant ships, had failed of Senate approval. Those final minutes, in view of all that had passed before, were comparatively calm. Too much energy and emotion had been expended.

I have felt, from that day to this, the filibuster was justified.

I never have apologized for the part I took in it.

The object we sought to attain was accomplished. Those of us who had become associated together honestly believed that, by our action in that struggle, we had averted American participation in the war.

It was only a temporary postponement of the issue, and a brief one at that.

President Wilson, within a few minutes after adjournment, called an extra session of Congress.

This session came together in great excitement and with an intensified bitterness of feeling against the filibusterers. While it had been summoned to pass upon nominations made by Mr. Wilson, the development which excited the largest public interest was Senate adoption of a rule which, under certain circumstances, limited debate.

The rule provided that upon motion by sixteen senators to bring discussion to a close on any pending measure, the presiding officer should have it read at once, and one hour after the Senate met on the following calendar day a roll call should be ordered.

The exact form, provided in this departure from the long-standing tradition of the Senate, was:

"Is it the sense of the Senate that the debate shall be brought to a close?"

If two-thirds of the members present voted in the affirmative, then the measure was to become the unfinished business to the exclusion of all other business until disposed of. And thereafter, no senator would be entitled to speak more than one hour on the pending measure and amendments thereto and motions affecting the same. It became the duty of the presiding officer to keep the time of each senator. Except by unanimous consent, no amendment could be in order after the vote to bring the debate to a close unless it had been presented and read prior to that time. No dilatory motion, no dilatory amendment, and no amendment not germane could be in order. Points of order, including questions of relevancy and appeals of decisions of the presiding officer, had to be decided without debate.

This cloture amendment adopted to the rules at this special session was a landmark in the history of the United States Senate.

I favored it.

I believe I would go still further in limiting debate, especially after a question has been discussed for some time by the Senate.

The Senate would be justified during those closing hours of a session in invoking the cloture rule by majority instead of two-thirds vote.

But, looking back, I believe this amendment would not have been adopted by the Senate except for the tense excitement that prevailed throughout the entire country, and especially in the Senate itself.

Woodrow Wilson publicly denounced the twelve senators who led this filibuster, and carried it on.

Wave after wave of indignation swept the country in unanimous condemnation. My own people at home generally condemned me with bitterness for my part in it and asserted that I was misrepresenting my state in the United States Senate.

In order to meet my accusers, I rented by telegram the auditorium in Lincoln, the state capital. So that there could be no question, I sent a check in payment of the rent. Then I announced a meeting for Monday March 26, 1917, in the auditorium at which I would be present and speak, inviting attendance by anyone who desired to hear. I planned to reach Lincoln Sunday morning, the day before the meeting was to take place.

I did not deem it necessary to advertise the gathering.

I felt that the occasion was of such importance that people from all sections of the state would fill the auditorium. By correspondence I arranged for the seats and for the stage, and for tables for the newspaper correspondents.

I assumed that when I got to the hotel the press, especially Omaha and Lincoln newspapers, would have reporters interview me as to the nature of my address. I was disappointed in my reception.

In the assumption that my friends at least would greet me, and some of them might congratulate me, I was sadly disappointed. I stayed at the hotel all day, alone, and no newspaper representative called upon me or asked for an interview. The few friends who did call were careful to avoid being seen with me.

It was not until daylight had waned and darkness set in that a newspaperman sought me out.

I was not personally acquainted with this young man, but he afterwards gained considerable national prominence. He was Frederick Babcock, a representative of the *Nebraska State Journal*, and he wanted to talk to me about the speech I was going to deliver.

I was suspicious at first and said:

"I will give you an interview if I can be sure you will print it as I give it."

This assurance was forthcoming; but I called attention to the fact that the editor of the *Journal* was bitter against me, and expressed the opinion that even if Mr. Babcock wrote the interview fairly it would be edited by those above him until it could not be recognized. He then told me that the editor would not be back in the office before the paper was printed, and that there was no one in the office with authority to change anything he wrote.

Under those circumstances I gave him the interview.

I told him that I would be chairman of the meeting but not that I had tried without avail to get someone to serve in that capacity. I told him that I had rented the hall and had paid for it; that I expected to tell the truth about the conditions in Washington, which the newspapers of Nebraska had not told. Then he asked for a copy of my manuscript, and I had to admit that I did not have a manuscript and would speak extemporaneously; that I did not have even penciled notes. I indicated the manager of the auditorium had been instructed to seat members of the legislature, if any of them desired, upon the stage, the legislature then being in session.

This interview appeared just as I gave it.

The auditorium was less than a block from the hotel where I was staying, and long before the hour announced it was filled to overflowing. Under the city ordinances it was a violation to fill the aisles with chairs or with standing listeners. But Mayor Charles W. Bryan, informed that hundreds of people were standing outside trying to get in, ordered the police to fill the aisles with chairs and seat as many as possible.

Not until the hour for speaking did I go to the auditorium. I went in by the rear entrance, and walked out on the stage to find the building literally packed with people, many of whom had traveled long distances. I had expected an unfriendly audience, and it was with some fear that I stepped forward.

I had tried to get Mr. R. Beecher Howell of Omaha, who was then Republican national committeeman, to act as chairman. He had come from Omaha on Sunday to see me, remained only a few minutes, and indicated it would be impossible for him to attend the meeting. Without any publicity, he returned to his home. I asked some other friends who they thought would be willing to act as chairman, but no one considered would accept. Mr. Howell, who afterwards became my colleague in the Senate, and whom I knew as my sincere friend, told me that he had come from Omaha to ask me not to make this speech.

"I do not believe it possible for this meeting to be held without trouble," Howell said. "I think your meeting will be broken up, or at least you will have such an unfriendly audience that it will be impossible for you to make any coherent speech."

I told him that, no matter what happened, I was going to carry out my part of the program, and that I would try to meet any contingency that arose.

Among other callers had been Mr. C. A. Epperson, then serving as chairman of the Progressive party in Nebraska; and he in effect told me the same thing Mr. Howell did. He said, all told, I had made a very sad mistake in returning to Nebraska; that he was fearful the meeting would break up in a row, and that he had been informed a large number of people were to be scattered through the audience to make it impossible for me to speak.

"You can easily arrange to get sick," he told me, "and leave on the afternoon train for your home in McCook. You can get a doctor's statement that you are physically unable to appear."

When I entered the rear of the auditorium and stepped out on the stage, there was a deathlike silence.

There was not a single handclap.

I had not expected applause; I was delighted that I was not hissed.

My friends had led me to believe that the people of Nebraska were almost unanimously against me. But the stage was crowded, and there was just enough room left for me to walk in near the footlights.

I remember I said first of all that I had come from Washington to my home state to tell its people the truth about what had happened, and that up to this time the newspapers had not told the truth.

Immediately there was a burst of applause from all parts of the audience.

Never in my lifetime has applause done me the good that did. It convinced me that I had friends enough in the audience to protect me; that the reports of everybody being against me were erroneous.

As I proceeded it appeared that the audience was sympathetic and generous, and with me heart and soul. Even while I was speaking, I looked over the sea of faces and came to the conclusion it was a fair criterion of the sentiment existing in Nebraska.

If my enemies had distributed hecklers in sections of the hall, these were overcome by the outburst of applause and made no attempts to interfere with me. I never received a heartier greeting in my life than the one that marked the termination of my address on that March night.

The Lincoln meeting was followed by several others that I was invited to address, and I became convinced that sentiment in Nebraska probably was in favor of the position I had taken.

I determined to test the charge that I was misrepresenting Nebraska.

To Governor Keith Neville I sent a letter proposing, as the legislature was in session and was of his political faith, that he recommend to the legislature, if he so wished, the passage of a resolution calling for a recall election in Nebraska. Saying that I realized there was no constitutional way to enforce a recall, I added that, if the legislature would pass the proper resolution for a recall election, and give at least thirty days' advance notice of date, I would abide by the result: if the election went against me, I would tender my resignation.

I also wrote a letter to John L. Kennedy of Omaha, then serving as chairman of the Republican state committee, in which I said that, if he would call a primary election of Republicans, I would abide by the result of the primary: if the vote went against me, I would resign.

Both offers were declined, and no further steps were taken in regard to a recall.

In Washington before the letters were mailed, there was a meeting in my office attended by those who had joined in the filibuster and a few others. In some way word had leaked out that I had written the letters, had rented a hall, and was going back to Nebraska to defend myself.

Senator Bob La Follette pleaded with me not to take this step. He said the people were in a state of excitement, and if the election were called by the governor I should be defeated.

All of these associates were against the action I had decided upon. When it became known that I was determined to see it through, every one of them volunteered to contribute money, and practically every one of them said he would go to Nebraska to campaign the state against recall.

Until those meetings in Nebraska I was uncertain of the outcome of a recall election. Even the encouragement they provided did not make the result sure. But I felt that I did not want to represent the people of Nebraska if they did not want me.

20

DECLARATION OF WAR

THAT TRIP TO NEBRASKA made little difference in the abusive letters which filled my mail.

Many were from my own people; many more came from correspondents living in other states. I made no effort to answer them individually: it would have been a physical impossibility. I cared little for the criticisms they contained, but was concerned that the members of my family should be so depressed by them.

Naturally, I resented deeply Woodrow Wilson's denunciation of the "little group of willful men" for defeat of his proposal to arm merchant ships. I knew the President was determined to preserve the doctrine of freedom of the seas with every resource at his command.

Within less than forty-eight hours of the termination of the successful filibuster, Mr. Wilson announced publicly that further examination of the laws defining executive power gave him the right to arm ships without any action by Congress.

He proceeded to take this step immediately.

By this action of executive authority, a successful filibuster was transformed into a losing fight. Sympathy throughout the country was with the President, and I think his action was approved by majority American sentiment under the feeling that existed then.

His triumph through executive action was his own undoing in the ultimate settlement of the issue of arming American merchant ships.

Within a few short weeks, the steps Mr. Wilson took established clear proof of the soundness of those fears which had been expressed so freely by that little group of senators. The logic and truth of the position they took were confirmed by swift development. The verdict was written in slightly more than a month when the American people found themselves confronted with a declaration of war.

Rarely has it happened that vindication of a specific legislative position came so speedily.

There was a new, an expectant quality in the atmosphere of Pennsylvania Avenue on the morning of April 2, 1917, when the Senate and the House, convening in a special session at the President's call, assembled jointly to receive a message from Woodrow Wilson. It was reflected in the faces and the talk of the people on the streets. Congress itself seemed to sense that the hour of decision had arrived.

In that message Mr. Wilson said:

"When I addressed the Congress on the 26th of February last, I thought it would suffice to assert our neutral right with arms, our right to use the seas against unlawful interference, our right to keep our people safe against unlawful violence. But armed neutrality, it now appears, is impracticable. Because submarines are in effect outlaws, and used as the German submarines have been used against merchant shipping, it is impossible to defend ships against their attacks, as the law of nations has assumed that merchantmen would defend themselves against privateers, cruisers, or visible craft giving chase upon the open sea. It is common prudence in such circumstances, grim necessity, indeed, to endeavor to destroy them before they have shown their own intention. They must be dealt with upon sight if dealt with at all.

"The German government denies the rights of neutrals to use arms at all within the areas of the sea which it has prescribed, even in the defense of rights which no modern government has ever before questioned the right to defend. The intimation is conveyed that the armed guards, which we have placed on our merchant ships, will be treated as beyond the pale of law and as such be dealt with as pirates would be. Armed neutrality is ineffectual enough at best; in such circumstances and in the face of such pretensions it is worse than ineffectual; it is likely only to produce what it was meant to prevent; it is practically certain to draw us into the war without either the rights or the effectiveness of belligerents."

A careful reexamination of those words in conjunction with the arguments that took place during the filibuster will reveal that in practical results Mr. Wilson had reached the conclusion determined upon by those of us who had filibustered the armed-ship proposal to death.

There could be no satisfaction for anyone in it.

Among that little group I felt then, and still think, that vindication was of slight consequence. All that mattered to me in those difficult hours was the hope and the desire of avoiding American participation in the struggle in progress in Europe. The fact that the President himself was now telling the nation armed neutrality was ineffectual, and likely only to produce what it was meant to prevent, brought scant comfort.

On that April morning, a gravity characterized Congress that had not been matched previously. Men sat silently weighing Mr. Wilson's words with great deliberation.

All of the glory of spring along the Potomac could not blot out the knowledge that war was very near to the United States.

* * *

I have been asked why I voted against war in 1917, and supported the declaration of war in December of 1941.

The circumstances were most dissimilar.

In 1917 there was no immediate threat of war reaching American soil. In 1941 an act of war was committed by Japan against the United States at Pearl Harbor under the most treacherous and despicable circumstances, and the following day Germany and Italy issued declarations of war against the American people.

In the present struggle, the Axis plan of aggression and conquest in my eyes constituted a direct threat to the safety and security of the United States.

* * *

Of course, I was opposed to the declaration of war in 1917, and I did everything I could to prevent it, knowing full well the resolution would pass virtually by unanimous vote. I knew men who dreaded war were going to vote for the resolution: they had told me privately that, while they were going to support the declaration, they would like to vote against it. I never have violated the confidence of those men.

The time for the final act was approaching.

Congress had before it a resolution embodying a declaration of war, and a vote upon it was not to be unnecessarily delayed by discussion. Curious impressions crowded themselves in. Out of the gathering shadows of Pennsylvania Avenue the street lights appeared. Outside, the air had that softness of an April night, with the sweet breath of spring in the breeze which blew in from the Potomac.

The war resolution came before Congress on April 2. On objection by Senator La Follette, it was laid over a day in the Senate under the rules, and taken up on April 4. It was approved by both houses on April 6. I recall the day I spoke.

The skies partially were overcast.

Inside the Senate chamber, that element of explosiveness which had been so near to the surface during the filibuster against the arming of merchant ships reappeared. To some of us, it seemed that only the striking of a match was needed to start a conflagration.

Long before, the outcome of the debate had been foretold. Before I spoke those words which aroused so much criticism, I knew discussion was useless; and yet I was powerless to follow any other course than the one I adopted.

There on the floor of the Senate it seemed to me, as I tried to say reason had fled and high excitement was going to stampede Congress, a gleam of hostility flashed back to me from the eyes of those with whom I had been associated. I could see in front of me the friendships of years dissolving into misunderstanding. I was sure that hatred would develop against those who by their vote opposed the resolution. I knew that what I intended to say would be condemned in the most severe terms. And in those closing hours

I knew I had become an outcast from a circle of men whom I loved, and in whose honesty of purpose and patriotism I had unlimited confidence. I was depressed only because it seemed to me that my colleagues were not giving me credit for being either honest or patriotic.

Certain as I was of the consequence, a calmness and serenity filled me in heart and soul, for I felt I was right. As I now look back over the years, while writing this, I still feel that I was right; right or wrong, I adhered to the only course which satisfied my own conscience.

I remember my opening words as I stood there on that night of April 4, facing my colleagues, who for the most part were grim and tense under the crucial decision that was to be reached, with galleries packed and equally taut:

"While I am most emphatically and sincerely opposed to taking any steps towards engaging in the war waged in Europe," I said, "yet if this resolution passes, I shall not permit my feeling of opposition to its passage to interfere in any way with my duty as a senator or as a citizen in bringing success and victory to the American armies. I am bitterly opposed to my country entering war, but if notwithstanding my opposition we do enter it, all of my energy and all of my power will be behind our flag to carry it on to victory."

* * *

In the months of conflict which followed, those opening words became my rule of life. I adhered to their spirit in every particular. Every measure of war which came before Congress for approval received my vote.

Every step essential to the progress of American armies had my support regardless of any misgivings or doubts of its wisdom. In matters of military appropriations and in all other proposals relating to the conduct of the war, I felt that, the decision having been made, unity of action and wholehearted efforts by Congress to aid constituted the only logical position a member could take.

* * *

I remember saying that the resolution before the Senate was a declaration of war and that, before taking this step, we ought to pause and consider judiciously the terrible consequences of the step we were about to take.

"We ought to consider likewise the route we have traveled recently and ascertain whether we have reached our present position in a way that is comportable with the neutral position we claimed to occupy at the beginning and throughout the various stages of this unholy and unrighteous war. No close student of recent history will deny that both Great Britain and Germany have on numerous occasions since the beginning of war flagrantly violated in the most serious manner the rights of neutral vessels and neutral nations under existing international law as recognized by the civilized world, up to the beginning of this war.

". . . Let us trace briefly the origin and history of these so-called war zones. The first war zone was declared by Great Britain. She gave us and the world notice of it on the fourth day of November, 1914, and it became effective the day after notice was given. This zone . . . covered the whole of the North Sea. . . . It sought to close the north of Scotland route around the British Isles, Denmark, Holland, Norway, Sweden, and the Baltic. The decree of establishment . . . warned neutral shipping that it would cross those lines at its peril.

"The first German war zone was declared on the fourth day of February, 1915, just three months after the British war zone was declared. Germany gave fifteen days' notice of the establishment of her zone . . . which covered the English Channel and the high sea waters around the British Isles. . . . The German war zone declared that neutral vessels would be exposed to danger in the English Channel route but that the route around the north of Scotland and in the eastern part of the North Sea in a strip thirty miles wide along the Dutch coast would be free from danger. It thus will be seen that the British government declared the north of Scotland route into the Baltic Sea as dangerous. . . .

"The German government in its order did exactly the reverse."

In great detail I told of the consequences of the establishment of those war zones. I said:

"There had been more ships sunk and more American lives lost from the action of submarines than from English mines in the North Sea for the simple reason that we finally acquiesced in the British zone and kept our ships out of it while in the German war zone we have refused to recognize its legality and have not kept either our ships or our citizens out of its area."

I could detect a growing restlessness on the part of my colleagues.

"It is unnecessary to cite authority to show that both of these orders declaring military zones are illegal and contrary to international law," I said. "It is sufficient to see that our government officially has declared both of them to be illegal and officially has protested against both of them. The only difference is that in the case of Germany we have persisted in our protest, while in the case of England we have submitted.

"What was our duty as a government and what were our rights when we were confronted with these extraordinary orders declaring these military zones?

"First, we could have defied both of them and could have gone to war against both of these nations for this violation of international law and interference with our neutral rights.

"Second, we had the technical right to defy one and to acquiesce in the other.

"Third, we could, while denouncing them both as illegal, have acquiesced in them both and thus remained neutral with both sides, although not agreeing with either as to the righteousness as to their respective orders. We could have said to American shipowners that while these orders are both contrary to international law and are both unjust, we do not believe that the provocation is sufficient to cause us to go to war in a defense of our rights as a neutral nation, and therefore American ships and the American citizens will go into these zones at their own peril and risk.

"Fourth, we might have declared an embargo against the shipping from American ports of any merchandise to either one of these governments that persisted in maintaining its military zone. . . . In my judgment if we had pursued this course, the zones would have been of a short duration. . . .

"There are a great many American citizens who feel that we owe it as a duty to humanity to take part in this war. Many instances of cruelty and inhumanity can be found on both sides. Men are often biased in their judgment on account of their sympathy and their interest. To my mind, what we ought to have maintained from the beginning was the strictest neutrality. If we had done this, I do not believe we would have been on the verge of war at the present time."

Up to that point, while I knew of the impatience for a vote, I saw no signs of the anger that followed my next statement.

"We have loaned many hundreds of millions of dollars to the Allies in this controversy," I said. "While such action was legal and countenanced by international law, there is no doubt in my mind but the enormous amount of money loaned to the Allies in this war has been instrumental in bringing out a public sentiment in favor of our country taking a course that would make every bond worth a hundred cents on the dollar and make a payment of every debt certain and sure. Through this instrumentality and all through the instrumentality of others who have not only made millions out of the war in the manufacture of munitions, and who would expect to make millions more if our country can be drawn into this catastrophe, a large number of great newspapers and news agencies of the country are controlled and enlisted in the greatest propaganda that the world has ever known to manufacture sentiment in favor of war. It is now demanded that the American citizens shall be used as insurance policies to guarantee the safe delivery of munitions of war to belligerent nations. The enormous profits of munitions manufacturers, stock brokers, and bond dealers must be still further increased by our entrance into the war."

I then read an extract from a letter written by a member of the New York Stock Exchange to his customer expressing clearly what he called the Wall Street view. I said the war brought no prosperity to the great mass of common patriotic citizens; that it increased the cost of living of those who toiled and those who already must strain every effort to keep soul and body together. After elaborating upon this, I then said:

"We are taking a step today that is fraught with untold danger. We are going into war upon the command of gold. We are going to run the risk of sacrificing millions of our countrymen's lives in order that other countrymen may coin their lifeblood into money. And even if we do not cross the Atlantic and go into the trenches, we are going to pile up a debt that the toiling masses many generations after us will have to pay. Unborn millions will bend their backs in toil in order to pay for the terrible step we are about to take. We are about to do the bidding of wealth's terrible mandate. By our action we will make millions of our countrymen suffer, and the consequences of it may well be that millions of our brethren must shed their lifeblood, millions of broken-hearted women must weep, millions of children must suffer with cold and millions of babes must die from hunger, and all because we want to preserve the commercial right of American citizens to deliver munitions of war to belligerent nations."

* * *

It was more than twenty-seven years ago that those words were spoken. Throughout all of the months preceding the declaration of war, I could look in no direction without seeing American policy crystallized into a determination to assert and maintain the doctrine of the freedom of the seas even at the price of war.

I had little patience with the stock expression of those days: "Too proud to fight."

The new prosperity which had come to America apparently created a fever for profits. No single group and no single industry could be charged with being wholly guilty or wholly innocent. It was a condition of the times. The foundation upon which the doctrine of freedom of the seas rested was the principle that the oceans should be open to commerce.

The reflections of all of these years have led me to believe that the developments to which I refer were widespread in their effect upon American thought and not restricted to any single individual or group.

* * *

The mounting temper of my colleagues in the Senate and the reaction that came from the crowd in the galleries warned me that I had ventured very near to the border of public resentment and indignation. But I was powerless, had I desired, to stop the flow of words coming from my heart.

"I know that I am powerless to stop it. . . . I feel that we are committing a sin against humanity and against our countrymen. I would like to say to this war god: 'You shall not coin into gold the lifeblood of my brethren!' . . . I feel we are about to put the dollar sign upon the American flag.

"I have no sympathy with the military spirit which dominates the Kaiser and his advisers. I do not believe that they represent the heart of the great German people. I have no more sympathy with the submarine policy of Germany than I have with the mine-laying policy of England. . . . I hope and pray that a revolution may take place in Germany, that the Kaiser may be overthrown, that on the ruins of his military despotism may be established a German republic where the German people may work out their world destiny. . . . The troubles of Europe ought to be settled by Europe; and wherever our sympathies may lie, disagreeing as we do, we ought to remain absolutely neutral and permit them to settle their questions without our interference. . . . Upon the passage of this resolution we will have joined Europe in the great catastrophe and taken America into entanglements that will not end with this war but will live and bring their evil influence upon many generations yet unborn."

I had no intention of attempting prophecy.

There could be but one result of entering the war, I felt.

Nor did I feel any particular resentment against the embittered replies by Senator James Reed, Senator John Sharp Williams, and others. I knew they felt just as strongly as I did. I recognized that in all that was said the effort was to force me to retract portions of the statements I had made, and this I had no intention of doing. Once or twice when direct observations seemed to call for something, I answered with as much calmness and freedom from feeling as I could.

The vote was taken.

There were only six of us in opposition: Gronna, Lane, Stone, La Follette, Norris, Vardaman.

Not one is alive today except me.

I know they suffered exactly as I suffered that night and in the weeks that followed.

From private conversations with members of both houses, I also know there were a few at least who voted for the war resolution feeling their votes to be wrong. Privately, I was congratulated for the course which I had taken by several senators and by several members of the House of Representatives, who stood recorded in favor of the resolution. They told me they believed I had been right and eventually would be justified by the historian.

The letter which I read from the New York stock broker had been given to me by Senator William S. Kenyon of Iowa, who assured me he believed I was taking the right course but felt unable to follow his own convictions because of the unanimity of war sentiment in his state.

In this connection, the war resolution, perhaps, more than any other issue upon which I voted during all the years in Congress, raised the issue of what should be the attitude of a member of Congress. Should he always follow what he believed to be the majority sentiment of his district, or should he obey his own conscience even when, in doing so, it appeared he was voting against the wishes of a majority of his constituents?

I have thought conscience was the guide.

Otherwise, a member of Congress giving weight to expressed public sentiment becomes only an automatic machine. If that is the line of duty of a member, then Congress requires no patriotism, no education, and no courage. All a member has to do, if he does follow that which he believes to be the will of his constituency at all times, is to attempt to take such action as will bring him the most votes in the next election.

In the end, the only worth-while pay in congressional service is that which comes from a satisfied conscience in the knowledge that you have done your duty as God gives you light, regardless of the effect it may have upon political fortunes.

I have no love for Germany.

That conflict in 1917 appeared to me to embody a clash of European imperialisms—the imperialism of Britain and her allies on one side, and the imperialism of the Central Powers on the other.

There was much in British life that aroused my admiration, and much in Germany that commanded my respect. In those years in Germany there was an opportunity of expression by the minority. I saw and sympathized with the criticism voiced by the German Social Democrats against the German militarists and the Kaiser.

I never have claimed any prescience in my anticipation of the war that followed. Hoping and praying that I should be proved wrong, I felt that the succeeding years fully justified the fears I then expressed.

The mounting power of American armies and American production made itself felt. German military power reached its height and ebbed.

In those months of war, I was concerned also with what seemed to me to be growing infringement of civil liberties, honestly proposed but nevertheless unfortunate and regrettable.

In my official life, I found myself spied upon.

I discovered efforts to obtain entrance to my files.

I was enraged when members of my family were harassed.

I recall that so-called investigators came to my home at Ross Place in Cleveland Park, when they knew I was absent, and made inquiries of my wife, sometimes of an almost insulting nature. Of course my life was made unhappy, and the nervous tension was almost beyond my control. I knew that efforts were made constantly through inquiry into my private life to classify me as "pro-German."

I knew I was innocent.

I did not believe all of the "war stories" circulating at that time. I thought my own government was guilty of dereliction in its failure to set at rest some of the falsehoods regarding conditions in the United States.

As a member of the Agriculture Committee, I received reports that broken glass had been mixed with food products and shipped all over the country. I was well acquainted with a chemist, Dr. Johns, in the Bureau of Chemistry of the Department of Agriculture. He lived not far from my Washington home. I had many conferences with him, great confidence in him, and I took up with him not only the one report that I have mentioned, but many others. His bureau investigated it but never found any basis for the stories.

There was that circulating tale of the American soldier taken prisoner, whose tongue was cut out, after which he was released and allowed to return to the American army. It was said that he had been confined in the hospital abroad for some time, brought home from across the Atlantic, and taken to the Walter Reed Hospital in Washington for treatment. I did not believe it a physical possibility, and I felt that these stories exciting our people were doing an injury to our cause. I determined to run it down with meticulous care, and wrote to the Surgeon General of the Army, detailing the reported circumstances and requesting him to tell me the facts. He answered promptly that the story was without foundation: no patient of this character was in Walter Reed Hospital and, as far as he knew, no such incident had taken place. I reported back to the man who had told me the atrocity story the letter I had received from the Surgeon General. He became angry and told me the Surgeon General knew nothing about it: only the superintendent of the hospital was informed. So I wrote to the superintendent of the Walter Reed Hospital, and promptly received a denial just as emphatic.

When I told the incident in the Senate cloakroom, to my surprise not a single senator present doubted the truth of the original story. We had quite an angry discussion. While it was in progress,

Dr. France, a senator from Maryland, came in; and I proposed this tale should be submitted to him. He enjoyed a high reputation as a physician, and we all had confidence in his integrity. After the circumstances had been outlined, he said without hesitation that it was impossible for a man to live with his tongue cut out at the root.

It did not convince my colleagues who were present. I was virtually without a friend in the cloakroom.

Because I thought these reports were doing harm, and because I was persistent in attacking them when perhaps I ought to have kept still, I made many enemies in those months, and I made life very disagreeable for myself.

Two men whom I had never seen and could not identify called at my home, summoned Mrs. Norris to the door, inquired for me, and when they found I was at my office, requested an interview with her. From previous unhappy experiences, she refused it and would not invite them inside.

"Well, Mrs. Norris, I want to ask you a question," one of them said. "It may seem like a personal one, but I assure you I mean no discourtesy. Is it true that Mr. Norris is of German descent?"

Mrs. Norris said:

"Yes, it is true. His stepfather was a Pennsylvania Dutchman."

The men smiled, tipped their hats, and departed.

That was the blackness and irony of those months.

In the fall of 1918, the German armies were in retreat. Yet no one anticipated that victory was so close at hand.

21

DEFEAT OF THE LEAGUE

My term in the Senate expired in 1918.

Deeply distressed by war critics, I thought seriously of quitting public life and even wrote to Norris Huse in New York City, the son of a pioneer Nebraska newspaperman, who was in charge of the Associated Press feature service, inquiring about the possibility of establishing a law practice in the nation's largest community. I had no well defined plan of seeking reelection until shortly ahead of the primary.

Both the primary campaign and the general election took the expected lines. My course in the filibuster and my vote on the war declaration were the chief targets for attack. The fact that I had given constant support to all steps in the war was ignored. I won an easy primary victory; and in the general election, held just six days before the armistice, I defeated Governor John H. Morehead, the Democratic nominee, and a very popular and able man, by a vote of 120,086 to 99,690. Mr. Morehead always had commanded substantial Republican support, and under the circumstances the result had promised to be much closer.

Then swiftly and incredibly the news of the Armistice turned loose a tumult of joyous rejoicing.

My spirits rose at the thought mass slaughter was over. I could see in the weeks and months ahead the legions of young Americans returning to their firesides.

The happiness of those weeks was short-lived.

There had been so little discussion and thought on the problems of peace. In the British Isles, Lloyd George had concluded a successful campaign on the principle of an eye for an eye and a tooth for a tooth. I could not ignore the unmistakable implications that the passions of the battlefield were to be carried to the peace table. Clemenceau, who so admirably incarnated the spirit of French resistance, likewise gave warning of the bitterness to reveal itself at Versailles.

Fully five years before the outbreak of the First World War and a decade in advance of the fight in the United States Senate over confirmation of the Versailles settlements, I had advocated a league of nations to prevent war and to insure permanent peace.

I had visited Brussels, and cities of France and Germany. It was in Brussels I had kindled with the hope nations and peoples would resort to orderly processes in the settlement of disputes. While still a member of the Lower House, I spoke of the desirability of a league to preserve peace during a chautauqua tour; but my audiences, with the deep sense of security of the American interior, were infinitely more interested in the fight to overthrow Joe Cannon than in any expression of my conceptions of a peaceful world.

I listened to the informal discussions in the Senate cloakroom and among small groups of the members in the months following the Armistice while the peace was being molded. These did not include Henry Cabot Lodge, under whose leadership the fight against the League was organized. I did not belong to his "lodge," and received no invitation to his home for the quiet Sabbath meeting in March, 1919, at which plans were discussed for this fight. I was not invited to join in the Round Robin setting forth American reservations which Senator Lodge and some of his close associates prepared and circulated, thus securing thirty-nine signers.

I was still very much under the displeasure of the Lodge group for my earlier vote on the war resolution, and my party irregularity.

While I could subscribe to some of the objections outlined in the reservations, and supported them with my vote, I had misgivings about the course which this opposition to the League was adopting. Discussion was wholesome and was of the greatest importance; the facts should be placed before the American people fully; but any agreement among nations to preserve peace necessarily imposed sacrifices upon each individual nation. If there was to be any agreement, no nation and no people could expect to have its own way entirely.

The possibility that American membership in the League might endanger the Monroe Doctrine did not frighten me. I told some of my colleagues that the proposed reservation protecting the Monroe Doctrine was not vital, because the right kind of league would make the Monroe Doctrine obsolete and unnecessary. If the League proved to be successful and received the genuine and honest support of all nations, the conditions that had inspired the Monroe Doctrine would not appear. Therefore, to incorporate the Doctrine in a reservation to American approval of the League appeared to me to be of no consequence even if it was not in direct contradiction of the purposes for which the League was to be established.

Long before the Covenant and the Treaty of Versailles reached the Senate, I endeavored to make my position clear in a letter to Walter Locke, a newspaper friend, then editing the *Nebraska State Journal,* but now editorial director of the Dayton *Daily News.*

On March 18, 1918, I wrote him:

During practically all of my public life, I have been a sincere advocate of an agreement between the leading nations of the world to set up all the necessary international machinery that would bring about a practical abolition of war between civilized nations. I advocated it long before the great world war commenced, and to keep the American government in a position to lead in such a movement, I used it as one of the arguments against our entering into the war. I thought we should be better able to lead if we stayed out. I may have been mistaken in this because subsequent events have determined that we are now in such a position that if we unite upon a fair and honorable plan, the entire civilized world will be disposed to follow. I realize that no such thing can be brought about unless every man and every nation approaches the subject with a willingness to compromise, with a willingness even to sacrifice some of his own cherished opinions, in order to bring the nations together. Nothing has ever happened in my life in which I felt a deeper interest or for which I would make a greater sacrifice. I am willing that somebody else shall get all the honor and all the praise if this cherished thing can be realized.

I think that is clear.

It not only embodied the requirements for the peace then, but suggests the difficulties that will follow the present conflict.

In that letter, I set forth that free debate and full discussion ought to be had. Secret diplomacy, secret agreements, and secret treaties should be abolished, and this doctrine should be practiced in trying to reach an agreement on peace.

Criticism, however, I said, ought to be constructive, genuine, and honest, and no man should criticize just for the sake of finding fault. No man should criticize except on the best of evidence.

The proposed constitution, I said, had provisions that were dangerous:

> I think we ought to take the world as it is and not as we would like to have it. It seems, therefore, inadvisable to me to enter into any agreement that would make it necessary for us or, for that matter, for any other nation to maintain standing armies for the support of new and independent governments that it is intended to establish among semi-civilized people. Such a course not only is dangerous and will in my judgment bring failure to that part of the enterprise, but it is in no sense necessary to maintain the peace of the world. The right kind of a league between nations that can be numbered on the fingers of one hand will insure a permanent peace.

I pointed out it would take centuries to develop some of the peoples of the earth, and we should not attempt at the cannon's mouth to impose our civilization upon any other people. Before permanent, stable, civilized governments could be established in many quarters of the globe, there would be strife, revolution, and bloodshed among such people.

This I could see no way of avoiding.

Russia was then in the throes of a revolution; and, to prevent this from running its course, maintenance there of a large army beyond the lives of those who were living would be necessary. Any effort we might make to impose a government under which another people was to live, was doomed to failure, and would compel the American people to support it with a standing army.

Our activities would not be confined to Europe and Asia [I wrote], but we would have on that theory ample reasons to go into Mexico and other countries located in the western hemisphere. There is not much danger of the smaller nations if the big nations will behave. . . .

We ought to disarm Germany completely. We ought to disarm Turkey completely. We ought to disarm Austria. We ought to destroy every fort along every international boundary line in Europe. This would be an easy thing to do if we and our allies would announce that it must be done. And when it is done, we ought to follow the example by disarming ourselves. No nation ought to keep a navy larger than is necessary to do police duty. If the world is disarmed, and remains disarmed, there will be no more world wars. If these leading nations would agree, in addition to this, that an international court of arbitration should be set up, that no nation should engage in conquest, that no secret treaty would be entered into or recognized, the danger of war would be as completely averted as it is possible for human beings to avert it. The constitution ought to specifically state that every nation is left entirely independent and supreme in its internal affairs, such as regulating emigration and all other similar matters.

President Wilson, I stated, had made his greatest mistake in not taking the Congress and the American people completely into his confidence (here voicing that criticism before Senate debate began). I expressed the feeling that full discussion and consideration would have crystallized a constitution for a league of nations that the European countries would have accepted in all of its essential provisions.

I said it looked as though the President had attempted to place the Senate in a position where it could do nothing except approve of a treaty he had made.

As a matter of policy, a wise man ought to see that such a course would have a tendency to cause the Senate to look upon his work with a suspicious eye. Without questioning his wisdom, or his leadership, or his sincerity, it seems to me he ought to have taken not only the Senate, but the House of Representatives and the entire country completely in his confidence.

SENATOR NORRIS AS CHAIRMAN OF THE SENATE JUDICIARY COMMITTEE CONSIDERING THE LEGISLATION ULTIMATELY APPROVED AS THE ANTI-INJUNCTION LAW, GENERALLY ACCEPTED BY ORGANIZED LABOR AS ITS MAGNA CHARTA.

I wrote rather sharply about the duly constituted American Peace Commission:

He [Wilson] went to Europe in a splendor and a gorgeousness never equaled in the history of the world. While his fellow citizens were sacrificing in every possible way, he used the money that came from millions of honest toilers in a display of wealth and pomp never equaled by any king, monarch, or a potentate. . . . It seems to me that, if he decided he should go in person to Europe, he ought to have given to the suffering beaten world an illustration of democracy's simplicity. I do not offer this as a reason for rejecting any proposition that he might propose; but the setting that he himself gave to the situation could have no tendency except to bring distrust and suspicion from those who were sacrificing to obtain the money that he was so lavishly spending. I am not one of the members of the Senate who have publicly on the floor of the Senate or elsewhere offered criticism. I have been so deeply in earnest that some agreements for permanent peace might come that I had some doubt as to the wisdom of public criticism . . .

There was another situation that distressed me:

It seems to me it is a sad commentary that the heads of practically all departments are now in Europe. The President himself is there, the Secretary of State is there, the morning papers announce that the Secretary of War and the Secretary of the Navy are to start; and yet, there is almost complete demoralization in every department of government here. Secretary Daniels is to go to France, to England, and to Italy. There are thousands of lesser lights who are now there and have been there, and more to follow . . . and the poor taxpayer, overburdened with toil and sacrifice, is beginning to realize that all of this wild and mad extravagance must be paid. . . . There is wide dissatisfaction all over the country. I think it comes from thousands of causes. I have mentioned only one. . . . All this has a tendency to put everybody on edge, and I fear the people are not in a state of mind where they can judiciously and logically pass on the various questions of government.

Late in June the Versailles Conference concluded its labors, and the treaty and the covenant were transmitted to the Senate Committee on Foreign Relations.

Its hearings were extensive.

And then debate opened and continued for weeks on the Senate floor. Mr. Wilson carried his fight to the country.

In all that debate, I devoted very little attention to the discussion of reservations. My concern was based upon what to me was much more substantial ground. I said little about Germany and the likelihood of its becoming another storm center in a world war. I centered my attention upon the secret treaties that I felt jeopardized the peace of the world gravely; and particularly I discussed at great length the partition of China to give Japan a slice of territory and the assignment to Japan of mandates over island groups in the Southwest Pacific. The bargaining that was plainly revealed in treaties between Britain, France, and Japan, over the distribution of German territory in the Far East had my particular contempt. It was the bribe to bring Japan into the war on the Allied side.

I could not believe Japan was any purer than militaristic Germany.

"No agreement," I said in the debate, in early October of 1919, "on any great question in the history of the world ever has been reached except on the basis of sacrifice and compromise. We could not expect to have our way in all things. We could only adopt a program of conciliation."

That rested upon mutual trust and faith.

I never trusted Japan.

My record of forty years in the House of Representatives and the Senate of the United States is free from the taint of racial prejudice; but I never knew whether the smile and the cultivated courtesy that covered the face and the bearing of the Japanese expressed friendliness or were only a mask.

These fears which I had of the Japanese government and of Japanese militarists developed from long study and observation. They grew as I watched Japan for years, and watched always with growing distrust, confirmed by the act of treachery at Pearl Harbor on December 7, 1941.

During my years in the House an American naval hero, Richmond Hobson, who became a member of Congress, was the foremost advocate of a powerful American navy. I was opposed to Hobson's plan of a great navy, but I listened intently to his arguments.

The Japanese government, in the Versailles Treaty, it is true, was on our side. Japan was one of the victorious nations.

Yet always, it seemed to me, every profession of faith and every action Japan took was taken with crossed fingers.

Japan had participated actively in the war only so long as was necessary to gain control and possession of the German possessions in the Pacific Ocean. There was no doubt in my mind but, if the war had continued for some time, she would have been on the other side of the conflict. Japan had made no sacrifices of consequence in the war; it appeared to me that she was only preparing for another war to follow, gathering unto herself all of the islands and all of the possible fortifications in the Pacific. When she had gained them she ceased her efforts.

And Japan was a part of the League of Nations.

Her heart was impure.

I felt that she had none of the genuine, humane intentions of a peaceful nation, and in her attitude toward China she was thinking only of Japan, and Japan alone, and of the day when she would establish her supremacy in the Orient.

There was that wicked, vicious provision under which Japan, through secret understandings with the Allies, had acquired the rights Germany formerly held in Shantung province of China.

It was compounding and perpetuating a crime against the Chinese people.

I attacked that transfer of Shantung to Japan. Nothing could have given greater sanction, in the new peaceful order to be established, to recognition of the practices of secret diplomacy; and nothing could have constituted a more direct repudiation of Mr. Wilson's principle of the rights of self-determination for peoples—a principle gladly and fully accepted in heart and conscience by the American people.

Here were thirty million people of Chinese blood to be placed under brutal Japanese rule. I knew of Japan's treatment of Korea, and of the massacre of hundreds of thousands of innocent Koreans in tyrannical rule. Here was the dynamite for revolt and war, if the long tradition of Chinese survival and ultimate triumph meant anything. Here was mockery of the high and noble purposes for which a league of nations was to be established. Here was repudiation of the decent objectives that had been set forth in the name of America throughout the progress of the war. Those boys who fell in battle had pressed forward with zeal for a peaceful world lighting their eyes.

These are not reflections brought by the fact we are now at war with Japan. They were put into the record more than twenty years before war came. I was indignant over the treatment accorded a nation not to be trusted.

I was outraged by the injustice to China.

Then and there I felt the Japanese militarist had tipped his hand to the world. I was disturbed by the prospect of a Japanese march in the Pacific, and plainly said so within the proper limitations of debate on the floor of the United States Senate.

Those mandates over groups of islands formerly German disturbed me.

In October of 1919, in a speech that extended over parts of several days, I said:

"If you will look at the map of the Pacific Ocean, you will realize that the giving of the German island possessions north of the equator to Japan means that Japan is brought thousands of miles nearer our coast. When she gets those islands fortified, she will not be so distant from us as she has been heretofore, and she will, as Krupensky [the Russian ambassador to Japan] says in his official correspondence, 'be at least in better shape to enforce her demands than she would be now.'"

So much precious American blood has been shed on the lands, in the skies, and on the waters adjacent to those Pacific islands to which I referred on that October afternoon in the course of the League debate. The Marshalls and the Carolines were the foundation of Japan's bid to overrun the Pacific.

A Japanese task force put out for Pearl Harbor from those newly acquired and secretly developed bases.

In the heat of the coral sands of Tarawa American marines wrote a new bright chapter in the history of America's oldest military organization, and three thousand and more lay dead or wounded at the close of seventy-two hours of savage fighting.

The engagement on Tarawa may have been among the inevitable developments which faced America, but it was hastened at least by the fatal mistake of mandating the German islands in the Pacific.

When I uttered that warning against turning the islands over to Japan, my Nebraska colleague, Senator Gilbert M. Hitchcock, entered objections, saying that Japan only would receive the islands in trust for the League of Nations and no fortifications would be permitted.

"It may be that Japan will not fortify these islands," I replied to Senator Hitchcock, "but when I realize that the representatives of all of these great nations stood on the rostrum with their pockets full of secret treaties without disclosing them to us, and when I know that they brought China into the war without letting her know that they had agreed already to carve her into mincemeat, I do not know how many secret agreements still exist and, regardless of anything that may be said in a treaty, may be carried out."

These fears were confirmed much earlier than I had any reason to anticipate. Germany had not undertaken serious development of those Pacific island possessions. Almost immediately the Japanese started out. Under the pretense that the simple, friendly, hospitable natives of the islands were opposed to outside visitors, a screen was pulled over the work of fortification. In defiance of the specific mandate of the League, Japan did not hold her newly acquired possessions in trust but proceeded with all the speed and zealousness of Japanese militarists to make them as impregnable as Japanese engineering skill could.

In the course of those debates, I quoted from an editorial in the periodical issued by the British Union of Democratic Control, *Foreign Affairs*, the words:

No man who realizes what this so-called peace treaty means, and the bitter mockery of the peace celebrations in connection with it, can pass a group of children playing in the streets or in the fields without saying: "Upon these innocents four men at Versailles have passed sentence of death; and that sentence will in due course be executed if I and my neighbors do not prevent it."

I commented:

"Mr. President, from the depth of my heart I believe that the last sentence I have read from the editorial is absolutely true."

How ghastly true!

They were the babes, now grown to manhood, who have died in the jungle, on the waters, or in the skies of the Southwest and Central Pacific, in the Aleutians, Burma, India, Malaya, and the Philippines.

I could not foresee in exact outline the developments which would come, and the developments that have come during the last two years. But my fears were real, and they took form in these spoken words:

"I have them—illustrations, posters, newspapers of all kinds—that go to show that the Japanese people believe Japan is destined to rule the world. This is one of the steps. There is not any question but what hidden in the heart of Japan is an idea that the Mikado some day will rule the world."

It was quite natural that in this historic struggle the more familiar argument relating to American responsibilities as a member of the proposed League overshadowed what to me were more fundamental weaknesses and sources of greater peril. The public devoted most of its attention to the discussions centering upon Article 10. And here we were giving Japan springboards from which to pounce upon us and strike us in the back.

I did not like the map making.

I did not believe it necessary, if hopes were to be entertained for a lasting peace, to subject the German representatives to humiliation at the peace table itself. There could be, it seemed to me, a courtesy in victory which in no way weakened justice. I did not believe that a people as virile as the Germans could be put in an economic strait-jacket and held in subjection without trouble.

There was still another serious defect in the Versailles settlements. I did not then know why Germany was not disarmed in such fashion that never again could a military group prepare the German people for war. I should have been happy to see every munitions factory in Germany destroyed. I should have been pleased if every facility for conducting war had been rendered useless. I should have said to the German people they never could countenance military leadership again.

One by one, as the reservations came to a vote, I supported them. I cast my lot with the group that opposed the treaty and covenant Mr. Wilson brought back from Europe.

I offer no apologies for my opposition to the Versailles League of Nations.

My only regret is that, out of all the agony and sacrifice, nothing came to insure peace.

The issues fought over in the fall of 1919 can provide most wholesome experience for the settlements of the present conflict. Those settlements are infinitely too important to become involved in petty partisanship. They are of too much consequence to civilization to be kicked around in party strife.

The months which followed Senate action on the League of Nations brought to me clearly the disillusionment of the American people.

Thinking they had emerged into the sunlight, they found themselves back in the shadows.

22

A SENATE SEAT FOR SALE

THE EXPECTED HAPPENED in the presidential election of 1920.

A Republican ticket composed of Warren G. Harding and Calvin Coolidge swept the country. The Democrats were turned out, and the Republicans not only gained control of the executive branch of government, but took over both houses of Congress.

Mr. Harding, a senatorial colleague, was not my choice in the Republican presidential primary of 1920. I had supported Senator Hiram Johnson of California, and had spoken in his behalf whenever the opportunity presented itself. I noted with deep regret the deadlock which developed in Chicago, and from out of which Mr. Harding emerged as a dark-horse candidate after the conferences of the inner circle in the hotel room.

With strong misgivings, I voted for Harding in the November election. I had no hope his elevation to the Presidency would contribute to the progress of liberal government. I knew his conservative tendencies but did not anticipate reactionary practices would run such riot in the next few years.

President Harding was one of the most kindly and amiable of men. It seemed to me that instinctively he reposed too much confidence in his friends, and that he shrank from giving hurt. That generous judgment did not account for the developments of the following months which shocked the American people.

In the Senate he had been a dependable conservative in all of his thought and his votes.

In the White House he symbolized Ohio political machine politics.

There came to Washington on the heels of this new administration a curious crew, with an amazingly blunted, repulsive conception of public service and the responsibilities of public office.

Even more significant, the currents of national thought reversed themselves. Great wealth took possession of the government. It was reflected in Mr. Harding's selection of a cabinet. It characterized all political utterances. The stock phrase, "Less government in business, and more business in government" was, I recognize, a natural reaction against the necessary regimentation of people in wartime. But it brought into the places of high responsibility men who could not be expected to have a far-sighted view of public service, combining qualities of unselfishness and high devotion to public trust.

It was not long before Washington, the most sensitive of all American cities to scandal, buzzed with gossip.

The letdown of American spirit affected not only the executive but the legislative branch. Reaction rushed eagerly forward to exploit its triumph to the fullest. Wealth was the thing, the American people were told. It was untrammeled enterprise which had made America strong and rich. The best brains of industry and of business were commissioned to lead the American people to the promised land.

It was under these conditions and in this spirit that an extraordinary senatorial campaign in Michigan became a subject of national discussion.

Huge sums of money had been spent there in the senatorial campaign. A very wealthy Michigan industrialist, Truman H. Newberry, defeated Henry Ford, one of America's richest men, in the primary election of 1918. Mr. Ford made no unusual effort and no unusual expenditures to gain a seat in the Senate. Newberry and his organization friends poured out hundreds of thousands of dollars, to offset Mr. Ford's popularity and prestige, and the dollars won.

So offensive had been the use of money in that Michigan election, the Newberry case came before the Senate Committee on Privileges and Elections for review on the question of seating the victorious candidate, and finally for discussion, on the Senate floor, although the full membership of the Senate never reached a final vote. Following his election in 1918 Mr. Newberry had taken his seat on March 4, 1919, but the peak violence of the angry storm of Senate discussion, and widespread magazine and press comment, did not develop until the Harding administration had taken over conduct of national affairs. He resigned on November 18, 1922, to be succeeded by James Couzens, another man of great wealth, of wholly different outlook.

Senator Couzens had outstanding ability and character, and I became greatly attached to him for his expression of liberal views. He gave the state of Michigan a distinguished representation that was recognized throughout the country.

I knew that in the atmosphere of Washington any orthodox attack upon Newberry would be futile. With the cynical philosophy of the day people were not greatly concerned over moral issues. They had surrendered fully to the reactionary leadership which promised them quiet, peace, and prosperity. If public attention was to be directed effectively to the circumstances of the Michigan election, different treatment would be required. So when the Newberry contest was before the Senate, I made a speech on the floor which drew nation-wide attention and was credited, perhaps unduly, with laughing Mr. Newberry out of public life. I selected, with some care, a time when the entire membership was present.

It was on the afternoon of January 11, 1922, while the Senate was proceeding sedately with the discussion of the Newberry case, that I gained the floor and said:

"Mr. President, they had a public sale up in Michigan. The property that was placed on the auction block was a seat in the United States Senate. The sale was public, the bidding was in the open, and the property was knocked down to the highest bidder. Every citizen of Michigan had an opportunity to get in and bid. Why, then, Mr. President, all this fussing and fuming? The only question before the Senate is: Shall that sale of a seat in this chamber be confirmed? It is a question of confirmation of a sale which is admitted, it seems to me, to have been made according to the rule."

I could see a slight awakening among my colleagues, and a developing interest.

I was encouraged to go on.

"The sale was public; the price was adequate. In fact, it seems to me as though the purchasers paid more than the blamed thing was worth. Why, then, should senators hesitate to confirm this sale so made and so conducted, before the people of the entire country?

"It is said by some of those who are opposing the confirmation that this would establish a precedent by which a poor man would be eliminated from the Senate chamber.

"Suppose it does. What business has the poor man here, anyway?

"If he catches cold, or some member of his family gets a toothache, so that he has to consult specialists or dentists in the city of Washington, he will be looking straight into the front door of the poorhouse.

"As I look at it, Mr. President, this is just exactly what it is intended it should be: the establishment of a precedent so that we will have more men of means in this chamber, and that seats will be put up in the market place just as seats on the stock exchange. This will insure a high-class membership, but, Mr. President, it does not follow that we mean any hardship for the poor man on that account. If the poor man has not money enough to put up the ante in the senatorial poker game, let him go to the back alley and engage in a game of craps. If he cannot raise money enough to run for the United States Senate, let him run for constable, road overseer, or even for the ancient and honorable office of justice of the peace.

"It is not intended by the establishment of this precedent to hurt the poor man. Senators do not realize how important a question this is. If we do not confirm this sale, the first thing we know we will have a lot of poor men here. Mr. President, there will be farmers in the Senate, a 'bloc' of farmers whom you cannot control by loaning public money on cotton or inviting them to a presidential dinner, farmers with whiskers, yes, whiskers that will put in the shade the beautifully trimmed beard which adorns the face of our illustrious leader."

I had gotten well along in this speech when an episode occurred in the gallery which a friend of mine described to me later.

He was seated behind two men, well advanced in years, who were listening to the discussion with intense interest, and whose sympathies were not to be misunderstood.

"Listen to that old fool!" one of the men said to the other while I was speaking in this vein. "If he isn't careful, his folks back home will hear about this and take care of him."

I was completely unaware at the time that there could be any possible misconstruction of my attempted satire. My colleagues did not misunderstand. I could see them enjoying it all, friend and foe alike, although I was speaking with the utmost seriousness, and not permitting myself even the luxury of a smile. There had been very few occasions when I enjoyed a Senate session more.

And so I continued:

"Mr. President, if we only knew it, we will accomplish much more when we confirm this sale than we realize; and it has been decreed by our masters that this sale be confirmed. It is all right for senators to insurge and go against the machine occasionally, but we have come to a time now when you have to show your colors, and obey the command, or in some future election you will find yourself without friends and without money.

"It is not for us to reason why, but it is for us to obey or die.

"It is said by some senators that if we confirm this sale we will be going contrary to the evidence.

"What has the evidence to do with this thing anyway?

"This is not a question of evidence.

"This is a question of obedience, and, after all, a great deal can be said, and even has been said by senators on this floor to the effect that the confirming of this sale is according to the evidence. It was said by the senator from Missouri, on some phases of it, that the evidence stands uncontradicted.

"For instance, one of the questions involved in this case is: 'Whose money was spent anyway?'

"The attorney for Mr. Newberry, and various other Newberry interests testified that he had ten, eleven, or twelve accounts, and that he transferred money from one to the other as occasion demanded.

"Now, some inquiring member of the committee said, 'Let us subpoena these bankers with their books, and that will throw some light on the ownership of the money that was really spent in this campaign.' But the committee very properly and very wisely decided that this could not be done. In other words, the evidence of this attorney who testified that Mr. Newberry knew nothing about it stands uncontradicted.

"So how dare you go back on it?

"The committee was so wise and so judicious as to see to it that it should remain uncontradicted.

"After all, the evidence does show in a good many respects just as has been claimed, and we should, I think, pass a resolution of thanks to that committee for making it so easy for us to follow the well marked-out path that is determined upon for us to follow. It was their wisdom that to some extent made this record so that it is easy for us to obey."

At this point I thought there was less enjoyment of the discussion. But I plunged ahead:

"It was proposed that Mr. Newberry be summoned before the committee. He had been silent. That was very properly blocked by this very dutiful committee, and he was not requested and not subpoenaed and he would not perhaps have been permitted to testify if he had appeared. That helped us out on the record a great deal, because there is not now anything to show that he knew anything about any of these things. It is uncontradicted. Again they prevented by their course of action what might have been embarrassing and made it embarrassing for us who are faithful to cast the vote here we are expected to cast. Think, Mr. President, how humiliating and embarrassing it would have been to have subjected a United States Senator to a cross-examination by any ordinary representative of the common people.

"It is said, Mr. President, by some of the senators that anyone who votes to confirm this sale will be defeated for reelection if he is a candidate for reelection to this body. Now, that is a threat unworthy of a senator to make. In addition to that, it is poppycock and there is nothing to it. His constituents will not read this. They will be too engrossed in other things that came into the campaign and they will forget about this.

"Let me say to my friends who are threatening us with the dire disaster before the people that that situation is pretty well cared for now.

"It always has been the custom of both great political parties to arrange soft berths for the lame ducks who are wounded while faithfully following the commands of our masters. If the people should be so unthinking and so unreasonable as to defeat any senator for reelection because he voted to confirm this sale, those senators who are still faithful and follow their leaders will find they will be properly cared for when the time comes, and some place somewhere they will be tucked away in a soft berth with a salary attached to it greater and larger than that which attaches to a place in this body. So you cannot scare us with that kind of talk. We are too well armed and too well fortified for that kind of threat to have any influence upon us.

"It is going to be said of us when we get through, as was said of some other great people:

"'He seen his duty and he done it.'

"Notwithstanding all that talk, we are going to carry out the program, do not worry about that. To the faithful, those who are faithful unto the end, will come the reward for hard labor and for duty conscientiously and faithfully performed, and when we have established this precedent we will have a Senate to be proud of composed of men of means.

"We will make Washington the social center of the world.

"We can then employ experts to do our thinking, and senators will have more time to give to golf and to the other kindred social duties."

The Newberry contest bore fruit, although it was a long time in maturing. The revelations brought to public notice the lavish expenditure of money, and the effect, while not immediately apparent, nevertheless was such as to effectively check unhealthy practices.

There were others to follow.

Among the cases was that of Frank Smith, a former member of the Illinois State Public Utilities Commission, who ran for the Senate; the evidence brought before the Privileges and Elections Committee sought to substantiate the charge that the utility interests had been active in his support, and had spent considerable sums of money. Once again I returned to the firing line to contest the seating of Smith, and this time in grim fight which swayed back and forth until finally he surrendered his seat to another.

It was the Vare election in Pennsylvania which was to present me with one of the greatest political battles of my career.

Those were days and years when America seemed lulled into indifference. They were dark days for the little progressive group in the House of Representatives and the Senate. We felt deeply the arrogant contempt of the regular old-line Republicans. It seemed to us that the fights which we had made, and which had given us high hope, had all been in vain.

At no period in my public life did I feel greater discouragement than during those years. The stories of Washington life grew in volume. There were ugly tales of the reckless handling of public business.

Mr. Harding's death brought Calvin Coolidge to the White House.

I think Mr. Coolidge's political technique is revealed best in this unimportant episode.

The telephone rang in my apartment one morning shortly after breakfast. The President's secretary was on the other end of the wire.

Mr. Coolidge wanted to see me.

I was somewhat indefinite in my reply—my desk had been piled with correspondence which required immediate attention; and I went to my Senate office. I had been there but a short time when the telephone rang again. It was the White House informing me Mr. Coolidge wanted to see me.

I told the President's secretary I would come right over, and on the way down the hall stopped a moment at the office of my colleague, Senator R. B. Howell. Mr. Howell, learning that I was on my way to the White House, told me his car and driver would take me there.

I was ushered in to the President, without delay, and Mr. Coolidge told me of an impending judicial appointment in California involving a bitter factional contest, and a candidate reputedly of dubious qualifications.

I was at the time the chairman of the Judiciary Committee.

"Your problem is simple, Mr. President," I told Mr. Coolidge. "You are convinced this man lacks the qualifications for a federal judge. Simply refuse to nominate him."

With that I left.

When I started to get into the waiting automobile, I discovered Senator Borah of Idaho in the back seat, waiting for me and a ride back up the hill. Apparently he had been summoned to the White House as a member of the Judiciary Committee, just ahead of me. We compared notes. It was clear Mr. Coolidge did not want to appoint the man but was making it possible to save face—either by saying he had consulted the Judiciary Committee, or by sending the appointment to the Senate with full knowledge it would be rejected.

Senator Borah, who was the ranking Judiciary Committee member under me, and I chuckled heartily to ourselves on our way back up the Hill. The nomination was sent to the Senate by the President, and was approved by the Judiciary Committee over my emphatic but futile protest, along with the opposition of several others. The appointment was confirmed in executive session of the Senate after I had led a fight against confirmation. A few years later that incident had its echoes in the Senate when impeachment charges were filed by the House.

There was no conviction, although a Senate majority voted to sustain the fifth of the five charges which constituted the basis of the proceeding, thus falling short of the required number for impeachment.

It seemed to me to be characteristic of some of the practices of that period and very symbolical of the tactics which produced that stuffy era of "good feeling."

23

TEAPOT DOME

STILL ANOTHER impressive bit of evidence of national apathy presented itself in the Teaport Dome scandal.

It had its origin in the early months of the Harding administration. It became the subject of common gossip in Washington, and yet no betrayal of public trust resisted exposure and punishment more tenaciously.

Teapot Dome involved the conservation of the oil resources of the United States, especially those situated upon the public lands. The investigation of alleged irregularities had been in progress for some time, under the auspices of the Senate Committee on Public Lands and Surveys, when the decision was reached to institute court action to cancel the leases granted to private interests at Teapot Dome and Elk Hills.

My old friend Robert M. La Follette of Wisconsin, always alert and vigilant, had introduced and procured passage of the two resolutions—Senate Resolution 282, and Senate Resolution 294—authorizing the Public Lands Committee to make the inquiry. Out of it came the evidence supporting the inescapable conviction that immense combinations of wealth, large corporations, under leases fraudulently obtained, were systematically robbing the government of the oil stored in the public lands by Nature. The evidence pointed straight to the guilt of a former colleague, A. B. Fall of New Mexico, who had become Secretary of the Interior.

As a senator, Mr. Fall impressed those with whom he came in contact as a picturesque character from the Southwest frontier.

Mr. Harding had placed him in charge of the Interior Department notwithstanding that Senator Fall had fought conservation policies consistently. Another former member of Congress, Edwin Denby, had been placed in the cabinet as Secretary of the Navy by Mr. Harding. Long before Secretary Denby emerged as a cabinet member, he had been denounced vigorously by Theodore Roosevelt, and had been defeated for reelection in his congressional district because of his attitude in the Ballinger case.

The circle was completed by the selection of a former Ohio politician, Harry M. Daugherty, for the cabinet post of Attorney General, at the head of the Department of Justice. Mr. Daugherty had been a close associate of Senator Foraker.

Before the gathering storm spent itself, three members of the cabinet had been forced from public life by the pressure of public opinion.

It was unfortunate that only those directly involved suffered the consequences. In a large sense, the condemnation that should have fallen upon Republican leadership in the National Committee of the party did not develop.

The initial court actions instituted by the government for cancellation of the oil leases were in charge of former Senator Atlee Pomerene of Ohio and Owen J. Roberts of Philadelphia (who has since become a distinguished member of the United States Supreme Court). Even in the early stages, the investigation by the Public Lands Committee, undertaken against the greatest opposition, and conducted under impressive difficulties, disclosed a disgraceful condition and revealed the illegal manner in which large corporations were appropriating the oil which underlay public lands, owned by the government.

The proceedings in the federal District Court of Wyoming, presided over by Judge T. Blake Kennedy at Cheyenne, disclosed that all the facts had not been brought out and there was urgent need for further inquiry on the part of the committee. Senator Pomerene and Mr. Roberts conducted the case with great ability and with equally great zeal and devotion, but found their hands tied when essential witnesses fled the jurisdiction of the court. One took refuge in

Africa hunting big game; another sought relaxation and peace in Paris and the watering spots of southern France.

Yet only under the crassly material atmosphere of those years could an investigation and trial involving the issues that were presented in the Teapot Dome have failed to arouse great popular indignation.

In those initial proceedings in the Federal Court, Judge Kennedy sustained a demurrer to the government's action, and the case then came before the Circuit Court of Appeals at St. Louis. Judge Kenyon who wrote the Court's opinion, one of the most vigorous of its day, reversed the ruling of the trial court.

It was under those circumstances, coupled with some new developments, that Teapot Dome came to my attention and inspired me to action. A second phase of the oil scandal opened.

Paul Y. Anderson, Washington correspondent of the St. Louis *Post-Dispatch*, one of the most fearless journalists I have ever known, who had been most active in assembling facts and in gathering information pointing to the guilt of other large oil companies and magnates robbing the government of its oil reserves, consulted continually with me on the Teapot Dome scandal. We had been friends for some years, and I had great faith in Mr. Anderson.

He had become convinced that millions of dollars had been made unlawfully and disgracefully. It is of more than passing interest that his distinguished service in connection with this case brought him the Pulitzer prize award of $1,000 for an outstanding example of reporting.

After some discussion the two of us came to the conclusion the Senate ought to instruct the Senate Committee on Public Lands and Surveys to renew its investigation.

I then prepared and introduced Senate Resolution 101 in the first session of the Seventieth Congress. The resolution set forth that the investigation provided for in Senator La Follette's measures had not been completed because of the refusal by Harry F. Sinclair to answer questions. It continued:

WHEREAS, In the case of the United States against Harry F. Sinclair and Albert B. Fall, it was disclosed upon trial that a fraudulent corporation, known as the Continental Trading Company of Canada, had been organized for the purpose of using the profits of its business in the bribing of public officials of the United States and for other dishonest, dishonorable and illegal purposes; and

WHEREAS, It was disclosed upon said trial that profits of said corporation were invested in Liberty bonds of the United States, that only a portion of said Liberty bonds so invested had been definitely traced and accounted for, and that a large amount of Liberty bonds coming into the hands of said fraudulent corporation had been unaccounted for and unexplained; therefore, be it

Resolved, That the said Committee on Public Lands be, and is hereby, authorized and directed to renew and to continue the investigation provided for in said resolutions No. 282 and No. 294, and said resolutions are hereby renewed as fully and as completely as though they were herein fully set forth; and be it further

Resolved, That said committee is specifically directed to make an investigation as to the transactions and activities of the said fraudulent corporation, the Continental Trading Company of Canada, and it is specifically directed to trace all the government bonds held and dealt in by said corporation, with the purpose of ascertaining the beneficiary or beneficiaries of all the illegal transactions connected with the fraudulent and dishonest sale or leasing of the said Naval oil reserves.

This resolution subsequently passed the Senate, and on the day after its passage, January 10, 1928, I spoke on the floor of the Senate, directing attention to the evidence, incomplete, that had been brought out in the earlier investigation:

"In November, 1921, Mr. Al Humphreys, an oil producer of Texas, entered into negotiations with Harry F. Sinclair, H. M. Blackmer, James O'Neil, and Robert W. Stewart for the purpose of selling to them oil that he was producing from his wells in Texas.

"On November 15, 1921, at a conference with these men in New York City, Mr. Humphreys sold them more than thirty-three million barrels of oil at an agreed price of $1.50 per barrel.

"On the next day when they met, for the purpose of putting

the contract in writing for the first time, these purchasers notified Mr. Humphreys that the real purchaser of the oil was the Continental Trading Company of Canada, and asked that the contract be drawn in the name of that Company. Mr. Humphreys had never heard of the Continental Trading Company, and because he knew nothing of its financial standing, he refused to enter into a contract for the sale of oil to that company.

"Thereupon, these men told Mr. Humphreys that they, on behalf of the companies which they represented, would guarantee the payment for the oil on behalf of the Continental Trading Company. The contract was drawn in the name of the Continental Trading Company, and payment of the price of the oil by the said trading company was guaranteed by Sinclair, Blackmer, O'Neil, and Stewart.

"At this time O'Neil was president of the Prairie Oil and Gas Company; Stewart was chairman of the board of directors of the Standard Oil Company of Indiana and still holds that position; and Blackmer was chairman of the board of directors of the Mid-West Refining Company which practically was owned outright at that time and still is by the Standard Oil Company of Indiana. Sinclair represented the Sinclair Consolidated Oil Corporation. This corporation, together with the Standard Oil Company of Indiana, represented by Stewart, jointly owned the Sinclair Crude Oil Purchasing Company.

"On the next day, November 17, 1921, Henry Smith Osler, an attorney of Toronto, Canada, appeared upon the scene and executed the contract as president of the Continental Trading Company, while Sinclair and Stewart 'for the directors' of the Sinclair Crude Oil Purchasing Company and O'Neil on behalf of the Prairie Oil and Gas Company, signed the contract as guarantors. On the same day the fraudulent Continental Trading Company thus assigned its contract and resold the oil it had contracted to buy to the Sinclair Crude Oil Purchasing Company and the Prairie Oil and Gas Company jointly.

"This sale was made at a profit of twenty-five cents on each barrel."

Now this was the plot hatched while the American people barely had emerged from a great war to make the world safe for democracy.

The steps as set forth in all of their careful planning were reviewed that day.

I pointed out that, under the terms of the contract between Humphreys and the Continental Trading Company, payments for oil deliveries were made on the fifteenth day of each month. The Continental Trading Company in its resale of the oil to the Stewart, Sinclair and O'Neil corporations got its payments on the tenth day of each month.

Thus it was possible for the fraudulent Continental Trading Company to get its money from the real purchasers of the oil five precious days before it was required to make payments to the man who actually produced and sold it. Under the contract, oil was delivered by Mr. Humphreys and turned over to these corporations until some time in May of 1923, when the Continental, through its president, Osler, assigned its interest in the contract to the Sinclair Crude Oil Purchasing Company.

At the time of the assignment, twenty-five millions of barrels of oil still were to be delivered.

The profit of the Continental Trading Company, at twenty-five cents a barrel on this remaining amount of oil, would have been at least $6,250,000. Yet Osler, on behalf of the Continental Trading Company, surrendered his contract to the Sinclair Crude Oil Purchasing Company for $400,000.

Immediately this fraudulent Canadian company went out of business. It had come into existence the day the contract originally was made. It never had any capital. It never had any property except the profit on this oil contract. It never did any business either before or after this oil transaction. When it went out of business, it destroyed its records and all of its documents.

I told the Senate:

"It is worthy of note that it went out of business about the time the Senate investigation of the Teapot Dome oil leases was threatened. While in business, its profit of twenty-five cents a barrel on this oil amounted to $3,800,000. All of this money was deposited under the direction of Osler at the New York agency of the Dominion Bank of Canada, and under his direction all of the money was invested in Liberty bonds of the United States government. These bonds were, by this Dominion bank, then turned over to Osler. In the trial of the Sinclair and Fall cases, $230,000 of these bonds were traced to Mr. Fall. The balance of the bonds have never been accounted for and the principal object in directing the committee to continue the investigation is to determine what became of the remainder of these bonds."

The obstructions which had interposed themselves in the trial of the civil actions largely escaped public attention.

I could sense that the dragnet was tightening. Government consent was obtained through a commission from the United States District Court to take the vital testimony of Osler in Canada. When placed upon the stand, however, he refused to testify on the ground that he was an attorney for the Continental Trading Company and its officials, and that all of the information which he possessed was privileged.

Thereupon he was cited for contempt of court and on December 13, 1924, Justice Riddell of the Supreme Court of Ontario delivering judgment against him, ordering him to testify. He then appealed to the Appellate Division of the Supreme Court of Ontario, which rejected his plea and reaffirmed the order compelling him to testify.

The speed and dispatch with which the Canadian courts disposed of the matter led me to say on the floor of the Senate:

"It may be worth while in passing to say that the Appellate Division of the Supreme Court of Ontario passed on the question on the twelfth day of March, 1925, just twenty-nine days after the matter had been submitted to it. I mention that to show how expeditious justice seems to be across the line as compared to the manner in which it is dragging along here for months at a time to find out whether or not somebody may be in contempt of court.

In Ontario the question went clear to the Appellate Division of the Supreme Court in less than eighty days, and the court rendered a decision."

And then came flight.

On the Senate floor while the case was pending, I said:

"Osler left Canada . . . went to Egypt, it is alleged on a lion hunt. It was therefore impossible to carry out an order of the court. He never returned until the case was disposed of when he knew his testimony would be of no value. . . . Blackmer and O'Neil left the country and went to France. Senators will remember that they were the representatives of oil corporations that really bought the oil and guaranteed payment. . . . Absence of Blackmer and O'Neil made it impossible for the government to get their testimony. Stewart, who represented the Standard Oil Company of Indiana, also left the country and went to South America. Stewart came back later and said he did not know they had been hunting for him, as they had been all over the United States, trying to get him on subpoena. . . . He was down in South America on some oil business. Blackmer and O'Neil are still in Europe, and it is supposed that they will remain there for the balance of their lives. . . . Both the Supreme Court of Ontario and the Supreme Court of the United States have branded the Continental Trading Company as a corrupt and fraudulent instrument of some illegitimate purpose."

I called my colleagues' attention to the language of the Supreme Court of the United States:

"The creation of the Continental Company, the purchase and resale of the contracts enabling it to make more than eight million dollars without capital, risk or effort; the assignment of the contract to the resale purchasers at a smaller fraction of its purchase value, and the effort to conceal the disposition of its assets, make it plain that the company was created for some illegitimate purpose. The record shows . . . that the government, notwithstanding the diligence reasonably to be expected, was unable to obtain the testimony of Blackmer, O'Neil, Stewart, Everhart, or Osler in respect to the transaction by which the Liberty bonds recently acquired by the Continental Trading Company were given to and used by Fall."

After observing that the Standard Oil Company was involved in the transaction, that use of the trading company, if the transaction was honest, could result only in cheating their own companies, I concluded:

"So that the stockholders of each one of these companies, assuming that this transaction had not some other ulterior purpose, were being robbed by their officials. Among the number comes the Standard Oil Company of Indiana, owned to a great extent, I am informed, by Mr. Rockefeller and the Rockefeller Foundation."

The investigation went forward energetically.

Two reports by the committee reached the Senate on May 29, 1928.

One by Senator Thomas J. Walsh of Montana, and another by Senator Gerald Nye of North Dakota, chairman of the committee—both unanimously concurred in—fully placed the facts before the American people.

The evidence presented pointed very strongly to the guilt of Doheny, Sinclair, a leading oil magnate, and also Blackmer, O'Neil, and Stewart.

In all of the actions brought, only the aged and failing Fall was found guilty. Doheny and Sinclair both were acquitted in jury court trials, although Mr. Sinclair served seven months in jail for contempt of court. The evidence had disclosed that, while trial was going on, Sinclair had employed detectives for illegal purposes. Mr. Doheny, old, with the adventurous career of a prospector in wild, rough country behind him, enlisted sympathy.

In the final termination of this fantastic conspiracy the illegal oil leases were set aside, a large amount of money was recovered, a large amount of income taxes collected.

Approximately six million dollars returned to the government as fruits of the investigations.

O'Neil, who like Blackmer went abroad to escape testifying against Sinclair in the oil trials, fled from the jurisdiction of the court and, beyond reach of a subpoena, paid the Treasury $151,597;

Blackmer, an equal amount; and from the president and general counsel of the Sinclair Crude Oil Petroleum Company $303,194 was obtained to meet the claims upon Sinclair and Stewart. Stewart was ousted as head of the Standard Oil Company of Indiana by the Rockefeller interests.

The great conspiracy seemed to pass quickly from the American mind.

Both Senator Tom Walsh and Senator Gerald Nye, prime movers in the investigation of the committee, are entitled to great credit for magnificent work. Walsh was a great lawyer. With infinite patience, matchless determination, unswerving purpose, he threw himself into this fight with all of the great ability he possessed, and his dauntless spirit overcame one obstacle after another. It was common knowledge that he had been selected by Franklin D. Roosevelt to be Attorney General, when death intervened. The country suffered a great loss in the high integrity and shining spirit of public service of this quiet-spoken, mild-mannered Montanan.

Nye applied himself with equal diligence.

It was during these days of discouragement that I first said that this disgraceful episode in national history came near demonstrating that under the American system of jurisprudence it was very difficult, if not impossible, to convict one hundred million dollars.

Delay, the weapon of great wealth, often nullifies justice. There will never be a day the American people can afford to be off guard. Only their vigilance will prevent misuse of the remaining resources of the nation. Its timber tracts, its oil, and its minerals have been used lavishly in recent years. Their conservation becomes of great concern.

24

LONELY PILGRIMAGE

I CONSIDER THE FIGHT to defeat William S. Vare as Republican senator elect from Pennsylvania to have been one of the most satisfying struggles of that era of reaction.

He had become the Republican nominee in 1926.

Largely unknown nationally, except as the dubious, legendary head of the Vare Republican machine in Philadelphia, he had developed great power in the state. His organization was most effective and efficient; its methods, most disgraceful.

In the primaries Mr. Vare had defeated Governor Pinchot for the nomination and it was the lavishness of the expenditures in his behalf, estimated at hundreds of thousands of dollars, together with voting frauds in Philadelphia, that crystallized belief throughout the country he had obtained his nomination by disreputable, illegal, and disgraceful methods.

There were many Republicans of national reputation who openly condemned the practices of the Vare machine. There was great agitation, which unfortunately ended at that point, without any common-sense proposal of a solution. In the Republican party especially, there was no definite program to curb the recognized abuses of the Vare machine.

The Democrats of Pennsylvania had nominated William B. Wilson. Mr. Wilson had grown up from babyhood in the ranks of labor and had become one of its leaders of the highest standing. As such he was elected to Congress, where his keen mind, fairness, and rugged honesty brought him recognition among his colleagues. Then President Wilson appointed him to the cabinet—to the universal satisfaction of the entire country—and he gave able and outstanding service as Secretary of Labor.

I listened carefully to the rising criticism of the Vare machine. While many Republicans felt they could not support Vare, they felt just as strongly they could not vote for Wilson because of his Democratic label. That was the only objection some of them raised to him. His fitness and his ability received no attention, inasmuch as he was a Democrat and had the Democratic nomination.

So these Republicans advocated a third or independent candidate for the senatorship in Pennsylvania.

It seemed suicidal to me.

I had no faith that an independent candidate in Pennsylvania could be elected to the United States Senate, and I thought any attempt would insure the election of Mr. Vare.

Most of the Republicans with whom I talked, strangely, admitted that would be the outcome, and expected to satisfy their conscience by voting for an independent rather than the Republican nominee. To this extent they were willing to cast aside their partisanship.

I took the position that the proper course was to support Mr. Wilson.

Having determined upon it, I wrote a short article for the *Nation* one Sunday morning while working at my office in the Senate office building, addressing it to an old friend, the editor, Oswald Garrison Villard.

In that article I took pains to emphasize that a third candidacy would only bring about the election of Mr. Vare. To defeat the Philadelphia boss, I urged direct support of William B. Wilson.

It was the first instance in a national contest in which I broke publicly from my traditional Republican moorings and urged the election of a Democrat.

Later I was to repeat the act.

The appearance of the plea in the *Nation* seemed to galvanize action immediately.

There were many organizations, chiefly among railroad men in Pennsylvania, who agreed with me, and who thought that the most effective way to defeat Vare would be to support the Democratic nominee.

Some of these men and some of the representatives of these organizations called on me in Washington, where I agreed to make a campaign in Pennsylvania on behalf of Mr. Wilson. When it became known that I had embarked upon this course, there was a sharply divided sentiment over the country as to whether I was pursuing proper methods.

An old friend living in Freeport, Illinois, a very progressive citizen, who always had been a firm supporter of the older La Follette, and who had reached down in his pocket to contribute liberally to the La Follette cause, wrote, expressing a desire to assist in this fight against Vare. He gave me the encouragement of expressing the thought I was taking the right course; and offered to make a financial contribution directly to me, which I declined.

The article I had written for the *Nation* was placed in the *Congressional Record* by Senator Copeland of New York. I suggested to my old Illinois friend that the circulation of the article through Pennsylvania during the campaign would be of very material help, and if he wanted to contribute and to take part he could do so very properly by having the article reprinted and sent out through Pennsylvania. He paid for the printing of 500,000 copies, which were mailed into Pennsylvania. It developed at the start that one of the main difficulties was a lack of organization. It was desirable that this article reach Pennsylvania voters generally but difficult to procure mailing lists of the voters, try as hard as the railroad men did.

Those few weeks in Pennsylvania, in a pilgrimage which I made largely by myself, without any associate, were most trying and discouraging and at the same time most satisfying.

Here was a battle in the great bastion of entrenched privilege. Here was a fight in the main battleground of intrenched wealth, of hereditary partisanship, and of a powerful corrupt political organization.

Here those groups against whom slowly I had been drawn into conflict had me in their own back yard, every square foot of which they knew and controlled.

I devoted all my time to that campaign until election day.

I spoke every day, frequently several times a day.

I spoke twice on Sunday.

I immediately sensed the deep feeling that lay beneath the surface in Pennsylvania.

My party heresy in openly campaigning for Mr. Wilson immediately brought caustic criticism from Republican colleagues and friends, but almost from the opening day of that campaign I sensed a great deal of uneasiness among the enemy. Letters, telegrams, and long-distance telephone calls dogged my footsteps from one town to another, hour after hour, and the only possible explanation was that this pilgrimage was stirring the country.

Usually when I reached a city and registered at the hotel the clerk, ascertaining who I was, would tell me of several long-distance telephone calls awaiting my consideration. Generally he handed me a batch of telegrams. Most of the telephone calls were from Republican associates, and most of the telegrams and letters came from Republicans who had been induced to write, wire, or call me from all parts of the United States. Among them were many from my most sincere friends in Nebraska, my home state. There were some from reputed Republican leaders in scattered sections of the country threatening me with all kinds of punishment if I persisted in attempting to break up the solidarity of the Republican front.

It was a gun which backfired. It had the tendency, naturally, to whip keen public interest in these matters and to bring out immense crowds. In fact, it was the most effective manner in which attention could be directed to the campaign I had undertaken. As a rule local newspapers were controlled by the Republican Pennsylvania machine; and from the time I reached the state, evidence came to light each day proving how energetically the machine was at work, how well oiled it was, and how determined it was to prevent me from continuing.

I spoke with infinite satisfaction that offset the tremendous physical strain and the bleak discouragement of that campaign. The only people openly active in behalf of my meetings were the railroad men. They came long distances to the meetings, and, looking out over the audiences, I saw the plain, hard-working successors of Pennsylvania folk who had followed my own pioneer mother, born in that state. These men vainly tried to publicize the meetings.

I was slated to speak at one of the larger cities, a coal-mining center, and arrived about the middle of the afternoon by automobile. I went to the best hotel, noticed that its lobby was deserted, and inquired of the clerk about a meeting that night. He knew nothing of it, and said he had seen no mention of it in the newspaper. I procured copies of the three daily papers serving the community and found no notice of the meeting. I next inquired of the clerk if any circulars had been distributed to announce the meeting, and again he replied in the negative, saying at least none had reached the hotel. So I concluded that something must have gone wrong and the meeting had been abandoned.

I had sat down, tired, weary, discouraged, and was thinking it over when three men came into the lobby, went to the clerk, examined the register, and discovered apparently I was in town. The clerk directed them to me, and they introduced themselves: one was a conductor, one a brakeman, and the third a mechanic in the railroad shops, and they were the committee of three in charge of the meeting I was to address. I pointed out there had been no announcement, and said I assumed the meeting had been abandoned.

Then they told me of their experience.

The community, they said, was controlled and practically owned by coal operators. They had had great difficulty in arranging for the meeting.

First they had gone to see the editor of the morning paper. They knew it was a very ardent Republican organ, devout in its support of the straight Republican ticket, but felt the editor, a man of ability and one of the most high-minded citizens of the community, would see to it announcement was made. They told him a Republican senator was going to make a speech in favor of the Democratic nominee. The editor evidently knew all about it, but he did not print a news story of the meeting. When they asked him to print an advertisement, he refused.

SENATOR NORRIS AND THE LATE SENATOR THOMAS J. WALSH IN CONFERENCE IN SENATOR NORRIS' OFFICE. FREQUENTLY CONGRESSIONAL CONFLICT FOUND THESE TWO STEADFAST LIBERALS FIGHTING SIDE BY SIDE, NOTABLY IN THE TEAPOT DOME INVESTIGATION, TO TRIUMPH OVER REACTION.

Virtually the same experience befell them when they called upon the second daily newspaper.

But the third paper, friendly to the candidacy of Mr. Wilson, had given mention several days in advance.

Equally disheartening had been their efforts to get a chairman for the meeting. My reputation as a progressive was fairly well known in Pennsylvania, and they were confident it would be sufficient to draw a crowd if people knew where the meeting was to take place. The first person they invited to serve as chairman was a minister. In his sermons he rather leaned toward the progressive program.

He was well known, and when they told him of the meeting he expressed great delight.

"We ought to have something of this kind in this town," they said he commented. "It is owned and controlled and run by the Republican machine, and their political methods are disreputable, and I am delighted to know you have succeeded in getting a Republican who will go after the machine."

But when they asked him to serve as chairman, he said he could not very well serve in that capacity, that he had another appointment; and after more excuses he suggested they try to get somebody else.

The men next called upon another minister, of fine reputation, recognized as one who took an advanced position in the religious world. He too was delighted but ended up by indicating to them he could not participate himself.

Still a third invitation brought the same result.

They all wanted the meeting. They thought it a step in the right direction, but they could not afford to identify themselves with such a campaign.

"We do not know what to do, and we are without a chairman," they said.

I told them the experience was common. Prominent men often disliked to participate in meetings of the type I was to address because I would advocate the principle of asking Republicans to vote for a Democrat. Rock-ribbed Republicans, I told them, would hesitate before publicly enlisting in such an enterprise; and the ministers they had called upon undoubtedly had in their congregations wealthy men who owned the coal mines, the railways, and otherwise were directly connected with the state machine I was trying to destroy. I suggested that one of them act as chairman, but they demurred. The conductor, apparently the spokesman, was urged by his two associates to preside; I gave approval, and finally we persuaded him to fill in.

When the hour arrived, the committee waited for me, and we proceeded to the meeting hall, large enough to seat about one thousand. The curtain on the stage was down when we arrived, and so all four of us went out and sat down waiting until time for the curtain to rise.

During the wait a man very well dressed in evening clothes came in and introduced himself to me as the editor of the morning paper. Unaware of what the committee told me, he expressed delight in meeting me and pleasure that I had come into Pennsylvania, and said he knew from grapevine reports that my appearance had excited a great deal of curiosity and had caused much apprehension. He wished more men would refuse to be partisan and would have the courage to support the best man for the office even though the man might be a candidate on the opposite ticket. He referred specifically to the candidacy of Vare.

While he was talking an attendant came and said it was time to start.

I suggested that the curtain be raised at once, and I never saw a man move more rapidly than this editor did. With the quickness and agility of youth he made a bee line for the nearest exit, and by speed won anonymity. The audience may have caught a fleeting, indistinct glimpse of his heels. The tails of his fashionable frock coat stood horizontal so cards could have been played upon them.

It was a fine meeting, the hall crowded to capacity, and the spirit strong and enthusiastic.

I was impressed, not only in this meeting but on many other occasions, by the exceptionally large number of fine citizens in

Pennsylvania who were afraid to show their colors in a political fight. Men of great ability, holding responsible positions, lacked the courage to stand up and do what their consciences told them was their duty.

Every day I saw a demonstration of the great power of a political machine superior to any that I had ever seen.

Uniformly in those speeches I delivered in Pennsylvania, I told the people that if they elected Vare, with his record of shortcomings, the Senate of the United States would not seat him in my judgment.

That turned out to be a prophetic utterance: Vare ultimately was refused a seat in the Senate.

During this campaign there was an incident that has lived in my memory ever since. In an earlier meeting a delegation of progressives had suggested that I visit their town, which was directly on my route of travel. This I agreed to do, and finally retired to my room in the hotel about two o'clock in the morning.

It had been arranged that these progressives would see to it I reach the next meeting place.

So the next morning a man with a boy, apparently sixteen years of age, drove up to the hotel in a rather dilapidated Ford to take me to my destination. I thought at first the man was a negro; but he was the father of the boy, perfectly white. My curiosity was aroused. There was only one white spot on the face of the man, a place about as large as a five-cent piece on his left cheek; and it was perfectly white. As we started off into the country, he told me his life story.

He was a miner; had worked a lifetime in a coal mine.

Years before, in an explosion that killed many miners, he was so terribly injured it was not believed that he could survive. Both arms, both legs, and his collarbone had been broken—one arm in two places. The force of the mine blast had injured his spinal cord, jammed his head out of shape, and seared every exposed spot on his body black. His case seemed so hopeless that little attention was paid to him in the beginning.

But visitors flocked to the scene from all sections of Pennsylvania, among them a surgeon from Philadelphia who, noting that no attention had been given to this unconscious man, made a careful examination. Immediately taking charge, he ordered the man taken to a hospital in Philadelphia, where he gave him the finest of medical attention and care, assumed every penny of expense himself, and through the months devoted himself unselfishly to the case until recovery was complete. That explosion left the miner unable to do heavy manual labor; nevertheless, he lived on and still was active in support of the miners' interests.

When he finished his story, I sat silent, deeply moved by its throbbing pathos.

Shortly after, we passed a cemetery where he showed me a cheap tombstone in a lonely corner. It had been there for years, marking the grave of a miner who, just before his death, wrote the epitaph that appeared. Enlisting from the mines at the outbreak of the Civil War, he had served through its four years. Then when the war ended, he had gone back to his original occupation as a coal miner.

My driver told me that in his own early experience the condition of the miners was much worse. The men who worked in the mines were compelled to trade at the company stores. Always at the end of the month the miner owed the operator instead of the operator owing the miner. Thus men were kept a little bit in debt; not permitted to join a union; not allowed to become affiliated with any organization for the improvement of their social conditions. At the time of his injury in the mine explosion he was the father of three children. He had been required to keep a small amount of money on deposit to cover any possible account he might contract. His wife and small children, without income, in those harrowing days, tried to get this money from the mining company, without success, and only the charity of neighbors averted starvation.

I sat there in the cemetery; it was not beautiful; it had grown to tall grass and weeds and plainly showed neglect.

In the tumbled masses of weeds we came to the small tombstone on which was inscribed this epitaph:

For 40 years beneath the sod, with pick and spade I did my task,
The coal king's slave, but now, thank God, I'm free at last.

It was written by a man on his deathbed, a man knowing he had not long to live, and who in dying expressed the desire to perpetuate his memory to the world.

I was impressed greatly by the experience of this day. While I think with satisfaction of the great improvement which has come in the years since that lonely grave was dug, I can see that even yet the coal miner's task is little understood by the American people. As a rule, he goes into the earth when only a boy, works there until he dies of old age, and in the end has not saved a competence to provide for his widow or minor children.

The flood tide of emotion aroused that afternoon had much to do with an activity in which I afterward became engaged in the Senate in passing the anti-injunction act that brought about abolition of the yellow-dog contract. In the course of the tumultuous debates over that legislation I stood in the center of the Senate chamber and repeated the lines of that epitaph to my colleagues.

There has always been a warm place in my heart for the miner who lives a life of toil with such meager results. And that sympathy was greatly strengthened by the impressions received in campaigning the coal-mining regions of Pennsylvania: impressions that stirred me to press legislation through Congress for labor's Magna Charta.

In the general election Vare won a close battle. Surprisingly the rock-ribbed Republican citadel of Pennsylvania had been so close to defeat the hot breath of repudiation was on the back of its neck.

Vare's election was contested by Wilson. When the former presented himself to the Senate and asked to be seated, I objected and insisted his credentials be referred to the Committee on Privileges and Elections. This was done, and in the investigation which followed it became the judgment of the committee no regular election had taken place.

That judgment was approved by the Senate with the result that the senatorship from Pennsylvania automatically became vacant and the governor on December 11, 1929, appointed Joseph R. Grundy to fill the vacancy.

James J. Davis became the Republican candidate in the next election and was successful.

25

A SECOND EMANCIPATION

The early twenties brought the American people to their knees in worship at the shrine of private business and industry.

It was said, and accepted without question by millions of Americans, that private enterprise could do no wrong.

In Mr. Harding's cabinet that philosophy probably was best exemplified by Andrew Mellon, the head of the Treasury, a man of enormous wealth, of widespread connections with industry, of great capacity. In the government of those years Mr. Mellon was a most able spokesman for huge industry and business, and that influence ran through Mr. Harding's cabinet and through all the administrative branches and agencies of government.

It dominated Congress.

Even more, it had the unmistakable support of the American people.

In the next twelve years it was to produce one of the great classic struggles of the legislative branch of the national government, through the battle for the Tennessee Valley Authority, better known as TVA, with which my name has been linked from the beginning.

My association with TVA was purely accidental and, at the start, very much against my personal wishes.

It represents the single outstanding development of the natural resources of a great American stream which has been undertaken in comprehensive fashion after long thought, study, and more than a decade of interminable conflict in the Congress.

It was not simply one struggle; more accurately, it was two, although the dividing line was indistinct, and always the issue was the same. From the first gun to the last, there was no armistice, no breathing space, and no truce. From the beginning to the end, there was that irreconcilable conflict between those who believed the natural wealth of the United States best can be developed by private capital and enterprise, and those who believe that in certain activities related to the natural resources only the great strength of the federal government itself can perform the most necessary task in the spirit of unselfishness, for the greatest good to the greatest number.

I did not ask for the job of leading in the battle for TVA.

I thought, as chairman of the Committee on Agriculture of the Senate, that I should be spared its great burden.

I felt deeply I lacked the strength, the time, and the technical background to discharge that task creditably.

I never have known how it came to be dumped upon my lap.

It was months and years of study and research which brought about my long championship of TVA. I entered upon that study without deeply rooted prejudices. I think I can say I had an open mind except for the feeling that congressional proposals, relating to the ultimate disposition of Muscle Shoals, more properly should have fallen to the Senate Military Affairs Committee, of which Senator Wadsworth of New York was chairman. He was a most able man, a conservative, and was courageous.

For some reason, he wanted the bill for the completion of Wilson Dam, then before Congress, referred to the committee of which I was chairman. He was most insistent this course be followed. The matter was debated at some length on the floor of the Senate. Secretly I hoped the bill would be referred to the Military Affairs Committee; but the Senate decided the issue as Senator Wadsworth wished, and thus I found myself confronted with a responsibility which I did not want.

I went to work.

In the years which followed, there were untold hearings, lasting for months, night sessions of the committee in order to expedite action, and a growing volume of controversies with each session of Congress.

At the close of the First World War, when the original dam of TVA was incomplete, the House of Representatives had dispatched a committee to investigate the subject of finishing it. The committee reported that the government should abandon the entire proposition; and the House, in which appropriation measures originate, consequently made no appropriation for continuing work on the dam.

I thought this was a grave mistake.

I had studied the matter enough to become convinced there were great possibilities for good in the completion of Wilson Dam and others like it in the Tennessee valley.

In the first crucial test, I endeavored to have an amendment inserted in the appropriation bill which had come over to the Senate, setting aside adequate funds for the continued construction of Wilson Dam. In this I failed, and work was suspended through the failure of Congress to provide funds. Right there the ultimate costs of TVA were increased because the organization for completion of Wilson Dam was destroyed by this brief, temporary abandonment of activity.

And I knew that all the work, upon which millions had been spent, would be lost unless future Congresses did something. For a year construction activities on Wilson Dam were suspended.

Fortunately, in the next Congress we obtained an appropriation permitting construction to be resumed.

From that point, throughout the next ten years, after beating back efforts of private interests to get Muscle Shoals, I introduced the several bills in different Congresses which, with only slight changes, followed the same general outline for the development of the entire Tennessee River and its tributaries. I came to the conclusion gradually that the possibilities were infinitely greater than had been first contemplated: while the production of nitrogen from the atmosphere was important to national defense in time of war, and while the manufacture of cheap fertilizer for use in reviving the productivity of exhausted soil was important in time of peace, there were other goals much to be desired.

I was impressed by the periodical floods exacting such an enormous economic toll in sections of the United States. In my own state, and in all of the Great Plains area, for example, there were rivers which frequently became unruly in flood season—and in those same valleys a few weeks later crops were destroyed by drouth.

It was so senseless and so useless.

I had come to the conclusion that many of the streams in the United States, flowing from the mountains through the meadows to the sea, presented the opportunity to produce great amounts of electricity for the homes and factories of the nation. I knew falling water, when properly harnessed, generated what men for want of a better name have called electricity. Its secret, even in the electrical age which is dawning, is but partially known and understood by science; but its service to mankind is recognized—relieving men and women of drudgery which cannot be discharged in any other way. It drives the machines of production.

I had lived the hard boyhood of a primitive Ohio farm, and the possibilities of electricity for lightening the drudgery of farms and urban homes, while revolutionizing the factories, fascinated me.

From that point, always the issue was the same.

It was uppermost some years later when I offered an amendment in the Senate to a pending bill which had for its object the prevention of floods in the great Mississippi valley. It underlies the conflict over Missouri River development. It extends to every great river valley in the United States where the questions of flood control, navigation, generation of electricity, and development of irrigation present themselves. For they are inseparably linked in any effective, intelligent, and internal economic developments of this nature.

All this I had written to a friend, associated with a midwestern newspaper, setting forth the source of opposition to TVA and the misunderstandings relating to it.

The source of that opposition can be stated clearly and simply.

It developed because of the necessity of taking the unconscionable profit out of the handling and development of property which belongs truly to the American people. It has seemed always to me that the development and conservation of such resources ought to be under public control, public operation, and public ownership. Equally clear to me was the fact that the maximum happiness and utility were attained only when a stream was developed as a whole, and not piecemeal.

So I wrote to this friend:

> Secretly I have hoped through the establishment of TVA, not daring to express it publicly, it would serve as a model by which this country could see the happiness, material progress, and prosperity to be attained if the American people act promptly and properly in the preservation of God-given natural resources of the country. The Tennessee Valley Authority does produce, in my judgment, the maximum benefits which come from the proper development of an entire waterway as one system. It does check and avert devastating floods in all of their economic waste. It does allay the forces of erosion of the land, and permit reforestation. It does provide cheap water transportation. It does produce enormous quantities of electricity for lighting the rural homes and the cities and for national defense. It represents the first attempt in history to coordinate all of these resources.

For whatever inspiration and encouragement it may be to the American people in their struggle against well-intrenched, enormously rich, and powerful forces, and the selfishness, confusion, and misunderstanding they inject, this "log" of some of the successive steps in the struggle for TVA furnishes some slight knowledge of the battle:

1921: Secretary of War Weeks asked for bids for the leasing of Muscle Shoals. The thought was private development and operation.

July 8, 1921: Henry Ford first submitted his bid. Committee hearings opened.

February 6, 1922: S.J. 159, for acceptance of Ford offer, introduced in Senate with committee support, together with other bills of a similar character.

December 5, 1923: House bill to dispose of properties to Ford again introduced; passed both House and Senate, but with amendments, and finally died through lack of action on conference committee report.

January 5, 1926: S.J. Res. 2147 introduced by Norris to provide for the operation of Dam No. 2 at Muscle Shoals, for the construction of other dams on the Tennessee River and its tributaries, and for the incorporation of the Federal Power Corporation. Referred to committee; no action taken.

December 15, 1927: S.J. Res. 46 by Norris providing for the completion of Dam No. 2 at Muscle Shoals and the steam plant at Nitrate Plant No. 2 for the manufacture and distribution of fertilizer and for other purposes. This passed both houses of Congress but received pocket veto by President Coolidge in June of 1928.

May 28, 1929: S.J. Res. 49 by Norris "to provide for the national defense by the creation of a corporation for the operation of the government properties at or near Muscle Shoals and for other purposes." It passed both branches of Congress and was vetoed by President Hoover, and the veto sustained March 3, 1931.

December 9, 1931: S.J. Res. 15 by Norris "to provide for the national defense by the creation of a corporation for the operation of government property at or near Muscle Shoals." No action taken.

April 11, 1933: S.J. 1272 by Norris "to improve the navigability and to provide for flood control of the Tennessee River, provide for reforestation and the proper use of marginal land in the Tennessee valley; to provide for the agricultural and industrial development of the valley; to provide for the national defense by the creation of a corporation for the operation of government property at or near Muscle Shoals, and for other purposes." In lieu of this, H.R. 5081 passed House, after introduction by Congressman Lister Hill, and Norris moved to take up the House bill, strike out all after the enacting clause, and substitute the Senate bill, which was done.

There, in most abbreviated form, are the milestones marking the legislative struggle over the Tennessee Valley Authority. There were many other resolutions and bills to turn Muscle Shoals to private interests in the opening phases of the fight.

It was a most natural opposition to the entire principle of TVA that developed in the beginning.

I was certain a majority of the members of Congress in both branches were against development of Muscle Shoals by the federal government.

If for no other reason than the conservative tendencies of those years, expressed on every street corner and throughout the rural regions, there was raised a nearly insurmountable barrier to TVA. Private enterprise, it was said, had built America. Its initiative, its energy, its genius, and its great vision had made the American people strong, sturdy, rich—the best fed and the best cared-for people in the world. Congress accepted that doctrine generally without reservations, gladly and honestly. People believed it. There was the proof in the young and vigorous nation, which had outstripped its older rivals, and enjoyed infinitely more comforts and luxuries than other nations. Governmental operation and ownership was looked upon with great suspicion, distaste, and open resentment.

It was by accident, the result of America's participation in World War No. 1, that the national government on its own initiative had taken the first, uncertain step for a development of this magnitude on a national scale. That war emergency was the chief reason, among many, why the Tennessee valley was selected as the proper site, or the testing ground, for this national movement.

War had made the question of nitrates a very critical and exceedingly important consideration. They were needed in all kinds of military operations, and for the production of explosives. To a very great extent, the United States, as well as other nations of the world, had been depending upon nitrates which came from Chile. Immediately submarine warfare, coupled with the sinking of ships by "surface raiders," raised a question of transportation of these nitrates from South America to the American mainland where they could be conserved properly, and utilized later to supply the American fighting forces with the necessary explosives to carry on and to win the war.

Nitrogen in its natural state was one of the most plentiful of all the ingredients which go into explosives.

It was in the air all around and about in inexhaustible quantities.

But to extract nitrogen from the air under the methods then prevailing required a vast amount of electricity. It could not be produced economically without fabulous amounts of cheap power. In

Norway, a nation blessed with swift, deep streams, lending themselves admirably to the development of cheap power and cheap electricity, one process for producing nitrogen had been in existence for a number of years.

Another, more effective and economical method, known as the cyanamide process, had been developed; but it too required a very great amount of electricity.

This was the emergency which led the federal government to undertake the development of cheap power by proper conservation on some of the streams of the United States. Congress had authorized the President, Woodrow Wilson, to select locations for such developments, and Mr. Wilson, upon recommendations by the engineering counsel, chose Muscle Shoals and began construction of Wilson Dam.

The intention was to make the United States independent of the necessity of importing nitrates from South America.

There also had been the hope that development at Muscle Shoals would result in the production of a cheaper form of commercial fertilizer for worn-out land as a permanent, valuable aid to agriculture. The two objectives fitted into each other. Through Muscle Shoals it was hoped to obtain adequate nitrogen for the explosives needed in war, and later for fertilizer in time of peace. A cheaper fertilizer would be a great boon to the older regions of the United States, making possible abundant crops, and an improvement in the status of farm families who were existing miserably on soil whose fertility had been depleted.

It was recognized that completion of Wilson Dam would take considerable time and was no overnight job.

As a short cut from dependence upon foreign nitrogen, it was determined to construct a steam plant at Muscle Shoals to supply the electric power for the production of nitrates while the war lasted. The steam plant was built, in a much shorter time than Wilson Dam, and the nitrate plant itself required much less time for construction. It became known as Nitrate Plant No. 2, built by the American Cyanamid Company under the supervision of the government, while work was being pushed rapidly on Wilson Dam.

It was known also Germany must have perfected some other process for the production of nitrates. That rigid blockade maintained by the vigilance of the navies of the Allied nations hemmed Germany in, and made it impossible for her to obtain Chilean nitrate. While American chemists and scientists were not sure of the secret methods employed by Germany, they thought they had uncovered them. So a pilot plant, known as nitrate plant, No. 1, and a second steam plant to provide the electricity which would be needed by it, were built near by, largely as an experiment.

This pilot nitrate plant naturally was not as large as its predecessor; and although it was completed it never was put into production. All the expenditures upon it, together with the outlay for a second steam plant, were lost. Never a pound of nitrate came from these developments, but the desperate condition which existed fully justified the attempts. There could be no complaint because of futile expenditures; under the circumstances, the necessity of producing nitrates constituted a national emergency. The cyanamide process adopted in Nitrate Plant No. 2 meant production was very costly—perhaps too costly to supply a cheap fertilizer in times of peace.

Before Wilson Dam was finished, war was over.

Then the scientific world learned of the process used by Germany in extracting nitrogen from the atmosphere, and thus carrying on the struggle even though the Allied blockade had cut her off from the South American source of supply.

The German method, known as the Haber process, was a very material improvement over the cyanamide formula and was much less costly.

Immediately private corporations in this country rushed to construct plants utilizing the Haber process.

It was then that it fell to Congress to determine the future of Muscle Shoals. It was then that the proposal for bids from private corporations received much public approval; it was then Mr. Ford made his offer and the congressional conflict began. Numbers of resolutions were offered to turn Wilson Dam over to private owners. There was the Underwood bill later, which in itself precipitated a bitter fight, and under the provisions of which the resources of the Tennessee valley would have fallen into private hands represented by a number of associated private corporations.

Of all the measures to turn over the resources of the Tennessee River to private development, I think that that of Henry Ford had more popular support than any other. A distinguished American, he is one of America's wealthiest and most successful men. He had captivated American imagination. He had produced a cheap automobile, established the most satisfactory relationships with the workers in his factories, and demonstrated he was a man of great vision, daring, and dreams. About that time the industrial giants of America had become the nation's heroes.

It was on July 8, 1921, that Henry Ford submitted his proposal for the leasing of Muscle Shoals. Nearly a year passed before House hearings were completed; and out of the hearings H.R. 11903 emerged in the House of Representatives, providing for acceptance of the Ford offer. There were other bills providing for the acceptance of Mr. Ford's offer, and for leasing Muscle Shoals to other interested groups. At the same session and subsequent sessions, there were resolutions and bills calling for new congressional surveys and for establishing commissions to complete studies. It was a period of great confusion and uncertainty of purpose in Congress.

Not until the opening days of December in 1923, did friendly sentiment towards acceptance of the Ford offer crystallize in the House and the Senate to bring about passage of H.R. 518, which was a duplicate of the Ford bill of the year before.

With many amendments added in the Senate, the measure went to conference; and agreement upon the differences was finally reached by the conferees in a report to both houses on February 6, 1925. It was a "Lame Duck" session of Congress, and adjournment was due in six days, so that no action was taken on the conference report by either branch of Congress.

Muscle Shoals occupied the same status after four years.

I fought all these bills.

In the main, the senators representing the southern states were in favor of accepting Mr. Ford's proposal.

After studying it, and the entire subject, to the best of my ability, I had reached the unalterable conclusion I could not support any proposition turning all of this property over to Mr. Ford. I had become convinced that every bill which had been introduced contained provisions which made it impossible for the plan to succeed. I argued at that time the cyanamide process of getting nitrogen from the atmosphere was too expensive to be of practical benefit in the production of cheap fertilizer for agriculture—the emergency of war, with the immediate need of nitrates for explosives, having passed.

I have no way of knowing how this blistering controversy, which Mr. Ford's offer had inspired in the Senate, would have ended had not he, himself, withdrawn the offer.

This withdrawal did not end it.

ANOTHER "GEORGE W." TRYING TO CROSS THE DELAWARE.

Still the fight between private interests on one side and government ownership and operation of Muscle Shoals on the other was far from settled. There was a very considerable sentiment remaining expressed in the Underwood bill, but I noted and took hope in the weakening of opposition. There were other aspects in which personal profit played a very large and agonizing part. The expectation that Mr. Ford or some other individual or group would obtain Muscle Shoals, upon which the government had expended millions, and would operate it for private gain and profit, ushered in an era of active real estate speculation in sections of the Tennessee valley. Thousands of honest men and women were led to invest their savings in real estate in the belief they were getting in on the ground floor of a new American wonderland.

I know Mr. Ford had no knowledge these real estate manipulations were going on.

I was burned in effigy in some communities because of my fight against his offer.

A flood of letters reached my office. Threats against my life, to which I paid no attention, were quite common. Among the thousands of letters undoubtedly were many from people who thought my advocacy of my plan was cheating them out of a profit legitimately theirs. I never believed that any of the threats represented any firm intention, although some men in high authority were inclined to look upon them as genuine, and some told me they thought a crazy assailant might attempt to carry out his threat against my life.

In that boom centering around the Muscle Shoals development, a town had been incorporated and platted, covering several square miles. It was these town lots which were being sold. Offices of the real estate speculators were established in some of the leading cities of the country, including Washington.

Special trains were run from New York City to Muscle Shoals, filled with prospective land purchasers. People were taken up in airplanes to view the wonderful sweep of country where a city, rivaling even New York, was to rise when this great power development had been turned over to Mr. Ford and his genius for ultimate development. In that boom thousands of lots were sold to people living in scattered sections of the United States so that every purchaser of a lot became a committee of one to help Mr. Ford gain possession of Muscle Shoals.

I am certain that, had Mr. Ford known of this, he would have frowned upon it and rebuked it with all the power at his command.

Thousands and thousands of dollars were siphoned out of the

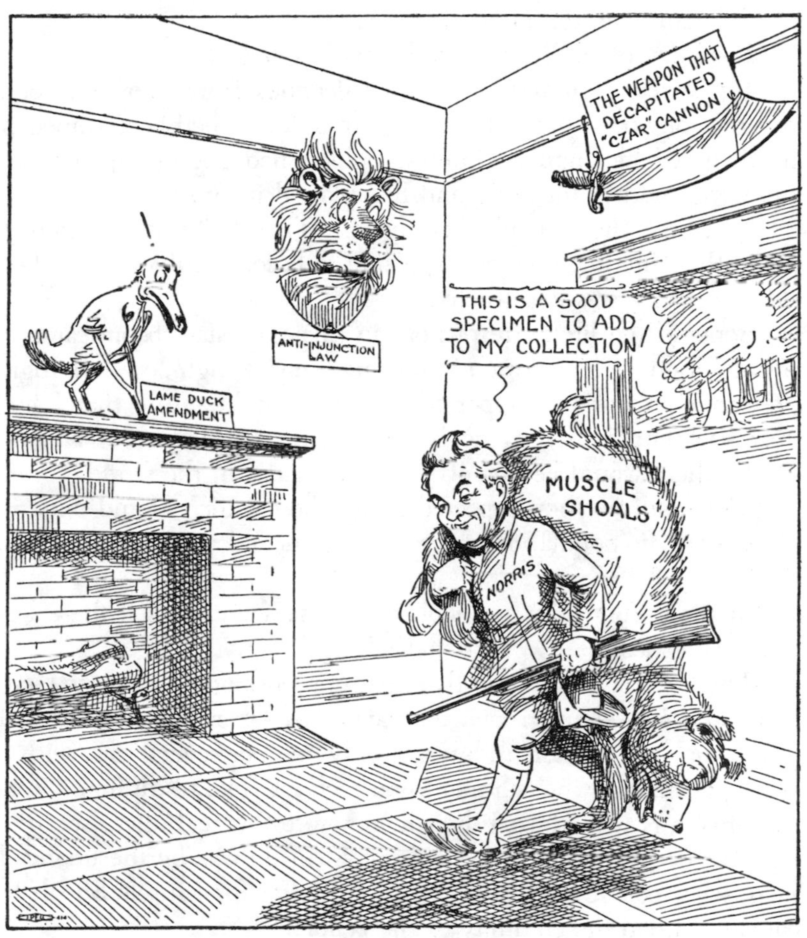

MORE BIG GAME!

pockets of poor people, principally laborers, by the installment method of selling lots in this great Muscle Shoals area. I have no idea what the ultimate profits were. I was distressed by the knowledge innocent men and women stood to lose their life savings. I was powerless to stop it. Congress was divided in its attitude toward Muscle Shoals, and no clear, distinct sentiment had manifested itself in support of a plan that promised effective, economical development.

The mail mounted in volume.

Each day my office was flooded with letters.

I received thousands of communications from people who, I became convinced beyond a shadow of a doubt, had been duped or hoodwinked by financial interests which had bought up the surrounding country for miles and had platted it into lots.

Of course these people were honest. They had invested money, many their lifetime savings, expecting to become millionaires when this great city was constructed.

Some of the literature put out in this real estate boom came to my attention. It was written in flowing terms, a high-powered, high-pressured promotion, supported by the finest literature that I had ever seen circulated, in the belief that in the vicinity of Muscle Shoals there would be one of the largest cities in the world.

Men told me they expected a city there which would outstrip New York in population. Men of wealth and power shared this belief.

In New York City a school to educate agents to sell these lots was established.

Those lots sold were mostly to persons working on a salary. Generous and liberal provisions for payments, extending over several years, enabled investors to buy not only one but several lots, with a small payment down each month on each lot. The result finally was that investors who poured their money into this real estate speculation lost everything, and the only profit made was by the financial men, who took advantage of Mr. Ford's offer for Muscle Shoals to capitalize upon the credulity of the people.

I made several trips to Muscle Shoals—one about the time that my mail was being flooded with letters from these poor investors. I was met by an army man, who showed me over the plant and all of the other developments. It was an inspection covering three days, partly by automobile.

Invariably, my guide had with him the same assistant—a man who took no part in any conversation, apparently knew nothing about Muscle Shoals, or anything about the controversy over it.

I was curious.

Then the awakening came. In getting into the automobile the man pushed an outer, heavy coat aside, and I saw a huge revolver strapped on his hip. At the first opportunity I asked my guide why his associate was accompanying us, to which he replied:

"That man is for your protection.

"I know of these land sales and I would be distressed beyond words, if, while you were under my guidance, some fool should take a shot at you in order to have what he feels to be his revenge."

There were weary years of fight still ahead.

26

TVA IN EXISTENCE

WITH WITHDRAWAL OF Mr. Ford's offer, the struggle over Muscle Shoals simplified itself to an issue between those who believed in public ownership and development of the power at Muscle Shoals and throughout the entire Tennessee valley, and the "power trust," seeking to prevent anything of the kind.

The private power companies never offered to develop the stream which it desired to prevent the government from touching.

Power, in reality, was not the first consideration of the Tennessee Valley Authority in any bill that I introduced in Congress over a period of years. Power was not even the most important of the the considerations.

I, at least, always have believed that the first and most important objective was the control of the flood waters of a great river, which in turn affected the Ohio from the mouth of the Tennessee to the mouth of the Ohio, and the Mississippi from the mouth of the Ohio to the Gulf of Mexico.

All the years I was in Congress until completion of the Tennessee Valley Authority, frightfully destructive floods had rolled down the tributaries of the Tennessee from their headwaters in the Alleghenies, in gathering volume to inflict great damage upon property and human life along the Tennessee, the Ohio, and finally the Mississippi.

In the months that followed these floods, there was not enough water left in the Tennessee to maintain navigation.

The bills which I introduced provided, without exception, for maintaining navigation on the Tennessee from Knoxville to the mouth in Kentucky, where it empties into the Ohio. They called for a normal channel, with a nine-foot flow of water. To accomplish it, flood waters had to be held back in the reservoirs and released during the seasons of low stream flow.

In this way, and only in this way, the destruction resulting from floods could be eliminated, or reduced to a minimum.

Up to this point, the fight had been much more confused.

Mr. Ford's offer, supported perhaps by a majority of the Senate, with nation-wide attention favorably focused upon it, had been clear, plain, and understandable to the people.

By contrast, I had no specific plan, and I realized all along my position did not present a practical method of utilizing all the power developed by the steam plant and the even greater electrical energy to be supplied by Wilson Dam.

I think I had demonstrated beyond argument that nitrogen from the atmosphere could be obtained much more cheaply by scrapping Nitrate Plant No. 2 and constructing an entirely new one embodying the Haber process.

That in itself had involved long study.

The Du Pont company (either a subsidiary or the parent corporation of the gigantic organization) had constructed a nitrogen plant near Charleston, West Virginia, utilizing the German Haber process for extracting nitrogen from the air.

I determined upon a personal examination of that plant at Charleston, and requested the War Department to assign to me one of its representatives who, while not a chemist, had had partial control of the construction of Nitrate Plant No. 2 at Muscle Shoals.

Secretary Weeks agreed to my request, and the examination was made.

The Du Ponts sent their principal chemist, a most generous and thoughtful aid, to meet me. He proceeded to make everything accessible to us; no objection was placed in the path of any investigation I desired to make. From what I saw, it became clear to me a new plant for Muscle Shoals could be constructed for much less money than the original one had cost, operated at much less expense, and would produce much more nitrogen.

Still the position I occupied was a very difficult one.

There was always the argument that since Uncle Sam had expended so many millions in the construction of this cyanamide plant, it should be utilized either under the Ford proposal or under some other, such as may have been contemplated in the Underwood bill.

There was only one answer.

I think I demonstrated before the Agricultural Committee of the Senate, through the testimony of the most eminent chemists and scientists, the cyanamide process never would be a success. New discoveries and new processes had antiquated its methods, although they were all right in their day.

And now the controversy was broadening infinitely.

It was my consistent argument that the construction of these reservoirs along the tributaries and on the Tennessee would prevent all damage from floods in the Tennessee valley and lessen the destruction on the Ohio and the Mississippi. The Tennessee, I pleaded, could be made navigable the year around. No longer was power the sole objective, or even the chief purpose.

If floods were controlled successfully, it followed naturally that erosion could be prevented to a very great extent. Already the winds whipping against the hillsides, the rains beating down, the floods churning through its valleys, had carried away into the river itself much of the fertile soil of the Tennessee region, with the result that the lands had lost some of their productivity and had become much less valuable for agricultural purposes.

The silt carried into the streams interfered seriously with navigation.

I thought I could look ahead to a time when thousands of people would be compelled either to abandon the land entirely, or to live in the utmost squalor and poverty.

If these flood waters were controlled by the construction of high dams to hold back the flow in reservoirs, necessarily it followed that, by the expenditure of comparatively small additional sums, electrical power could be generated at the dams as a by-product and dis-

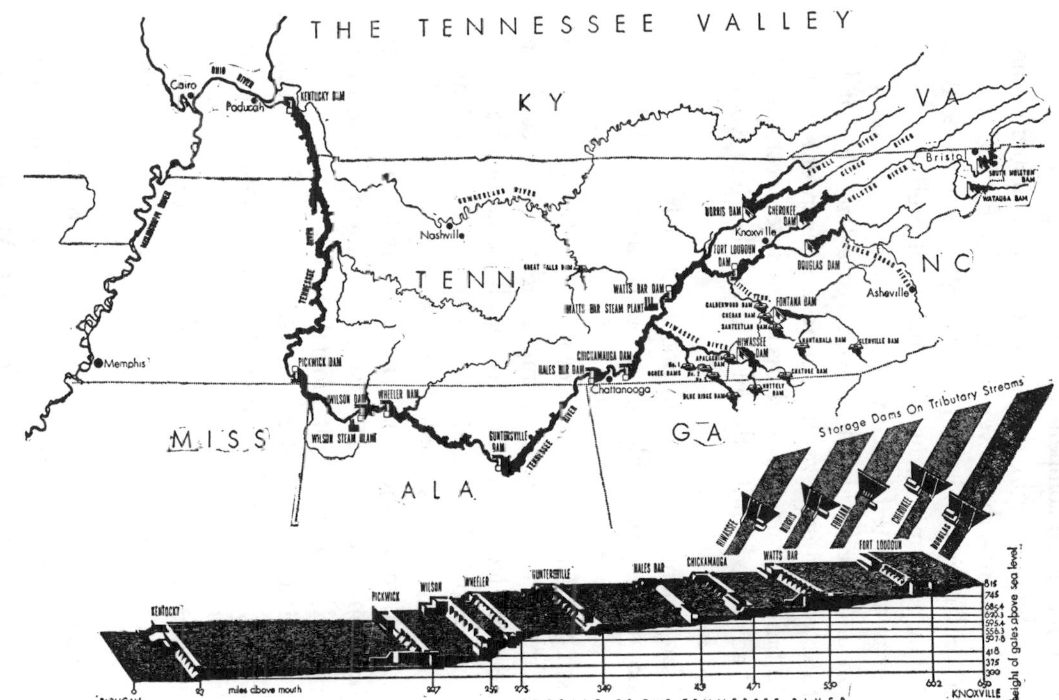

The TVA represents the first comprehensive development of a river and its tributaries to insure the maximum benefits of flood control, navigation, conservation of the soil, reforestation and cheap electricity. At the top is the map showing the dam sites on the Tennessee and its tributaries; at the bottom a profile of the river and the dams situated upon it. Twelve years of struggle went into this development which now has attracted national and international attention.

tributed freely to the people of the entire region at prices much lower than they had been compelled to pay.

It was this which brought the irreconcilable, embittered, and uncompromising enemy—the power trust—into the fight.

It had no fundamental objection to making the Tennessee River navigable, but in pursuance of its own interest it preferred an unnavigable river to any interference with its monopolistic control of the generation and sale of electric power. For a long time it had claimed that the way to improve the Tennessee River, or any other stream, was to build low navigation dams at much less cost than the dams which I advocated; and in this plan it said the river would be navigable even in low water.

It was an argument which would not stand analysis.

Navigation, to be practicable, must be as unimpeded as possible.

Ships passing through fifty, sixty, or more low navigation dams would be confronted with impossible impediments. The great reservoirs, some of them located on the river itself, some on the tributaries, by the use of the high dam, would expedite navigation through sets of locks. Vessels would be elevated from a lower level to a higher level through the locks, and they could sail for miles without impediment over artificial lakes, speeding up navigation, making it practical, and making it profitable.

At the same time these artificial lakes and high dams would produce electricity, all of which would be lost by the construction of only low navigation dams.

One high dam could make the river navigable for many miles and eliminate the necessity of constructing scores of low navigation dams.

The largest dam in the TVA program is named Kentucky Dam, and, at the time of writing, is not yet completed. It is approximately twenty miles from the mouth of the Tennessee. When finished, it will make the Tennessee navigable for a distance of 180 miles to the site of the next dam, known as Pickwick Landing, which has been in operation for several years. Together they will provide a stretch of water 220 miles in length, on which ships can navigate freely without any impediment and without any use of navigation locks.

Norris Dam, provided for under the original TVA act, is about twenty miles to the northwest of Knoxville on the Clinch River, a Tennessee tributary. It holds back the largest amount of flood waters except that which will be impounded by Kentucky Dam. Norris Dam has had a very material effect upon the navigability of the Tennessee River itself and upon the floods of the Tennessee, Ohio, and the Mississippi. It holds back the surplus waters of a number of Tennessee tributaries which otherwise would discharge a huge volume of water into the main river at a time when flood conditions are aggravated.

In 1937 one of the most damaging floods east of the Mississippi that have ever been recorded would have been intensified had it not been for the effect of Norris Dam upon the flow of the Ohio and the Mississippi.

The city of Cairo, located on the Ohio River, between the mouth of the Ohio and the mouth of the Tennessee, often has been damaged greatly by floods. There is no doubt but the city would have been engulfed and possibly destroyed in this particular case had it not been for Norris Dam.

It may seem impossible that Norris Dam, roughly seven hundred miles distant from Cairo by river, should have saved that city from destruction. Yet the waters of the Ohio at Cairo had risen to the danger point and then above, the levees for the city's protection were in danger of being washed out. At the critical hour, eminent engineers, making careful computations, reached the conclusion that the huge volume of flood waters stored back of Norris Dam had saved Cairo and had greatly diminished the floods along the entire Ohio and Mississippi.

Again, there was an extremely dry year. Less water came down from the mountain streams that form the Tennessee River than in many years. All the tributaries were very low, and navigation of the Tennessee would have been impossible but for the water that had been stored behind these dams, particularly Norris Dam, which was released gradually. The stream was open to navigation throughout the entire period. Engineers again estimated that the navigability of the Mississippi itself had been increased materially by the release of these flood waters from the Norris Reservoir.

It has been demonstrated that the fears of the power trust that competition by the TVA would prevent it from selling its own electricity had no solid basis.

All over the civilized world, when electric power is produced and sold at reasonable rates its use is multiplied manifold. In many cases the cheapening of hydroelectric power has brought greater financial progress because then the ordinary customer can afford to use more electricity.

In the closing stages of this fight, all the forces that could be mobilized against the Tennessee Valley Authority were drawn in.

There were the coal companies.

Their opposition was inspired by an argument that labor in the coal mines would be the loser if TVA developed the vast amount of power that was contemplated. The figures have shown that the coal companies have not come into competition with TVA activities but actually have made more money and have sold more coal since TVA than they sold before.

The truth is that electric power is rapidly becoming a necessity in every modern community, but until recent years the prices for it have been so high that its full use has been denied to millions of people.

I remember the case of John L. Lewis.

Mr. Lewis always had been opposed to the TVA Act—honestly, no doubt, believing that the generation of vast amounts of electric power would deprive many of his miners of their jobs. The TVA purchases and uses a large amount of coal; has constructed and built several generating plants where coal is used exclusively for the generation of power. Mr. Lewis' attitude simply demonstrated that any man who stands in the way of human progress and seeks to prevent the use of technological improvements is standing in his own way and blocking his own progress.

Not only has TVA brought reduced prices to the firesides in the homes where electricity is consumed; but it has improved agricultural conditions in the great Tennessee valley beyond all hopes and expectations of those who favored the TVA legislation. This was inherently a part of the struggle for final congressional approval of the bill I introduced at the opening of each session of Congress.

At the end of seven years' fight, following months of congressional battle, TVA passed both branches in June of 1928; but President Coolidge killed it by pocket veto. Again, two years later Congress passed TVA; but President Herbert Hoover sent my hopes crashing to the lowest point they reached in all those years when he vetoed it in a sharp message assailing the principles of government ownership and operation.

I tried unsuccessfully to override the veto.

The power trust with all the vast resources at its command, utilizing fully every ounce of influence it could wield in a last-ditch fight, naturally had sought to create the impression that nothing more was concerned in the TVA program than the generation of electricity through harnessing the streams under a program of public ownership and operation.

The truth was that power was only a by-product—important because it would contribute most to the recovery of the necessary outlays of public funds to carry out all of the objectives of the TVA. This I repeated session after session until TVA passed Congress for the third time in April of 1933 and was signed by President Roosevelt.

The TVA Act in express language states that its object is:

1—To improve the navigability and to provide for flood control of the Tennessee River.

2—To provide for reforestation and the proper use of marginal lands in the Tennessee valley.

3—To provide for the agricultural and industrial development of the Tennessee valley.

4—To provide for the national defense by the creation of a corporation for the operation of government property at or near Muscle Shoals, Ala., and for other purposes.

East of the Mississippi, the question of irrigation does not enter, at least in any material sense; but in the Great Plains to the west, stretching all the way to the foothills of the Rockies, irrigation probably is the most important consideration.

Irrigation is a form of flood control, although generally unrecognized as such, and contributes very materially to navigation by the regulation of the tributaries of the Mississippi. The best and the most effective way to store water is in the soil itself. The water that piles up behind flood-control dams, and is turned out upon thirsty and parched soil, to a very great degree finds its way back to the stream; but in its return, slowly and gradually, it alleviates those conditions which produce floods.

All these different uses of water are embraced in the plan of the TVA; and all these beneficial uses should be involved in every act that attempts to restore the natural resources of the United States and conserve them.

No private corporation ever organized under any law has been large enough to handle the conservation of all natural resources.

The dam that holds back water for irrigation, makes its contribution to the prevention of floods in the lower course of a stream; and water held back for irrigation, flood control, or navigation may be released in such a way as to produce electric power. We should commit an economic sin, a folly, if we built large dams to control floods or improve navigation or irrigate the fertile soil of the western plains without utilizing the water to produce electric power.

The low navigation dam advocated by the power trust to serve its own purposes is a thing of the past. The "multiple-purpose dam" now is acknowledge by all engineers of intelligence and patriotism to be the efficient means by which natural resources will be preserved and made beneficial and useful to man. It is only by scientific, thoughtful, unselfish, and inspired action that full conservation of natural resources will be achieved.

TVA alone has greatly extended America's system of navigable rivers, stretching from the Rockies to the Alleghenies, and from the Gulf of Mexico to the upper Mississippi. Some day industry and business, frequently critical, will prosper even more through those benefits.

It would be impossible to project the complete panorama of TVA. On the main stream of the Tennessee, as this is written, nine great dams are complete—all constructed by TVA itself with the exception of two. The first, Wilson Dam, was built by the government before TVA was born. The second, Hale's Bar Dam, was constructed by private corporations under special statute quite a number of years before TVA came upon the scene.

On the tributary streams of the Tennessee fourteen dams have been built, acquired, are under construction, or are authorized.

The aggregate power capacity, either already installed or under construction for early installation, for the nine main-stream dams is 1,123,600 kilowatts. The total power capacity of these dams on the main stream will be, it is estimated, 1,634,100 kilowatts. The number of acre-feet of useful flood control of the nine great reservoirs on the Tennessee is 6,808,900. On the tributary streams of the Tennessee the fourteen dams furnish 605,160 kilowatts, but the estimated capacity in all these dams when finished is 1,015,260 kilowatts. The number of acre-feet of useful flood storage in these tributary reservoirs is 8,625,290.

The ultimate useful storage of both main and tributary streams then is 15,434,190 acre-feet, and the total electric generation is 2,757,700 kilowatts.

TVA's steam plants, built or acquired, have a total power capacity of 2,093,960 kilowatts, which ultimately will be increased, through both hydro and steam plants, to 3,134,360 kilowatts.

This is the great giant whom the American people have at their service to obey their will, and perform their labors, and gladden their lives. This is the giant who was ready and willing at a time when the demands of war, involving a serious need for great electrical power, presented a grave crisis to the American people. This is the giant who will brighten the lives and bring laughter to the lips of many generations of children in the old Southland where poverty and national neglect have brought sorrow. And this giant, striding across America, begetting stalwart sons in other river valleys, will fight the battle of the American people to realize the hopes of happiness to which all peoples aspire.

It is such a simple process.

For full comprehension of the system, it need only be recalled that water used to generate electricity at the various dams is used time and again—the same water. The turbines generating power at Douglas Dam turn the water they use back to the Tennessee above the Fort Loudoun Dam—the last situated on the upper reaches of the Tennessee. Thus this water, which already has been used to generate electricity in the turbines of the Douglas Dam, is used nine times more as it flows down past the nine main dams in the river.

That process is repeated by the water caught behind the Cherokee and by the waters stored by the dams in all these tributaries.

In this fashion are revealed the benefits that come from flood control, navigation, and power generation in a comprehensive program for a river system.

It has been estimated by capable and qualified engineers that as a result of the flood storage provided in the basin of the Tennessee and its tributaries, already from two to three feet has been cut from the crests of the Mississippi River floods. In the Tennessee River basin as a whole the flood problem has been brought under complete control.

Of the many dams along the Tennessee the poorest was Hale's Bar Dam, privately constructed by a corporation under special legislation by Congress. It is west of Chattanooga. When the TVA purchased it from the Tennessee Electric Company, through its holding company, the Commonwealth and Southern, immediate steps were taken to improve the Hale's Bar Dam. Up to now TVA has spent three million dollars in repair work; but in order to attain the greatest efficiency, and to realize its possibilities fully, the dam will have to be increased in height at an additional cost of perhaps twelve to thirteen million dollars.

From its humble beginnings, TVA has grown until the net

© *International News Photos, Inc.*

PRESIDENT FRANKLIN D. ROOSEVELT, AFTER SIGNING THE BILL CREATING THE TENNESSEE VALLEY AUTHORITY, PRESENTS TO SENATOR NORRIS, FATHER OF TVA, THE PEN WITH WHICH HE APPROVED THE LEGISLATION.

income from the sale of power for the fiscal year ending June 30, 1943, was $13,148,653.44. This income, in all probability, will be greatly increased when the dams now under construction are finished. I am confident it will be only a comparatively few years before the net income from the sale of power will be sufficient to pay the cost of the entire system.

At the same time TVA paid in lieu of taxes more money to the various political subdivisions than was paid by the private owners of the properties when that part of TVA was privately owned and operated by the Commonwealth and Southern Corporation.

In the fiscal year of 1943, TVA paid to states and counties $1,960,492 in lieu of taxes; municipalities and other distributors of TVA power paid in lieu of taxes an aggregate of $1,914,300; the two together total $3,874,792, or practically a million dollars more than was paid in taxes when the properties were in private hands. The consumers of electric power now are buying it at savings in excess of ten million dollars a year.

The use of electricity, of course, has increased at a tremendous rate in all of this region. Average consumption per residential customer served at TVA rates advanced to 1,596 kilowatt-hours, as compared with a national average for the entire United States of 1,044 kilowatt-hours.

At the same time the average cost per kilowatt-hour declined to 1.96 cents compared to 3.66 cents per kilowatt-hour for residential service in the United States as a whole. During this last fiscal year the average residential consumer of TVA power received 50 per cent more electricity during the twelve months and paid 18 per cent less.

During the first years of its life, TVA was prevented from going on in its development and from realizing any substantial revenues from power as a result of a series of injunction suits instigated and pressed by the power trust. The expense of this litigation has cost TVA many millions of dollars. In the suits of any consequence whatsoever (every vital suit finally has been won by TVA), it was necessary to fight to the Supreme Court of the United States, where finally, when TVA itself was under direct fire, the high tribunal said it was constitutional in all its ramifications and fundamental operations.

There was that inspired investigation of TVA after it had been in operation for several years and was at the peak of its construction, brought about by unfounded charges, and resulting in the appointment of a joint committee composed of members of the Senate and the House.

The chairman was Senator Vic Donahey of Ohio. For months this joint committee continued its labors, at a cost of many thousands of dollars.

Its method of procedure sometimes was unfair. Anonymous letters were introduced as evidence; no one even now knows who wrote them. Other evidence was admitted by the committee that no court under similar conditions would have permitted.

These anonymous charges were sifted thoroughly. Senator Donahey, who was not a lawyer, paid little attention to legal distinctions in ruling on the admission of evidence: he let everything in, but only in the most honest spirit and the best of intentions, with the idea of letting the opposition to TVA have full rein to produce anything it wanted to present or felt or pretended to think would have any bearing on the issue.

Officials and employees of TVA were subjected to questioning—frequently questioning that had nothing whatsoever to do with the issue involved. The result when the committee prepared its findings was a complete vindication of the TVA officials and employees, with no evidence of dishonesty on the part of any of them. Its officials and its workers came out with unblemished and unsullied reputations.

But this investigation, to some extent, was brought about by a very unfortunate condition in the membership of the board of TVA.

Its first chairman was Dr. Arthur E. Morgan, an eminent engineer, conscientious and honest in all that he did, although in the later phases of the bitter controversy that developed it was difficult to harmonize his attitude then with the history of developments that took place in TVA itself.

It has seemed to me that, although magnificently qualified as an engineer, and perfectly conscientious, he did not give his associates on the TVA board proper consideration. Unconsciously he was unfair to them; disregarded their advice and counsel and seemed at times desirous of establishing himself as a dictator in control of every activity of the board.

As the controversy festered and became an ugly sore, I gained the impression he had formed a dislike and eventually a hatred for other members of the board, against whom he made serious charges which were found on investigation to be groundless and without merit. He was particularly bitter against David E. Lilienthal, one of the three members.

Mr. Lilienthal's term was about to expire, and Dr. Morgan apparently was determined to prevent him from being reappointed. That disagreement reached the White House, with charges made to President Roosevelt, which at the same time were brought to me by Dr. Morgan: charges which if they had been true, would have made Mr. Lilienthal an unfit man for reappointment. I had many conferences with Dr. Morgan; and I know that President Roosevelt conferred with him several times. I went over those matters in controversy at various times with the President. I had asked Dr. Morgan to be specific, insisting that general charges would not do: he must reveal concretely why David Lilienthal was unfit to serve on the board. Never in a single instance did Dr. Morgan ever make a charge or make a claim that would have received any consideration by reasonable men. Mr. Roosevelt revealed to me he had had the same experience with Dr. Morgan, who several times said to me (and, I understand, to the President) that if Lilienthal was reappointed he would resign.

Because of Dr. Morgan's great ability as an engineer I thought, and I know the President thought, his retirement should be avoided if possible. During those months I was much disturbed by the fear that Dr. Morgan would carry out his determination to retire. I investigated every charge he made. I conferred with him upon my conclusions, and still never on a single occasion did he produce a thread of evidence that Mr. Lilienthal had been untrue to his trust.

David Lilienthal was a much younger man than Dr. Morgan;

an able lawyer who previous to his initial appointment on the board had been a member of the Wisconsin Public Service Commission. It appeared to me he had been contributing an excellent service as a TVA board member. I was impressed with his comprehension of the full and real objectives of TVA and with his efforts to carry them out.

When Dr. Morgan and Mr. Lilienthal differed on questions of policy which were discussed at board sessions, the third member, Harcourt Morgan, nearly always agreed with Mr. Lilienthal. Dr. Morgan appeared to become very arbitrary at some of these meetings of the board, finding fault with all that his colleagues did or proposed. I tried to persuade Dr. Morgan to change his course; urged him to forget his idea of retiring; and told him that any differences of opinion among the members of the board should be discussed fully until a decision was reached, after which all three should unite in carrying it out.

Through those months I was conscious of making no headway with Dr. Morgan.

Mr. Roosevelt was holding up the reappointment of Mr. Lilienthal until harmony could be restored. Finally I reached the conclusion there was but one course to pursue—to reappoint Mr. Lilienthal; and the President arrived at the same conclusion.

The reappointment was made.

Dr. Morgan's enmity became aggravated, and the controversy grew worse. It seemed to me he had become so unreasonable it was impossible to work with him and to settle these disagreements in the normal manner.

My attitude changed then. I came to feel he was not going to carry out his threat to resign, and the deeper I went into the subject, the more I regretted this.

He did not retire.

Conditions on the board deteriorated.

Reluctantly I came to the conclusion there could be no improvement without the removal of Dr. Morgan. About that time Mr. Roosevelt arrived at the same decision when he issued the order directing the removal of Dr. Morgan from the TVA board.

His action came after he had summoned Dr. Morgan before him, and gave him an opportunity to state his case, of which a record was made. Subsequently the President issued an order directing his removal from the board. Dr. Morgan appealed the order to the courts, which sustained it. The investigation by the congressional committee also supported the President.

In all of this my affection for Dr. Morgan and my respect for his capabilities as an engineer never diminished. I had become intimately acquainted with him and had been deeply impressed with his powers.

From many sections of the world, engineers came to me to discuss TVA: from old and wearied countries; countries where for centuries the increasing pinch of poverty had bred stoicism and a spirit of defeat. They were caught up by the glory of the re-created land. It brought to them, they told me, a new faith and a new hope in the destinies of their own nations, long bogged down by the exhaustion of the natural wealth within their borders.

They went back, back home, where in part the miracle of the development of streams has been repeated on a large or a small scale; back to carry a gospel of hope in a world that some day will be peaceful, where men and women will seek to utilize the gifts of God for the greatest good of all.

TVA's services in the Second World War, now in progress, have been recognized by all who are responsible for the mobilization and the equipment of America's fighting forces. Its facilities have made possible a great development in war activities that could not otherwise have been.

I am grateful for the part I was privileged to play in the Tennessee Valley Authority. I did not know, when those congressional battles were in progress, that another world war was to be fought; I hoped war never again would come to the American people; but I have been everlastingly proud of the great contribution TVA has made, which cannot be fully revealed until peace returns to a tortured world.

But before Hitler's legions had broken over the frontiers of Poland it was clear to all thinking men that the present global conflict to a great extent was going to be fought in the skies. The airplane was a necessity. And American production of airplanes, requiring a vast amount of aluminum, which in turn requires a vast amount of electric power, was wholly inadequate. Aluminum production had to be greatly and rapidly increased. Production of electricity had to be increased.

Those in control of America's affairs, looking over the country with a view to a rapid stepping up of the production of electrical power, came to TVA for assistance—many of them men who had bitterly opposed its construction. Among them were the distinguished engineers of the great Commonwealth and Southern Corporation, one of the bitterest enemies TVA ever had; but, imbued with a patriotic spirit of doing a job and doing it quickly, they buried their ancient antipathies and joined hands with TVA in the construction of a dam which was needed urgently. The dam was completed in less time than the estimates indicated, and began to contribute its power to the production of aluminum for airplanes much sooner than had been believed possible. The officials of the Commonwealth and Southern saw still more was necessary, and again they came to the TVA, and TVA constructed another dam in less time and at less cost than the estimates allowed.

Airplanes made and equipped with the help of TVA electric power are fighting on every battlefront where American boys are fighting. They are fighting the same battle, wherever the young men are waging the struggle for human freedom. It can be said the TVA played an important part in the victories of our armies over tyrants.

My memory goes back to one of the delightful events associated with the long battle for TVA, shortly before I took farewell of the national capital, which for forty years had been my home and my field of action.

It was mid-December of 1942, and friends in Boston had arranged a dinner in my honor in a great hotel dining room crowded to capacity, at which there was a list of distinguished speakers.

During my brief stay a small group on the faculty of Harvard University gave a small luncheon, informal and intimate, in my honor. I was told it was the desire of my hosts that I speak to them.

Frankly, I was nervous; puzzled as to what subject would interest men on the staff of one of America's most distinguished and oldest educational institutions.

Then it was suggested to me that the group would like to hear about the TVA.

Imagine my surprise!

Here were men learned in the classics, in science, in the humanities, in every field of study the human mind has probed. And they wanted to hear me tell of an effort to reclaim an exhausted region of the United States. They wanted to learn of the fight to restore a region of woods and streams and bleeding hills where more then a century earlier Daniel Boone had extended the American frontier.

After talking to that group considerably in excess of an hour, I thought I had talked long enough. Then there were questions. I have never encountered any group of men with a more avid interest.

My years are measured.

Today TVA is a sturdy soldier in the ranks; its strength devoted to overcoming evil tyranny.

Through all these ages the tyranny of poverty has been the unseen enemy of people. It has been the provoker of wars between people.

If in the peaceful years ahead new vigor comes to old and wooded hills not only in the basin of the Tennessee but throughout America, and in other regions of the world, and laughter replaces the silence of impoverished peoples, that is well.

27

RELIEF FOR THE FARMER

I WAS FOR MORE than five years chairman of the Committee on Agriculture and Forestry in the early part of my service in the United States Senate: an assignment much to my liking.

I gave as much attention to the work as my limited abilities permitted.

After long investigation and thought, I came to the conclusion that America's role involved two responsibilities. In a long-range, broad program the greatest usefulness of the American people was in furnishing food to the crowded, undernourished peoples of Europe and other sections of the world. And at the same time I was strongly impressed with the necessity of finding a market for the products of the American soil that were so abundant.

That period of agricultural distress which followed World War No. 1 offered the paradox of abundant harvests and increasing economic distress for the farmer. He had developed vast acreages of new land to produce food for a starving world. His market was gone as suddenly as it was developed.

A part of the gospel of my party in which I never had any faith was that the imposition of heavy tariff duties upon the manufacturers of other countries would bring prosperity to the American people.

Nothing in my experience and philosophy had led me to believe that we as a people could prosper and achieve happiness through the want and misery of others.

It seemed contrary to the experience of every civilization, where intercourse and trade had been the life line of human vitality; but

I was a Republican, and tariff was one of the foundation stones of my party. From those early days in the House when I fought against the duty on petroleum products, through all the years in Congress, I opposed the mounting trends of tariff duties; and I felt strongly that the future of American agriculture could not be guaranteed by the exclusion of products of other countries.

I had lived much too close to the growing desperation on the farms arising from glutted markets and depressed prices and high interest rates and slowly reduced fertility of the soil to be indifferent. I had seen the bright hope of the countryside flicker and sputter and die.

In the years immediately following World War No. 1, when Congress and the country looked out upon the strange contrast between overproduction in the United States of many of the essential articles of food and clothing, and suffering in many of the European countries for lack of food and enough warm clothing, I felt something should be done about it.

So after investigation and study I introduced a bill in the opening days of the special session of the Sixty-seventh Congress to perform the dual service of giving relief to the suffering people of Europe, and at the same time, eliminating the paralyzing surpluses that depressed farm prices and created a very critical emergency for farm people. In the preparation of this bill I was assisted very materially by Louis Crossette, who had been confidential adviser to Herbert Hoover while he was Secretary of Commerce in the Harding cabinet; and by Carl Vrooman, Assistant Secretary of Agriculture under Woodrow Wilson.

This bill in brief provided for a government corporation, to be financed through government funds, with power to purchase agricultural and manufactured products in this country and sell them, under generous terms of credit and adequate periods for payment, to the starving peoples of Europe. Under its terms a board was to be created to administer the affairs of the corporation, with authority to purchase the products of farms and factories from cooperative organizations of farmers, or from any other source, to ship them to different parts of the world, and to dispose of them by establishing selling agencies. Sales were to be made "on time" with such security as the corporation was able to obtain, and as in its judgment was sufficient to guarantee payment of the debt.

The Secretary of Commerce was to be ex-officio chairman of the board in general charge of the business of the corporation.

Automatically under that provision of my bill, Herbert Hoover, who then was Secretary of Commerce, would have been in charge.

It was provided that the merchant marine built during the war by the government, and tied up at docks in idleness at the time I introduced my bill, should be turned over to this governmental corporation free of cost with the only condition that the corporation keep the ships in reasonable repair and in turn surrender them to the government in case of emergency or at any time when the government desired. It was also stipulated the Interstate Commerce Commission should have authority to reduce rates upon all products dealt in by this corporation from the place of purchase to the point of exportation.

It would have given the necessary cheap transportation rates and would have added tremendously to the volume of freight movements.

Products sold on time were to be paid for by debentures issued by the purchaser; the debentures to be sold for cash, and the cash in turn used to purchase more goods, thus establishing a stable, practical period of operation.

I thought Mr. Hoover's experience in handling relief measures in Europe fitted him admirably to take charge of these operations. I feared, and my fears subsequently proved to be well founded, that President Harding would be opposed to the proposed legislation. That made me all the more anxious to secure the influence of Mr. Hoover, not only to have it enacted but to see, when the law was passed, that it was properly administered. I thought that through Louis Crossette, who had assisted me originally in the preparation of the bill and who had exceedingly close relations with Mr. Hoover, the opposition might be won over. I think Mr. Hoover had appointed Mr. Crossette on several occasions to make secret missions to foreign countries where the Department of Commerce was interested in increasing the trade between these foreign countries and the United States.

We held extended hearings on the bill before the Agricultural Committee. Present at these hearings were representatives of foreign countries to outline their views, among them three spokesmen from Poland. I had several private conferences not only with them, but with many others, who understood European conditions and appreciated fully the desperation of many of these nations.

The Polish representatives told the committee that war had destroyed Poland's industries; that her factories had been tumbled to ruins or damaged, her cotton mills being idle because of the lack of capital to make the necessary repairs.

Agriculture in Poland, they said, had been destroyed to a great extent, and the people were suffering through the lack of necessities of life. They expressed a desire to purchase large quantities of cotton and other raw products; while repayment would have to be spread over a period of years, they were willing to give a security ample to insure payment for all products secured from the corporation. They wanted also to purchase clothing and food while Poland was reconstructing its farms and its factories. In the more temporary needs they expressed the belief repayment could be made within a year and a half of purchase.

The purchases of cotton to feed their reconstructed mills, they told the committee, should be based upon repayment in three years.

As security, they agreed debentures could be issued by the local municipal authority and in turn guaranteed by the Polish government. They were willing to pay any reasonable rate of interest, not to exceed 7 per cent, and were willing to enter into any other co-arrangement deemed necessary to provide additional security.

The bill met with serious opposition from powerful, wealthy, and influential citizens of our country, as well as from the White House.

Many of the cotton men of the South expressed opposition because they thought that the rehabilitation of European factories might mean destructive competition later on.

American shipping interests, eyeing the idle merchant marine and affected personally, were unanimously against the bill.

In spite of his testimony I always have believed Mr. Hoover at heart favored the legislation and would have made a great success in management and control of the governmental corporation it proposed.

Immediately it was revealed that a large majority of the committee was favorably disposed to the bill; but among them there always was a doubt as to what the final position of Mr. Hoover would be. Mr. Crossette was of the opinion that if Mr. Hoover acted entirely upon his own judgment, he would favor the legislation.

He was in an embarrassing position.

So bitter had become President Harding's opposition that if Mr. Hoover had supported the legislation actively he might have been compelled to resign from the cabinet. When the hearings had been practically completed, Mr. Hoover was asked to appear before the committee and give his views, it not then being clear whether he would favor or oppose the bill. He did not take a very positive stand either way, although there was the echo of the White House slogan "Less government in business" in what he said. He expressed the belief private agencies should work out the problems. Yet he was most careful in his appearance before the committee to indicate that if the bill passed in the present form he would do his best to carry out its provisions and to make a success of the operations of the corporation. As food administrator in Belgium, I felt, without much delay he could determine wisely and soundly where agencies should be established, and could make the act effective within a few months after its passage.

I had no doubts about Mr. Hoover's fitness for this particular role.

The powerful opposition was still to play its last card. With Senator Kellogg of Minnesota as the apparent author, it had a substitute bill up its sleeve.

Many of the more prominent Republican leaders and a number of Democrats were organized under the leadership of President Harding to oppose the enactment of my bill. Members of the Agricultural Committee who in the beginning had been favorable gradually became hesitant and timid and finally veered to follow the presidential leadership.

Among these committee members was Senator William S. Kenyon of Iowa, at the start one of the principal supporters of my proposal. Senator Furnifold M. Simmons of North Carolina, not a member of the Agricultural Committee but a leader of the Senate Democrats, was won over by the presidential opposition. Senator Simmons was followed by many of his southern colleagues who feared that the plan might interfere seriously with the prosperity of the cotton producers.

The agricultural bloc, which in the beginning had been enthusiastically back of the plan, melted away.

It injured the protective tariff, if not destroying it entirely, the opponents charged.

Most formidable of all, however, were the shipping interests, a practical monopoly of the most powerful of the financial economic powers, aggressive, determined in their opposition.

The fight against this agricultural program was not lacking in patriotism. It was conscientious but narrow-minded, and selfishly and blindly indifferent to the fact that half the world was starving, and the other half suffering from a surplus of products which, if carefully distributed, would have added to the happiness of both.

I recognized the problem involved in transport. Products handled by the corporation would have received the lowest rates enjoyed by any agency. The costs of transporting food and other commodities from the point of production to the place of exportation were to be slashed materially. And then the cost of transport from the point of exportation to the ultimate destination would have been without profit. I proposed that these transport charges, cut to the bone, should be added to the price of food commodities. It would have been possible, therefore, to pay the American farmer and the manufacturer higher prices for the articles they produced and to deliver them to all parts of the world at a cost lower than had been possible heretofore.

I had been working night and day for months upon the bill.

Winter gave way to spring, spring yielded to summer, and the heat of the Capital told heavily upon my physical strength. I had been ill and dispirited. This bill had buoyed me in the beginning by a belief that it would pass; in the mounting opposition inspired by presidential hostility, I saw its certain defeat.

In the July debates that followed the appearance of the bill, and the Kellogg compromise measure that had been agreed to, under the leadership of the President, I collapsed. I was taken to an adjoining committee room where a doctor was summoned; and later I was carried to my home in Cleveland Park. For several days there were doubts of my recovery. I had fought for three days without rest, in Washington's heat of late July, to beat down the opposition in a debate that suddenly had become sharp and at times personal. In the closing stages it was Vice President Coolidge and Charley Curtis, the Republican whip, who manipulated the parliamentary tactics through which the Kellogg substitute superseded my bill.

Word reached Nebraska that I would not recover, and discussion arose immediately over the appointment of my successor in the Senate. The governor of the state, Samuel R. McKelvie, at that time had aspirations for a seat in the Senate, and the lieutenant governor, P. A. Barrows, was ambitious to serve as governor. During those days of illness the reports trickling in from the outside told of a plan under which the governor would resign, the lieutenant governor automatically become his successor, and in turn, his immediate predecessor would be appointed to the position I had occupied. These ambitions were frustrated because I did not die.

I fooled them.

I recovered.

After a period of convalescence at the lakes I returned to the Senate the following October.

The defeat of that legislation was the greatest single disappointment of all of my public service in Congress. I had grown accustomed to the ebb and flow of battle. I had seen men in highest purpose fight for legislation dear to them and had seen them bow to defeat. I myself had known what it was to lose fights. Yet I could not reconcile myself to the thought that one populous region in the world was desperate, undernourished, starving in thousands of instances, for the simple necessities of human life—and at the same time millions in another part of the world, separated by oceans and land, were suffering and agonized because of the overproduction of these same necessities.

It is not a credit to human intelligence that conditions of this character can prevail in this world. Somehow, in some manner, there should be the intelligence, the human capacity, to avoid the tragedy of a great abundance accompanied by a great hunger.

Poverty there is, and poverty there always will be, men say—hunger and starvation, desperation and futility. That is not a civilized state. It is a confession that with inherent selfishness men have not progressed sufficiently to protect themselves. Poverty and hunger breed desperation, and desperation breeds contempt for law, and contempt for law breeds anarchy in the affairs of the world.

I am wondering what the world will do about it again. Why should not a bill similar to the one I proposed be brought forward again? It would go far toward meeting the postwar conditions that we sensibly can anticipate and that shortly will be upon us.

We should plan now to meet hunger in these war-devastated countries more than halfway, without hope of exorbitant profits but with hand and heart that are merciful.

In the peace that will follow the war, we must be on guard to see that the great corporations, the monopolies, and the aggregates of wealth shall not extort from the men, women, and little children of the world who will be on the verge of starvation, and dependent chiefly upon us for food and clothing. If we fail, then our failure will return to us with double penalty.

28

"GROCER NORRIS"

THE ACCUMULATED DISPLEASURE of Republican leadership against the independent attitude I had taken in public life finally caught up with me.

It had been smoldering among those leaders for years.

Only the faint outlines of the revolt which I led against Cannonism remained in the long, sharp memories of the more elderly counselors of the Republican party. A new generation of voters had acquired the privilege of the franchise, and they were infected by the hostility of the elders. In the eyes of these older party leaders, and some of the younger men who had risen to places in the high command, inheriting naturally the hatred my course inspired, I had sinned again and again against my party.

There were innumerable instances in congressional deliberation in which I was rebellious—the Cannon struggle and the refusal to be bound by party caucus only being the more conspicuous cases which came to public attention.

In 1924 as a successful Republican candidate for reelection to the Senate, I had supported my old friend and senatorial colleague Robert M. La Follette against Calvin Coolidge. There was nothing hidden, secretive, nor subtle about it. I had indicated plainly by letter to the Republican leaders in Nebraska my inalterable purpose. There was nothing in common between my conceptions of national policy and Mr. Coolidge's philosophy of American welfare. I sympathized with the independent candidacy of Bob La Follette in no less degree than I had supported Theodore Roosevelt in his organization of the Bull Moose movement. I told those leaders if people in the audience asked me to state my position I would outline it.

I had turned down the plea of Republican leaders for the seating of Senator Newberry, to permit the Republicans to gain control of the Senate. All of this added to the mounting resentment against me of those who worshiped at the party shrine.

Then came the crossing of party lines in a Pennsylvania campaign in behalf of the Democratic senatorial standard-bearer against "Boss" Vare.

My mail was filled with party denunciations.

From Nebraska, and from other sections of the country, the devoted party leaders condemned me in the most severe terms.

I crossed the political Rubicon in the presidential election of 1928. I bolted the Republican candidate, Herbert Hoover, publicly announced my support of Alfred E. Smith, and near the close of the campaign spoke in his behalf over a radio "hook-up" out of Omaha, and at other points.

It was well that I had had some training in the matter of abuse.

The storm which followed that Omaha pronouncement for Smith was more violent than any I had encountered. In the personal sense, I had not known Governor Smith. There had been only the most casual correspondence between us. But I had followed with intense interest his position on the development of water power in New York State while he was governor. I had been attracted to him by his liberal and farsighted position on that issue. I knew where Mr. Hoover stood. Later he vetoed TVA in the most outspoken terms. He had demonstrated to my satisfaction that, whatever other claims he might have to a liberal outlook on the question of conservation of American resources, he was most backward and reactionary.

I felt that, in spite of his professions, he was equally shortsighted in his views relating to agriculture.

I recognized that throughout the Harding-Coolidge administrations he had occupied a chair at the cabinet table, and it seemed to me he must have been fully cognizant of what was going on although, perhaps, powerless to do anything about it short of resigning.

There was that June episode during the Republican national convention which nominated Mr. Hoover, when friends brought the indirect word I was under consideration as Mr. Hoover's running mate. I know nothing about the truth or falsity of that reputed plan. It may have had no basis in fact. Possibly some of my associates felt accounts could be balanced by nominating Mr. Hoover for the Presidency, and selecting me for the Vice Presidency. I was in no mood to give it any thought. I would not consider it and indicated my distaste far more forcefully than the circumstances justified. Then in the fall campaign, I spoke bluntly of my opposition to Mr. Hoover.

There was more.

In December of 1925, in a public statement I branded the pending Mellon tax bill, which had the administration's blessing, with unfairness toward those of scanty or moderate means and favoritism toward those of huge incomes and immense wealth.

In that statement I said:

> The revenue bill as passed in the House is indefensible. In a nutshell it is a millionaires' bill. Practically all the reductions made are on the taxes of the incomes of those who are immensely wealthy. . . . Mr. Mellon himself gets a larger personal reduction than the aggregate of practically all the taxpayers in the state of Nebraska. The reduction of inheritance taxes on big fortunes contained in this bill is a greater step backward than has been taken by Congress since the war. . . . It was passed by the House without fair consideration, without reasonable opportunity for debate, and is a demonstration of the working of the new rules just adopted by that body, enabling a few men who are alleged leaders to dominate the House and handle it as completely as the master controls his servant.

Every mile of the road, it seemed to me, I had been in conflict with the Republican leadership; and I knew it considered me as a thorn in its side.

Again a Senate term was drawing to a close, and the election of

1930 was ahead. There had been a period in the summer and fall of 1929 during which I was uncertain whether I would become a candidate for reelection. I had written to a friend in Grand Island I would wait and then announce my retirement. A series of letters and telegrams forced me to change my plans.

Actually, I served five terms of six years each in the Senate. The first four terms I was nominated and elected as the regular Republican nominee, but I never engaged in a primary conflict in which I was not bitterly opposed by the Republican machine. As a rule, it carried its opposition to the general election.

In all four contests, there was never any charge made against me that I had obtained my primary nomination as the party candidate otherwise than honestly, openly, and fairly. I had been chosen under the law applying to primary elections, and even my bitterest enemies never raised any doubt that I had obtained nomination openly and legally.

The leaders of the Republican machine in Nebraska always had advocated voting the party ticket straight.

But they violated their party doctrine by opposing my election after I had received the regular Republican nomination.

My first term in the Senate came after Nebraska had adopted the so called "Oregon plan"—of which Senator Jonathan Bourne, Jr., of Oregon was the author, and under which he himself had been elected as a Republican senator from the state of Oregon. This law provided that the candidates for the state legislature had the right to have a pledge printed on the primary ballot that, if elected to the state legislature, they would vote for the candidate for United States senator who had received the highest number of votes in the preceding general election, regardless of such person's political affiliation. In effect, it was a pledge to carry out the expressed popular will, regardless of party loyalty and personal convictions. Practically every candidate for the state legislature made this pledge in order to strengthen his own candidacy.

The legislature in Nebraska elected after adoption of the Bourne plan had a Democratic majority, but the members fulfilled their pledges by electing me to the United States Senate—for, under the same law, I had carried the state. Thus, while a Republican, I owed my seat in the Senate to a legislature a majority of the members of which were Democrats.

I received practically the unanimous vote of that Democratic state legislature.

IN NEBRASKA AS NOVEMBER 4TH NEARS.

After that, of course, the constitutional change under which members of the United States Senate were to be chosen by direct vote of the people meant that, in all subsequent elections, except my last successful battle, I was the regular nominee of the Republican party in the primaries, and was elected as a Republican.

I realized, however, that in every primary contest I was receiving a large number of Democratic votes. There were only seven cities in Nebraska where registration was a requirement for voting either in the primaries or in the general election. In all the remaining voting precincts in the state, all the voter in the primaries did was to call for the party ballot he desired; and many Democrats in my state called for a Republican ballot in every one of my primary contests. Where registration was required, the voter had to designate his party affiliation; and voters normally Democratic who desired to cast a Republican ballot in the primary election for United States senator had to change their party registration, well in advance of the primary election day.

In this way a large number of progressive Democrats were following me faithfully in full acceptance of the fundamental philosophy of government I was trying my best to achieve.

This was the situation in the primary election of 1930, when the Republican "bosses" concocted a very clever scheme to defeat me.

They discovered another man bearing my name, George W. Norris, and they induced him to become a Republican candidate for United States senator in the regular primary election.

He was a clerk in a grocery store at Broken Bow, the county seat of the second-largest county geographically in Nebraska, on the fringes of the sand hills in the old cattle domain. He appeared to be a quiet, untutored, and gullible young man, lending himself easily to pliant manipulation.

Later it was established he was not well known in the state, never had participated prominently in politics; and to the best of my knowledge he never had been a candidate for any public office. Even among the people of Broken Bow, he was known personally by comparatively few. He had no financial means—which was no objection to his candidacy, but meant that he could not put up the money which this disreputable plan would have required.

Of course, the Republican machine did not anticipate he would be either nominated or elected.

The object of the machine's plan simply was to make it impossible to count any votes cast in the primary election for any senatorial candidate who bore the name George W. Norris.

It would have been absolutely impossible for any honest local election board to discriminate between the votes cast for Senator George W. Norris and those for "Grocer" Norris of Broken Bow.

There would have been no way legally to canvass this vote. Under the provisions of the state election law, the secretary of state was prohibited from placing any mark or identification on the ballot to serve as a guide for the voter; any ballot so marked could not be counted, so that the voters themselves could not designate for which Norris they were voting without invalidating their ballots.

The result was that all votes cast for George W. Norris would have been thrown out.

In this way, I should have been eliminated completely and entirely in the primary by subtle trickery and exceedingly disreputable political tactics.

All the primary voters who marked the ballot for George W. Norris would have been disfranchised. Through this device the machine intended, therefore, to accomplish my elimination as a candidate; and it came very near succeeding.

Except through a mistake by "Grocer" Norris himself, there would have been no alternative to throwing out all the ballots cast either for me or for him.

There were several candidates for the Republican nomination, among whom the leader was W. B. Stebbins (at the time, state treasurer). Another receptive candidate was former Governor Samuel R. McKelvie.

A plan was devised for taking a straw vote to ascertain who would be the strongest candidate. In charge of it was Victor Seymour, who had been active in both state and national politics for more than thirty years.

In a summary of the evidence filed with the report of the Senate committee, which made an investigation of the "Grocer" Norris conspiracy, Mr. Seymour is described as a

Nebraskan, who had had various appointive offices and in 1928 led the McKelvie forces at the Republican national convention in support of the Hoover ticket. Seymour is shown by the testimony of several witnesses to have handled the negotiations which led "Grocer" Norris to file as a candidate for the Senate, transmitted to him the money to pay his expenses, drafted his announcement, and arranged for the employment of his attorney.

In the main, the poll was financed by Walter W. Head, who was treasurer of the Republican state committee, chairman of the board of the Omaha National Bank, chairman of the board of the Nebraska Power Company (a subsidiary of one of the large electric concerns in the United States), and president of the Foreman-State National Bank of Chicago. He also was a director of the New York Life Insurance Company and of the Chicago & North Western Railway Company.

In his business connections, he was a man of some consequence. He often was advertised as the teacher of the largest Sunday-school class in the state of Nebraska. He was active and prominent in the Boy Scout movement, and for a time was president of the national council of the Boy Scouts of America. He was chairman of the finance committee of the Y.M.C.A. and was either an officer or a director of various other character-building, religious, charitable, or philanthropic organizations.

All of this is set forth in the record of his testimony on page 485 of the committee report.

There was an element of caution apparent in former Governor McKelvie's candidacy. It was being held in abeyance awaiting the result of this poll. Mr. McKelvie, it is to be concluded, would have become a candidate in the primary if the poll had suggested he had equal or superior support to mine in the Republican primary.

But this poll turned out to be a great disappointment.

Its results, in so far as possible, remained a carefully guarded secret known only to those it was intended should be informed. It did appear in the investigation that when the poll which was taken by secret agents sent into different parts of the state showed that I was getting more votes than any of the other candidates, it was abandoned and Mr. McKelvie did not become an actual candidate.

Stebbins thus occupied the role of the leading, outstanding candidate against me in the primary. When the investigation undertaken by the Senate committee disclosed the attempt then being made secretly to get "Grocer" Norris to file as a candidate, and when it was shown rather definitely over the state that the object was to eliminate me by this disreputable method from the senatorial contest, an attempt was made to convince the voters of Nebraska that, actually, I myself had instigated "Grocer" Norris in his candidacy.

It was charged that he was a relative of mine and that I was responsible for his attempted filing.

Mr. Stebbins' publicity agent, Will M. Maupin, who had been a particularly vicious critic, issued a number of statements to this effect. Mr. Stebbins himself publicly and brazenly charged me with the political chicanery for which he afterwards assumed complete responsibility.

In a radio speech to the people of Nebraska, Mr. Stebbins used this language during the primary:

"Both myself and my supporters have denounced the Broken Bow affair. . . . As a scheme framed by long-time friends and political supporters of Senator Norris to win for him sympathy, using his cousin as, perhaps, the unwitting tool of their evil design . . . He, who would profit politically by the violation of an election law, is not better than the bootlegger who profits by the violation of the Volstead Act."

This statement of Mr. Stebbins is set forth on page 6 of the committee report.

However, when Mr. Stebbins was put upon the stand and sworn as a witness by the committee, he admitted that he had furnished fifty dollars in cash to pay "Grocer" Norris' filing fee and later gave him a Liberty bond for five hundred dollars.

It was a fantastic, amazing, and depressing case.

Stebbins was a very prominent Methodist. An attempt was made in the campaign to control the Methodist vote. Actually one of the bishops of the Methodist church wrote a letter to the Methodist ministers of the state in which he set forth the importance of nominating Mr. Stebbins as the Republican candidate for the United States Senate. His standing as a temperance leader, his position in the church, and his reputation as a Christian gentleman were set forth in elaborate, laudatory terms. I never knew how widely that letter was circulated, but I assumed it was sent to every Methodist minister in Nebraska.

How near this scheme came to succeeding may be judged by the facts.

Word trickled to Washington that another George W. Norris had filed for the United States Senate. I had made my filing in person during a Christmas holiday visit in Nebraska and under the election laws had bound myself to abide by the primary results and, if defeated for the nomination, not to run as an independent. Who was this new Norris, and what did he represent? No one seemed to possess any reliable information about him.

When the tangled skein of fact and fiction finally was separated, it developed "Grocer" Norris had undertaken a filing calculated to beat the dead line by the narrowest squeeze. He had enclosed his filing, with the proper receipt for the filing fee, in a letter addressed to Secretary of State Frank Marsh at the capital in Lincoln. He gave instructions specifically that the letter was not to be placed on the train until the morning of July 3.

It was the fringe of the dead line for filings, and his letter had to reach the Secretary of State.

Evidently "Grocer" Norris overlooked the fact that the next day, July 4, was a national holiday, so that in reality, his filing did not reach the secretary of state until July 5. An old friend, Attorney General C. A. Sorensen, indicated in his opinion the filing was invalid because it reached the secretary of state's office July 5, more than a day after the dead line of July 3.

But the Secretary of State, a Republican "regular," ruled that inasmuch as it was postmarked July 3, it came within the requirements of the law.

My secretary, John P. Robertson, had gone to Nebraska to open campaign headquarters.

In those days of uncertainty I had the choice between continuing as a candidate in the primary in a hopeless, futile struggle with the cards stacked against me in the event "Grocer" Norris' name appeared on the primary ballot, and withdrawing to become an independent candidate in November.

The time was exceedingly limited.

Under the law, my withdrawal from the Republican primary had to be filed with the Secretary of State before midnight, July 18.

Not until July 17 did Secretary of State Marsh announce his ruling.

I had given Mr. Robertson my withdrawal with instructions to file it if necessary, and with the very strong feeling on my own part that I should stake my political life upon an independent candidacy. I left the ultimate decision entirely to my secretary, Mr. Robertson, Attorney General Sorensen, and other friends on the scene.

Mr. Robertson, who had served me with devoted loyalty and much ability, had gone to Nebraska uncertain of the conditions he would find, but in establishing headquarters issued a statement, which appears in part:

> The entrance into the senatorial race of another man by the name of George W. Norris, who is a clerk in a chain store, is just another demonstration of the dishonorable and disreputable means which are resorted to by the standpat enemies of Senator Norris. . . . I do not believe the people of Nebraska will stand for this latest dishonest political trick sought to be perpetrated by trusts, machine politicians to defeat Senator Norris for reelection. . . . I am not prepared to say at this time just what steps will be taken in the matter.

On the day following Mr. Marsh's ruling, Attorney General Sorensen perfected his appeal from the ruling of the Secretary of State, appeared before the Chief Justice of the Nebraska Supreme Court, Charles A. Goss, with the plea that a legal filing had to be received physically by July 3, to meet the legal requirements.

In this hearing "Grocer" Norris was represented by a North Platte attorney, W. E. Shuman, who also represented the Burlington Railroad.

The day dragged slowly.

When night was closing in, after careful study of the record, Chief Justice Goss announced his decision, finding that "Grocer" Norris' attempted filing had not been received in accordance with the provisions of the election law and his name could not appear on the primary ballot. With that ending, there was the beginning of an investigation that consumed months.

What forces were back of "Grocer" Norris?

Why had he suddenly disappeared from Broken Bow?

Efforts of federal marshals to serve him with a subpoena and attempts of representatives of the special Senate committee to locate him were unavailing. He had disappeared as mysteriously as he had projected himself as a candidate.

Then in the morning of one of those dusty, steaming July days, Saturday, July 19, Senator Gerald Nye of North Dakota turned up in Broken Bow to open a hearing. He had abruptly abandoned an investigation in Illinois to sift the mystery of "Grocer" Norris. The first witness called for by Senator Nye was "Mr. George W. Norris, late of Broken Bow, Nebraska."

And then the committee chairman asked:

"Is Mr. Norris present?"

There was no response.

In rapid order, the testimony of United States Marshal Dennis H. Cronin, and of a number of local witnesses, was taken. Among them was County Treasurer Guy Dady, who told of an earlier primary filing by "Grocer" Norris for railway commissioner, and then of subsequent appearance by him to pay a filing fee of $50 for United States senator, on July 2.

In both instances, "Grocer" Norris put up cash for the filing costs.

The testimony of Walter Schnabel, a Broken Bow postal clerk, next was taken. He told of meeting "Grocer" Norris outside the store where Norris was employed, of being handed a letter with a request that it be registered; it was not to be dispatched on the night train of July 2, but held until the following morning, when the registration record was to be completed. Then witness Schnabel created a ripple of excitement by acknowledging he had received a statement as to the "Grocer" Norris senatorial candidacy from A. Paul Johnson, Broken Bow attorney.

Johnson, called as a witness, admitted under close questioning he had prepared "Grocer" Norris' application as a candidate for railway commissioner, which was not sent to Lincoln. More than that he tossed a bombshell into the hearing when he revealed that, only a day before, he had been in contact with the missing Norris in Lincoln.

Hour after hour the questioning went on without definite results.

It was like beating against stone at this point. Whatever the plot was, it had been developed carefully and with some planning. I felt keenly here was a struggle of no small magnitude. There was more than the Broken Bow incident of the country boy.

The Nye hearings moved on into Lincoln. One of the first witnesses was Victor Seymour, who under oath and questioning testified he did not have any acquaintance with Norris of Broken Bow, never had seen him or heard of him until the name appeared in the newspapers.

But by now men were running to cover.

It seemed that the element of glibness which had characterized the earlier stages of the investigation evaporated, to be replaced by a certain grimness in the relentless determination of Senator Nye and his Senate colleagues to get at the bottom of the mystery of the "Grocer" Norris filing.

In three or four appearances on the stand, "Grocer" Norris himself contributed very little real information. At one stage of the proceedings, I examined him.

The transcript of the testimony showed this exchange between us:

SENATOR NORRIS: Now I ask you, were you a candidate for senator in good faith?

MR. NORRIS: Yes, sir.

SENATOR NORRIS: And yet you knew that if the court had not put you off, you could not have been nominated because your name was the same as mine and we would both have been eliminated? You say that, too, under oath?

MR. NORRIS: Yes, sir.

SENATOR NORRIS: Then it must follow that you could not have been nominated as United States senator.

MR. NORRIS: Unless you had withdrawn.

SENATOR NORRIS: You hadn't any promise from me that I would withdraw, had you?

MR. NORRIS: No, sir.

Thus, it went along for hours.

It is likely that the full facts never would have been ascertained had it not been for a young lady engaged in a stenographic role by Mr. Seymour, and her testimony came quite by chance.

Paul Y. Anderson, the representative of the *St. Louis Post-Dispatch,* who was reporting the hearings for his paper, had contacted her during the lunch hour, and at the resumption of the hearing in the afternoon, informed Senator Nye of his discovery. The young woman, Esther Marie Alton, had accepted employment with Victor Seymour in January, after he had opened the office and had conducted the straw poll. Miss Alton remained until July and noted that regularly checks came in from outside the state, apparently from the East, for the maintenance of the office. She also told of the visits of a field agent of the Republican National Committee, posing as a newspaperman. She had typed the statements given out in connection with "Grocer" Norris' candidacy for the Senate.

The testimony on that point in the record reads:

CHAIRMAN NYE: Can you recall, Miss Alton, about what time you typed that statement?

MISS ALTON: Let me see. I don't think it was very long before the primaries.

SENATOR NYE: Anyway, when you read it in the paper, you having typed it, it was all very fresh in your mind?

MISS ALTON: At the time I read it, one of my girl friends was there and I said, "Well, here's the article that I typed."

There was one more clincher.

SENATOR NYE: When Mr. Seymour wanted you to type this statement which it appears evident was the statement announcing the candidacy of George W. Norris of Broken Bow, Mr. Seymour gave you a copy of what you were to type, which was written in longhand, did he?

MISS ALTON: He did.

SENATOR NYE: What made you think it was Mr. Seymour's handwriting?

MISS ALTON: I know his handwriting when I see it.

SENATOR NYE: And then you knew that was his handwriting?

MISS ALTON: Yes, sir.

At last the plot was bared.

Attorney Paul Johnson was recalled, and voluntarily made a statement that he had not only evaded but had evaded to a very great extent. He said he had not done so for his own protection so much as for others, naming Mr. Seymour and Mr. Norris. "Grocer" Norris admitted his candidacy had been suggested by somebody else.

I threw myself into the most vigorous campaign of my senatorial career.

I spoke in a majority of the counties in Nebraska; spoke frequently two and three times a day. I had won an easy primary nomination. In a three-cornered contest Stebbins received 84,486; Aaron C. Read, 6,458; and I got 108,471. Up to that point the plan had failed.

But in the general election in November, I found myself confronted by Gilbert M. Hitchcock, nominated by the Democrats, of a pioneer Nebraska family, with a distinguished record in Congress behind him, and the publisher and owner of the Omaha *World-Herald*. There was a third candidacy, an independent filing, by Mrs. Beatrice Craig. Under the leadership of Elmer B. Stephenson, of Lincoln, a Republican "Hitchcock for Senator Club" was organized throughout the state. It was plentifully supplied with funds. Mr. Stephenson had been identified with "old guard" Republican leadership in Nebraska for years, and he drew to his side hundreds of regular Republicans throughout the state. Again the bulk of the press was unfriendly, and full-page advertisements bearing the signature of the Hitchcock Republican club made their appearance in the weekly papers of every county as well as the dailies. An intensive radio program supplemented the drive for my opponent, and sacks of the most defamatory literature were circulated broadside in all sections.

The K.K.K. was active. Women workers were enlisted in the fight.

Senator Hitchcock himself addressed Republican clubs, advising party workers in Republican ranks they had no candidate to represent them except him.

I was not seriously disturbed.

I realized this, perhaps, was the greatest fight in which I had ever become engaged, but I sensed the voters were enraged by the plot which had been hatched; and when the votes were counted I had triumphed by the most decisive majority I ever received.

The official count was: Norris, 247,118; Hitchcock, 172,795; Craig (by petition), 14,884.

There was still the final clean-up.

Stebbins earlier had confessed to the committee his full part in the "Grocer" Norris candidacy, the paying of the filing fee, later the gift of a $500 bond to the Broken Bow Norris. He told his story unblushingly, shrugged aside a question by Senator Nye why he had not made the facts known before, and attempted to assume full responsibility for all the funds back of the "Grocer" Norris candidacy.

But in the plentiful spending of money throughout the campaign, additional evidence was brought to light.

The laws of Nebraska limited contributions that could be made in primary campaigns to $1,000. There is no doubt but this law was circumvented in many cases. It was developed later in the investigation that Charles A. McCloud, Republican national committeeman of York, Nebraska, had contributed to the Stebbins fund an amount in excess of $1,000. He gave his own money to various individuals, taking their checks for the respective amounts, and sending these alleged contributions to E. B. Stephenson, who was treasurer of the Stebbins fund. This appeared to be a direct violation of the law, without any doubt.

Mr. McKelvie was a Hoover appointee to the Federal Farm Board. He placed in the hands of Max V. Beghtol a total of $10,000. This fund is described in the Senate committee's report, pages 7 and 8, as follows:

> The method of handling this $10,000 fund, contributed by a high federal official, merits attention. According to McKelvie's testimony, the entire amount was placed in Beghtol's hands to be used in the campaign against Senator Norris. Not a dollar of it, however, appears in the report filed on behalf of Stebbins or any other candidate as being contributed by either McKelvie or Beghtol. On the contrary, $2,500 appears in the report of Stebbins as having been contributed by Charles T. Knapp with the designation "personal and miscellaneous contributions."
>
> According to Knapp's testimony, Beghtol on a visit to Chicago gave him his personal check for $2,500 which was deposited in the Harris Trust Company to the account of Charles T. Knapp Company, and Knapp in return gave Beghtol a check of the Charles T. Knapp Company in the amount of $2,500 payable to Charles T. Knapp and endorsed by him in blank. This check was in turn contributed to the Stebbins campaign fund of which E. B. Stephenson was treasurer. Thus the identity of the real contributor, McKelvie, was completely concealed. A further concealed contribution out of this fund is said to have been made in the name of F. C. Foster. McKelvie testified that the balance of the $10,000 fund, amounting to $7,150, was retained by Beghtol until after the November election, when it was applied to the payment of a note previously given by McKelvie to Knapp for the purchase of bank stock.
>
> This transaction violates the spirit, if not the letter, of the Nebraska election laws in two particulars: First, the amount contributed was in excess of the legal limitations of $1,000 from any individual (32–2222 compiled statutes of Nebraska, 1929). The use of the designation "personal and miscellaneous contributions" in connection with the Knapp contribution would indicate a knowledge of this provision and a desire to evade it. Second, McKelvie did not report the making of this contribution to the clerk of the county as provided by the Nebraska law (32–2023, 2024, 2027 supra), requiring every individual contributing in excess of $250 to make such a report.

It seemed to me enough evidence was developed by the investigating committee to show that a large number of prominent officials in Nebraska had violated the state law with impunity. Yet none of these men ever has been prosecuted. The only prosecutions that were brought were against "Grocer" Norris and Victor Seymour. Both were charged with and convicted of perjury, arising in connection with their testimony before a Senate investigating committee. Seymour was sentenced to six months in prison by Judge T. C. Munger of the United States District Court; "Grocer" Norris, to ninety days.

I felt the sentences wholly inadequate in the nature of Mr. Seymour's offense. Seymour deserved the full penalty provided by law; Norris clearly was only a tool. Seymour carried his case to the United States Supreme Court, but it refused to review the Circuit Court of Appeals' finding.

After Seymour had taken advantage of every technicality of law and had served a portion of his sentence, the late Arthur F. Mullen called me in Washington and told me he wanted to talk to me about the Seymour case. Mr. Mullen visited me in the Senate Office Building and tried to get me to sign a petition for a pardon for Mr. Seymour. It was said Mr. Seymour's wife was critically ill, and it was feared she would not survive her husband's term. I flatly refused to join in a recommendation for parole or pardon for Mr. Seymour (for which I was sharply criticized by many Nebraskans), and I cut the conference short by telling Mr. Mullen I thought Seymour should have been given the limit of the law instead of six months.

The Masons got into it. The Grand Master of the state wrote me a letter, in the best of faith, seeking to induce me to be merciful to a Masonic brother. I wrote him I myself was a Mason but had asked no sympathy nor support on that score, and felt if the Masons were going to intercede they should have done so in the beginning.

I was deeply interested in the activities of an organization which masqueraded during the campaign under a very high-sounding patriotic name, but which really was projected by the Ku Klux Klan.

Its object was to distribute literature brought into Nebraska from the East. In the Senate investigation, only two witnesses appeared—the driver of a laundry wagon in Lincoln, and a common laborer. Yet this organization distributed about a quarter of a million copies of literature over the state through the Ku Klux Klan membership.

It must have expended a considerable sum of money.

The simple item of postage must have aggregated a large amount.

No evidence was disclosed as to who financed these expensive activities. The two men, so far as the testimony was concerned, seemed to compose the entire organization, and yet everybody who heard the testimony knew that not all of the facts came out, and that there must have been a considerable financial investment in this phase of the campaign against me.

I also was interested in the petition candidacy of Mrs. Beatrice Craig, a schoolteacher and a very intelligent, respectable woman, who seemed to be completely under the domination and control of a few alleged leaders of the Republican party who were enemies of mine. Her husband, Jesse Craig, was well known among the politicians of the state. With him she made a campaign covering Nebraska. Her entire energies were devoted to opposition to me, but her candidacy did not excite the interest anticipated.

It was quite apparent that everything she said and did had but one object in view, and that was my defeat, and while she devoted considerable time her efforts did little damage.

It is only another indication that the opposition to me in this particular senatorial campaign had all the money it could use. It appeared that opposition was prepared to put into the campaign as many people as it desired. But what money actually was spent was never known fully by the public.

Finally the concluding hearings of the Senate investigation committee shifted from Nebraska to Washington.

Senator Nye and his colleagues had become convinced Stebbins and the others were shielding higher-ups. Again it appeared a dead end would balk final solution of the source of some of the sums of money spent in the campaign, and a knowledge of the higher-ups involved.

There had been detailed questioning of the foreman of the Independent Publishing Company in Washington, John F. Blackwell, when the hearing was interrupted by the cry:

"Mr. Chairman, in the interest of truth—"

The speaker was Charles I. Stengle.

Chairman Nye inquired of Mr. Stengle if he was willing to be sworn, and, upon receiving an affirmative answer, invited him to take the witness stand, where he made this statement:

> I am about to make a statement to the committee, and I make it in the interest of truth and because of my long friendship for the two members of this committee, who are seeking the truth, one of whom I have known for twenty-five years. Mr. Blackwell, to the best of his knowledge and belief, told the truth. The real truth is I am compelled to violate confidence in order to put into your record. The real truth is that I placed those orders in his hands, that I gave him that yellow slip and told him that the order [for printing] was to be booked in that name. The real truth is that that order was obtained by me from Robert H. Lucas, director of the Republican National Committee. . . . The letter that you are seeking, the original of that, was also placed in my hands by Mr. Lucas.

It developed from Stengle's testimony that Mr. Lucas furnished the addresses to which the literature was to be mailed.

Then followed the admission by William E. Murray, assistant to Franklin W. Fort, who was secretary of the Republican National Committee, that he had made a trip to Nebraska, had worked with Seymour in making a survey. On the witness stand Mr. Murray admitted that during the hearings in Washington he had put in telephone calls first to the Republican National Committee quarters, and later to the White House to reach Mr. Lucas.

Robert Lucas made a clean breast. He said that in the committee activity of which he had knowledge, he was trying to beat "a Democrat."

He told the committee that I was a Democrat by all the rules, and ought to be. He explained he was not complaining of my policies and stand but was complaining, as an executive officer in the Republican party, against a Democrat holding high office in the party and constantly fighting the party administration, opposing party policy, and attempting to call that situation to the attention of the country.

"I think," Mr. Lucas concluded, "if Senator Norris is to be classed as a Republican, you might as well tear up the Republican platform and turn Abraham Lincoln's picture to the wall."

When questioned about the source of the funds he had spent for printing, which he had caused to be sent into Nebraska in opposition to me, in the amount of $4,237, Mr. Lucas testified he had borrowed it on his own note. The treasurer of the Republican National Committee, J. R. Nutt, testified that Lucas had no right to pledge a special account which the committee maintained for his convenience, as security for the loan. Nutt added he had given Lucas his own personal check to pay for the loan and said I should have been kicked out of the party in 1928.

Two of my associates, Senators R. B. Howell and Bronson Cutting, the latter representing New Mexico, demanded of Senator Fess, chairman of the Republican National Committee, that Lucas resign, but the demand was refused.

I was embittered and depressed.

This trail, it seemed to me, led directly to high quarters, the Republican National Committee.

Publicly I announced that I would not be driven out of the party by a renegade or a band of renegades.

I never have known whether the Republican leadership of the National Committee ever discussed with President Hoover in any form any part of this attempt to defeat me in that election of 1930. I have always felt that, informed or uninformed, the activities of the Republican National Committee through Robert Lucas had Mr. Hoover's sympathy.

And in that belief, my determination to fight was strengthened.

I did fight

I demanded Lucas be prosecuted, in a letter to the Attorney General. No action along this line resulted.

I had met up with the force great wealth and Big Business could bring against the political life of a rebel fighting its rule.

29

YELLOW DOG CONTRACT

For many years there had existed a most deplorable labor condition in the coal mines of the United States, particularly in Pennsylvania.

It approached semi-servitude.

Gradually that condition came to my attention. I was more conscious of it as a result of the campaign I had made in Pennsylvania against "Boss" Vare, during which I came in contact with, and had the opportunity to observe first-hand, the miners and their families. That knowledge was augmented by talks with spokesmen for organized labor.

I had relinquished the chairmanship of the Agricultural Committee, feeling its duties had become too heavy and should go to a younger man.

Senator Charles McNary of Oregon was next in line; we had worked together, and I had the highest regard for him and for his outlook on national affairs. I wanted him to have the chairmanship, and my resignation paved the way for his advancement. As ranking member next to Senator Borah on the Judiciary Committee, I became its chairman, Borah being chairman of the powerful Committee on Foreign Relations.

I was criticized by some for giving up the Agriculture chairmanship, but it was this transition which brought me squarely into some of the most important struggles—among them, that of the miners.

There had been a close organization among the coal-mine operators. They fought organized labor very bitterly, and through their close interlinking of interests, gradually had developed what became known over the country as the "yellow dog contract."

Under it, the miner practically signed away his liberties. He surrendered his right to ask for increased wages, for better working conditions, or to associate with his fellow workers in giving effectiveness to any attempt to procure changes in these working conditions. As a rule, this contract provided that he would not join a union, and that he would not associate with his fellow miners in giving effectiveness to any attempt looking toward a change in the conditions.

In the more extreme instances of the yellow dog contract, I was shocked profoundly. Through the agency of the company store I discovered that the miner and his family, accepting all of the great hazards of his occupation, its toil and its dangers, usually found himself in debt for the bare necessities of life. I found that miners or members of their families who became ill usually relied upon the company physician for medical care. The conditions in many of these mines were horrible.

The courts generally had been rather unfriendly to organizations of labor. Immense combinations of capital and monopoly had had their own way in this field of human operations. That miner who signed a yellow dog contract relinquished freedom of action. If he left one job because of dissatisfaction with conditions, his contract made it impossible for him to get another. Thus, there developed under the system a type of human bondage that enslaved the miner to a life of toil without any opportunity to make a decent effort to improve or to better his position.

The mine operators in some of these coal fields ruled the community without mercy, without compassion, without sympathy for the men who actually dug the coal out of the ground, and without respect for the rights of workmen. The condition had become intolerable. Courts had issued injunctions of the most restrictive character, and through resort to law the mine operators had invoked the aid of government to make it impossible for miners to organize and to strike.

Through the medium of the yellow dog contract, thousands of American citizens were compelled to labor under conditions too horrible to tolerate in any free country. Not only were they compelled to live under this system, but through the medium of the injunction as a process of law, government was legalizing a system that constituted a reproach to the conscience of free men.

I gave a great deal of attention to that subject long before formulating legislation to deal with it. Whenever the opportunity presented itself, I studied it to the best of my ability. I followed the developments in investigations that already had taken place, covering a period of eight years of research and legislative fight before an adequate law was enacted.

The committee had before it a bill introduced by Senator Henrik Shipstead of Minnesota.

It was well known and understood among members of the Senate that the Shipstead bill had been prepared by Andrew Furuseth. Furuseth was not a miner. He was a sailor, representing the seamen's union; but something of his ardor and his zeal in the interest of organized labor, something of his rugged, blunt honesty, something of his primitive force, had caught the attention of Washington, and he was a well known man in the nation's capital.

He had spent his entire life in the interest of labor.

I think Andrew Furuseth in time came to command the respect of all the members of Congress who became acquainted with him. They might not agree with his passionate espousal of organized labor, but his utter sincerity and forthrightness commanded their respect. He had started life without the advantages of education—he was untutored in letters; but long experience, diligence, and unswerving loyalty to his cause had remedied the defect of early education, and at the time that I knew him there was a brilliance of mind far overshadowing his obvious defects of schooling. He understood the labor question from labor's view as completely and fully as any man I ever knew. He was perfectly conscientious. Through his years at sea in storm and in calm he knew intimately just how the seamen on the high seas were treated.

His word was good.

That rough exterior, heightened by a bluntness of speech that at times was almost offensive, melted away, once you got to know

Andrew Furuseth and once you understood him. You recognized that here was a man true as burnished steel, with a throbbing sympathy for the misfortunes and struggles of his fellow men. The depth of his convictions and the strength of his philosophy were such as to inspire faith in the man and interest in the aims to which he devoted his life.

I do not know how Andrew Furuseth became interested in the coal miner; but he had very definite ideas upon coal mining, and the bill which he had prepared embraced those views. It was not a lengthy bill.

Principally it undertook to make the yellow dog contract illegal.

Beyond invalidation of the yellow dog contract, Andrew Furuseth aspired to put labor on a higher and nobler standard and to give the miner a measure of equality in his fight against the organization of mine operators, who through great wealth and unlimited monopoly had been able to control the conditions in the mines and the lives of the men who worked way below the ground.

He believed his bill would accomplish its purpose.

Senator Shipstead, a man of liberal tendencies, was not very familiar with the problems of the coal miners. He was in complete sympathy with the attempts being made to improve the status of labor, and especially interested in the laboring conditions in mining; but under the pressure of his work he paid very little attention to the bill after he had introduced it.

The Judiciary Committee of the Senate selected me as chairman of a subcommittee appointed to study the Shipstead bill and to hold such hearings as were deemed necessary. It authorized me to appoint two other members as my associates.

Senator William E. Borah, as a member of the Judiciary Committee, would have been entitled to be chairman of it if he had not held the chairmanship of the Foreign Affairs Committee. I endeavored to persuade him to serve with me on the subcommittee; he was sympathetic, but felt strongly he had not the time for proper investigation. Whereupon I appointed Senator Thomas J. Walsh of Montana and Senator John J. Blaine of Wisconsin, as my associates on the subcommittee.

Unanimously, we reached the conclusion that the bill introduced by Senator Shipstead, as drawn by Andrew Furuseth, did not meet the requirements fully; and especially we feared it would be held unconstitutional. We decided to prepare a new substitute bill. I was to tell Andrew Furuseth of our decision. I remember calling him to my office, and discussing with him at great length what we regarded as the defects of his proposal. He became impatient with me, and I think his anger was aroused because I did not believe his bill would meet the situation.

The subcommittee held unlimited hearings, which were very extensive.

From the very beginning, as was to be anticipated, the proposed legislation was fought bitterly by the National Association of Manufacturers. I remember that its representative, James A. Emery, a very able attorney seasoned and experienced in legislation, and a veteran of many years of struggle before various committees of Congress, appeared in opposition. He was assisted by a number of other attorneys, but he was in general command of presenting the case against any legislation relating to labor conditions in the coal mines.

No attempt was made to limit testimony. The subcommittee permitted anybody to appear. In addition to direct evidence, every witness who took the stand was open to cross-examination if either side desired.

I believe it was one of the most comprehensive, conscientious investigations a congressional subcommittee has undertaken. I heard every syllable of testimony that was given, and my two loyal and conscientious associates heard nearly all of it. At the completion of the hearings, my associates directed me to summon to our assistance some noted attorneys, who had had long experience with labor legislation and with the trial of labor cases in the courts. The result was that I requested Felix Frankfurter of the Harvard Law School (now a justice of the United States Supreme Court), Donald Richberg of Chicago, Professor Herman Oliphant of Johns Hopkins, Edwin E. Witte, of the University of Wisconsin, and Francis B. Sayre of Harvard to aid in the preparation of the substitute bill; and they all agreed to undertake the labor. I urged them to arrange to come to Washington at the same time, so that they might not only counsel with the subcommittee but also confer and deliberate among themselves.

And then I turned over the Judiciary Committee rooms to these men.

I have always thought that the method of procedure which was adopted was significant. They locked themselves in, and for forty-eight hours gave their undivided attention and study to every court decision bearing upon the rights of organized labor. They reviewed the decisions of the United States Supreme Court with the most scrupulous care, aware that in the great conflict of interest certain to arise from legislation of this character, the constitutionality of the law would be subjected to challenge immediately.

When they had completed painstaking study of the court decisions, they consulted Senator Walsh, Senator Blaine, and myself and placed before us the results of their conclusions. The subcommittee then took the subject up again in active session and prepared a report for the full membership of the Judiciary Committee. As a result we struck from the Shipstead bill all of the provisions after the enactment clause and substituted a much more comprehensive piece of legislation. After all of the study and research and energies devoted to hearings, and the deep desire among the members of the subcommittee to remedy frightful conditions in the coal-mining industry, we were concerned chiefly with framing legislation that would pass the test of the courts. We also recognized that whatever legislation was passed would be subjected to court attack, and we felt that the failure or success of our efforts would be determined largely by perfecting a bill that could come through its legal ordeal, survive all legal assaults, and still exist as law.

I reported the redrafted bill to the Senate with the change which had been agreed upon by the subcommittee.

In the House a companion bill was introduced by Representative Fiorello La Guardia, who conducted it through the House Judiciary Committee and successfully championed its passage in the House.

As the bill passed the House, it was substantially the original draft. Mr. La Guardia performed a very great service in the fight which he made for it.

In the Senate the opposition was better organized. There was a bitter contest within the Judiciary Committee, with Senator Frederick Steiwer of Oregon leading the attack. He was a very bright and able lawyer, and a fine man who had won a wide circle of friends. He wrote the opposing opinion. The Republicans were in control of the Judiciary Committee and dominated the Senate. Mr. Hoover was in the White House. So far as I know, he did not come out openly in opposition to the bill; but we never received any assistance of any kind from the Department of Justice in the Hoover administration. There was that impenetrable wall of opposition, an opposition not voiced, not out in the open, but under cover, silent and effective. The yellow dog contract legislation failed to pass the Senate of the Seventieth Congress.

Immediately upon convening of the next Congress, I reintroduced the bill in the exact form it had been reported out previously. I knew there had been a considerable shift in sentiment in the country in regard to the legislation. Many of those previously opposed had changed their attitude, and a majority of the members of the Judiciary Committee this time favored the bill. It could not have been better illustrated than by the position taken by Senator Steiwer of Oregon. Not only did he drop his opposition, but he voted for the bill in exactly the same language which he had previously opposed. Many of the Republican leaders in the Senate swung from opposition to support, either as honest and genuine converts to the purposes of the legislation, or fearful of sentiment that had developed in support of the bill.

In all of this struggle organized labor, at the time of the passage of the legislation invalidating the yellow dog contract, more completely impressed the consciousness of the American people with the inequalities which then existed in the economic structure than at any time in American history.

I always have believed and still believe that it was this remarkable upsurge of sentiment in the United States that led President

Hoover to sign, instead of veto, the bill. I had no doubt then that, if he did veto it, it could be passed over his presidential veto. In the light of developments it was most fortunate that the first attempt to pass the bill had failed. I am equally certain that passage by the Seventy-first Congress, followed by a veto, would have made it fail in the next Congress.

I believe now just as firmly as I believed at the time I was sponsoring this legislation there has been written into the law of the United States a labor enactment which should appeal to the fairness and the honest judgment of any person who has given study to the subject. It embodies only matters of simple justice. The right of men to organize for the improvement of conditions under which they labor should not be open to question. The right of collective bargaining has been determined in this country. The opportunity of labor to fight for its rights should not be limited by court restrictions that in practical effect impose a condition of servitude upon men who daily go down into the bowels of the earth to extract the fuel that heats millions of homes and turns the wheels of American industry.

All that the Norris-La Guardia bill did was to give the miner emancipation from the slavery that had prevailed for years in the coal mines of America.

I believe that the anti-injunction act already has brought and will continue to bring full and honest consideration of labor questions by the American people.

I believe that in their mature judgment, with full knowledge of the facts, the new freedom for these toilers will be sustained.

Never will man's conscience permit him to restore the tyranny and injustice which long bound men to the earth in unwilling and unremitting toil.

As this is written, the American people have become concerned over labor disturbances. They are fighting a war. They are attempting to defeat armies bent upon destroying human freedom. They are endeavoring to save American civilization for posterity.

Coal miners often have been led astray, in my judgment, by ill advised leaders; and they are now thwarting the government in its greatest war by failing to maintain production so vital to victory.

I have had few personal contacts with John L. Lewis, or with any large number of his associates, but I feel strongly that no man should strike against his country in time of war. No man, representing either management or labor, should resort to strike methods in order to enforce demands in time of deadly national peril. It seems to me that the miners have forgotten the blessings and the rights given them by the anti-injunction law, and have followed false leaders who care more for their own ambitions than they do for freedom and civilization in the world.

Nothing contained in the provisions of the Norris-La Guardia law, however, made it possible for the striking miners to take the course mapped in the recent crisis by miner leadership. Nothing in the fundamental decent principles embodied in that law—a law that attempts to safeguard and protect the liberties of the individual man—justified anyone in staying the hands of government in its glorious, noble attempts to save a civilized world from European dictatorship. Wrong committed in equalizing earlier injustices never becomes right. Right and justice are not achieved by piling wrong upon wrong.

In those quiet discussions within the circle of the Senate subcommittee I listened to the expressed aspirations of Americans to bring a larger measure of understanding and justice between the employer and the employee. Senator Walsh and Senator Blaine both were very eminent attorneys, men of judicial temperament and the very highest character. Walsh's place is secure in the hearts of his countrymen for the brave and courageous fights which he made. Senator Blaine had served as governor of Wisconsin and in that role had given great attention and energy to the type of legislation embodied in the anti-injunction law. So far as I could observe, he was as free from prejudice as any man I ever have met. The members of the committee who assisted us were outstanding lawyers; had attained prominence through their study of the subject, and commanded public confidence.

This law is labor's charter—to be guarded and protected against attack both from without and from within. It can be weakened by abuses within through the destruction of the sustaining faith of the American public. It can be destroyed only if those whom it emancipates enable those who always have opposed it to seize upon the temporary tides of American public opinion. Labor in the mines, labor everywhere, should be free from contractual relationships in its employment that strip the individual of the rights of American citizenship. The charter for labor embraced in this legislation gave labor no right that any American citizen ought not to possess in his daily life and in his day in court.

30

LIGHTING THE FARMS

NATURALLY DEVELOPMENT of the TVA was followed by the establishment of the Rural Electrification Administration, the object of which was to carry electricity to the farms of America.

It was an undertaking that had my deepest interest and sympathy.

From boyhood, I had seen first-hand the grim drudgery and grind which had been the common lot of eight generations of American farm women, seeking happiness and contentment on the soil. I had seen the tallow candle in my own home followed by the coal-oil lamp. I knew what it was to take care of the farm chores by the flickering, undependable light of the lantern in the mud and cold rains of the fall, and the snow and icy winds of winter.

I had seen the cities gradually acquire a night as light as day.

Anyone giving extended study to electrical developments in America could come to no other conclusion as a simple matter of equity, justice, and progress than that the farmers of the United States should have the benefit of cheap electricity to the same extent and in the same way that villages, towns, and cities would possess it under the TVA Act.

Fundamentally I felt the farmer would become a better and a more satisfactory consumer of electricity than the individual in the town and city. His needs were greater. In the farm home there were or should be all of the various applications of electricity that the city dweller made, and there were so many additional requirements. Electric power could be used to pump water, to grind feed, to meet all of the needs of the dairy, and to perform other useful and beneficial services not within the grasp of a city home.

I therefore regarded the REA not only as a necessary twin development of the TVA, but as a step which would extend the blessings of electricity to agriculture throughout the nation.

It was a great national undertaking, the utility of which is clothed with the most decent, sentimental aspirations.

I knew the heat of those summer days in a farm kitchen in the deep South or the Great Plains, where humidity and the blazing sun combined with the stove to create unbearable temperatures. I had seen the drudgery of washing and ironing and sewing without any of the labor-saving electrical devices. I could close my eyes and recall the innumerable scenes of the harvest and the unending, punishing tasks performed by hundreds of thousands of women, uncomplainingly and even gayly and happily, growing old prematurely; dying before their time; conscious of the great gap between their lives and the lives of those whom the accident of birth or choice placed in the towns and cities.

Why shouldn't I have been interested in the emancipation of hundreds of thousands of farm women?

It was an executive order issued by President Roosevelt, not legislative action, that established the first Rural Electrification Administration in 1936. The President set aside $100,000,000 of work relief funds appropriated by the Seventy-fourth Congress in S.J. Res. 117 to launch this program.

Early in 1936, shortly after REA had been created by executive order and had gone into operation, I introduced a bill in the Senate to make it permanent, and to effect some changes in the plan of operation and administration that I thought were desirable. Under the provisions of the bill I introduced, rural electrification was made nation-wide in scope and in jurisdiction. It was greater than TVA, which was necessarily limited in its objectives. I was thinking then that, with TVA as a model, the United States would move forward to the construction of similar projects on all the streams of the country where it was practical to preserve and protect the natural resources effectively and economically.

My bill did not meet with very serious objection either in the Senate or in the House. I was surprised, although I might have anticipated that a proposal to extend the blessings of electric power to the farmers of America would have behind it the friendly sympathy and backing of hundreds of thousands of rural homes.

In its simple provisions, it stipulated that farm organizations might be established to construct the necessary transmission lines and distributing systems to deliver electricity directly to the farm homes within such districts. The logical lines of geography were to be followed in the establishment of these districts. And while the act permitted the building of generating plants, it was intended primarily that electric power should be purchased either from private or from public owners of generating plants at fair wholesale rates to permit liquidation of the financial obligations incurred in the building of transmission and distributing lines.

It provided that the government of the United States should loan the money required in the beginning for such undertakings.

Under the law, any REA organization might apply to the federal government for such loans to serve the territory incorporated in the district. Each district obligated all of its facilities to the REA for repayment of the funds advanced to it.

The bill passed by the Senate established the interest to be paid to the federal government at a rate not to exceed 3 per cent; incorporated the rigid provisions of Civil Service under which the administrator in the appointment of officials or employees was required not to give partisan, political consideration to selections, and stipulated that promotion was contingent upon efficiency and merit.

When the bill reached the House, that provision to base the entire operation of rural electrification upon efficiency and merit was stricken out as a whole, while the provision covering the loan of funds to these farm organizations was modified materially. The House provided that the loans should be based on an interest rate of not less than 3 per cent, where the Senate had provided that the charge should not exceed 3 per cent. Under the terms of the House bill, the interest rate never could have been less than 3 per cent and might be placed at any figure which the administrator established.

In this restrictive step, it seemed to me, the entire intent and purpose of the legislation to provide electricity for farms was in danger. If that interest rate was advanced high enough, either farmers would be discouraged in their efforts to procure the blessings of electricity for their homes and farm operations, or their undertakings would be financially unsound. It was an attack which I felt well might kill rural electrification under certain developments.

The bill went to conference, with these two principal changes and some changes of lesser importance at issue. It was in the conference committee, where no record vote was taken, and where the meetings were held in secret, that the real battle developed.

I discovered at the very first meeting I had a stubborn, embittered fight upon my hands.

House conferees were most insistent upon retention of the House amendments to the Senate bill.

I was chairman of the Senate conferees, and at most of the meetings my colleagues named by the Senate did not attend. I had a proxy from each Senate conferee with the exception of the chairman of the Senate committee, "Cotton Ed" Smith of South Carolina. He was irregular in his attendance at these gatherings of the conference committee so that on most occasions I was the sole representative of the Senate.

I made it a practice to keep my Senate conferees informed of what was going on; advised carefully with them; but since we all were in agreement the other members, who perhaps had not followed the bill as closely as I had, saw no purpose in attending these sessions during a congressional period when the demand upon the strength and energy of members was exceptionally heavy.

Days and weeks passed.

We held many conferences, and while in those deliberations discussion always was courteous, conducted in a high moral tone, the issue was sharply joined and exceedingly bitter. I could see no progress towards reconciliation. It was clear to me that the House conferees would not agree to eliminate partisanship in the selection of officials and employees in charge of rural electrification. The House conferees were equally determined that the rate of interest to be paid by the REA districts for federal loans never should be less than 3 per cent and might be any rate higher than that at the discretion of whoever should be in charge of rural electrification.

I despaired of reaching an agreement.

Finally I told the House conferees that in my judgment there was no necessity for spending any more time in discussion; that the issue had become very simple; and that it would be raised effectively in the next congressional campaign. I told the House conferees I was going to see to it that the question of rural electrification was carried directly to the people of the country, and thought the voters would be solid in support of me. In my judgment, I said, it would be one of the principal issues of the campaign.

Then I concluded with these words:

"I am going to quit the conference. I will not call another meeting of the conference committee."

Following adjournment, I left the committee room where the conference had been meeting; strolled into the lobby of the Senate a few minutes in advance of the hour it was to meet. I was joined there by one of the members of the House REA bloc, Representative John Rankin.

I knew he was a real friend of rural electrification, and trusted him.

He told me he thought I had been too hasty in reaching a conclusion we never would agree. He expressed the hope I would reconsider my decision, permit some time to elapse to enable him to talk the matter over with his associates on the conference committee; and he said he was satisfied we then could reach an agreement.

On the issue of nonpartisan selection of employees, he assured me the House conferees would recede from the ground they had taken rather than to permit the bill to die through failure to reach an agreement. He added that he thought we could reach a decision on the issue of interest rates.

I told him I was willing to call the conferees together any time when there was any disposition by the House conferees to compromise, but unless there was, no reason existed for continuing the battle longer. Again I repeated that in my opinion it would be necessary to make a national issue of rural electrification; I had no doubt that it could be done easily; and if it became necessary it was perfectly plain that the position I had taken would prevail.

He agreed with me in these conclusions, and I do not think personally he was opposed; but he did regard himself as being under obligations to stay with the House conferees until agreement could be reached.

We separated with the definite understanding he would work with the House conferees and, after sufficient time, let me know what the result was.

I got notice from him asking me to call another meeting of the conferees, which I did at once, and at that meeting a settlement was reached in a very few minutes after weeks of discussion.

The House members indicated they would recede from the House amendment that struck out the Senate provision embodying the nonpartisan selection of officials and employees. On the question of rates, Representative Huddleston proposed a compromise fixing the interest rate at the identical figure that the government had to pay in its financing program.

I agreed to this at once, and the struggle was over.

As a result of the House proposal on interest, the conference compromise turned out to be much more favorable to the farmers than the provision I had written into the Senate bill. From that time on, the rate of interest paid by farm electrification districts to the federal government never has reached 3 per cent; and it has been materially below that during the entire operation of the law.

As finally agreed to, the act contained a provision I had incorporated in the Senate bill under which rural projects could not be established in communities where farm organizations already were supplied with electric power from central service institutions.

I had never liked this provision of my own bill.

In introducing it, I had thought the limitation would avoid some very bitter controversies that could be brought in opposition to the law on the inspiration of the power trust. Reluctantly I had incorporated it in the bill after counseling with quite a number of friends and after having become convinced the bill would not pass the Senate without such a provision.

It pulled the teeth of any opposition which anyone could raise on the ground of interference in localities where rural electric power already existed and was supplied by private utilities. I was confident that the cost to the farmer of electricity in those localities would remain higher, but there had to be a start to get it. I felt it would be better to submit than to defeat rural electrification entirely.

My fears were justified.

There was trouble with that provision of the law.

By virtue of it, private power interests immediately began to build so-called "spite lines," and some extremely bitter fights developed in widespread sections of the country. The private utilities had done little to develop rural service. It had been their position that the cost of supplying electricity to the farmer in the construction of lines and of maintenance was prohibitive. The utilities were opposed to the entire law.

Immediately these companies, without notice in many cases, started to run a line through the middle of a contemplated rural electrification district, and in a practical sense, cut up territory which otherwise might have been sufficient for organization. The private power companies in developing these "spite lines," skimmed off the cream, leaving territory insufficient to form a new district, and often leaving farmers helpless to procure cheap electricity. By supplying part of the territory from a central service station they left the part unserved helpless, because under the provision it was illegal to organize a district that would not effectively serve the entire region, and it was impossible to construct a competing line.

After nine years, the REA has developed into a wonderful success. In its early beginnings, the farm people of America did not realize fully that it was nation-wide in scope, and that its provisions could be invoked in rural regions anywhere in America. Particularly it failed to be recognized that under the provisions of the law farmers even could construct generating plants to supply electricity to the countryside. Now the REA constitutes one of the largest organizations of a governmental nature ever undertaken in the United States. Its benefits to the rural population have been of mammoth proportions and will grow constantly as electricity is carried to thousands more of farms in all areas of the country. More than 1,200,000 American farm homes have electricity as a result.

In my judgment, President Roosevelt made a grave mistake when, under the reorganization bill passed by Congress, he transferred the administration of REA to the Department of Agriculture. Under the action of Congress originally establishing it, it was an independent agency similar to TVA, and not under the jurisdiction of any cabinet officer.

In time, REA bids fair to become greater in its effect upon agricultural life than the Department of Agriculture itself. My objection to placing it under the Agriculture Department is not from hostility or dissatisfaction, but solely from the desire to keep REA administration out of partisan politics. It was with the same desire that, in the drafting of TVA, I stipulated that all appointments, promotions, and demotions should be on the basis of merit.

The appointments of cabinet officers, however able and worthy, are based primarily on party considerations. If the REA or the TVA should ever get into politics, and should come under the control of politicians, then it will fail. I do not believe it possible to conduct the activities of agencies of this character upon the basis of proficiency and merit when the appointment of the head is influenced by partisan reasons.

TVA went through this ordeal when the act originally passed. It was the belief of many members of the House and the Senate, and political leaders outside, that thousands of appointments could be given to faithful party workers. Party-machine men always said that the provisions of the two laws could not be enforced and represented only dressing.

I had a conference with the personnel manager of the TVA, honest and upright, endeavoring to comply with the law both in letter and in spirit. He told me it would have been impossible to retain his position thirty days if the provisions of nonpartisanship had not been written into the law: political pull, and the influence of party bosses and machines, were so great that no man could stand up under the pressure without a rigid provision written into the law.

Because in each instance I was the author, I was beset, probably, with applications from all sections of the United States for positions in TVA and REA. I made some bitter enemies because I would not use my influence as a member of the Senate to get anyone a place in either agency.

Invariably I reminded these applicants I was the author of that section of the law, I believed its success depended upon its rigid observance, and I meant every word written into that regulation.

Colleagues in both branches of Congress told me that they thought these critics of the nonpartisan provision were right, and they wanted to know, confidentially, whether I had succeeded in getting appointments under the TVA Act. I told them I had no patronage and I had never written a recommendation for anybody.

If attempts to mix politics with electricity succeed, two great benefits which have come to the American people will be jeopardized.

That final journey to my home in McCook from Washington was marked by an incident which, entirely aside from the personal pleasure it gave me, seemed to lift the curtain upon the future.

In St. Louis at the national convention of the National Rural Electric Cooperative Association, at which 725 rural electrification projects were represented, I was given a silver plaque upon which were engraved farm buildings connected with REA lines, and the Norris Dam. In the accompanying resolution, it was set forth that a million farmers were receiving the benefits of cheap electricity. There were kind words for my "independence of partisan politics, for the fight for political and economic freedom for all human beings, for the suppression of monopoly and special privilege, for honesty and efficiency in government, for elimination of racial and religious prejudices and for economic security and freedom from want for all."

These young men and young women, America's farmers of the future, observing all the wonders of the modern age of electricity, will not be content with the homes of earlier America. Unless those homes in the countrysides are lighted electrically, and equipped with the devices electricity provides—for comfort, convenience, and efficiency—they will not be content. They will have been trained in the colleges and universities of this country for the most efficient agricultural methods, and electricity will be a part of their lives.

31

THE LAME DUCK AMENDMENT

It was the conservative swing of the years immediately following World War No. 1 that prepared the ground for the long congressional struggle finally ending in adoption of the Lame Duck Amendment to the American Constitution.

In the congressional campaign of 1922 one of the very material issues raised was what became known as the ship subsidy bill.

Popular sentiment was divided sharply.

There had developed in Congress a formidable bloc of supporters for a ship subsidy: a bloc that met a smashing repudiation in the fall elections of 1922. Members of Congress committed to the subsidy program went down to defeat, and the new Congress was bitterly opposed to any subsidy legislation. Wherever the issue became dominant in congressional fights, the American people spoke most emphatically.

It seemed to me that sentiment was expressed fairly in the November election of 1922.

Still President Harding favored, and was committed to, ship subsidy legislation. It followed, therefore, that if the advocates of ship subsidy were to salvage anything, it had to be rammed through the old Congress before the new members elected in November took office.

In order to accomplish this, Mr. Harding called a special session of Congress to meet on November 20, 1922. The short special session continued until the regular session of the old Congress in December. In this fashion, the advocates of ship subsidy had all the time from November 20 to March 4, 1923, to enact ship subsidy legislation against which the American people had spoken emphatically.

The lamentable, illogical, repellent condition was brought graphically to the attention of Congress and the American people by Senator Thaddeus Caraway of Arkansas. He introduced a concurrent resolution in the Senate directing attention to the fact that the question of a ship subsidy had been one of the material issues of the preceding congressional campaign, that many advocates of it, who were members of the present Congress, had been rejected decisively by large majorities of their constituents, and that the President had called Congress in extraordinary session for the purpose of passing legislation which the people in the general election by "imperative and unmistakable mandate repudiated."

One of the provisions of Senator Caraway's resolution stipulated that no member of Congress in either branch "has the moral right to support or vote for any measure which the people by their votes have repudiated."

The resolution concluded that it was the sense of the Senate and of the House of Representatives that "all members defeated at the recent polls abstain from voting on any but routine legislation, such as necessary supply bills, etc." Going one step further, it proposed "that chairmen of committees not in sympathy with the people's wishes expressed at the polls, and who have an important effect on legislation, resign from their respective chairmanships."

It is true Senator Caraway's resolution did not suggest a remedy to the difficulty; but it was revolutionary in its language, and it outlined clearly one of the evils long existent in American legislative machinery. Without suggesting an amendment to the Constitution as a cure it turned the light in striking fashion upon a condition that had been the subject of grave abuses.

I assume that Senator Caraway wished to call the attention of the country to the deplorable enactment, about to take place, of important legislation by men who had been defeated for election, while their successors, duly elected but unable to take office, representing the sentiment of their constituencies, were helpless to prevent it.

Senator Caraway requested his resolution be referred to the Committee on Agriculture and Forestry. I remember vividly the laughter that swept the floor of the Senate when he presented his request; and the merriment that mounted when the chair stated that the Caraway resolution would be so referred unless objection was made. There being no objection, the resolution was referred to the Agriculture Committee, of which I was chairman at the time.

I called the resolution up before the committee at the very earliest possible moment, and the committee referred it to me as a subcommittee of one. When I reported back to the committee, I expressed the opinion that in my judgment it would require an amendment to the Constitution to remedy the abuses so clearly projected by the resolution. I told my colleagues I had prepared, in lieu of the Caraway resolution, a substitute amending the Constitution of the United States.

The Agriculture Committee, by unanimous vote, directed me to make a favorable report to the entire membership of the Senate on the substitute I had drawn.

Thus, what now is known as the Lame Duck Amendment came into existence. And thus was born the first resolution proposing an amendment to the Constitution of the United States to do away with the Lame Duck Congress. Under the direction of my committee associates I reported the resolution to the Senate with a recommendation that it pass.

* * *

Under the provisions of the Constitution agreed upon by the Constitutional Convention, the terms of the President, and of the Vice President were established at four years; terms of senators, six years; and terms of the members of the House of Representatives two years.

Nowhere in that document was there any provision stipulating when those terms should begin or end. The Constitution provided in Article VII: "The ratification of the conventions of nine States shall be sufficient for the establishment of this Constitution between the States so ratifying the same."

Then when a sufficient number had approved it to make it effective the Congress of the Confederation by act of September 13, 1788, provided "that the first Wednesday in March next be the time . . . for commencing proceedings under the said constitution."

This act of the Congress of the Confederation therefore fixed the date when the new American government should commence to operate as the first Wednesday in March, 1789.

The first Wednesday in March of 1789 happened to be the fourth day of March, and thus by accident for more than one hundred years the terms of President, Vice President and members of Congress began on the fourth day of March.

In practice, that decision by the Congress of 1788 established a long session of Congress and a short session—which in due time came to be known as the lame-duck session. Since the terms of all members of the House of Representatives and of one-third of the members of the Senate ended every second year on the fourth day of March, the second session of every Congress, beginning on the first Monday in December, ended on the fourth day of the following March. On that day the terms of the newly elected members began, and automatically the old Congress had to come to an end.

When America was young and the burdens of Congress comparatively light, there were no serious difficulties. But as the country grew and reached West, and as the business of Congress became heavy, it became impossible for any group of men at a short session of Congress to transact properly the business of the nation.

Men elected to the House of Representatives in November could not enter upon performance of their duties until the fourth day of the following March. Yet the date fixed for the beginning of Congress was the first Monday in December, so that, unless a special session was called, members of the House of Representatives and one-third of the members of the Senate elected in November were not sworn into office until approximately thirteen months after their election. It created the abnormal condition of members of Congress holding office and performing their functions after they had been defeated for office.

It was contrary to all reason and precedent that men who had been repudiated by their own people should continue to mold legislation as representatives of those people. This gave any President who desired to use it enormous power over legislation. On several occasions, it was revealed, many of these lame-duck members of Congress were willing to follow the command of the executive and to adopt legislation which he desired. For their subservience, they were given fat executive appointments. Not all defeated members of Congress were guilty of this subservience—many remained loyal to their conscientious convictions; but it had become quite common for men retired to private life by their people to do the bidding of the President of the United States in legislation of the gravest national importance.

The ship subsidy legislation was only one example.

No congressional fight of protracted duration more clearly projected the difficulties of achieving sensible and necessary change in institutions of government than the struggle over the Lame Duck Amendment.

The substitute resolution to amend the Constitution of the United States, which I reported from the Committee on Agriculture, contained a provision doing away with the antiquated Electoral College, and provided for the election of President and Vice President by the direct vote of the people. Long before the Caraway resolution, I had given considerable thought to an amendment to the Constitution doing away with the Electoral College. I thought then and believe now it is entirely undemocratic: it has no place in the American Constitution, under which the voice of the people should dominate in the most simple, direct fashion in the election of a chief magistrate. I added that provision thinking that it was a good time to get it before the Congress of the United States, that it would not excite any opposition, and that, under the favorable atmosphere that existed, a long-neglected change would be accomplished easily in this way.

In this I was mistaken badly.

The proposal to abolish the Electoral College strangely excited a great deal of staunch opposition from high and influential sources. Liberal leaders whom I consulted, both in and out of Congress, universally advised me to strike out that part of the resolution, and to confine the resolution to a provision fixing the beginning and ending of the terms of the President, Vice President, senators, and representatives. That section was not necessary to remedy the condition to which the Caraway resolution directed attention.

Among distinguished Americans with whom I consulted was William Jennings Bryan, of my own state. He was so interested in the lame-duck proposal he came to Washington to see me, and passed the better part of a day with me.

Mr. Bryan was not so much opposed to the abolishment of the Electoral College as he was fearful that including it in the resolution would bring the defeat of the resolution. He promised me, if I would amend my resolution to strike out all references to the Electoral College, he would do everything within his power to enlist support in Congress, especially in the House of Representatives. It was plain that he was convinced sufficient support could be mustered in the House to carry the resolution by the two-thirds majority required for a constitutional amendment.

With great reluctance I yielded. True to his promise, Mr. Bryan labored with the members of the House of Representatives; but he was mistaken in his ability to procure the necessary votes.

In the Senate when my resolution came to the floor, Senator Knute Nelson, who was chairman of the Judiciary Committee, expressed criticism that the Caraway resolution had been referred to the Agriculture Committee instead of the Judiciary Committee. Normally, under Senate procedure, the Judiciary Committee always had jurisdiction of all legislation relating to the amendments of the Constitution of the United States.

In reply, I called the Senate's attention to the fact the Caraway resolution had not proposed an amendment to the Constitution but simply had expressed a sentiment "that all members defeated at the recent polls abstain from voting on any but routine legislation." There was the Senate record itself, examination of which revealed that the Caraway resolution had been referred to the Agriculture Committee through action of the Senate itself. I had not requested that it be sent to the committee of which I was chairman, and had had nothing to do with the decision of the Senate to place the Caraway resolution with the Agriculture Committee for study and action.

I had prepared a most voluminous report, which was submitted to the Senate on February 12, 1923, in which it was said:

> The passage of such a resolution [S. Con. Res. 29, the Caraway resolution] would not only be unwise, but if it were complied with, would interfere with the constitutional right and privilege of many members of Congress. Under our Constitution, a member's right, if not his duty, to participate fully in all legislation up to the close of his constitutional term, cannot be questioned or denied. The resolution, however, does call attention to a very serious defect in some of the provisions of the Constitution. The passage of the resolution, however, would not bring a remedy, and your committee, after due consideration, has reached the conclusion that it should report to the Senate for its action a proposal to amend the Constitution of the United States that would in the judgment of the committee be certain to bring relief from the conditions pointed out by the concurrent resolution. . . .
>
> There is no reason why the Congress elected in November should not be sworn in and actually enter upon the duties of office at least as soon as the beginning of the new year following their election. . . . In a Government "by the people" the wishes of a majority should be crystallized into legislation as soon as possible after these wishes have been made known. These mandates should be obeyed within a reasonable time. Under existing conditions, however, more than a year lapses before the will of the people expressed at the election can be put into statutory law. This condition of affairs is not only unfair to the citizenship at large, it is likewise unfair to their servants whom they have elected to carry out this will. . . . It is conceded by all that the best time for legislators to do good work is during the winter months. . . .

Under existing conditions, a member of the House of Representatives does not get started in his work until the time has arrived for renominations in his district. He has accomplished nothing and has not had an opportunity to accomplish anything because Congress has not been in session. He has made no record on which to go before his people for election. It is unfair both to him and to the people of his district.

In the case of a contest over a seat in the House of Representatives, history has shown that the term of office has expired practically before the House is able to settle the question as to who is entitled to the contested seat. During all of this time the occupant of the seat has been drawing the salary, and if it is decided in the end that the occupant was wrongfully seated, then the entire salary must again be paid to the person who has been deprived of his seat. Double pay, therefore, is drawn from the Treasury of the United States and the people of the district have not been represented by the member whom they selected for that purpose.

In that report I discussed at considerable length the direct election of the President and the Vice President. I pointed out that the method provided in the Constitution not only is archaic but stands as a barrier to progress and makes it impossible for people to enjoy to the fullest extent the freedom and rights that ought to come to the citizenship of a free democracy.

No reason [I reported] can be given why an independent people, capable of self-government, should not have the right to vote directly for the chief magistrate, who has more power than any other official in our government. While the system [of the Electoral College] is unnecessary, cumbersome, and confusing, and has no merit whatever that can be mentioned in its favor, it has a severe and disastrous effect, and as a matter of fact, often indirectly, but certainly, takes away from the voter the right to effectively express his will. . . . Everybody knows that political conventions are very frequently manipulated and controlled by powerful secret influences that have selfish ends in view rather than the benefit of all the people. The machinery of a great political party of national scope is sufficient to enable those in control of that machinery to control the action of a national convention. . . . All of us have seen such control exercised, sometimes completely, and almost universally to a partial extent.

If a few men under existing conditions are able to control nominations without consulting the wishes or wants of the voters, and if a nomination is necessary for election, then the only right given to the voter is that of choosing between two samples which are set before him. This is in reality a denial of suffrage. At least, the right of suffrage so given is not absolute, and is little more than a hollow sham and mockery. As a matter of fact, the actual practice always has been and perhaps as long as the system lasts always will be that the man or men who control political parties do it from selfish motives. They care but little about the wishes of the people. They are sometimes the representatives of special interests, and even though those who do the work directly may not ask or expect any benefit, those whom they in reality represent and who furnish the sinews of political warfare expect to benefit by national legislation or by presidential appointments of administrative officials.

The people are not consulted, and the people have in reality no voice in the selection of their own President, whose power and influence in administrative directions is almost unlimited. . . . Even though the people are dissatisfied, they are helpless because it is practically impossible for anyone to be an independent candidate for President, no matter what demand there may be from the people in this respect. The Electoral College stands in the way. In order to run for President, it is necessary to organize in every state and in every congressional district of every state and select candidates to become electors, pledged to the man who is to become a candidate. This takes not only time, but a vast amount of money.

If the Electoral College were abolished, and the people allowed to vote directly for President, it naturally would follow that those who control political conventions would be more careful in the selection of nominees. . . . If national political conventions nominated candidates unsatisfactorily, it would be easy for the people to defeat such nominees by rallying behind an independent candidate for President. It would be an easy matter to have printed on the official ballot in all states the name of an independent candidate. This could be done without the organization of a new party, and at very little expense, and when the voter went to the polls to cast his ballot, instead of a ballot ten or twenty feet in length, he would be confronted with the names of actual presidential candidates on a space two or three inches in length. It would be a very simple procedure, inexpensive, and perfectly practical.

I do not believe that the American people ever will attain their full freedom until they win emancipation from convention manipulation through the privilege of voting directly upon the President and the Vice President of the United States.

In the ten-year battle that got under way, I saw enough of the intrenched defenses of politicians to lead me to believe that here was the last citadel of reaction and of reactionary thought in the United States. With heavy heart I relinquished that portion of a fight that I believed would be vital to the welfare of the American people.

It was on December 5, 1922, that I filed the report on the Lame Duck Amendment. For the first time the amended resolution, with all reference to the Electoral College stricken out, was taken up in the Senate on February 12 and 13, 1923, and, well towards the close of the 13th, passed by a vote of 63 to 6. Yet, in the opposition of the years ahead, that Lame Duck Amendment was not adopted finally until 1933, and for ten years a simple, common-sense reform of the Constitution was defeated and nullified openly and under cover.

Such is the slow march of progress.

After its passage in the Senate, in 1923, the amended Lame Duck Amendment was sent to the House, where it was referred to the Committee on the Election of President, Vice President, and Representatives in Congress, to get quicker action this time. Strangely, that amendment, in its initial struggle for recognition, was associated with the birthdays of two great Americans. Debate started in the Senate on the anniversary of Abraham Lincoln, and favorable action followed forty-eight hours later. Initial action in the House came on Washington's Birthday when the committee made a favorable report on my resolution, and the resolution itself was placed on the House calendar. There it died, for lack of action, with the expiration of the Sixty-seventh Congress.

In the Sixty-eighth Congress, I introduced the resolution again in practically the same form, and it passed the Senate the second time on March 18, 1924. In the House, another House committee made a favorable report on April 15, 1924, and it was placed on the calendar, where it remained without action until the expiration of the Congress on March 4, 1925.

I reintroduced the resolution in the Sixty-ninth Congress, and for the third time it passed the Senate on February 24, 1926; the

MODERNIZING THE CONSTITUTION

House committee reported it favorably on January 24, 1926, but it remained on the House calendar without action until the expiration of the Congress on March 4, 1927.

There was the record.

Three times it had passed the Senate; three times it had gone to the House; three times it had been favorably reported by the House committee, and three times it had been smothered to death on the House calendar without debate or the lifting of a hand.

Again I reintroduced the resolution in the Seventieth Congress, and the Senate passed it on January 4, 1928. When it reached the House, again it received a favorable report; this time the House discussed it on March 9, 1928, and gave it a gratifying majority of votes but less than the two-thirds majority required by the Constitution.

For the fifth time in the Seventy-first Congress I introduced the resolution. It passed the Senate on June 7, 1929, and reached the House a day later, but was held on the Speaker's desk until April 17, 1930.

Representative Nicholas Longworth of Ohio, son-in-law of Theodore Roosevelt, was Speaker. By arbitrarily holding back the Lame Duck resolution to the House committee more than ten months, he violently abused the parliamentary authority of the House and showed discourtesy to the Senate.

I have no idea how long Speaker Longworth would have persisted. Early in April I decided to do something about it. On April 9, 1930, while the Lame Duck resolution was slumbering on his desk, I introduced a resolution (S. Res. 245) calling attention to what was going on in the House, and asking a committee of the Senate be appointed to ascertain why no action had been taken in the House during that long period of time. Nothing was done with my resolution, but it brought the desired results, because Speaker Longworth, after having had the earlier resolution on his desk so long, referred it to the proper committee of the House.

In the meantime, while my resolution was slumbering under Speaker Longworth's anesthetic, the House Committee on the Election of President, Vice President, and Representatives in Congress reported a similar House resolution introduced by its chairman, Representative Gifford of Massachusetts, and it was placed on the calendar of the House.

Here was fresh delay.

The House committee truthfully could say the resolution passed by the Senate had not been before it, and therefore it was justified in acting on the House resolution. Then within a few days Speaker Longworth referred the Senate resolution to that committee. This irregular action could not have come about by accident, and it could only result in delay. The House committee should have acted on the Senate resolution instead of taking up a House resolution which had not passed the Senate. It is fair to conclude that whatever conspiracy the House leaders had in mind was frustrated when I introduced my resolution asking for an investigation of the delay.

The committee took no action on the Senate Lame Duck resolution; but on February 24, 1931, the House took up the House resolution, and the Senate resolution was taken out of the hands of the committee and laid before the House. It was amended by striking out all after the enactment clause and inserting the words of the House resolution. In this form, it passed the House of Representatives on the same day and was reported to the Senate. On the following day, February 25, the Senate disagreed to the action of the House and requested a conference, resulting in the appointment of myself, Senator Borah of Idaho, and Senator Walsh of Montana as the Senate conferees. The Senate reported its disagreement the same day to the House, and the Speaker appointed Representatives Gifford, Perkins, and Jeffers as conferees.

Time was running out when the House managed to toss the Lame Duck Amendment into conference, and it named its conferees on the afternoon of February 25, when the expiration of the Seventy-fourth Congress was only a few days away. In between was Sunday, so that there were only five working days for agreement in the conference committee and approval by both the Senate and the House. It was clear that, unless the conferees revealed a desire to reach an agreement, it would be impossible to get final action on the resolution.

To speed matters, I called a meeting of the conferees at once.

Within a few minutes it was apparent no agreement could be reached in conference. The House bill contained some minor amendments to my Senate resolution which might have been adjusted easily; but the main House amendment embraced a provision that the Congress must adjourn by the fourth day of March.

It was an amendment that the Senate conferees never could accept.

One of the main objectives of the Lame Duck Amendment had been to abolish the fourth day of March as the date of final adjournment of Congress. This was destroyed by the House amendment. The second session of Congress—the shorter, lame-duck session—would have been unlimited, like the first session.

In that first meeting of the conferees it was revealed that a majority of the House conferees would not agree upon any report. Senator Borah, Senator Walsh, and I met by ourselves later and decided it was impossible to get a report before adjournment. The House had held the resolution without action for nearly a year, plainly determined to defeat it by delay.

It had succeeded.

The trail was indubitably clear to the three of us as we sat there talking.

The attitude of the Speaker was established.

There were a number of very important appropriation bills awaiting action that required passage to keep the government going. There was little chance of obtaining action on the conference report, so regretfully we agreed to let the resolution fail. It therefore died in conference, and the fifth attempt to amend the Constitution by eliminating the Lame Duck session of Congress had failed.

When the next Congress convened, I introduced my resolution for the sixth time on December 9, 1931. It was referred to the Judiciary Committee, was reported back promptly to the Senate, and on January 6, 1932, the Senate passed it for the sixth time. It went to the House, was amended, and passed on February 16, 1932. The next day the Senate disagreed to the House amendment, requested a conference to which the House promptly agreed, appointing conferees.

The sun had broken through the clouds after ten years of frustration.

It is important to note that the House had changed its political character in the preceding election.

It was now under control by the Democrats; Speaker Longworth had been succeeded by John Garner of Texas, and the control which had successfully defeated every attempt to pass the resolution had been terminated. Again I had the assistance of Senator Walsh and Senator Borah as conferees, and this time a majority of the House conferees were friendly. There was no difficulty in reaching an agreement. The conferees' report was accepted by the House on March 1, 1932; by the Senate on March 2; and thus the resolution after passing the Senate in six different Congresses became a reality and was submitted to the states for approval. So long as the House had been controlled by the Republicans, it was unfriendly to the legislation; when the Republicans lost control, the days of the lame-duck sessions were numbered.

Under the Constitution an amendment required the approval of three-fourths of the state legislatures.

I was gratified by its rapid acceptance.

On January 23, 1933, a sufficient number of state legislatures had voted ratification to make the amendment effective. It was one of the most rapidly approved constitutional amendments ever submitted to the states, demonstrating conclusively the general support for the change throughout the country.

I know of no state legislature where the issue precipitated a partisan struggle. Partisanship revealed itself only in the House of Representatives, and there only because of Republican leadership.

This Twentieth Amendment to the American Constitution, for which I fought and finally won, not only cured a genuine evil that progressively became more serious, but also corrected two significant omissions in the original Constitution. They are covered in Sections 3 and 4—designed to meet contingencies liable to arise after every presidential election.

These two sections prescribe the steps to be taken in the event of death of the President elect or the Vice President elect.

As a result, those omissions in the original Constitution have been so clarified it is believed there never can arise a contingency where the country will be without a chief magistrate or without the method of selecting a chief magistrate.

Those sections provide:

Section 3. If, at the time fixed for the beginning of the term of the President, the President elect shall have died, the Vice President elect shall become President. If a President shall not have been chosen before the time fixed for the beginning of his term, or if the President elect shall have failed to qualify, then the Vice President elect shall act as President until a President shall have qualified; and the Congress may by law provide for the case wherein neither a President elect nor a Vice President elect shall have qualified, declaring who shall then act as President, or the manner in which one who is to act shall be selected, and such person shall act accordingly until a President or Vice President shall have qualified.

Section 4. The Congress may by law provide for the case of the death of any of the persons from whom the House of Representatives may choose a President whenever the right of choice shall have devolved upon them, and for the case of the death of any of the persons from whom the Senate may choose a Vice President whenever the right of choice shall have devolved upon them.

I think it remarkable that, in a country grown to maturity, rich, prosperous, soundly established in democratic ideals, accepted throughout the world as the fortress of democratic thought, ten years should be required to effect a simple, common-sense change in government in keeping with physical and social changes in a nation. The founding fathers drew a constitution that has been adequate for America in its elemental principles in a fraction of the time.

32

UNICAMERAL LEGISLATURE

It was a cold Sabbath morning close after New Year's Day of 1937 that I stepped from the train which had brought me from McCook to Lincoln.

There were splashes of white covering the frozen fields, and the wind from out of the north cut sharply.

In the warmth of the hotel lobby the crowds were assembling.

A new legislature was to convene in the Nebraska capital; a unicameral, or one-house legislature. Among the crowds there was an undercurrent created by those who knew that the experiment would fail, and those equally certain it would succeed.

I was stopping in Lincoln briefly for the ceremonies attending a governmental reformation for which I was responsible.

I was on my way to Washington where the inaugural ceremony had been advanced two months and a President of the United States was to take the oath of office in January as a result of the Lame Duck Amendment that I had proposed to the federal Constitution—adopted by the American people after more than a decade of battle.

The unicameral legislature was no sudden fantasy on my part. For quite a number of years I had given study to the idea of providing a unicameral legislature in my home state by amendment to the state constitution.

While living at Beaver City, I had been importuned by Republican leaders in Furnas County to become a candidate for the legislature. They wanted me to run sometimes for the house and sometimes for the senate. Always I had refused purely for business reasons:

As an attorney without a partner, even if elected unopposed, I could not afford to serve in the Nebraska legislature. Its session came at a time when ordinarily I was most active in my work as an attorney. If I went to the legislature, I practically should have to close my law office. The pay of a Nebraskan legislator was very small, $300 a term—insufficient even to meet living expenses on a modest scale. Which meant that either I should have to neglect my duties as a legislator, or I should have to give up my law practice.

It was then that I first became interested in the unicameral legislature; and my interest continued throughout my five terms in the Lower House of Congress and my service in the United States Senate. Midway in my fourth term in the United States Senate, I still was anxious that the State of Nebraska abolish its illogical and clumsy two-house legislature and substitute the unicameral plan for it.

I promised some Nebraska friends in 1934 to help in a movement to bring about the adoption of the proper amendment to establish the single chamber. Out of these preliminary discussions came plans for a public, state-wide meeting to be held in Lincoln on Washington's Birthday, February 22, 1934. An old-time friend and supporter, Colonel John G. Maher, called the conference, which everybody interested was invited to attend, in the auditorium of the Cornhusker Hotel.

I journeyed from Washington to address this meeting—at which, to my surprise, eight hundred men and women, from all parts of the state, were present—and proposed in my address adoption of an amendment to Nebraska's constitution providing for a unicameral legislature.

In the discussion which followed, Colonel Maher was authorized to appoint a committee, of which he would be chairman, to conduct a campaign and circulate petitions under the initiative and referendum provisions of the constitution for a constitutional amendment to appear upon the official ballot of the following November election. I submitted at that time a tentative proposal, which the committee changed in subsequent meetings, unanimous agreement being reached upon the final form of amendment.

That tentative proposal called for a limited legislative membership, twenty-five, and a salary of $2,500.

When Colonel Maher's committee gathered, there was spirited discussion. I had proposed election of the members of the one-house legislature on a nonpartisan ballot. While every member of the committee wished partisanship to be eliminated from the legislature, yet the committee members believed that adding such a provision to the amendment would be at the risk of its defeat by the people.

But I insisted strenuously that the nonpartisan feature be retained, expressing the opinion to the committee that when the campaign got under way the nonpartisan feature would present one of the strongest appeals of the proposed amendment.

There also was much discussion of salaries. The committee agreed that the salaries of the members should be increased, but were unanimous in expressing the opinion that to increase them in the amendment would bring defeat at the election because of the expense incurred. Finally agreement was reached by placing a salary limitation of $75,000 for the biennium on the basis of a membership of not fewer than thirty or more than fifty. The exact membership was to be determined by the legislature itself. The larger the membership, the smaller the salary of the individual member; and the smaller the membership, the larger the salary. I was satisfied to leave it to the discretion of the legislature with the limitations of not more than fifty nor fewer than thirty.

In all of this campaign the greatest difficulty encountered was in procuring the number of signatures the initiative and referendum petitions required in order to obtain a place on the official ballot for the proposed amendment. Under the constitutional procedure which was then in force, great care had to be taken to guard against signing of the petition by persons not qualified to vote. The constitution stipulated that not more than twenty names might appear on any one petition, and that each petition should contain an affidavit properly sworn to by the circulator that he himself had seen each person sign it whose name appeared on the petition—that it was signed in his presence, and the address given was the proper address of the signer. These proper initiative safeguards made it absolutely essential that the petitions be circulated by residents of the communities where the signers lived. The constitutional safeguard contained a penalty that if in any court or elsewhere any name on any petition was found to be illegal for any reason, all the signatures to that petition would be invalidated.

In our enthusiasm at that first meeting it was not thought likely that a large amount of money would be necessary to initiate the unicameral amendment.

The committee upon organizing made provision for the collection of contributions to defray the expense of circulating the petitions. It was certain that, after the petitions were printed, they could be sent to individuals in various parts of the state, acquainted with the localities who would obtain the necessary signatures without great expense.

That hope was uprooted quickly.

We soon discovered that it was not so easy to obtain circulators of petitions and signatures to the petitions, and that, if the amendment was to be submitted, it would be necessary to compensate the circulators for the time needed in obtaining the requisite number of signers. This number, based by the law upon the vote cast for governor in the preceding general election, was 65,000, to be distributed among not fewer than two-thirds of the ninety-three counties of the state.

The committee chose Donald Gallagher to take charge of the campaign to obtain the requisite signatures. After it had been in progress for several weeks, he wrote me of his great discouragement and of his conclusion that it would be impossible to obtain the necessary number unless a stipulated amount was paid for each name obtained. He soon used all the money that had been contributed. Finally he wrote me in Washington it would be impossible to obtain the number but he did not want the matter to fail entirely, and suggested I write a letter, addressed to him, calling attention to the lack of money to submit the proposal in the November election. He apparently had in mind a campaign to submit the issue two years later.

Instead of writing this kind of letter, I wrote him we had gone too far to stop, and even if we had to admit failure it would be better to fight and lose than to discontinue the efforts. I enclosed a check for $1,000 and wrote to other people, with the result that several made contributions. The campaign again was under way, circulators receiving five cents for every name on the petitions.

The opposition was not idle.

The Omaha *World-Herald,* a powerful, widely read newspaper, fought the amendment bitterly. The leaders of both political parties were opposed to it. Among the farmers there was a feeling that the membership of the unicameral legislature should be larger, the majority of those in opposition expressing the opinion there should be at least 100 members.

The banks, the market, and the provision men mostly were against the amendment, so far as we could determine.

It was the nonpartisan feature that aroused the enmity of the politicians. Early in the campaign Arthur F. Mullen, the acknowledged leader of the Democratic party in Nebraska, came to my office in Washington and frankly told me he was opposed to the amendment because of the nonpartisan feature, and would fight it; but if I would agree to retention of the party basis in election of members he would promise the active support of the Democratic organization. I answered with equal frankness, although with much regret, that I would not surrender the nonpartisan election feature, that I saw no reason why election to the legislature should be on a partisan basis and was going to continue the fight for a nonpartisan unicameral legislature, win or lose.

I knew fully while talking to Mr. Mullen the difficulties to be overcome.

We had no broad organization supporting the amendment. We could count on the opposition of political machines of every description. We knew the farm vote was divided, some of the organizations supporting us, and others opposing us. Most of the newspapers in Nebraska, the majority of the bankers, the lawyers, the utilities, and the railroads were hostile to the amendment.

In the daily newspaper field only the Lincoln *Star* and the Hastings *Tribune* actively supported the amendment.

When at last the requisite number of signatures to the petitions to place the amendment on the official ballot had been procured, the battle became easier. Support grew like a snowball rolling down hill. I was amazed in the unanimous support of educators in the state.

Once the campaign got under way, it was unnecessary to spend money. All the work for the amendment was volunteer; and, so far as I know, the only pay workers received was to defray expenses incurred—most of the supporters paying their own expenses.

Before the campaign for a unicameral legislature ended, I saw one of the best organizations with which I have ever been associated, laboring without money or pay.

I was particularly inspired by the thousands of young people who, not old enough yet to vote, nevertheless revealed deep interest and voluntarily made speeches in the campaign. Joint debates were held in nearly every town and city. Young girls and young boys, with chips on their shoulders, made door-to-door canvasses distributing literature. After the campaign had terminated with a victory, I was told of a weekly gathering of a ministerial association in one of the larger cities. The association's work was not political in any sense, but a few days before the election one of the members proposed a straw vote on the one-house legislature amendment; and surprisingly every minister in the association favored its adoption. Not one believed it would be approved.

I never made a more complete campaign in Nebraska, or in any other political contest in which I became engaged. I traveled every section of the state, nearly wearing out my automobile.

I paid my own expenses. It was an intensely interesting fight and a gratifying campaign, for I never have had larger or more sympathetic audiences in my political experiences.

Well towards the close I felt, or thought I felt, a sentiment more and more favorable to the adoption of the amendment. I was certain it was going to receive a much larger vote than people expected. It came to my attention that many men of prominence were supporting the proposition without saying anything about it; I talked confidentially with hundreds of these men all over the state, and invariably they told me they did not want to support it openly, for fear their activity might injure them in some future political contest.

It was the type of fear that I had encountered years before in the campaign in Pennsylvania.

On the eve of the election the politicians in Nebraska were confident the amendment would be defeated overwhelmingly.

However, when the people went to the polls and marked their ballots, surprisingly it had been approved by a majority of 92,934.

If the campaign had lasted two weeks longer we might have doubled the majority.

The vote was for the amendment, 286,086; against it, 193,152.

Out of the ninety-three counties, eighty-five gave majorities for the amendment; and only eight against. The eight were Arthur, Banner, Clay, Dundy, Hayes, Keya Paha, Merrick, and Rock. Only two were populous; the others were ranching regions, sparsely settled.

There is no logical argument in favor of a two-house legislature as against the unicameral assembly. It is illogical to elect members of two separate bodies when the qualifications are identical, the tenure of office is the same, the salary is the same, and the duties, responsibilities, and jurisdiction are the same.

The two-house legislature is a relic of the past.

We have adhered to it for many years because it was preferred by our forefathers, and because the politicians found it convenient for their purposes. The two-house legislature, in existence largely over the country, is out of date and incompetent. In the membership generally are men not interested in the welfare of the state or the laws of the state; more interested in employing the legislature as a steppingstone to something else. Often they use their positions as a lever to obtain financial advancement. Most of them are honest, but sometimes it is as easy to fool the honest man as it is to buy the dishonest one.

Salaries paid are woefully inadequate.

The legislature should be a business institution, with the state compared to a great corporation. The governor is its president; the legislature, the board of directors; the people, the stockholders. There is no more reason for a state to have a two-house legislature than there is for a bank to have two boards of directors or a city to have two boards of aldermen. There is no reason why the politics of a legislature should conform to the politics of Congress or the national administration in Washington.

The issues usually are entirely different.

The greatest evil of a two-house legislature is its institution of the conference committee. When a bill passes one house and is amended by the other, however slightly, it then must go to a conference committee, the source of numerous errors and frauds. And in this conference committee the "jokers" are placed in otherwise good laws. There the "bosses" and the special interests and the monopolies get in their secret work behind the scenes. There the elimination of a sentence or a paragraph, or even a word, may change the meaning of an entire law.

Frequently a conference committee does not report until the eve of adjournment, and when the report is made it cannot be amended. Both branches must take it or reject it entirely. And conference committees universally are appointed by the presiding officer.

If a monopoly controls the presiding officer of either house, it can control through him the action of the conference committee. It is this which makes it easier as a rule for the lobbyist to control a two-house legislature than a unicameral body.

Many times in two-house legislatures amendments have been put on bills in order to shift the responsibility for legislation to the other house; conference committees have been unable to agree, and when that has taken place proposed legislation has died.

It has been the stock argument that in a two-house legislature one branch serves as a check upon the other in the ultimate molding of good and wholesome legislation. As a matter of practice, it has developed frequently that, through the conference committee, the politicians have the checks, and the special interests the balances.

The simplified procedure of the unicameral legislature eliminates the possibility of shifting responsibility. In the one-house legislature there is no way a member can evade his duty. Under the unicameral plan it is easy for the ordinary citizen to place responsibility for the passage or defeat of legislation where it belongs. There is the opportunity to reward the faithful representative and to hold to account the unfaithful.

I watched one fight in Nebraska where the existence of the conference committee made possible parliamentary tactics that not only smothered a deserving and popular proposal, but covered the matter up so completely that the ordinary citizen could not find out what really happened.

The proposal was to amend the law to permit municipalities to extend the lines of publicly owned utilities beyond their corporate limits. Under the existing statute a city owning its electric or water system did not have that right, and any suburb that might grow up could not be served. A private corporation supplying electric service could extend its lines to such an area, but not a municipally owned utility. It was this unfair limitation that the friends of municipal ownership undertook to remedy.

A bill was introduced in the Nebraska legislature permitting municipally owned electric-light plants to build lines beyond their corporate limits to furnish service for homes outside. It was not thought that there would be opposition. Hardly any member of the legislature could have opposed it openly and retained his seat. But, after parliamentary juggling, the legislature adjourned without passing the bill.

Two years later the same bill was introduced, with the same results. Two years later still, the same bill was introduced; but this time the municipalities in Nebraska owning their electric facilities took pains to insure its passage—obtaining in advance promises of support from a majority of the members of both branches of the legislature. But the bill failed again, not because any member violated his pledge, but because the bill passed by one house was amended in minor particulars in the other house, and died in the conference committee.

Still every member of the legislature could go back home and say truthfully that he had voted for the bill. The conference committee had provided the utilities with the weapon to accomplish their purpose.

Thus frustrated for six years, the proposal was submitted through initiative and referendum; and Nebraska, voting directly, approved the bill by over a 100,000 majority.

This could not have happened in a one-house legislature. Under its procedure one member demanding a roll call upon any proposition can place every member of the legislature on record for or against any bill.

I have had extensive correspondence with individuals in nearly every state of the Union on the subject of the unicameral legislature. I have sent literature and have written extensively to men and women seeking to reform legislative methods in their own states. I believe it would not be difficult to establish the unicameral system among the states if the right organization undertook it, and it would be approved in each of the forty-eight states.

In Washington nearly all of the so-called progressive members of the United States Senate have discussed the unicameral legislature with me.

When Phil La Follette was governor of Wisconsin, I sought to persuade him to undertake the unicameral reform there. The chief difficulty in all undertakings of this kind is that the outstanding political leaders do not take kindly to a movement of this nature unless it originates with them. So often they seem to be jealous if it develops outside their own domain.

I think this was the trouble with Governor La Follette.

Like most progressives he agreed with me that a one-house legislature in every state would be a great forward step. Action through the initiative, in those states that possess the initiative, naturally provides the easiest method. It is more difficult where an amendment must be submitted by legislative action, most legislatures being opposed because the unicameral plan would put the majority of them out of office—invariably it brings a vast reduction in the membership. (In Nebraska there were thirty-three members of the senate and one hundred members of the house.)

Had we been forced to depend upon the submission of an amendment by legislative action in Nebraska, the plan never would have been submitted to the people.

One episode in the Nebraska campaign deserves particular notice.

The colored vote in the state is concentrated almost entirely in Omaha and Lincoln. One district in Omaha almost solidly made up of negroes had been electing a negro to the legislature.

The opponents of the unicameral plan shrewdly and subtly planted the idea among the negroes that the plan would cost them their representation. They sent a delegation to see me, and it was decided that I should address a meeting in the colored district. A large hall was rented, seating about eight hundred people, and the meeting was well advertised.

When I arrived at the hall I found only seven or eight present—the only time in the campaign that I was not greeted by a capacity audience. So well had the opposition exploited the fears of the colored voters. I was prepared to meet the issue squarely, but intended to suggest that if that traditional seat were lost there was a principle involved that was fundamentally right.

As a climax, in spite of the fact that the negro vote was nearly solid against the unicameral plan, the colored voters succeeded in electing a member of their race to the legislature after it went into effect.

I have been asked why if a unicameral legislature is adapted to state government, I never have made an effort to reorganize Congress along similar lines. Hundreds of letters have come to me from many people over the country, pointing to what has seemed to be an inconsistency, or prompted in some cases by a genuine desire to see a one-house Congress. I am sure that these really overlooked the influences determining the organization of Congress. The two houses are a compromise between the large and the small states, the populous and the unpopulous regions—each state having two representatives in the Senate and having representation based upon population in the Lower House. Under the circumstances it was impossible to secure support, if it had been desired, for reorganization of the Congress along the pattern of the unicameral plan.

The results of the unicameral legislature have exceeded many expectations. In four regular sessions of a two-house legislature in Nebraska, coupled with one special session in 1935, a total of 3,960 bills was introduced, of which 754 were passed. In four regular sessions of the unicameral legislature, coupled with a special session in 1940, 2,073 bills were introduced, of which 794 were passed. The reduction in number of bills was 1,897—eliminating the waste of printing, the waste of time and energy of committees, and the waste of the people's money.

The legislative costs of the four sessions of the two-house legislature were $775,517.95; of the unicameral, $411,903.21.

We pay a pretty penny for our indifference to the necessity of constantly improving government and bringing it down to date.

33

LIMITATIONS UPON VOTING

WHILE IN THE SENATE, I became interested in the poll-tax laws.

Several of the southern states had written such voting qualifications, sometimes as a part of the state constitution, and sometimes as a statutory provisions, independent of the constitution. Often it was both.

It was, in effect, an effort on the part of some of the states of the Old South to prevent the negro race from enjoying the privilege of the elective franchise. Yet, the people against whom these laws were passed were shouldered with all the responsibilities of citizenship. Many of them were finely educated. In those instances where educational qualification was not an issue, it could be only a prejudice against permitting the negro to vote that furnished the background for such legislation.

This developed notwithstanding amendment of the federal Constitution after the Civil War to protect the right of these citizens to vote. There logically could have been a question at the time the Constitution was amended of the wisdom of such action. It was true, possibly in hundreds of thousands of cases, that the negroes were not prepared for citizenship as suddenly as it came upon them. But whatever may have been the case, the American people did amend the Constitution to give the negro full rights of citizenship, including the right to vote, by specific amendment of the Constitution of the United States; and that right was given at a time when there was some question as to its wisdom.

Through education and training, the negro has been prepared for citizenship.

I am conscious of the tragedy of the Reconstruction days in the Old South.

Many evils came to these southern states as a result of the control of legislatures in the states by men incompetent to enact laws for intelligent people. It brought about great suffering and hardship to all classes. I always have sympathized with the people who had to live under these laws, which were made by men under the control of northern "carpetbaggers." My study of the developments of those years immediately following the Civil War led me to the conclusion that many of the laws written into the statute books at that time hindered progress instead of aiding it

I am sure there were great injustices to all classes of people.

In that difficult period, responsibility and blame for the disorganization that took place were not entirely on one side. The enactment of laws by men who were not prepared for self-government, and who were subject to control by disreputable elements, brought about a condition which never should be thrust upon any free people. Developments projecting economic and moral mistakes, and ushering in ruin and suffering in their wake, cannot be defended.

More than half a century has elapsed, however, and it seems to me we should not prevent the colored race from voting—a privilege which the Constitution, the fundamental law of our land, gives them.

As the writing of this book comes to an end, again that issue has flared forth in all its bitterness in the ugly controversy over a federal soldier voting law. I could appreciate some of the fundamental passion that characterized the congressional discussion of a measure making it possible for American soldiers, now engaged in war, to vote while far from their homes. The issue always has contained explosive qualities. In the debate in Congress that began in December, 1943, and continued until March, 1944, the issue of the poll-tax laws was one of the main difficulties.

The poll-tax laws are intended, and were enacted, to frustrate many American citizens in the exercise of rights given by the Constitution of the United States. In order to avoid constitutional challenge in the courts, the poll-tax laws were not drafted on the theory that the right to vote should be denied on account of race. Clearly such a law would have been unconstitutional. The same objective could be accomplished by giving other reasons than race or previous condition of servitude. It was therefore devised that men or women, in order to vote, should pay a poll tax each year, which directly violated the sacred right to vote under the Constitution.

These laws, then, not only struck at the negroes but disfranchised thousands of legal white voters.

It was said openly on the floor of the Senate that in Mississippi, for instance, 250,000 white people were disfranchised as well as the negroes.

In my judgment, it is just as unconstitutional to tax a citizen for the right to vote as it would be to preclude him from voting because he happens to belong to the negro race.

I have regretted deeply the development of racial hatreds in the United States. During my service there were attempts extending over a period of years to enact legislation to prevent mobs—often mobs of intelligent citizens—from taking the law in their own hands and lynching men of the negro race, sometimes condemning them without a trial and lynching them without a hearing.

In the Seventy-fifth Congress an anti-lynching bill, which had been introduced several times, was before the Senate for consideration.

I thought the bill unconstitutional.

In an examination of the record, I find that I was alleged to have stated in a speech to the Senate that in my judgment this bill was unconstitutional, but that it had "other objectionable features which ought to condemn it."

My speech on that day, February 21, 1938, was entirely extemporaneous, and I had never looked over the report of it in the *Congressional Record* until a few weeks ago when I engaged in the research for this work. I was astonished to read there this expression of opinion that the law was constitutional, and I believe that the reporter who took down the speech erred. As it appears, I am quoted as saying that I thought the proposal was constitutional when in reality I said that it was unconstitutional in my judgment but my objection to it was as much on the issue of constitutionality as it was on other grounds.

In part I said in that speech:

"I think it would be a bad mistake if Congress should pass the so-called anti-lynching bill. Much as many of its features appeal to me, after as mature consideration as I am able to give it, I have reached the conclusion it never ought to be enacted into law. . . . I am opposed to the bill for reasons which have, perhaps, not been given during the debate. . . . I am opposed to it because I think it would have a tendency to raise again that slumbering monster which came into being as a result of the Civil War. I am opposed to the bill because I believe it would do more harm than good even to the colored race.

"I had a brother, Mr. President, an only brother, who breathed out his life in the battle of Resaca while serving with the Union army. I got my first lesson in the details of the Civil War when, standing as a child at my mother's knee, I heard her read the letters which had been written by her elder son by the campfire's light in the Southland. One of the letters received was after the fatal bullet had done its deadly work. I saw that mother, although she lived for many years afterward, go to her grave with a broken heart. The packet of letters which she read to me was tied up, I remember so well, with a little red ribbon, and was enclosed in a little tin box. When my mother died many years after I had grown to manhood, she left me no material riches, nothing of intrinsic value, but she gave to me something more precious than gold of the kingdom. She gave me that little packet of letters, stained with a mother's tears, tied up with a little red ribbon, enclosed in a little tin box. She carried to her grave a heart broken by the loss of her boy in the Civil War. My mother was only one of millions of others, both in the North and the South, whom that terrible conflict made unhappy for life. . . .

"When I read of the terrible things that happened to the South after the Civil War; the Reconstruction days, and the days when the carpetbaggers were running riot, adding misery and ruin to the homes which had already been desecrated as a result of the war

. . . I wonder how the South has done such remarkable work in the way of recovery. With many of their boys, their brothers, their sons, and husbands killed in the Civil War, their homes destroyed, their country laid waste, seeing them, a proud people, subjected by the cruelties of the Reconstruction days to the domination of the carpetbaggers . . . controlled in their legislatures and in their executive offices by officials who were corrupt and ignorant, and who added insult to injury, I wonder at the great improvement that has come about in the South in the years since the Civil War. The people of the South have done a wonderful job. . . .

"The people of the South have made a record of which they have a right to be proud.

"We have forgotten the Reconstruction days. The agonizing animosities which came about from the Civil War and the Reconstruction period have been largely forgotten, thank God. If enacted into law, this bill would revive them all. It would have a tendency, I think, to halt the progress which has been made during eventful years. We could not improve upon what has been done. . . . Why should we interfere now? Why should the federal government undertake to step in now? . . . I know that I was expected to vote for the bill. Until I thought it out myself, until I began to realize what I believe would be an affliction instead of a blessing, I was not looking upon the measure with disfavor. . . . I do not want the federal government to take up this burden which the people of the South have carried so well. I think it is certain we should fail where they have succeeded. . . .

"Whatever may be the result so far as my vote and voice against the proposed legislation are concerned, I take the responsibility, and I am willing to abide the consequences."

I set this down because I have been criticized by some for the inconsistency in opposing the anti-lynching bill and supporting the so-called poll-tax bill.

In these individual attitudes upon two distinct legislative proposals, I felt there was no inconsistency.

The poll-tax bill, as I saw it in the debate on the floor of the Senate, and still see it, was designed and intended to preserve a right not only for the negro, but for all citizens. It was the right to vote given to all citizens by the Constitution and protected by laws passed after the Civil War. The so-called poll-tax bill which came before Congress was a matter of law, entirely; the only issue, protection of a constitutional right.

After listening to all the evidence in the hearings, and giving it long study and consideration, I became convinced that the anti-poll-tax bill before Congress was constitutional and was necessary for the protection of citizens of the United States, especially those citizens belonging to the negro race.

I was on the subcommittee of the Senate Judiciary Committee to which the controversial measure was referred. I not only attended every hearing, and listened intently to the testimony, but gave the subject a great deal of independent research. When I became convinced that the proposal was constitutional, and that the right of voting it sought to protect was a sacred right derived through amendment of the American Constitution, I fought as best I could to procure adoption of the bill.

The subcommittee had reported its findings to the full Judiciary Committee. I found myself in the minority on the subcommittee, but when the bill came before the full committee additional amendments and consideration led to its sustaining the position I had taken by a large majority. I was appointed by the chairman of the Judiciary Committee to make a favorable report on the bill to the Senate.

Then began a historic fight.

I made the report, and the bill went on the calendar of the Senate, defeated through a filibuster, and never reached a vote on its merits.

On November 23, 1942, after the filibuster had become well developed in the Senate and there no longer was doubt but the opponents would undertake to talk it to death, I and other supporters undertook to invoke the cloture rule, which requires a two-thirds vote.

Cloture did not get even a majority; the vote was 37 for cloture to 41 against it, and as a result the bill died.

In view of the bitter fight in Congress in recent months, I can only feel that it was a most lamentable climax to a long struggle. Had decision been reached in 1942, disposing of the poll-tax issue, much of the controversy that has consumed months, added to the confusion of the American people, and contributed to disunity and dissension in a mounting tide of war, might have been averted.

There was no doubt the bill would have been passed by a large majority if it could have gone before the Senate on its merits.

I was very much disappointed by the vote on cloture, especially on the Republican side. I had taken it for granted that the leader of the Republicans, Senator Charles McNary of Oregon, would look with favor upon cloture because he, a good parliamentarian, knew that the Senate had to vote cloture in order to reach a vote; and in practical consequences a vote against the cloture was in reality a vote against the bill itself.

A few days before vote on cloture came on the Senate floor, a private conference was held by friends of the poll-tax legislation, with Senator McNary in attendance. He had been invited to the conference at my request. I assumed he would be favorable to the legislation. I was dumfounded when at the conference he announced to his colleagues he would vote against cloture.

I think judgment on this legislation is best expressed in the report which I made on behalf of the Judiciary Committee in favor of the passage of the poll-tax bill. I said in part:

"Practically the only question involved in this legislation is the constitutionality of the proposed legislation. The committee has reached the conclusion that the proposed legislation is constitutional and therefore should be enacted into law. Those who believe the proposed law is unconstitutional rely upon Section 2, Article I, of the Constitution which reads as follows:

"The House of Representatives shall be composed of members chosen every second year by the people of the several States; and the electors in each State shall have the qualifications requisite for electors of the most numerous branch of the State legislature.

"The qualification of a voter generally is believed to have something to do with the capacity of a voter. We think it would be admitted by all that no state, or state legislature, would have the constitutional authority to disqualify a voter otherwise qualified to vote by setting up a 'pretended' qualification that in fact has nothing whatever to do with the real qualifications of the voter. No one can claim that the provision of the federal Constitution quoted above would give a legislature the right to say that no one should be entitled to vote unless, for instance, he had red hair, or had attained the age of 100 years, or any other artificial, pretended qualification which, in fact, had nothing to do with the capacity of or real qualification of the voter.

"The evil that the legislation seeks to correct is, in effect, that in taking advantage of the constitutional provision regarding qualifications, the states have no right to set up a perfectly arbitrary and meaningless pretended qualification. . . .

"Can it be said in view of the civilization of the present day that a man's poverty has anything to do with his qualification to vote? Can it be claimed that a man is incapacitated from voting simply because he is not able to pay the fee which is required of him when he goes to vote? Is it not a plain attempt to take advantage of this provision of the Constitution and prevent citizens from voting by setting up a pretended qualification which, in fact, is no qualification at all?

". . . There are other provisions in the Constitution and amendments to the Constitution to which we desire to call attention. Section 4 of Article 1 on the original Constitution reads as follows:

"The times, places, and manner of holding elections for senators and representatives shall be prescribed in each State by the legislature thereof; but the Congress may at any time by law make or alter such regulations, except as to the places of choosing senators.

"The subcommittee to which this proposed legislation was referred has held rather extended hearings and has listened to very able constitutional lawyers . . . These two provisions of the Constitution above quoted have been discussed at great length and with great ability by some of the ablest constitutional lawyers in the country.

"The pretended poll-tax qualifications for voting have no place in any modern system of government. We believe it is only a means illegal and unconstitutional in its nature, that is set up for the purpose of depriving thousands of citizens of the privilege of participating in governmental affairs by denying them a fundamental right, the right to vote. . . . The most sacred and highest of all federal functions is the right to vote."

On that point in the report, I called attention to the decision of the Supreme Court of the United States in the Yarborough case, in which the court said:

> The right to vote for members of Congress is fundamentally based upon the Constitution of the United States, and was not intended to be left within the exclusive control of the State.

In emphasis of that, Justice Miller added:

> It is not correct to say that the right to vote for a member of Congress does not depend upon the Constitution of the United States.

In the Classic case which was decided in 1941, Justice Stone of the Supreme Court elaborated upon that point; and his opinion was set forth more fully in the report to the Senate:

> While in a loose sense the right to vote for representatives in Congress is sometimes spoken of as a right derived from the state . . . this statement is true only in the sense that the states are authorized by the Constitution to legislate on the subject as provided by Section 2, Article I, to the extent that Congress has not restricted state action by the exercise of its powers to regulate elections under Section 4 and its more general power under Article I, Section 8, clause 18, of the Constitution "to make all laws which shall be necessary and proper for carrying into execution the foregoing powers."

One might add that, since voting is one of the fundamental governmental rights, the right to tax this fundamental privilege by a state would be giving to the state the power to destroy the federal government. No state can tax any federal function. This is a proposition which will have to be admitted by all, and, if this federal function—the right to vote—can be taxed by a state, then the state has a right to destroy this federal function which is, if at all, the foundation of any government. As a matter of self-preservation, the Congress, in order to save the federal government from possible destruction, must have the right to prevent any state authority from destroying this cornerstone of government itself.

The right to vote for members of Congress is a right, as the Supreme Court has said, granted under the Constitution of the United States and, therefore, any law, constitutional or statutory, of a state which taxes this fundamental privilege is contrary to the provision of the federal Constitution. It could be said, of course, if these poll-tax laws are unconstitutional, they could be taken to the Supreme Court and there challenged directly and that a law of Congress is therefore unnecessary to protect this constitutional right. This undoubtedly is correct but it does not follow that, when the Congress of the United States has had brought to its attention these poll-tax laws, by which millions of our citizens are in effect deprived of their right to vote, that it would not be the duty of Congress itself to pass the necessary legislation to nullify such unconstitutional state laws. Most of these people are deprived of their right to vote by these poll-tax laws which are a method of taxation. As a rule, they are poor people and are unable to vote because they are poor. The very fact that because this class of people whose rights are being taken away are without financial means to fight makes it clear that they could not rely upon their constitutional rights of carrying their cases to the Supreme Court of the United States. The expense would be absolutely prohibitive and it is therefore the duty of Congress to protect these millions of citizens in their most sacred right as citizens—the right to vote.

In that report I called attention to the Virginia constitutional convention which submitted an amendment to the constitution of Virginia, by which it was intended to disfranchise a large number of Virginia citizens. I said the convention could be regarded as a fair sample of conventions in other poll-tax states.

I said Carter Glass then was a member of that convention, and early in its deliberations made a forceful speech. In the report I quoted his words:

"Chief purpose of this convention is to amend the suffrage clause of the existing constitution. It does not require much prescience to foretell that the alterations which we shall make will not apply to 'all persons and classes without distinction.' We were sent here to make distinctions. We expect to make distinctions. We will make distinctions."

And then in the report I referred again to a speech by Senator Glass in which he reviewed work already performed and then said, referring to the beginning of the convention and the debate on the oath:

"I declared then that no body of Virginia gentlemen could frame a constitution so obnoxious to my sense of right and morality that would be willing to submit its fate to 146,000 ignorant Negro voters [great applause] whose capacity for self-government we have been challenging for thirty years past."

The report continued:

> Under the circumstances, can there be any doubt when perhaps the greatest leader of all stated what the object was and what was expected to be accomplished by the so-called poll-tax laws? If we concede that this was the object of the law, then we admit it is unconstitutional because, if this was the effect of the law, it in fact made an artificial qualification, which in itself is illegal and unconstitutional.

I summed up the question involved in the proposed poll-tax legislation in this lanuage:

> It is quite clear that the so-called poll-tax laws do abridge the privileges and immunities of citizens of the United States. If any citizen of the United States is deprived of the privilege of voting by any of these poll-tax laws, it seems a clear abridgment of privileges of citizens of the United States. One of the greatest privileges, and a fundamental one, of every citizen of the United States is the right to vote. If he is deprived of this right, he is denied the right to participate in governmental affairs. Such a citizen becomes an outcast. He is subject to all the laws of the state. His citizenship is admitted and the burdens which rest upon him are the same as rest upon all other citizens. He can be drafted into the army and be compelled to face the foe and give up his life to protect

the lives of his fellow citizens. Yet he is deprived of the most sacred privilege of all—the right to vote. It is quite evident that all these poll-tax laws are in direct violation of Section 1 of the Fourteenth Amendment to the Constitution as well as being in violation of other constitutional and federal laws heretofore referred to.

This poll-tax question will continue to be of the greatest importance until disposed of, and disposed of properly and lawfully.

The American people are engaged in a war in which the life of the nation is at stake. The question of human freedom and human liberty is involved. Every American realizes that if the United States fails in this war, his liberties are destroyed and civilization ruined. The choice in this conflict is either victory or slavery and death.

In it millions of Americans are fighting, suffering and dying on the battle fronts of the world. Many thousands of these soldiers, giving up their lives to preserve civilization and freedom, are poor. Some of them if at home, undertaking to vote in any of the so-called poll-tax states, would be denied the right of franchise unless they paid the poll tax.

I felt very strongly on this issue in that fight in the fall of 1942. I still feel strongly.

A nation which boasts of the liberties which its citizens enjoy—which flaunts the freedom its government gives to the individual—is demanding of men, regardless of their financial condition, that they shall meet the foe, murderous and ingenious, in the jungles and on the mountain sides, on the sea, in the air, and beneath the sea; and yet it denies these men, in isolated regions, the right to participate in the selection of public officials.

We have called upon them to protect the American home; we have demanded they suffer and die in order to preserve our freedom; and yet in the poll-tax states they are cast aside with impunity, denied the right to vote and a voice in their own government for which they have suffered and risked their lives.

Such an attitude is obnoxious to the sense of honor and uprightness.

34

AMERICA TAKING SHAPE

MUCH OF WHAT I had long dreamed took place in that ten-year sweep between 1930 and 1940.

Developments which had seemed fantastic to many became commonplace.

Old and familiar political battlecries mingled with new.

There is in this country a far more competent, effective, and judicial judgment upon national policy than that rendered by any single individual. It is the deliberate, considered will of the American people. It has not been their tradition to retreat. I served in Congress throughout the entire period when the most sweeping adjustments of national life came, with two possible exceptions: the period immediately following the Revolution, with the formulation of an American Bill of Rights, with judicial interpretation of the practical meaning of American freedom and independence; and the period which followed the Civil War, with the ultimate settlement of the West.

The course of American life has been impressive throughout all the years the nation temporarily rested upon the oars, or in those periods of crisis when great decisions were made.

Yet I think that the three eras to which I have referred generally will be recognized as the months and years of high controversy, so wholesome and so good for the spirit of democracy.

Among the little noted developments which have come to pass is the growth of nonpartisanship in the administration of government agencies. Its greatest efficiency will be attained only when Civil Service, or the merit system, is applied in genuine fashion to all employees of government. It means better public service. It will bring to political parties a new appreciation of political responsibility beyond the spoils involved in the reward of faithful party workers.

I have fought for the extension and improvement of Civil Service for more than thirty years. In agencies in whose creation it was my privilege to have a share, I refused to compromise upon the ideal of the merit system. In TVA and REA, and in all other developments in which I could exert an influence, I insisted that appointment, tenure of service, and promotion be upon the basis of ability and efficiency.

I watched the mad scramble for jobs for forty years. I know that the mail of a member of Congress is doubled and trebled by letters from those seeking appointment to government posts.

When Mr. Roosevelt came into office, I intensified my efforts in behalf of the extension of Civil Service, recognizing the President's sympathy in that direction. Publicly I criticized the dual role which James A. Farley occupied as chairman of the Democratic National Committee, and as a member of the President's cabinet in the office of Postmaster General. I intended no reflection upon Mr. Farley, whose abilities and services have been recognized. My constant efforts simply sought improvement in the quality of public service through its divorce from party politics.

After the experiences in 1930, when I became the target of organized wealth and intrenched selfish interests and was confronted with the plotting of Republican party leaders in Nebraska and outside the state, I was ready to retire. I had no desire to be the candidate of a party whose state and national leaders had undertaken to steal an election by imposing a dummy candidate bearing my name unknown to the people of Nebraska. That decision was genuine, whatever others may think. Under no circumstances could I have been induced to have become a Republican candidate for the United States Senate in 1936. Under no circumstances would I have accepted a Democratic nomination.

Thus it was that an independent candidacy for reelection took form, and something upon which I had set my heart many years before was realized. I had contemplated an independent candidacy in 1924 and, in the development of the "Grocer" Norris episode, again in 1930. It advanced further than the record reveals.

In 1936 petitions were put into circulation by the associate who has assisted me in this book, J. E. Lawrence, the editor of the Lincoln *Star*, filed, and accepted by me. It was a candidacy born under conditions of most unusual character. The heat that summer was intense, frequently ranging for day after day well above 100 degrees. The countryside in July and August was as brown and sear as in late fall. People in Nebraska were in great distress, for this was the third consecutive year of a drouth which was to continue unbroken for seven years. Thousands had left the state. In this heat and in "black blizzards," men and women circulated petitions until more than 41,000 signatures had been secured.

I could not refuse those petitions.

Then, in October, I returned to Nebraska for a personal three weeks' campaign in every section of the state. I was reelected over former Representative Robert G. Simmons, now chief justice of the Nebraska Supreme Court, the Republican candidate, and Terry Carpenter, the Democratic nominee.

The vote was: Norris, 258,700; Simmons, 223,770; Carpenter, 108,391.

I think that was the only successful independent candidacy for the United States Senate without an independent slate involving other offices.

Again in 1942, I accepted petitions for an independent candidacy and was defeated. Nebraska had become strongly Republican in its political faith in the election of 1940. In the heat of the campaign, I found myself engaged in one of the great congressional struggles over the poll-tax legislation, and I remained in the national capital until the Friday preceding the election. The vote was: Kenneth S. Wherry, 186,207; Norris, 108,151; Foster May, 83,763.

It was a deep disappointment after what I had thought was forty years of faithful service, but a judgment under the prevailing conditions by my own people which they had a perfect right to render, even without giving any reason for their action. I loved the people I was serving, and I love them still, and I have no desire, no wish to find fault with any action they have taken.

Why these independent candidacies?

If the circumstances have not been made clear, I became convinced firmly there is in reality no difference between a Republican political machine and a Democratic political machine. Gradually it came to me that the evil in American life, the corruption that takes its toll of the American people, uses political parties for its convenience. When I became convinced that the corruption which existed in my party was just as great, or seemed to be just as great, as that which existed in any other party, I became a disappointment to many of my Republican friends. It was impossible for me to draw any difference between a Republican political machine and a Democratic political machine. Their methods were identical; their purposes, the same. The corporations and monopolies furnishing the sinews of war, putting up the finances which brought Republican victories, were obnoxious and detrimental to public good, and I could not abstain from fighting them, even though they were in my own party. In fact, I believed and still believe that one ought to be more careful, desirous, and anxious to expose wrong or evil in his own party than in the opposing party.

With the true spirit of public service, every member of Congress in his loyalty to his country ought to expose wrong or evil whenever he finds it; and when he finds it in his own party he ought to be doubly anxious to condemn it, because there he finds not only a duty to his country but a duty to his party to keep its machinery clean and undefiled.

I have thought that one of the great misfortunes which befall splendid men is the natural, understandable budding of political ambition. When their eyes become fixed upon distant horizons, and their thoughts turn to posts of greater importance, they lose the effectiveness, the courage, and frequently the high purpose which previously characterized their utterances and their votes—I have seen scores of such cases. When that political "bee" gets to buzzing, a new caution seizes them, and a new spirit of partisanship grips them in high fever. I have known it to change the entire public life of men with whom I have been associated. I have seen them retrace their steps, and retreat, when actually realization of their ambitions might better have come through continued obedience to their own conscience.

Through the years, frequently, men wrote and talked to me of the Presidency and the Vice-Presidency. Delegates were pledged to me in the convention of 1928 in the selection of Republican standard-bearers. I have had no ambition for office other than which I occupied. I was happy in the fights in Congress. There was a great satisfaction in those fights even in the hours of despair, desolation, and defeat. I refused to take seriously all of those generous and kindly letters and proposals which reached me at various times. It has seemed to me that in the legislative branch of government, there is infinite opportunity for public service.

What of those changes that have come in recent years: the social security program, the farm program, the plans for river development, and many other departures in American life?

They will not be uprooted completely, and tossed aside. The changes which come will be such as improve and strengthen, instead of destroying them. I supported them with my voice and vote. They did not always represent my precise idea. Frequently I felt I could suggest, and on occasions did suggest, changes which would improve them.

But the permanent stability and security of agriculture is a consideration of the utmost concern to the United States. Agriculture is more than the food which it contributes to satisfying the hunger of the United States and of the world; it has made invaluable contributions to the design of American living, and of democratic government itself.

I supported these agricultural programs; regretted that decision by the United States Supreme Court declaring unconstitutional the original Triple-A law; and joined vigorously in the efforts to draft and to pass its successor for soil conservation, parity payments, and crop insurance.

I have always felt a tender interest in the labors of the Forest Service. I have supported legislation strengthening it, have talked innumerable hours with the chief foresters about their enlightened efforts to reestablish the forests of this country.

One of the undertakings which had my particular interest was the effort to create the Halsey Forest Reserve in the sand hills of Nebraska. It is a monument to the late Dr. Charles E. Bessey, one of the great botanists of this country, for years associated with the faculty of the University of Nebraska. Dr. Bessey always insisted that trees would grow in a region which, during the days of the California gold rush, was marked on the map as a part of the "Great American Desert." There between the Middle Loup River and the Dismal a tract of 90,000 acres of sand hills was set aside for a national forest, and there now more than 30,000 acres of pines, many of them thirty and forty feet in height, blanket the hills and the grass with their dark green robe. I spent a day, a happy day, visiting the Halsey Forest, marveled at the remarkable adaptation made by seedlings which had been brought down from the pines of the Black Hills, and caught occasional glimpses of beautiful specimens from a herd of more than 750 deer.

Always on such occasions, the lines come back to me:

> I love thy rocks and rills,
> Thy woods and templed hills.

I was taken sick suddenly at the height of the controversy over the proposed reorganization of the United States Supreme Court, and went to the hospital. Later, when I had regained some of my strength, I went to the lake to recuperate completely. There were phases of the court plan which I did not like, much as I sympathized with the objectives which it seemed to me would strengthen the courts and justice in the United States.

Through the years I had fought when issues of judicial confirmation arose. Some of those battles reflected no great credit. I was cool to confirmation of Justice Stone, nominated by Calvin Coolidge, and he, now Chief Justice, has been one of the great jurists of America. I opposed confirmation of Chief Justice Hughes, although recognizing his great talents as a lawyer. I fought the nomination of Judge Parker of North Carolina, rejected by a single vote, convinced that his record in labor cases made him unsuitable for the United States Supreme Court. I had many conferences and much correspondence with Justice William Howard Taft bearing upon the celerity of justice, with suggested modifications of court rules.

In forty years only once did I prepare in writing a speech given on the floor of the United States Senate or in the House of Representatives. When it came to opposing the nomination of Mr. Justice Hughes, I felt that the distinction which had come to him required that I write what I intended to say so that there could be no possible misunderstanding or misinterpretation of my words.

Years later, when Chief Justice Hughes retired I took the floor at a Senate session to urge Justice Stone be elected to the post of Chief Justice of the United States Supreme Court.

I remember that Mr. Stone wrote me a very beautiful letter, and it lifted a load from my heart. The compensation of righting an unintentional wrong brings to any man a great deal of satisfaction.

Law in the United States is of such great consequence. Its failure, when justice miscarries (which does happen), strikes at the very foundation of democratic faith. It is upon law that democratic institutions of government rest in the capacity and ability of people to govern themselves.

In 1933 a dream long in the back of my mind began to take shape. It embraced a little TVA in Nebraska, including the Platte and its tributaries; the Loup and its feeder streams; and the Republican valley to which I had come as a young man. It was a long fight extending over years, with much confusion of honest origin and with the opposition, inevitably, of the private power interests contributing greatly to misinformation and conflict. It has in part been realized. On the upper Platte is Kingsley Dam, back of which is a great artificial lake containing, as this is written, nearly a million acre-feet of water for the expansion and strengthening of irrigation in a semiarid region where all that fertile soil needs in order to produce abundantly is water at stated seasons of the year. On the upper Loup, other productive valleys are under irrigation, and immense quantities of electricity are being produced to light the towns and cities and the farms, and during the present emergency to provide for war plants.

I spent enormous energy upon those projects. I fought days and months against opposition. Now they are taking form. In my own valley, against heavy odds, only the Republican remains for incorporation in the program of conservation of natural resources. On several occasions, I rescued it from the dump heap. I had been accused of a deeper concern for the Tennessee valley than for my own homeland. Strangely, I had also been accused of seeking "pork" for my own state. But in the revival of these ancient river valleys, in the security and stability which irrigation provides, and in the cheap electricity of the years ahead, I am sure this river plan will justify itself.

I recall that attack, midway in my senatorial service, by the Hearst newspapers, which accused Senator Borah, Senator Heflin, Senator La Follette, and me of receiving large sums of money from the Mexican government. It came at a time when Washington's intense heat (which always afflicted me sorely) together with a minor indisposition had sent me to the hospital. From my hospital bed, I issued a statement riddling the charges which appeared to owe their paternity to Mr. Hearst himself. I was furious. The investigation which followed effectively exploded them, and left Mr. Hearst in all his nakedness. It, together with other experiences, frequently left me with the feeling that the American press needed a regeneration and, most of all, emancipation from the business office.

Among the reforms in the first years of Mr. Roosevelt's administration that I think represent a great improvement in American life were the act providing for the regulation of the New York Stock Exchange; the act establishing a securities commission; and finally, the utility holding company death sentence act.

I threw myself into this fight with a thoroughness of preparation that I have rarely given to legislation. I had drawn up a chart showing the wide ramifications of holding companies throughout the United States, and I used that chart in the fight. The abuses which had developed called for drastic treatment. There was great satisfaction in the final approval of legislation which affects the American people so profoundly. In time the American people will appreciate even more than now the vast benefits of that legislation in the war years, in guarding the nation against pitfalls which are especially dangerous when abnormal conditions prevail.

Some of the unforgettable visits of those years are linked closely with present developments. In the fight over Muscle Shoals, and the development of the Tennessee valley, I had become acquainted with a distinguished engineer, Colonel Hugh L. Cooper. He built the great dam across the Dnieper River, which Russian armies blew up in their retreat to the east, and later retook in the great Russian offensive which began with the German defeat at Stalingrad. Colonel Cooper had an international as well as a national reputation, was consulting engineer and devised the plan for the Wilson Dam at Muscle Shoals, as well as the great dam across the Mississippi at Keokuk. He was bitterly opposed to the sale of Muscle Shoals to Henry Ford and appeared many times as a witness in the investigation, but he did not agree with me in the question of public ownership.

I had not seen him for nearly a year when he came into my office and said:

"I am going to take your breath away when I tell you what I have been wanting to tell you."

I knew that he was very bitterly opposed to the Russian government. We did not agree upon that subject, and I was startled by his next words:

"I am going to start to Russia next week. I have been employed by the Soviet government to come to Russia and look over some of their power possibilities on the Dnieper River. A short time ago I was waited upon by an agent of the Soviet government, who wanted me to go to Russia to look over the ground. I thought I would fix the price of my employment so high Russia would not pay it, but immediately the agent accepted. It goes without saying that, having agreed to accept the responsibility, I will do my level best to give them a right judgment in accordance with my professional opinion as an engineer. In other words, I am going to serve them just as faithfully and honestly as I would serve my own government under the circumstances, although I am not in sympathy with the Soviet government."

I exacted one promise from him.

I asked him to come back to my office the first time he was in Washington after his return and tell me not only of the Russian government but of the possibilities of power development there.

Thus we parted.

I did not see him again for several years, but through the press and in the magazines I knew what had taken place on the Dnieper.

Then one day Colonel Cooper came in to see me.

He said his relationships with Soviet Russia in the enterprise he had directed had been very satisfactory; the Russians had complied fully and fairly with every agreement he had with them. He said he did not know of a single instance of a breach in the arrangements. The government had assigned a group of expert engineers to work with him, and he found them uniformly of great ability. He told me that he had made a mistake in connection with some engineering data he had prepared; it was against him, and would have cost him quite a large sum of money. The Russian experts discovered it, and although it would have meant quite a large sum for the Russian government they reported it to him promptly.

At the conclusion of his studies, Colonel Cooper told me, he was engaged to supervise directly the construction of Dnepropetrovsk Dam. His arrangements gave him absolute power, complete freedom to employ assistants, including some Americans and some Germans, with whom he was acquainted both personally and professionally. The manual labor was done by the Russians. He was paid every penny the Russians had agreed to pay him at the time payments were due. He came back with his judgment of the Soviet government somewhat modified by his experience.

It happened that at this time the Teapot Dome case was undecided.

"If this had happened in Russia," Colonel Cooper told me, "there would have been a different result. There would have been a committee appointed, and Mr. Fall and his associates would have been called before it, charged with crime. The prosecution would have been allowed to offer any evidence it desired, and at its conclusion the defendant would have been given the same privilege. There would have been no lawyers present to offer objections on the ground of irrelevance or immateriality. Not more than three or four days would have been consumed. There would have been no lawyers to call attention to technicalities or to make pleas for mercy. At the conclusion of the evidence, everybody would have been put out of the room except the committee. The committee would have been in session perhaps a day, would then have brought in its verdict, and that would have ended it."

He did not agree that this was a proper procedure, but he did call attention to the fact the Russians went about as far to one extreme as we have frequently gone to the other. He did think we might improve conditions if we took on some of the elements of Russian procedure.

I was so impressed with Colonel Cooper that later I made arrangements through which he talked with the President; and I think that the several years of personal contact with the Russians not only was extremely valuable to him, but turned out to be valuable to American officials called upon to deal with the Russian government in later years.

These changes arising in part from conditions within, and in equal degree from conditions without, presented America with ten years of tumultuous action. In their objective and in their possible mechanical mistakes, they have carried the American people through days of extreme peril with remarkable facility. Health slowly returned to a nation that had been very sick. Inherently the strength and vigor of a young race was there to meet the challenge as that challenge arose in the form of great changes in other regions of the world. There was a new, mounting spirit of conquest abroad, and there were other struggles here at home.

35

STEPS TOWARD PEACE

No one at the present time entertains doubts of the ultimate victory that will come to the American people and their allies; or that such victory will come as a result of a military triumph symbolized by the collapse and unconditional surrender of our enemies.

But this victory will be of a temporary nature unless proper provision is made in the treaty of peace to give permanency to the natural peaceful aspirations of peaceful peoples and nations. It seems to me that to do this properly, certain steps are absolutely essential:

(1) Germany and Japan must be absolutely and completely disarmed. It will not be easy to uproot the military traditions instilled by long teaching in the minds and the flesh of the peoples of these countries. So every vestige of military strength in these nations that have chosen the path of military aggression must be destroyed.

(2) Manufacture of all kinds of military weapons must be made impossible by the complete destruction of every industrial factory and plant primarily devoted to war production. Not only must the factories be destroyed, but every lathe, every piece of machinery housed under their roofs must be destroyed. Every tank, every war plane, every gun, every piece of equipment employed in the specialized age of modern mechanized warfare must be destroyed. The materials which they embody must be utilized for peaceful existence and not for war. Not only must the submarines be sunk and sent to resting places on the bottom of the sea, but it must be made impossible for these countries to build new submarines. Every capital ship, every auxiliary battle wagon, every unit of a modern navy must be

destroyed. Every plant and every machine contributing to the production of military explosives must be eliminated.

(3) The maintenance of a standing army by any of these enemy countries must be forever and absolutely prohibited. To make sure that such terms are followed implicitly, there must be punishment for the people or the government that violates those stipulations; and there must be the enforcement agency to make sure those conditions are obeyed.

(4) It will be necessary in order to do this and do it right, to maintain complete supervision or policing of these aggressor nations for a period of time at least.

It will not be so difficult as most people think to maintain a peace resting upon these foundations.

Any country which is disarmed completely, and which lacks the weapons to carry on war, will not be able to resist any armed force, however small, which undertakes to enforce the treaty stipulations. If the destruction of war plants and the confiscation of weapons is systematic and thorough, it will not be long before it will be unnecessary to maintain standing armies in any of the conquered territories. The size of the occupational forces which in the beginning may be necessary to enforce the treaty of peace can be diminished gradually until at last they can be withdrawn entirely.

Under the treaty, there should be an international commission with adequate power and facilities to investigate any possible move to violate the treaty. An energetic, active, and alert police force should experience little difficulty in uncovering any attempt on the part of the aggressor nations to rebuild war production plants or to rearm. Upon the first evidence of manufacture of arms or ammunition, an armed police force, however small, could be sent immediately into the region, not only to punish those undertaking to violate the condition of complete disarmament written into the treaty, but to destroy every vestige of factory or munitions plant that has been started.

I do not believe an unarmed nation would make any serious attempts to violate such a treaty, to re-create an army involving long and arduous training of soldiers, or to build plants for the construction of weapons of war and explosives. Its government and its people would know in advance that any such attempt would subject the guilty to civil punishment and could end only in absolute failure.

It is in this particular that the peace treaty drafted at the close of the present conflict must be rigid, uncompromising, and, perhaps, to some, harsh.

There can be no sentimentality, no misguided sympathies, no softness in this respect. Those governments which have fostered ideals of aggression, our enemies in this present struggle, must be made to understand that any attempt to violate this basic provision of the treaty will be dealt with promptly and effectively, and will meet with immediate failure.

We must be firm because it is absolutely necessary to preserve the peace of the world. It is vital not only to our own hopes and aspirations for a permanent peace, but to a realization for the enemy peoples of the great blessing of peaceful living.

They, as well as the victorious nations, must understand that not only peaceful, happy living in a world emancipated from the misery and horror of war is at stake in such a disarmament program, but also the one most certain hope of economic recovery vital to a healthy civilization.

I think in time—in less time than could be anticipated—the people of Germany and Japan especially will come to see that a disarmament program is more to their benefit than to the benefit of anyone else. These peoples, freed of the bruising burden of maintaining armaments, will find new hope and a new philosophy of life.

They will be freed from the drudgery and the slave labor to which they have been subjected under a way of life that involves devoting their energies and the wealth they have created to making the weapons and munitions of war. The disarmament programs will strip them of their arms but, in place of a gun, will give them many of the necessities and comforts of life. They will emerge from the grimness of clanking tanks and roaring airplanes and shining guns into the sunlight of better home furnishings, modern transportation, improved health, and a new, wholesome leisure. They will be liberated from the heavy taxation imposed upon them, generation after generation, to maintain armies and navies and to pension a military class which at stated periods has sent their fathers, husbands, and sons to distant battlefields to kill or to be killed.

Their streeets will echo to laughter instead of sobs.

Their homes will reflect the comforts made possible through science instead of the sorrow of empty chairs. Their manhood will be trained to produce the commodities that enrich and perpetuate life rather than destroy life.

How long, then, will it be before these countries come to realize that such a program of disarmament, instead of contributing to degradation and humiliation, actually for the first time in all of their existence frees them from their burden and their curse! How long will it be before they come to look upon a program of disarmament as the turning point in their history when the heaviest burdens falling to them were lifted and they emerged into a life never known since compulsory militarism stamped the die of German culture and Japanese ambition!

We must remember not to be too ambitious in our thoughts of peace.

By attempting too much, we may lose all.

But by ignoring the basic, contributing causes of war, we may fail completely. War involves men and weapons. Men without weapons cannot wage war. At the bottom of war is the capacity to make war. And at the bottom of the capacity to make war are weapons.

We must remember that this peace treaty, if it proves anything more than a temporary stopgap, looks to the unborn generations no less than to those now living. It is going to take off the shoulders of those unborn millions the heavy burden of devoting most of their energies to the sacrifices and labors inevitably necessary to maintain huge military establishments. Shall the baby now in its mother's arms grow into a manhood or womanhood in which it will devote a major portion of its daily and weekly wage to the making of weapons of war? Those babies who shall be born twenty-five years hence, and who shall emerge into manhood and womanhood fifty years hence: shall they bear the expense of maintaining modern mechanized warfare?

No nation has fought effectively in this present conflict without learning how costly war has become. The delicate instruments, frightfully expensive, which are a part of aerial conflict, cost as much as the equipment for a regiment in earlier wars. The feverish research in the laboratories, involving constant change in the perfection of destructiveness, cries out for billions. The medical care, so properly and humanely provided for fighting armies, which people must and should furnish their soldiers, involves a humanitarian burden of expense that cannot be denied.

We are not drafting this peace for those now living; we are making the peace for those who will live.

But no world can be fashioned intelligently if molded only for those now living. While the world belongs to the living, it is the duty and the responsibility of the living to build for those who will follow.

We have found that in any war, or in any armament race, equality of arms is not enough. The ultimate success or failure in the majority of battles of the present conflict has been determined by superior arms and equipment. It means superiority in planes, tanks, guns and explosives, with the ability to use those weapons effectively.

In a world in which peoples seek to outrival each other in navies and armies and air strength, clear and disputed superiority will be the only assurance of a peaceful existence—peaceful in the event that any nation possessing superiority indicates clearly its willingness to fight if the occasion arises.

I cannot think in terms of peace except with reference to the future generations.

When I think of peace I am concerned not only with the welfare of the living, but with a future in which men and women and babies can live in neighborly fashion. We should require the governments established in the enemy countries to repudiate all national debts incurred for military purposes. Such action would relieve their peoples of unbearable burdens. It would enable those governments to pay reasonable indemnities to the Allied nations for the destruction of war.

Absolute prohibition of armament and reasonable indemnities embrace the two most important punitive steps related to the peace.

It seems to me that the question of the punishment of war criminals is an abstract issue of justice. Where there has been wanton violation of ordinary conceptions of justice and decency, even in war, the course seems clear and simple. Those men who are guilty should be brought to trial. Punishment meted out should be based upon the conceptions of justice which have governed civilization in its wisdom. For some it may mean death; for others, loss of citizenship and liberty. That is a detail and not a foundation stone of permanent peace, for the life span is short under the law of nature and permanent peace is enduring and ageless.

There is the matter of the Prussian Junker, and the Japanese militarist.

What is to be done with them?

The Prussian Junker has been the disturbing force in modern Germany. He has planned and plotted war and has lived only for war.

He must cease to be a continuing force in Germany.

The Japanese militarist has twisted and distorted the minds of his people in adulation of the immortality of the warrior who finds heaven in death upon the battlefield.

He must be removed from the dominant role in Japan.

But this peace must be born in a spirit of fairness, friendship, and reconciliation. It must be clothed with ideals of human justice and civilization. It must be nursed upon sincerity. We must show the peoples of Germany, Japan, and Italy that the peace which is being drafted is as much in their interest as it is in that of the victors upon the battlefields. It was the failure to convince defeated nations of their interest in a peace imposed which basically doomed previous attempts to establish permanent peace and led again to fresh conflicts.

Our present enemies must become our friends and our neighbors.

They must be made to understand that, while disarmament is to be enforced permanently, it is in a spirit of justice and friendship.

They must be helped back along the road to prosperity. It will not be long before the guilty—the men in the ranks as well as the leaders—who brought on this terrible catastrophe of suffering and death, pass into eternity and are succeeded on the earth by those unborn.

In wisdom and justice how can we now pronounce sentence upon hundreds of millions not yet on this earth?

How can we justly establish a world unfair to hundreds of millions innocent of any wrong, and innocent of any participation in bringing on this murderous and unholy war?

We shall be called upon to feed a starving world. When quiet replaces din, cities upon three continents of the earth and many of its islands will lie in blackened ruins. Factories will have been tumbled in ruins or blackened by fire. Vast stretches of fields will have been ruined or will have grown to weeds or fallen to waste. Peoples will have been weakened in body and spirit.

I venture no guess upon the time required to rehabilitate devastated and occupied countries. The damage, however, is irreparably greater than in any war previously fought. The regions affected are infinitely larger. The peoples engaged are much greater. The possibilities of famine, starvation, disease, and epidemic are augmented beyond accurate, intelligent comprehension.

We shall feed a starving world through no mistaken conceptions of generosity and humanitarianism. It is in the interest of our own security and safety. Unless we feed and aid in rehabilitating a starving, wounded world, we shall run grave danger of chaos and continuing conflict. For hunger and sickness breed desperation, and desperation breeds bitterness and hate, and hate spawns war.

When the decency back of this peace has become established, and the suspicion and distrust have vanished, we shall be met by penitent peoples just as anxious as we to maintain peace.

I know the first question which will arise.

If we disarm our enemies, why not disarm ourselves?

That, I admit, would be an ideal development which cannot

now be attained. America, and all the Allied nations, ought not to be expected to disarm until experience has shown that the disarmament of aggressor nations permanently has uprooted the passion for conquest that led them to initiate this present conflict.

I am confident that the gradual disarmament of the world, including disarmament of powerful nations allied in the struggle against the Axis powers, will take care of itself. The longer the disarmament program in the storm centers operates successfully, the less necessity there will be for peaceful governments and peoples to bear the enormous burden of great armies and navies. Naturally, those armies and navies will be decreased until their burden will disappear substantially or entirely.

An "armed" neutrality never has succeeded in preserving a peaceful world.

Inevitably the day arrives when temporary irritations, which could and should be composed by peaceful means, tempt some nation possessing considerable military strength to use it. It is a simple corollary established in history that the basis of aggression is military strength. The large standing army has been the symbol of conquest; never the emblem of peace. The existence of great military force perpetuates the temptation to use it.

That is history.

Wars do not spring up overnight.

They represent long and deliberate planning and plotting by military leadership.

They embrace careful preparation and training. Without exception, all of the great major developments between nations have involved the problem of aggression and conquest. No nation can fight that is disarmed, and a war without adequate weapons is impossible.

There is one other impelling reason why the absolute disarmament of our enemies, and the ultimate, gradual disarmament of ourselves should be the basis of the permanent peace.

Permanent maintenance of the present armaments of America and her allies could only bring bankruptcy and destruction to nations and peoples. The wealth of this world has not been created by war. War only has destroyed what men created, and burdened succeeding generations with its losses. There is no long life span for weapons. Guns quickly become outmoded, tanks and ships and planes over-age. Maintenance of the weapons we now possess is no assurance of security against the weapons some other nation may develop. We can devote our energies and our wealth to keeping pace with invention and developing new weapons—or we can encourage gradual disarmament.

We have professed, and do now profess, that we are fighting this war in defense of human liberty.

To these shores, thousands came to escape the compulsory military service of European nations.

When they turned their eyes to America, they knew very little about its freedom and its liberties, except that it was established upon the principle that a man was not ordained to spend a portion of his young manhood away from peaceful pursuits in military training. And that frequently was the reason why they came here. The principle succeeded here to a reasonable degree; and there is no valid reason for believing it would not succeed equally among the peoples who have been enslaved by the doctrine of vast armaments.

I like to think that the way of life that has proved so successful in a nation where armament programs have been looked upon with distaste will prove equally successful in the world at large.

Let us not repeat the mistake of thinking we are going to write an American peace in its entirety.

We are not.

First, we should agree upon a program among ourselves (which we have not yet done). When we have agreed, we still have to agree upon a permanent program with our allies, considering their wishes and their demands in a spirit of understanding, friendship, and equality.

We cannot claim justly that we have won this war alone.

It is doubtful whether we could have won the war alone; and certain that alone we could have triumphed only after many years of strife and turmoil. These simple facts must and do give our allies a voice in the peace. If we fail to recognize the contributions made by China, Russia, and Britain, we cannot expect to command either respect or trust among their peoples.

They know, far better than we know, the sacrifices they have made.

There is the isolated case of China. Her men and women have been murdered by the millions, and still, after seven years of war, she fights on bravely.

There is the case of Russia. Her millions, unlike some of Hitler's earlier victims, did not give way to panic and despair. They fought mile by mile, their lands overrun, their cities in ruins, their homes despoiled, and their families scattered or killed. When the figures of Russian losses become known to the world, it may be found that millions have perished, and yet Russia carries on with a unanimity and a courage unexcelled and unsurpassed in all human history. On the banks of Mother Volga her men stood at Stalingrad, and there in the rivers of their blood created a Russian spirit that truly breathes the essence of a national immortality. I have a faith in Russia.

There is the case of Britain. In northern France and Belgium the British left the pitifully few weapons they possessed. At Dunkirk they crossed the English Channel empty-handed. And in the succeeding months of Hitler's blitz, in the darkness of night hours, their cities were rocked and crumbled by the exploding bombs of the Luftwaffe.

Great Britain defended the cause of human freedom in those days and months, at a time when it seemed her free people could not resist successfully the Axis hordes pounding her from the skies. I mention this because we shall not write a peace solely upon lines laid down by the American people.

We should not expect those who have fought shoulder to shoulder with us to abandon their ideals of peace completely and stand by while we define the course of life in every quarter of the globe for time immemorial. We must meet these allies in understanding spirit, not in the belief that we alone have won the victory and we alone have the formula for permanent peace.

We must recognize their greatness in the struggle that they have made, and trust in their greatness in the peace that will be drawn.

We have paid more money, perhaps, for triumph than any of them, but we have also shed less blood and suffered less devastation.

Upon each and all the noble allies there is the necessity of attaining a unanimity of agreement. It means that America may have to surrender some of her cherished hopes. It means that, if we are called upon to make a sacrifice, our choice lies between the sacrifice involved and the failure of permanent peace. And failure this time projects a world more bankrupt in hope than modern civilization has known.

36

LEND-LEASE

Europe's freshly gathering war clouds in the late thirties deserved more attention than the American people were willing to accord. It was unfortunate that the intensity of political partisanship in those years immediately following Hitler's rise to power seemed to make the American people wholly unconscious of the new danger facing the world.

When Japan marched into Manchuria to establish the puppet state of Manchukuo, President Hoover filed formal protest for the American government; but only Stalin's Russia joined him. Nations showed a curious indifference to the indisputable evidence that the spirit of aggression again was loose.

No fifteen-year sweep of modern civilization reveals more national recklessness on the part of the great powers of the world than the era which began in 1925. Governments were falling and rising in Europe. The naval disarmament treaty negotiated by Secretary of State Charles Evans Hughes became a scrap of paper. The German republic under the aged Hindenburg was headed for the rapids. France was shaky in its sharp divisions, and the mounting economic difficulties confronting hundreds of millions of people portended a grave world crisis. Nations were so concerned with their troubles that they rarely gazed beyond their own borders.

Hitler's rise to power created far less alarm in the United States than the outlines of communism in Russia. In those days it was not unusual, but proper and popular, to speak admiringly of the strong government Mussolini had established in Italy and the fascism of Hitler, which was to restore Germany to her old efficiency and dignity. There was no shock in Hitler's racial oppressions or in his frequent purges. There was no reaction to Hitler's and Mussolini's bitter denunciations of democratic ideals and democratic processes of government. A remarkable apathy had settled upon the free peoples of the world and left them wholly numb.

I have wondered what would have happened if the free peoples of the world had been vigilant and keenly alive in the early years when dictatorship was sinking its roots in Europe.

Certain developments in both Germany and Italy caught the imagination of large and powerful groups in the United States. Mussolini abolished holidays and put the Italian people to work in his announced plan to revive the glories of ancient Rome, and people said work was good. Mussolini abolished the Italian Chamber of Deputies, brought the Italian courts under his control, abolished the Italian press as a free agency, and developed the fascist code; and here in the United States that transition brought only mild interest.

Hitler and his gangsters overran Germany, but the one thing that attracted American attention was his handling of German labor in the destruction of the unions. Step by step, the military spirit of Germany revealed itself while the peaceful peoples and nations were occupied with other matters. German youth was being molded in the Prussian design. Not even Spain's bloody civil war nor Mussolini's new African empire penetrated the consciousness of the free peoples.

The Spanish struggle had no significance, and Ethiopia was fair game in the thoughtlessness of the hour.

In 1933 President Roosevelt proposed to the Geneva Assembly that the tank and the airplane be outlawed as weapons of war; and in practical effect, armed conflict be limited to stationary warfare. That proposal died of disinterest. Its death was solemnized by the thirty-day conquest of Poland, the speedy subjugation of Norway, the triumphant German blitz of the Low Countries and France, and the quick Axis victories in Yugoslavia and Greece.

I hope the United States never again will be so indifferent to world developments.

Frequently the votes I cast in the Senate on measures necessitated by a fresh world conflict have been compared with those which defined my position in the First World War. It seemed to me there was no similarity in the challenge which confronted the American people. I voted for every step of American preparedness. I wanted to strengthen the army and the navy, and I voted for the extension of conscription after originally opposing it.

I supported appropriations to fortify America's outposts.

No single piece of legislation attracted my attention more than the program of Lend-Lease. I took a great interest in its passage by Congress; and I believe that it not only has shortened the war, perhaps by years, but may have saved the free peoples of the world.

In the Senate the Lend-Lease bill produced one of the bitterest struggles of a bitter period. I never could understand from the arguments developed in the debate why any member of the Senate objected to the passage of the act. In all of the discussion, it seemed to me, the opposition to Lend-Lease closed its eyes and refused to recognize the circumstances responsible for the proposal.

Hitler's triumphs had simplified America's choice.

Either this country could accept him and try to get along with him, or it had to stem the march of his armies in his plan of world conquest. I place no faith in his protestation of a peaceful attitude toward the countries of the western hemisphere. His every deed and utterance established that once he had made himself supreme in Europe, Africa, and Asia, the next step would be conquest of the Americas.

When I voted for Lend-Lease, under which the President was authorized to make contracts with the governments of nations opposing the Axis powers for weapons and supplies of war, it was a very minor consideration to me whether the beneficiaries of Lend-Lease made repayment for the material furnished them.

I felt strongly that the United States should be glad to furnish this assistance, even if it never was repaid, because the sacrifice of human life which our ultimate allies made was infinitely greater than the financial sacrifice involved.

Lend-Lease, it seemed to me, embraced so much of the elements of inspired vision. It replaced the American Embargo Act. Under the provisions of the latter, the sale and shipment of munitions and supplies of war was strictly forbidden. The Embargo Act placed responsibility upon the American government, acting through the President, for defining a belligerent and a neutral. Japan was buying huge quantities of scrap iron, copper, gasoline, and other essential war materials in the United States. In its undeclared war against China, there was sharp criticism of these purchases; but Japan never formally admitted a state of war with China. The presence of its armies in the richest, most populous regions of China and in its seaports was explained on the ground the Japanese government was protecting Japanese interests and Japanese citizens, and was maintaining law and order in the policing of China.

In all of this earlier aggression, the Japanese militarists and Hitler did not take the trouble to observe the basic principle of international law: that the violation of territorial rights was to be preceded by a declaration of war.

Under the provisions of the Embargo Act, the suspension of shipments of scrap iron and other war materials to Japan only could come about by action of the American government in declaring Japan to be a belligerent. And frequently on the floor of the Senate it was said that the United States should stamp Japan as a belligerent.

It was also my understanding China did not want supplies cut off; it would have applied to China also.

There was much in that Lend-Lease bill that I liked, and much that was consistent with beliefs I had expressed earlier. Under its terms, I thought we could fulfill our responsibilities to civilization.

Hitler and his Axis associates had succeeded until Great Britain, Russia, and China furnished the chief obstables to his complete victory. All three were short, and woefully short, of airplanes, tanks, guns, and other armored equipment, munitions, and food. Dunkirk had left the British virtually without equipment and supplies. Russia, it seemed, could not stand up under the weight of Hitler's legions. The spirit to fight was strong in Russia, and it had the men to do the fighting. I felt we should be delighted to furnish

Russia the weapons and the explosives and the food needed to wage war against world aggressors. China had the brave soldiers to fight, and the will to survive. I thought we should be happy to place the implements in her hands to defend herself and at the same time contribute to the ultimate defeat of Japan.

More than $22,000,000,000 have gone into Lend-Lease at the time of writing. The course of the war has been changed. What our sacrifices in young manhood may be, before final, complete victory, cannot be anticipated; but, whatever they are, they will be infinitely less than they would have been except through congressional passage of the Lend-Lease program. In slightly more than nineteen months, in World War No. 1, our losses in killed, wounded, missing, and prisoners were nearly double the American casualties of twenty-six months of participation in World War No. 2.

We have seen the tide of German aggression in Russia roll east until it reached the banks of the Volga at Stalingrad, and then recede until Russian soil is virtually cleared of the invader, and the strength and spirit of Germany are broken. In the hour of his victory, Marshal Stalin acknowledged that it had been American assistance in supplies and equipment that had made Russian victories possible. Lend-Lease, in the hands of British soldiers and sailors, with the help of comparatively small American forces, quickly cleared all of the western Mediterranean, and seized Sicily and Corsica.

Lend-Lease contributed much to destroying the effectiveness of Hitler's submarine campaign and to reestablishing Allied domination of the oceans.

Lend-Lease in the effectiveness that it gave to Russian, British, and Chinese armies, brought new hope to the peoples of the free nations of the world.

It has furnished the basis for the belief that the war will be brought to a triumphant conclusion much sooner than seemed possible in the beginning.

Without the repayment of one penny, this contribution the United States has made, the Lend-Lease program, has ample justification in the result it has attained.

It turned possible defeat into certain victory.

The American people merely gave their dollars instead of thousands, perhaps hundreds of thousands, of their young men. Their towns and cities and their countryside have been spared the ravages of war.

Publicly Russia has given notice of her intention to repay. The United States can use enormous amounts of raw materials—metals, and a thousand products.

It may develop in the postwar world that Lend-Lease provides the basis for more amicable trade relations with those nations toward which America has been drawn in the global crisis. The interchange of goods in a time of war may facilitate the interchange of products so vital to economic health in times of peace.

Lend-Lease can stand on its own record.

So many times it has seemed to be the unknown soldier whose presence in fierce battle is too infrequently recognized, but whose devotion and high purpose leaves its impression upon the course of history.

37

INFLATION

I CAME TO THE CONCLUSION in the late fall of 1943 that despite all efforts, one of the great dangers which confront the United States is inflation.

It is the natural accompaniment of great spending. It was apparent in the price levels reached during the Civil War and much more visible in the years following World War No. 1. Ten years of my service in the Senate were concerned with legislative efforts in the United States to undo the consequences of the inflation that became a part of World War No. 1 and the rehabilitation period.

Inflation is an unseen enemy.

It does not attack with a blare of trumpets; on the contrary, it gives its victims no warning.

If the production of commodities for civilian use is restricted or short, and any considerable portion of people have the money to purchase available goods, the inevitable result is to raise the prices of these commodities, and thus increase the cost of living. This means that wages have to be increased, and the increased wages mean increased costs of production, which can be met only by an increase in the prices of commodities and again by fresh increases in wages and salaries.

Thus the spiral of inflation gets under way.

No one escapes.

The evils of a spiral inflation may delay or impede military activities, depending upon the length of the conflict; and, even without prolonging the war, inflation would add infinitely to its unprecedented costs. The American people are clothing, feeding, and maintaining ten million men in the armed services. They are furnishing medical supplies; providing every care and precaution that can be given. This is the least that they can do for the men who fight for them. The food bill is enormous. It takes untold quantities of meat, vegetables, flour, and other articles of food to satisfy the appetites of the men of the armed forces. It takes vast amounts of cloth to keep them warm and healthy. It calls for staggering amounts of materials to shelter, equip, and arm them. If prices get out of control in this country in the closing months of the war, and inflation sets in, many billions in costs will be added to the already fabulous billions required to wage the war.

That is why I voted for all proposed controls in my closing months in the Senate. There are some things I do not like in regimentation, but I like price-control measures and rationing much better than the ruin of inflation. I supported the OPA. I approved of every control measure. I favored the tax bills.

Lend-Lease, its effectiveness tapering off, either would be destroyed, or its burden cruelly increased in the vast amounts of equipment and supplies sent to America's allies. It might prove that the actual development of inflation, symbolized by runaway prices, would destroy Lend-Lease in its final, useful service.

There is still one other American responsibility directly a part of the war effort which will be complicated infinitely if the controls are taken off.

We know now it will be necessary to feed and clothe and nurse back to health and strength elements of the peoples of these occupied countries. After all of the agony of occupation by Germany military forces, the sacrifice to liberate them will be nullified if they are left to die of starvation or to drift into lawlessness and anarchy.

The plan for joint contributions by the victorious Allies to a fund for reestablishing the peoples and the governments of Axis-occupied territories would be disrupted seriously, even destroyed, by inflation in the United States in the closing stages of the war. We could not make our necessary contribution, and we would disarrange, if not destroy, the entire undertaking. If prices do get out of control, the chances of an orderly postwar era will be diminished a thousandfold. It will be months after liberation before these countries begin to resume production on a considerable scale. The exact condition of the occupied countries is unknown; but in all of them industry has been diverted chiefly to war production. Axis powers have drawn heavily upon their resources.

Inflation in the United States will defeat any effective postwar program.

The civilian population of the United States will suffer more terribly than in any previous war. That civilian population is making a great sacrifice at the present time. It patriotically is doing everything necessary for victory. It is ready to make the additional sacrifices essential to a successful prosecution of the war to full and complete victory.

The members of Congress should realize fully the dangers inevitable if the spiral of inflation is not prevented during the war and the difficult period which will follow. Congress should know that living costs will soar to unlimited heights. It should recognize that even those groups of workers for whom the avenues to wage advances appear to be open will be unable to procure wage increases rapidly enough to keep pace with the rising cost of living; and it should recognize that every wage increase adding to the cost of production will contribute to the vicious circle of increased costs of production and fresh wage increases, to which there is no end.

Congress should know that men with fixed salaries will find it impossible to support their families unless salaries are increased.

If inflation gets under way in the postwar years, it will be the beginning of disunity and dissension. Labor will be arrayed against capital in new malignant growth. Under uncontrolled inflation it is each man for himself in a new and terrible struggle.

While I always resented encroachment upon the individual in the enjoyment of his rights, I was glad to vote for measures designed to avert inflation.

I recognized the great difficulties of administration of price control, and the frequent mistakes inevitable in an undertaking of this magnitude; but I had a great deal of sympathy for those charged with the undertaking. In a period when reasonable price control was so vital to success, and so essential to the welfare of the American people, it seemed to me at times that in all the criticism perhaps we had not learned how to use liberty, or how to safeguard it. There is no greater enemy to the economic and political independence of a free people than inflation. In the ruin, the destruction of people's savings and life accumulations, liberty becomes a mockery.

It is so difficult to draw the line between property and freedom, between the pocketbook and political ideals of liberty. Men frequently talk about profits and property as though they constituted the essence of freedom. Misuse or misunderstanding of wealth or property can destroy human liberty.

This is the essence of resentment against price controls and wage controls so essential to averting inflation. Men strike out against controls when thinking primarily of temporary profits. Labor resents wage controls when weighing temporary wage levels. Regimentation during a war period, and its abnormal spending, are a cheap price to pay in order to escape the great evils of inflation.

I saw a prosperous agricultural region receive fabulous prices for the food which it produced, and then, when deflation set in, I saw many thousands of those farm families lose everything they possessed. I received thousands of letters of distress from men and women who had lost their farms and their homes and were filled with despair. I had a part in the legislative measures that were deemed necessary to offset the ruinous deflation that followed the last war.

I voted for the revenue legislation in the early months of the war. One of the best ways to prevent inflation is to increase taxes, so that the American people will not have a large amount of spending money to purchase from the meager supplies of the necessities and luxuries. Only through taxation of the most drastic character can the greatly increased money be siphoned off safely and, at the same time, America's national debt be held within bounds.

Congress must be on guard, and back of Congress, the American people must man the ramparts against an insidious enemy. Let inflation get the upper hand, and the American people will sow to the wind. Its danger becomes greater, strangely, with military success on the battlefields, and its danger is greatest when finally peace arrives.

38

BY WAY OF FAREWELL

MANY WASHINGTON correspondents of the American press were generous, kind, and helpful to me through the years of my service in Washington as a member of the American Congress.

One of them said recently my life was the story of America's struggle in its more mature years.

I am wholly unconscious of it, if this observation is correct.

In my early boyhood, my young manhood, and for much of my life, the frontier of the settlements of new land was an important reality. The struggle to preserve the Union started almost with the start of my life, and its years of conflict and of Reconstruction are contained in my earlier memories. I saw the American people push westward, and ever westward to the mountains and the sea. I tried faithfully as a public servant to aid in their decent aspirations, and to contribute in such fashion as I could to a leadership in the nation under which the American people would come to the fullest enjoyment of the physical and spiritual blessings placed at their disposal.

Undoubtedly many times I was wrong in my estimates of men, and in my attitude upon issues embodying national policy.

In forty years in the Congress, I have been impressed most by the great strength and vitality of the American people. In the spirit of democratic institutions of government, they have made, and they will make, their mistakes. But so long as an unselfish leadership remains for their guidance—a leadership untainted by corrupting personal ambition—a leadership inspired by the simple strength that oozes from the soil and the humble ranks of the poor—and at times is enriched and fortified enormously by the support and voice of those who wear purple robes of great wealth—I am sure America can continue to be the bright beacon toward which the eyes of the world's oppressed and downtrodden ever will turn for inspiration and hope.

Only by faith are men and women sustained.

And what is faith?

It is not born solely or largely by the actions of one but through the contributions of millions living in the spirit of justice, with due consideration for the burdens and the rights of all others.

In America under a capitalistic system, resting upon democratic institutions of government, for more than a century the chief concern has not been infringement by the masses upon the rights of the rich, the powerful, and the strong. They have taken care of themselves. Largely until now the unceasing struggle has been to protect the helpless, the weak, and the poor from exploitation by the strong. In the main, the fight has been against the consuming ambitions, both for power and for wealth; the greed and avarice of individuals and groups for wealth; the injection of privilege, favoritism, and discrimination in national policy.

It will be recognized generally that those forces represent the greatest danger which American faith has faced.

In the way our life has been molded, there is a spirit in all of us that resents injustice.

We want to see honest service rewarded.

We demand that ability and loyalty be recognized.

We accord our respect, our admiration, and our love to those millions of Americans who live quietly and simply, without pretense, envy, malice, or ill will.

Among my favorite passages are the words of the ancient philosopher by the roadside, who spoke of one's love for his fellow men.

To an amazing degree, the miracle of this America of which we all are a part is not only its high living standards, its comforts and conveniences, its wealth, its education, its scientific progress, its great cities and its farms, its earlier absorption of millions from the old world of different languages and races who have come to live in communities side by side in peace and harmony, but also its widespread understanding and sympathy for those living in poverty, and its fair and liberal attitude to those living in riches.

Nowhere else in the world do I know of a land of such amazing paradoxes which I have watched unfold in front of my eyes in the years which followed the Civil War and the years which now are drawing to a close for me.

I have no bitterness in my heart.

I have no ill will towards any man.

If there are those who in the heat of conflict retain a lingering bitterness towards me—on my part, all the differences have faded into the mists of forgiveness.

At the completion of my final Senate term, I came home to McCook.

There were many opportunities to remain in public life in one capacity or another. During those closing weeks, many friends scattered throughout the country were solicitous and kind. My mail was filled to overflowing with thousands of letters, hundreds of them from Nebraska, and hundreds more from other sections of the country, containing expressions of comfort and continuing loyalty.

I could not read them all.

I could not assume the great physical burden of attempting to answer even a small part of them. For the first time during my career in Congress, it became necessary to send to all of these kind friends a simple, printed expression of appreciation.

I remember the day I reached McCook.

In leaving Washington, which for a good share of each year had been my home, I traveled by way of the valley of the Tennessee and St. Louis. Among many meetings which had stirred me deeply, one had been arranged by leaders and the people of the Tennessee valley.

It was dark when the train reached McCook in the early morning of a day in January, 1943, and Mrs. Norris and I stepped from the Pullman. I had been long awake; always it was difficult to sleep on a train, and this was home-coming for me. Purposely I had not let it be known when I would arrive.

An old friend, Carl Marsh, was waiting for us. We drove

through the dark streets to our home to take up our life among the people who had permitted me to represent them in the House of Representatives and in the Senate for forty years. They had been loyal to me. I had been commissioned by them to represent them in Congress until only a few who had been with me in those earlier days of initiation to America's legislative branch of government, were left on that afternoon when I took leave of Washington with mingled emotions of sadness and relief at being free of responsibility constantly growing heavier. I entered the house which I had built, and turned on the lights, illuminating those familiar rooms. I was home to spend my remaining days.

Across the street through the months, I have looked out upon the park where as a young man I had a part in planting and watching over these great trees which provide shade throughout the day.

There in the chill fall last year, I saw the birds gather for their trip to the Southland.

Here to my home many visitors have come to enliven my hours and to seek advice.

Here in my home I have maintained my correspondence as far as my strength permits, and Mrs. Norris and I have read and have watched the progress of another great conflict, in the supreme faith that justice again will triumph. Here we have prayed that, this time, decency will be enthroned permanently in the world.

I know of no better way of setting forth my creed of life than to quote generously from a letter which I wrote in the early days of 1929 to an old associate and friend, now dead, John F. Cordeal of McCook. We had shared a law office together; had been much together through the years. I was conscious of his loyalty, his ability, and his high integrity.

He had written me in some critical spirit, it will be observed, at a time when many Nebraskans were indignant at my support of Al Smith, and my differences with Republican leadership. I felt sure none of that feeling of religious bigotry tinctured Mr. Cordeal basically. I had written:

I am devoting this Sabbath day to an effort of cleaning up my desk. I am answering your letter among the first. I read it and reread it last night when I was all alone. I entirely agree with most of what you say. Other things you mention I agree with in part, and for nothing you have said do I feel in the least as though I want to criticize it. . . . Although you have said some things to me which I do not think I deserve, from your point of view, as I understand it, you were perhaps fully justified in saying everything you have said. . . . It is not for me to say that you are wrong and I am right. The reverse may be true. I respect you for everything even though I think you are wrong.

Whatever you or other people may say or think, I do love my friends. I am delighted when I please them. I am brokenhearted when I lose them. About the only thing in life that makes it worth while is the enjoyment of friendly relations. . . . About the only enjoyment I get in my innermost soul is that I try to do that which, in the light God gives me, I believe to be right. . . .

The truth is that my religion and my politics are one and the same. It has not always been so. I have come to this belief, not because I tried to, perhaps, not even because I wanted to, but because I have been led to it by what I believe to be the irresistible logic of human events. Politics, in my belief, is the science of government, and political parties are only instruments—imperfect instruments—to bring about good government. A government, in its truest sense, is only a method to bring to humanity the greatest amount of happiness and is founded, after all, upon the love of man for man.

True love for humanity is an unselfish desire to perpetuate the welfare and happiness of all the people comprising the government.

I think religion is the same thing.

True religion is founded on human love. As I look at it, it is not the love of self. It is not a means to save one's soul from a future punishment, to the neglect of human beings. I am not trying to make a theological definition or to place myself in harmony with those who believe in any Eternity. "True religion exists where charity is seen, and if we mount to Heaven, 'twill be on the rounds of love to man." . . . I can conceive of no God except a just God, and I cannot understand how a just God, knowing the frailties and the weaknesses of human nature, can punish His imperfect creatures for wrongs which come about on account of the very weaknesses which He has, Himself, planted in the minds and hearts of all of us. I agree heartily with the lowly Nazarene when he said: "The Kingdom of God is religion." By no means do I want to set myself up as an example. I realize that I have frailties and weaknesses, perhaps, even in a larger degree than most of my fellow men, but I cannot be anything but myself. If I attempted to do so, I know in advance I would make a complete failure of it.

This is my creed of life.

There are many problems ahead, of both foreign and domestic character.

Some of the latter can be mentioned only superficially.

Religious prejudice is the most deeply imbued prejudice that exists in the human heart. I have found it from the highest to the lowest; from the wisest to the most ignorant.

Next to religious bigotry, sometimes the intolerance that exists on the prohibition question takes second rank. I have been an abstainer throughout my life. I believe temperance is the only rule of life. Yet on both sides of this issue are prohibitionists supporting a prohibitionist, regardless of how he may stand on any other governmental question, and wet bigots, narrow-minded enough to support a man opposed to prohibition regardless of how he may stand on other questions.

I am sorry these things exist.

There must be room in a successful democracy for differences of opinion. It is the true leavening process which produces the best flower of thought.

And what about this country, and the future course of liberalism? No matter how temporarily dark and depressing the skies may be, social progress, despite its setbacks, always has been upward and onward. Each reverse resulting from a reappearance of reactionary practices and thought has been followed by new peaks of enlightened social conceptions. No one can say what challenge the American liberal will face. He must be prepared to block the path to brutality and greed.

I recognize now some of the more apparent problems of the years which will follow the final thunder of war.

At the root of all these problems is human nature itself, craving quiet, rest, and serenity when there is no rest in view. People are exhausted, emotionally and spiritually no less than physically, by the demands of sacrifice and the necessities of a great struggle. They are weary at a time which calls for great efforts. They will seek relief from worry when, most of all, they must be vigilant.

It will be necessary for the American people to decide in their wisdom what shall be done with those islands in the oceans, and with those sections of continental areas which have been reclaimed from Axis militarism by American soldiers. The United States in this new world of a "war of movement" will need bases far from the soil of continental America. It should not permanently undertake to retain vast amounts of territory. It should not embark upon imperialism. Never in its entire history has America coveted the lands and the wealth of other peoples, and nothing in the present struggle suggests a departure from its fixed tradition of good will toward all the other peoples and races of the world. Quite to the contrary, the expressed aims of the American people renounce all thought of territorial enrichment as a result of this war, and its frightful financial burden. In the maintenance of law and order, the reestablishment of governments, and the rehabilitation of regions destroyed or damaged by war, the American people should interfere as little as possible with the life of the people of those regions.

If out of this war the world wins emancipation from conflict, the United States should see to it that such territory as has been occupied for military purposes should be returned to the rightful owners, together with all the natural resources.

The United States, through the expenditure of billions, has developed great resources for future use.

It has built the greatest merchant marine any nation ever possessed. The hundreds of ships of that merchant marine now sail the seas, transporting men, equipment, and supplies vast distances. At the close of the last war, those ships needed for it offered a difficult problem. There were proposals they be turned over to private owners, proposals for government subsidies for their operation, and in the protracted controversy they remained idle for a long period. America's new merchant marine should be utilized for the good of the people.

Men have been trained to man these ships. Enough of the ships should be retained by the American people to insure that no great shipping monopoly shall rise upon foundations created to defeat a tyranny which was established by military means.

In this war the American people have built factories to produce basic metals and materials for all of the thousand items needed in war. They have built factories to produce airplanes, tanks, explosives, and guns. I am told that in some isolated cases, 90 per cent of the materials used for purposes of war come from factories built by the American people. I am told that a large proportion of the planes and the tanks and other armor used by American soldiers and their allies has been produced in factories belonging to the American people.

What shall be done with them?

Shall they be placed on the auction block and sold to the highest bidder, to become the basis of powerful monopolies?

Shall they be sold so that at least a fair portion of the enormous expenditures necessary to establish them will be returned to the people who built them?

The American people, it seems to me, should not be so anxious to dispose of these plants as to be devoid of facilities to defend themselves against a relentless foe. I never have believed in great armaments, and I do not now believe in huge ones as a permanent national policy. Just as soon as possible we should undertake to disarm ourselves, in the event that a genuine effort for the establishment of permanent peace emerges from the conferences which will follow this war. But the American people will need to be alert in all these matters relating to the enormous means of production which they have created.

They will need to be on guard.

The stakes are the greatest in the nation's history.

There is the foundation for the most gigantic organizations, for the greatest corporations, and for the most powerful monopolies the American people have ever known.

The people will need to be more alert against the rise of monopoly than ever before.

Here at home we shall face the great problem of millions of

returning soldiers, coming home from triumphs on the battlefield to again take up a peaceful life. Perhaps no single program will be sufficient to meet the impact of the return of more than ten million young Americans. The solution may rest in a combination of several programs. Private industry and enterprise will be strained sorely to absorb the returning men. It is to be assumed that their return will be gradual. Thousands will be needed temporarily for policing the countries of an occupied continent, the condition of which is not known. A combination of public works of permanent character and private employment may offer the only solution for the stability and security which employment alone provides.

There may be the mad rush to convert war bonds to spending, with all of the grave danger of inflation which that involves.

There will be the stupendous burden of taxation with the innumerable efforts to shift it from one shoulder to another. Yet drastic levies under inheritance-tax and income-tax plans offer the only just and acceptable method of meeting the burdens of war.

In these recent months, letters have reached me from men in the armed services. They express a strong, sweet faith born on the fringes of battlefields.

One of them reads:

> I have started to write to you many times but have hesitated for want of a theme. I don't have any more definite idea now than on those other occasions. It all started, sir, way back when I was in high school. When I was a sophomore, it seemed to me you were quoted as an authority. . . . I discovered that you were sincere in whatever it was you said. I discovered that you were honest, kind, and had an intelligence that comes only from a union of both heart and mind. This understanding of you has grown since high-school days. No eulogy could express the deep feeling of debt that I feel this country owes to you. No other man has been courageous enough to stand firm on such a course as yours with the obvious pains.

This young voice, and others echoing its appeal, it seems to me, are seeking reassurance that a world will emerge in which the plain, industrious, honest, and God-fearing man will find satisfaction in his quest for happiness.

I know from letters received that these men on the ragged fringes of jungle, desert, or mountains, are thinking of the world which they hope to see. I know from what they write their hopes rest upon a good world in which man has triumphed over himself.

What shall I say to them?

The answer is faith. The world for which they long is not only soil, rock, water, space, man, and animals, but it is built of the faith which has sustained humankind throughout all of its evolution. I am sure they are thinking of a world in which justice gives confirmation to faith, in which existing opportunities not only feed and clothe but permit peace of mind.

It will take more than this war to destroy the leadership that has made great accomplishments possible.

I am sure that, from among America's fighting men and others, warriors will appear to fight the unending battle for good government. I am sure that, so long as there are men, there will be knights to lift their swords and press their shields against the enemies, corruption and evil.

Liberalism will not die.

It is as indispensable to life as the pure air all around about.

It is deathless—it marches forward—and it will continue to march long after those who have carried its standards in past struggles are gone from this earth.

This is my faith in America.

INDEX